W9-ADI-195

Intellectual Foundations of the Nicaraguan Revolution

Intellectual Foundations of the Nicaraguan Revolution

by DONALD C. HODGES

University of Texas Press ◆ Austin

First Edition, 1986

Requests for permission to reproduce material from this work
should be sent to Permissions, University of Texas Press, Box 7819,
Austin, Texas 78713-7819.

Library of Congress Cataloging-in-Publication Data

Hodges, Donald Clark, 1923–
    Intellectual foundations of the Nicaraguan revolution.

    Bibliography: p.
    Includes index.
    1. Sandino, Augusto César, 1895–1934—Political and social views.
2. Nicaragua—History—1909–1937.   3.   Frent Sandinista de Liberación Nacional.   4. Nicaragua—History—1937–1979.   5. Nicaragua—History—Revolution, 1979—Influence.   I. Title.
F1526.3.S24H63   1986   972.85'051   86-6937
ISBN 0-292-73838-2
ISBN 0-292-73843-9 (pbk.)

Contents

Abbreviations

APIA Agencia Periodística de Información Alternativa (Alternative Information News Agency)

APRA Alianza Popular Revolucionaria Americana (American Popular Revolutionary Alliance)

CESO Centro de Estudios Socio-Económicos (Center of Socioeconomic Studies)

CGT Confederación General de Trabajadores (General Confederation of Workers)

ED de la SN de N Ejército Defensor de la Soberanía Nacional de Nicaragua (Defending Army of Nicaragua's National Sovereignty)

ELN Ejército de Liberación Nacional (National Liberation Army)

FAPU Frente de Acción Popular Unificada (Unified Popular Action Front)

FER Frente Estudiantil Revolucionario (Revolutionary Student Front)

FMLN Frente "Farabundo Martí" de Liberación Nacional (Farabundo Martí National Liberation Front)

FPN Frente Patriótico Nacional (National Patriotic Front)

FSLN Frente Sandinista de Liberación Nacional (Sandinista Front of National Liberation)

FUN Frente Unitario Nicaragüense (Nicaraguan Unitary Front)

GPP Guerra Popular Prolongada (Prolonged People's War)

INRA Instituto Nicaragüense de Reforma Agraria (Nicaraguan Institute of Agrarian Reform)

IS Internacional Socialista (Socialist International)

JPN Juventud Patriótica Nicaragüense (Nicaraguan Patriotic Youth)

JRN   Juventud Revolucionaria Nicaragüense (Nicaraguan Revolutionary Youth)

MAP   Movimiento de Acción Popular (People's Action Movement)

MCR   Movimiento Cristiano Revolucionario (Christian Revolutionary Movement)

MIR   Movimiento de Izquierda Revolucionaria (Movement of the Revolutionary Left)

MPU   Movimiento Pueblo Unido (United People's Movement)

PC de N   Partido Comunista de Nicaragua (Communist Party of Nicaragua)

PLI   Partido Liberal Independiente (Independent Liberal party)

PLM   Partido Liberal Mexicano (Mexican Liberal party)

PPSC   Partido Popular Social Cristiano (Popular Social Christian party)

PSN   Partido Socialista Nicaragüense (Nicaraguan Socialist party)

UHAO   Unión Hispano-Americano Oceánica (Hispano-American Oceanic Union)

Preface

In the introduction to his book covering fifty years of Sandinista
struggles, Nicaragua's minister of defense, Humberto Ortega,
claims that the Sandinista offensive, which culminated in the overthrow of the Somoza dynasty in July 1979, formed part of a
long-term revolutionary process that began with Augusto César
Sandino.[1] In this reassessment of Nicaraguan history, Sandino
served as an enduring catalyst of revolutionary struggle that lasted
more than half a century.

For the Sandinistas, Sandino's example is important but so is
his political thought. The latter is crucial to understanding the
Nicaraguan revolution not only because it has influenced the
thinking of the past and present Sandinista leadership, but also because the leadership believes the Revolution began with Sandino
rather than with the Sandinista movement reconstituted thirty
years after his death.

Whatever the economic, political, and sociological explanations of the revolution, the intellectual factors behind it derive
from Sandino's unique blend of revolutionary ideas. Although obsessed with U.S. domination and repeated political and military intervention in Nicaragua and the rest of Central America, Sandino
did more than wage a war of liberation against a foreign intruder.
Whereas he was astute enough to hide his political intentions from
his immediate followers until conditions might be ripe for revealing them, his long-range goal was an economic, political, and cultural transformation that would have ended in revolution—it finally did.

The present work examines the intellectual sources and foundations of the Nicaraguan revolution identified in the writings of
Sandino and the Sandinistas. It is an essay in intellectual history
aimed at clarifying the philosophy of the revolution. Given the no-
toriety attained by the new revolutionary government, the controversy surrounding it, and the foreign intervention directed at
toppling it, this is one way of understanding the issues at stake.

Most interpretations of the Nicaraguan Revolution have been animated by undisguised political passions. From one quarter we hear that Nicaragua is tantamount to a second Cuba, that the Sandinista Front of National Liberation (FSLN) is the political shell of a Marxist-Leninist vanguard, that this revolutionary elite is steamrolling the country in the direction of totalitarianism, that Nicaragua's new democracy is a sham, and that behind the government's alleged policy of nonalignment is its actual alignment with the Soviet Union.[2] From another quarter we are told that the Sandinista revolution is kin to the American struggle for independence, that it is a revolution of, by, and for the people, that the Marxists in the leadership are closer to being social democrats than Marxist-Leninists, that Christians are a real power in the government and are shaping both the country's culture and its new education system, and that totalitarianism is not a threat because of the FSLN's commitment to human rights, political pluralism, and a mixed economy.[3]

Highly respected scholars, including Latin America specialists, are sharply divided over how to interpret the revolution. Yet there is surprising agreement in their assessments of Sandino. Sandino's struggle against the U.S. Marines who occupied his country from December 1926 to January 1933 is widely interpreted as nationalist and populist and unhampered by doctrinaire ideological beliefs of any sort.[4]

An understanding of the philosophy of the revolution may be helpful not only in resolving these intellectual disputes, but also in disputing this ill-fitting consensus. As we shall see, each side is mistaken in its assessment of Sandino and in its interpretation of the Sandinista leaders. A careful examination of the intellectual sources indicates that Sandino was a dedicated revolutionary on the border between anarchism and communism, and that the FSLN's leaders are neither Marxist-Leninists nor social democrats but representatives of a Marxist and Leninist New Left that incorporates anarchist elements.

In Nicaragua the people's revolutionary initiatives seem to have surpassed most previous records. But public participation in an insurrection tells us nothing about the other face of the revolution, its private life. A balanced account of the Nicaraguan revolution must consider its esoteric inner workings as well as its popular dimension.

Both Sandino's Defending Army of Nicaragua's National Sovereignty and the Sandinista Front of National Liberation belong to the category of secret societies or conspiratorial organizations. In the struggle against what each identified as the fundamental enemy, they were acutely aware of the need not only to conceal, but also to dissemble their political objectives. It is ironical that some of the most hostile critics of the Sandinistas, such as former ambassador to the United Nations, Jeane Kirkpatrick, have expressed strong sympathies for Sandino.[5] Yet Sandino more than most revolutionary leaders successfully disguised the aims of his movement behind a bizarre and mysterious symbolism that even the Sandinistas have failed to decipher.

The tradition behind the top leadership of the Nicaraguan revolution, the nine-man National Directorate of the FSLN, may be traced to François Noël Babeuf's "Conspiracy of Equals" during the Great French Revolution. Transmitted by Auguste Blanqui's "Society of the Seasons" and by Michael Bakunin's secret alliance within the International Workingmen's Association, it came to fruition in the twentieth century with Lenin's creation of a vanguard party. Not for nothing was Lenin repeatedly charged by his social-democratic critics with "Blanquism." To understand Sandino and the Sandinistas, it is necessary to examine their roots in this conspiratorial tradition, in its antecedents and post-Leninist developments.

If the FSLN's leaders have disguised their long-range objectives, it has been to protect themselves from criticism. The belated discovery of Sandinista duplicity accounts for the sense of betrayal experienced by disillusioned Sandinistas such as Edén Pastora, and by former allies of the FSLN such as Dr. Arturo Cruz and Alfonso Robelo.[6] They and others like them initially supported the FSLN because they were taken in by its public image. Not privy to what was taking place behind the scenes, they believed that the original revolutionary leadership of the Sandinistas had given way to a new breed of reformists.

They have learned their lesson. Today Edén Pastora is the leader of a social democratic wing of the *contras*, Robelo has given his support to the *contras'* liberal wing, and in Washington, D.C., Cruz backs the campaign to get the United States to recognize a provisional government in exile.[7] Cruz's humiliation at being deceived still rankles, as evidenced by his recent declaration, "But the Sandinistas are totalitarians!"[8]

Are they? The question I raise is, What corresponds to the realities? The popular image of Sandinismo that makes its leaders appear to be only loosely Marxist in their sympathies, the *contras'* image of them as hard-core Marxist-Leninists contemptuous of the people's beliefs, or the image of a new kind of revolutionary van-

guard that has learned to temper its Marxism-Leninism by adjust-
ing to the patriotic sentiments and Christian traditions of the
Nicaraguan people?

Following a precedent established by Marx and Engels in the
Communist Manifesto and adopted by most Marxist-Leninist parties, the report by the party's secretary to its national congress is
designed to update the party's intelligence since the previous report. Periodically, responses are sought to Marx and Engels's three
questions crucial to the revolutionary enterprise: What is happening in the world and within one's particular national reality? What
do the people want and how do they justify it? What is to be done?
The answers provide, respectively, the party's assessment of a given
political situation, its activating ideology, and its strategy.

Sandino and the Sandinistas also responded to these questions.
For Sandino, the fundamental question was ideological, concerned
with ideals and program. Then came the strategical decisions that
were modified according to his assessment of the realities. This was
a principled approach rooted in moral conviction and supported by
faith. In contrast, the Sandinistas give first place to theory, to assessments of the balance of social forces at a particular political
conjuncture.[9] For them strategy is mainly a function of theory, and
beliefs rooted in sentiment and faith instead of knowledge are
judged according to whether they help or hinder a particular strategy. Theirs is an instrumental approach stressing the conditions of
victory and the means of achieving it.

Begun after my return from Nicaragua in January 1981, this
study of the Nicaraguan Revolution has gone through more revi-
sions than I care to remember. Ross Gandy and Deborah Hepburn
of the Cuernavaca Research Center read the original draft and
helped me with their criticism, as did my colleagues in philosophy,
Michael Hand of Florida State University and Douglas Kellner at
the University of Texas. A second draft was read by Latin Ameri-
canists Michael Conroy and John Booth, and a third draft by
Michael Dodson and also by John Booth. Their probing questions
led to an almost complete overhaul of the original manuscript. My
sponsoring editor, David Catron, has labored with me over the second, third, and now the fourth version.

In this research I am indebted to libraries and to librarians in
Nicaragua, Mexico, and Argentina. In Nicaragua I received invalu-
able help from the Ministry of Culture; from the editor of *Barri-
cada,* Onofre Guevara; from the director of Importaciones y
Exportaciones Literarias, S.A., Adolfo Alfaro; from Larry Boyd of
Agencia Periodística de Información Alternativa; and from Fred

Murphy of Intercontinental Press, who went to considerable trouble to provide me with needed documents. In Mexico I became aware of the importance of Ricardo Flores Magón's thought for an understanding of Sandino's philosophy through the intermediary of Mexican sociologist Juan de Dios Vargas, and Magonist activist, Mónico Rodríguez. In Argentina, if it had not been for the patience and kindness of Juan D. Trincado, director of the Magnetic-Spiritual School of the Universal Commune in Buenos Aires, I would have passed over the single most important source of Sandino's rational communism in the school's philosophy of rational austerity.

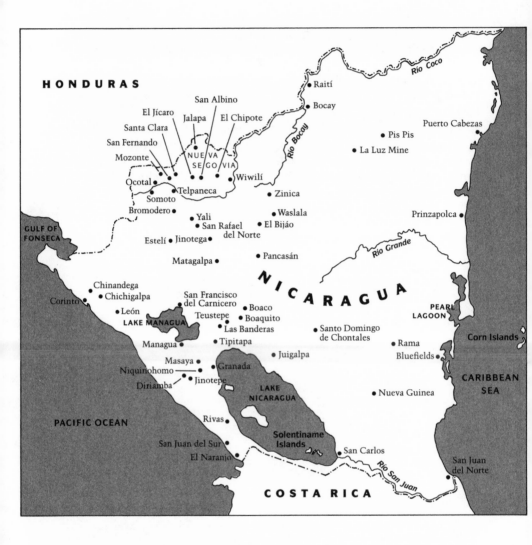

HONDURAS

Río Coco

Raití
Bocay
Río Bocay

Puerto Cabezas
Pis Pis
La Luz Mine

San Albino
El Jícaro   El Chipote
        Jalapa
Santa Clara
San Fernando
Mozonte   NUEVA
                 SEGOVIA
Ocotal   Wiwilí
         Telpaneca
   Somoto   Zinica
Bromodero
         Yali   Waslala
      San Rafael   El Bijáo   Prinzapolca
         del Norte
GULF OF   Estelí Jinotega
FONSECA   Río Grande
         Matagalpa   Pancasán

                        NICARAGUA

Chinandega
   Chichigalpa   San Francisco
Corinto   del Carnicero   PEARL
         León   Teustepe   Boaco   LAGOON
         LAKE MANAGUA   Boaquito
                    Las Banderas   Santo Domingo   Corn Islands
         Managua   Tipitapa   de Chontales
                                        Rama
         Masaya   Juigalpa   Bluefields
Niquinohomo   Granada   CARIBBEAN
   Diriamba   Jinotepe   SEA
                         LAKE   Nueva Guinea
                      NICARAGUA
                  Rivas
PACIFIC OCEAN
San Juan del Sur   Solentiname
   El Naranjo   Islands   San Carlos
                                                    San Juan
                                  Río San Juan   del Norte

                  COSTA RICA

PART ONE. *Sandino*

Because there have been no really profound studies of Sandino's thought, I believe that one of the principal tasks of the revolution will be to . . . systematize the study of his thought. There ought to be departments of Sandinista studies in the universities, there ought to be standing seminars on Sandinista studies in Nicaragua. Every day that passes it will become more important to explain not only Sandino's thought in his letters, proclamations, and addresses, but also the direct and indirect influence that he exerted on revolutionary thought since his time. . . . I would say that, just as none of the post-modernist or vanguard poets in Nicaragua can be understood without Darío, so no ideologist, no Nicaraguan revolutionary can explain his own thought without referring to the origins of Sandinista thought.

— SERGIO RAMÍREZ MERCADO
Análisis histórico-social del movimiento sandinista

Revolutions are not made only through bloodshedding and great sacrifices. They are also made with intelligence. . . . Sandino was a valuable source of political and military experiences. He left many teachings indispensable to building a revolutionary vanguard. . . . A group of young men rescued those teachings, studied, analyzed, and elaborated his doctrine. But the one who launched and completed this demanding task was Carlos Fonseca. To the entire revolutionary movement he proclaimed that Sandino's ideas were still in force, that Sandino was not just of historical interest but represented a guide to action. . . . I am convinced that in converting Sandino's thought into the doctrine of the Front of National Liberation, Carlos provided the key to the Nicaraguan revolution.

— VÍCTOR MANUEL TIRADO LÓPEZ
El pensamiento político de Carlos Fonseca Amador

1. The Making of a Revolutionary

If Sandino's political philosophy is an essential part of the Nicaraguan Revolution, then the foundations of the revolution must be sought in his own formation as a revolutionary. Basic to that intellectual formation was his experience of the aftereffects of the Mexican upheaval of 1910–1920—the first great social explosion of its kind. "It is in Tampico," writes Gregorio Selser, "that every biographer must begin to search for the origins of Sandino's later struggle."[1] An avid reader with a strong claim to being an independent thinker, Sandino assimilated the teachings of the principal revolutionary currents of his day along with their exotic counterparts in religious protest movements against the Roman Catholic church. Although he absorbed elements of other political ideologies, including that of Mexico's moderate revolutionary government, the more extreme currents proved to be decisive in his intellectual formation.

The Mexican Experience

Augusto César Sandino was born in the tiny town of Niquinohomo, thirty kilometers southeast of Managua, in 1895. He was the illegitimate son of a small but moderately prosperous landowner of Spanish descent and an Indian woman who worked for the Sandino family. He was reared by his mother, who had become an agricultural day laborer and lived in a shack on the town's outskirts. He took her surname, Calderón.

Several experiences in his youth contributed to the shaping of the future revolutionary. One was his mother's mistreatment and miscarriage in an unhygienic prison cell. Attended only by Sandino, then a lad not quite ten years old, she almost died of a hemorrhage. Sandino first thought only of revenge.[2] But aware of his impotence, he soon began raising fundamental questions concerning God and society. "I remember vividly my infantile reflections on philosophy: Why is God the way he is? . . . And what is law? If, as the priest and therefore authority says, law is the voice of God aimed at protecting the people, then why does it favor the lazy instead of helping us who are poor? Why does God love Sócrates [Sandino's half-brother] more than me, when I have to work and he doesn't? God and life are pure shit! Only we poor get screwed!"[3]

The contrast between his miserable existence and that of his brother Sócrates provided another source of bitterness. "When I compared my brother's situation with my own, the injustices of life made me indignant."[4] Encountering his father by chance in the street one day, he blurted out, "'Listen, sir, am I your son or not?' And when his father replied, 'Yes, son, I am your father,' he retorted, 'Sir, if I am your son, why don't you treat me like you treat Sócrates?'"[5]

It was after this experience that his father invited his eleven-year-old son to move into the family home at the center of town. Augusto then adopted his father's name. Resented by his step-mother, though, he was obliged to eat in the kitchen with the servants and to perform humiliating chores for the rest of the household.[6]

Although his father was generous, Sandino suffered over the disparity between his mother's poverty and his father's affluence: "My father is a proprietor and I considered him to be taking advantage of the people's circumstances. . . . He must have been surprised when I asked him if he did not consider the way in which he maintained his small capital unjust. He replied that he did not wish to exploit people in their situation but that if he did not, then he would be exploited by the exploiters."[7] During those early years Sandino was already beginning to see behind appearances. "One can say that since that time [age twelve] I began to take stock of the way things were."[8]

At age fifteen Sandino's schooling was interrupted and he had to begin working for a living. He worked for his father as a grains jobber until 1916, when he left home to become a mechanic's helper near the Costa Rican border. Returning to Niquinohomo after several years, he established his own small business as a grains dealer. His budding business came to an abrupt end in 1920 when he had to abandon Nicaragua after shooting a man during a quarrel.

For the next five years, beginning in Honduras, then in Guatemala, and finally in Mexico, he worked as a mechanic until promoted to bookkeeper in a U.S.-owned oil company near Tam-

pico.[9] The fires of the Mexican Revolution were still being fanned
in the oil fields of Tampico when he arrived in the summer of 1923.
There he acquired not only his eclectic political and spiritual
philosophy, but also his first experience and impressions of the
Mexican Revolution and its relevance to the political struggles
in Nicaragua.

Tampico was a hotbed of political agitation among oil workers.
It was where the U.S.-Mexican petroleum dispute came to a head.
The movement each month of some two hundred ships in and out
of this city of one hundred thousand testified to the crucial role of
this industrial port. From his companions on the job, Selser tells
us, Sandino assimilated his first notions of the most generalized
struggle being waged at that time, the struggle by workers to
organize their own unions.[10] When the dispute over petroleum
reached its climax and the oil firms threatened to close down the
wells, the entire city felt endangered and the workers retaliated
with demands for nationalizing the oil companies. Whether or not
Sandino participated in the agitation against the foreign owners,
he began to consider them his enemies.

Tampico's oil fields became a recruiting ground for the followers of Mexico's immensely popular anarchist, Ricardo Flores
Magón. According to Neill Macaulay, "[t]he anarchist Industrial
Workers of the World dominated the Tampico labor movement until
seriously challenged in the 1920s by newly formed communist
groups, by purely Mexican radical unions, and by a more conservative government-backed labor federation."[11] The socialists un-
reservedly defended Mexico's new revolutionary government, and
by 1925 Tampico also had a Communist cell. The charismatic
Melquíades Tobías, an organizer for the Mexican Communist party,
was active among Tampico's oil workers.[12] Unlike the banana republics of Central America, which still had one foot in the Middle
Ages, Mexico was an inferno of competing revolutionary ideas.
Sandino could not have remained immune to this social ferment.
The doctrines of Flores Magón in particular made a lasting impression on him.

Sandino assimilated anarchist, socialist, and communist ideas
from these agitators claiming to represent workers like himself.
Mexican anarchists stressed the need for a sustained struggle
against political authority, capital, and the clergy in the hope of
eventually replacing them with self-governing "communes"—associations owning property in common. Mexican socialists insisted
that the land should be worked cooperatively, that nationalization

of the means of production would have to be achieved piecemeal through reforms, and that an advanced system of social legislation was all that workers and peasants might expect, given Mexico's economic backwardness. Mexican Communists argued that the workers' fundamental enemy was international capitalism or "imperialism," that the Mexican government and Mexico's capitalists were incapable of acting independently of pressures from the major centers of world power, and that the violent seizure of the state by a united front of workers and peasants led by a revolutionary vanguard was a necessary step toward national and social liberation. Although they all had a classless society as their ultimate objective, they clashed over how to get there and over the form the new society might take. In the last analysis all were "communists," but only in the loose sense of advocating property in common.

From the anarchists Sandino absorbed a strong dose of antiauthoritarianism, anticlericalism, and anticapitalism; from the socialists, his advanced program of social legislation and strategy of alliances with other progressive forces, including hoped-for material and moral support from Mexico's revolutionary government; and from the Communists, his commitment to a struggle to the death against imperialism through a worldwide proletarian revolution.

In Tampico Sandino also lent a sympathetic ear to the religious currents that supported the Mexican Revolution. César Escobar Morales notes that from 1923 to 1926, Sandino "attended the meetings of Masons that were then fashionable, and absorbed their revolutionary ideas."[13] He adds that Freemasonry played a major role during the French Revolution of 1789 and the struggles for independence in Central and South America. Under the spell of the Mexican Revolution, Freemasonry recovered its earlier revolutionary élan.

The revolution had aroused a number of Masonic lodges to disown their nominal grand master, the dictator Porfirio Díaz, and to support Francisco Madero's constitutionalist movement. Others seceded from the National Rite of Freemasonry and, under the influence of anarchist ideas, set up their own lodges. Valentín Campa provides a glimpse of this revolutionary tendency within Freemasonry in his autobiography on the experiences of a Mexican Communist.[14]

He was invited to join the Grand Lodge of Nuevo León in Monterrey and noted that it had a revolutionary offshoot known as the Bolshevik Grand Lodge. Unlike the traditional lodge, dominated by reactionary intellectuals and large landowners, the bolshevik lodge was overrun by industrial and railroad workers. These Masons, Campa discovered, were partisans of a Russian or bolshevik-type world proletarian revolution without themselves being Communists. Instead, they espoused the doctrines of anarcho-syndicalism, a variant of anarchism based on organized labor and the belief in a general strike that would paralyze the state and replace it with government by revolutionary "syndicates" or trade unions. Flying from the Bolshevik Grand Lodge was a banner combining the black flag of anarchism and the red flag of socialism. Sandino may have joined a similar lodge in Tampico in 1923.

That the Mexican experience was decisive in shaping Sandino's outlook is evident from his own account. "Around the year 1925 . . . I succeeded in surrounding myself with a group of Spiritualist friends with whom I discussed daily the submission of our people in Latin America to either the hypocritical advances or violent interventions of the Yankee imperial assassin."[15] From these friends Sandino acquired his knowledge of Mexican Spiritualism, a nineteenth-century countercultural movement closely tied to political dissidence.

Like Mexican Freemasonry, Mexican Spiritualism was an identifiable sect organized into temples or lodges whose manifest purpose was to form the nucleus of the coming brotherhood of man.[16] The oneness of God and the final redemption of humanity were doctrines common to both. In most other respects they differed. From Mexican Freemasonry Sandino acquired a belief in an impersonal God who supervises human destinies from afar, a hidden or secret doctrine learned through degrees by illumination, and a strategy of revealing this doctrine through small doses to a select few. Through Mexican Spiritualism he came to believe in communication with the spirits of the dead, in a cycle of birth and rebirth, in extrasensory perception, in the power of prophecy, and in the continuing struggle between good and evil spirits for control of the universe.

Common to Mexican Freemasonry and Spiritualism was the doctrine that all men are brothers because they are born of the same holy spirit, and that all men should behave as brothers toward one another. "Brother" and "comrade" were terms of address used by anarchists, socialists, and communists because of their commitment to a fraternal or classless society. Thus there was a common denominator in Sandino's political and spiritual beliefs. Such was the ideological baggage, in the form of a peculiar blend of revolutionary politics and theology, that Sandino carried back to Nicaragua in 1926.

The Struggle in Nicaragua

After learning about the unsuccessful Liberal revolt on his country's east coast in May 1926, Sandino returned home to fight for the
Liberal and Constitutionalist cause. This first Liberal revolt was
followed by a second in August and a third in December in the form
of expeditionary forces armed and trained in Mexico with the support of Mexico's revolutionary government. In the struggle against
the Conservative dictator Emiliano Chamorro, the Liberal party
christened its forces the "Constitutionalist Army" after its Mexican Revolution counterpart. Apparently, Sandino believed that
Nicaraguan Liberals were about to make a revolution like the
Mexican that would be both antioligarchical and anti-imperialist.

Nicaraguan Liberals professed the same political philosophy as
Mexican Liberals. They believed in constitutional government, the
rule of law, and government by the consent of the governed through
a freely elected legislative body. They believed that people had certain natural and inalienable rights, of which the most important
was freedom from the exercise of arbitrary and unlimited authority.
They believed in the right to property; they were modernizers and
defenders of capitalism; they opposed government interference in
the economy; and they supported the separation of church and
state. Many were anticlerical, and some, like Sandino's father, were
also ardent nationalists. And they constituted the only effective
opposition to the Conservative party, which had been in power
since 1909, after a military rebellion incited and supported by the
United States.

Sandino's father was a prominent figure in the Liberal party and
had raised Sandino on the liberal ideology. Although Sandino questioned the sources of his father's wealth, he proudly related how his
father had resisted the onerous Bryan-Chamorro Treaty, in which
Nicaragua conceded to the United States important naval and military rights—an act of defiance for which Don Gregorio had gone to
prison.[17] Liberalism also had a revolutionary past in which Sandino
took pride. It was the political philosophy of the great liberators
of Latin America, Simón Bolívar, San Martín, and Benito Juárez.
The question is whether Sandino was still a liberal when he decided to participate in the constitutional struggle in Nicaragua.

Sandino's personal account of his motives suggests a different
interpretation. "About the year 1925 I was ready to believe that
everything in Nicaragua had become a disgrace and that honor had
completely disappeared among the people. . . . One day I told my
friends that if in Nicaragua there were one hundred men who loved

it as much as I did, our nation would recover its absolute sovereignty, endangered by the Yankee empire."[18] He said this to a group of Spiritualist friends in and around Tampico, who replied that there might be that many men but that the difficulty would be to find them. At issue was not only ordinary patriotism—liberal opposition to Chamorro's regime could be described as patriotic. Sandino meant something more, an extraordinary patriotism tied to the belief that national salvation hinged on the formation of a one-hundred-man revolutionary vanguard.

He recalled that the Mexican people and most of the peoples of Central America felt contempt for Nicaraguans because of the dishonorable treaties signed with the United States. Sandino had personally suffered from their reproaches: "I felt wounded to the core when they called me 'sell-out, shameless, traitor.'"[19] He initially replied to those accusations by explaining that, not being a statesman himself, he was not to blame. Later he realized that they were right. Thus, as soon as he learned that a revolutionary movement had flared up in his country, he quit his job in Mexico and with his three thousand dollars in savings returned "for the purpose of finding those one hundred legitimate sons of Nicaragua."[20]

There are strong indications that Sandino was already a revolutionary firebrand in 1926. We have his own statement as reported by the biographer he trusted most. During three weeks of conversations with Sandino (23 February–16 March 1933), the Nicaraguan journalist José Román learned some of the most intimate details of Sandino's life. Said Sandino concerning his efforts to revolutionize the miners of San Albino, where he was employed after returning to his country in May 1926, "I explained to them the system of [workers'] cooperatives in other countries and the sad fact that we were exploited and that we ought to have a government really concerned for the people to stop the vile exploitation by the capitalists and big foreign enterprises. . . . I explained that I was not a Communist [bolshevik], but rather a socialist!"[21]

This was an understatement. Anastasio Somoza García, founder of the Somoza dynasty, recalled in his biography of Sandino the feeling of distrust when Sandino appeared at Liberal headquarters on the Atlantic coast to ask for arms. The petition was denied after the head of the Liberal or Constitutionalist Army, Gen. José María Moncada, listened to Sandino's reasons for overthrowing the Conservative dictator. Sandino wanted to pursue his own political ideas, which appeared to Moncada to be at variance with the Liberal cause.[22] Moncada was incapable of fully piecing those ideas together, not understanding their precise sources in the Mexican

Revolution and their relevance to Nicaragua. But he did perceive that Sandino espoused a subversive doctrine alien to Nicaraguan liberalism.

Somoza relied on General Moncada's personal testimony to support the charge that Sandino was not a liberal. Said Moncada, "I saw Augusto Sandino for the first time in Prinzapolca. He addressed me, saying that he wanted to go to fight in the interior. . . . At the same time he gave me a written statement concerning his ideas, the concluding sentence of which proclaimed that 'PROPERTY IS THEFT.'"[23] This was the thesis of a book by the father of modern anarchism, Pierre Joseph Proudhon.[24] Sandino's conception of the struggle against the Chamorro dictatorship was understandably not shared by the leaders of the Liberal party.

Sandino learned a lesson from this humiliating experience. From then on he was careful to keep his deepest political convictions to himself and to stress the patriotic motives of his struggle.

This was not his only humiliating experience in the presence of Moncada. Several months later, after ordering Sandino to get rid of his red and black flag with a skull and crossbones in the center, Moncada contemptuously added, "Our enemies are trying to discredit us by calling us bolsheviks, and we must not give them the opportunity of having others believe this or of making us appear ridiculous!"[25] Sandino complied in tears. But he never forgave the insult both to himself and to the cherished principles symbolized by his emblem.

Not long afterwards, when General Moncada decided to collaborate with the U.S. forces of occupation that had intervened during the civil war, Sandino rebelled and refused to accept the general's authority. As he sarcastically replied to Moncada's veiled threats of retaliation, "I don't know why you wish to command me now. I remember that you always regarded me badly when you were commander-in-chief. You never accepted my request for troops to fight the enemy. . . . It seems that you were jealous of me. You undoubtedly know my temperament and that I am unbreakable. Now I want you to come disarm me. I await you at my post. You will not make me cede by any other means. *I am not for sale, I do not give up.* You will have to defeat me!"[26]

Nonetheless, one must give Moncada credit for perceiving that Sandino was not a bolshevik. Sandino's flag suggested a contempt for all authority. As he later wrote, "Sandino's ideas are something more than socialist. . . . It seems that in Mexico he made contact with elements opposed to all authority, and now these connections are helping him."[27] As Selser notes, Sandino eventually obtained the support of anarchists not only in Mexico and the United States, but also in many other parts of the world.[28]

Despite his difficulties with Moncada, Sandino managed to arm his men from other sources and to fight in the Constitutionalist war under Moncada's overall command. Promoted to the rank of general by his little army of volunteers, he led his column from victory to victory until it swelled in numbers and surpassed in popularity the other Liberal columns. His soldiers were grateful to have a general who did not lord it over them, who practiced an ordinary trade and could qualify as a gunsmith. According to Gen. Luis Mena's account, Sandino spent almost two weeks repairing the rifles of Mexican origin finally granted him at Dr. Sacasa's headquarters in Puerto Cabezas, some without triggers, others without breeches, and many with maladjusted sights.[29]

By then the U.S. government had pressured Emiliano Chamorro to resign. When he was replaced by Chamorro's fellow Conservative and U.S. faithful Adolfo Díaz, the White House recognized the new government. Shortly afterward the marines returned to Nicaragua to stabilize the situation and to forestall a second edition of the Mexican Revolution. When victory for the Liberal, or Constitutionalist, Army was imminent, the United States threatened to enter the war against the Liberals unless they agreed to the American peace terms.

In May 1927 General Moncada and the other Liberal generals capitulated—all except Sandino. Reorganizing his forces as the Defending Army of Nicaragua's National Sovereignty, he waged a guerrilla war of attrition against the U.S. Marines. Soon revolutionary intellectuals from other countries joined his cause to expel the foreign invader.

In the liberated territory under his control in northwestern Nicaragua, the mountainous region known as the Segovias, Sandino had the support of local sections of the Liberal party reorganized as the Liberal party of the Segovias. Ostensibly, he continued fighting in defense of the liberal principles he believed had been betrayed. But when elections were held in November 1928 and the Liberal Moncada was elected president, Sandino adopted a more radical policy.

At that time he came under the influence of Agustín Farabundo Martí, the Salvadoran Communist and representative of the Communist International on Sandino's general staff. Martí encouraged him to break with the Liberals and to continue the war against the newly elected government because of Moncada's record of continuing collaboration with the American forces of occupation. Although the marines were scheduled to withdraw after the new president's inauguration, they remained to safeguard the new Liberal government against the threat of Sandino's armed opposition.

Sandino responded to Moncada's election and to the continued presence of the marines by launching a new program of social legislation for Nicaragua's workers and peasants. Simultaneously, he called for the political unification of the Central American republics to defend his country's sovereignty and to combat U.S. "imperialism." Sometimes characterized as a "populist" program, to distinguish it from the liberal one it replaced, it questioned the representative character of Moncada's administration by demanding a government not just of the people, but also for the people.

Unlike liberals for whom individual liberty is the supreme political end, populists (from the Latin *populus,* the people) give precedence to collective interests. In opposition to the classical liberal credo of each for himself or herself, populists stress the general welfare. Instead of "sink or swim," the injunction to "help and be helped" would prevent anyone from sinking. In defending minimum standards below which no Nicaraguan citizen would be allowed to fall, Sandino's new program could be called a populist one.

Sandino's program gave the impression of threatening the established order. In Mexico populism had led to a policy of partial nationalizations and labor legislation that infringed on the rights of property. In practice, the populist credo had converged on a socialist one. Such was the impression created by the program, in essence a social democratic program like that of Mexico's revolutionary government.

Abandoned by Nicaragua's Liberals, Sandino relied on his populist program to court Mexico's revolutionary government and the representatives of the Communist International. In search of arms and moral support, he made a second trip to Mexico in May 1929, from which he did not return until June 1930. In Mexico he idled in Yucatán until the Mexican president finally received him some six months later, only to reject his request for arms. His bid for Communist support also fell on deaf ears. Although supported by the Communists during 1928 and 1929, they broke off relations with him in 1930, when he refused to agree to their terms.

Revitalizing an Ailing Cause

When Sandino failed to obtain support from the Mexican government and lost the backing of the Mexican Communists and the

Comintern, he turned to other groups for help. Among these was the brotherhood of Mexican Freemasons. In Mérida Sandino joined the Masonic Grand Lodge, where he immersed himself in secrets accessible only to the initiated. A member of his general staff reported that "Sandino acquired the third degree, passing on . . . to the degree of Master Mason."[30] Attesting to the importance of his Masonic connections, Sandino deposited in the Masonic Grand Lodge through a notary public the treasured archives of his Defending Army.

But Sandino's most important backing was to follow from his studies "at Spiritist [not to be confused with Spiritualist] institutions in Mexico that still operated underground."[31] In addition to becoming a Master Mason, he attended meetings of the "Spiritism of Light and Truth" Provincial Cathedra of Yucatán in the port city of Progreso, only a few miles from Mérida.[32] This cathedra was one of several Mexican branches of an international Spiritist society with its headquarters in Buenos Aires. Known as the Magnetic-Spiritual School of the Universal Commune, its founder was the Basque Spiritist Joaquín Trincado, who had emigrated to Argentina at the turn of the century. Eventually, he would become Sandino's official representative in Argentina, with powers and privileges equal to those of Sandino's representative in Mexico.[33] By then the school could count on more than four thousand adepts throughout Latin America, who were devoted supporters of Sandino's cause. Sandino was to become the school's official representative in his country, the head of its Nicaraguan branch.[34]

In Mérida, Sandino steeped himself in the doctrines of the Magnetic-Spiritual School, which reinforced what he had learned from Mexican Spiritualists. Spiritism shares with Spiritualism the same basic doctrines and may be considered an offshoot of it, except that the former holds that not just the human body but all things are full of spirits. Trincado's Spiritism further distinguished itself by its universal rejection of all forms of religious faith and worship, including efforts to reconcile religion and modern science.[35]

Trincado's major work, an eight-hundred-page treatise on austere rational philosophy, was required reading for all would-be members of his school. Apparently, Sandino spent long hours in solitary reading in an effort to master this particular work, not to mention other books the school published. An American journalist, Thomas L. Stockes, reported in September 1929 that Sandino had taken refuge in the top story of a Mérida apartment building, "where he passed almost all his time living the life of an anchorite!"[36] The downstairs entrance was carefully guarded by members of his Defending Army to prevent his being disturbed.

José Román, one of his few trusted biographers, interviewed him after the war was over and recalled how Sandino enjoyed expounding what he called his "philosophical ideas." On one occasion he talked at length about "reincarnation, the Rosicrucians, Spiritism, yoga, theosophy, and his many invaluable intuitions during the war."[37] Sandino was especially impressed by Trincado's works. "Apropos of philosophy," he said to Román, "you should have read something by or heard about Martín [sic] Trincado. . . . Unquestionably, Trincado is one of the great contemporary philosophers. . . . He is the Great Master of Cosmogony."[38]

From his first arrival in Mexico in 1923 until his death in Nicaragua in 1934, Sandino came under the influence of two thinkers, primarily: the anarchist Ricardo Flores Magón, and the Spiritist Joaquín Trincado. Flores Magón's thought prevailed until Sandino returned to Mexico in 1929, after which Trincado became his chief mentor.

Since Trincado shared with the Mexican anarchist a commitment to anarcho-communism, his thought did not replace but rather complemented that of Flores Magón by adding a spiritual dimension to it. What endeared Trincado and his school to Sandino was their conviction of the importance of spiritual reform and their hope of establishing a universal commune with the help of his Defending Army. The first step was to be a Spiritist government in Central America as part of an ambitious plan to implement Trincado's doctrine of universal fraternity. In this respect, Trincado's philosophy corresponded to Flores Magón's.[39]

Abandoned by his former allies, Sandino had to rely on his own spiritual resources to revitalize an ailing cause.[40] He combined the anarcho-communism learned during his first stay in Mexico with the ready-made synthesis of anarchism and Spiritism taught him by the Magnetic-Spiritual School. It was an almost perfect fit.

Besides Román, Sandino confided his Spiritist worldview to the Basque journalist Ramón de Belausteguigoitia. The first of his biographers to have a knowledge of oriental philosophy, Belausteguigoitia perceived that Sandino was a student of theosophy.[41] Theosophy is not so much a religion as a tradition of occult wisdom transmitted by superior beings known as mahatmas or guiding spirits of humanity. These seers or sages lay claim to an inner light, to a unique form of knowledge derived from long hours of meditation assisted by extrasensory perception (clairvoyance)

and communication (telepathy). Belausteguigoitia believed that
Sandino exhibited the same extraordinary powers.[42]

Sandino spoke of "guiding spirits of mankind, among whom he
listed Adam, Moses, Jesus, Bolívar."[43] He admitted to being clair-
voyant and to receiving and transmitting extrasensory messages.[44]
There were moments in his conversations with Belausteguigoitia
that he appeared to enter a trancelike state preparatory to receiving
a new vision. Thus to Belausteguigoitia he gave the impression of
being "a cultivator of yoga, a disciple of the Orient."[45]

Sandino was cautious about revealing his theosophical convictions in public. He was especially concerned that they might un-
dermine his political credibility. As Belausteguigoitia noted, "On
one occasion, speaking to me about his belief in . . . incarnate spirits and of the future of communization, by which he meant fraternization, Sandino added with a jovial air: 'But look, if I were to say
this openly, people would take me for a screwball or a drunkard!'"[46]
What Belausteguigoitia did not know was that Sandino was a member of the Magnetic-Spiritual School and shared its commitment
to a universal anarchist commune.

The substance of Sandino's Spiritism was expressed in a letter
to Col. Abraham Rivera in October 1930, shortly after Sandino's return to Nicaragua.[47] At first he revealed his belief only to his most
spiritually adept and trusted officers. Encouraged by their response,
he proclaimed it to all the soldiers under his command. Sandino
had been educating his men in spiritual matters as early as February 1928, when the American journalist Carleton Beals visited his
camp and commented on the role of religious ideas in strengthening their morale.[48] But it was not until February 1931 that he presented a public statement of his anarcho-Spiritism in his famous
Light and Truth Manifesto.[49] Apparently, it had a remarkable effect.
It went hand in hand with an escalation of Sandino's armed struggle
and the spread of Sandinismo to the remotest corners of Nicaragua.

"There was a moment," wrote Belausteguigoitia, "when I realized that the strange and profound soul of Sandino had created in
his army a religious sect imbued with the fire of a new revelation."[50] He attributed the composure of Sandino's soldiers less to
exacting discipline than to the extraordinary comradeship that
united them. "The absence of distinctions in the distribution of
food and clothing, in which all shared equally regardless of rank,"
compensated for strict subordination to their military superiors.[51]
How to explain, then, that Sandino's army consisted exclusively
of volunteers, that they were shabbily clothed and inadequately

armed, that they seldom enjoyed a full meal, and that they served
without pay—except by the spiritual force and ideas of their
leader?

His soldiers recognized the spirituality of this remarkable man
who became their teacher as well as general: "Despite the lack of
contact . . . all his soldiers adored him. The 'old man,' as they
called him, was like a father. . . . The day he left for Managua the
hardened soldiers in his camp burst out in tears, because they
feared they might never see him again."[52] The worship of Sandino's
person reached ridiculous heights. Belausteguigoitia listened to
stories of how, at the end of a rainfall, his soldiers had collectively
witnessed a double rainbow about the general's head, which they
interpreted as a halo. He also heard how the mountain people followed Sandino in hopes of obtaining some object he might have
touched, which then became a precious relic. Thus "the reverence
of his soldiers helped endow the general with fantastic and supernatural attributes . . . to the point of inspiring a kind of blind
fanaticism."[53]

From his return to Nicaragua in June 1930 until the marines
withdrew in January 1933, the escalation of his armed struggle continued. It came to an abrupt halt when Dr. Juan Bautista Sacasa,
who was the former leader of the Constitutionalist movement and
who shared some of Sandino's idealism, replaced Moncada as the
new Liberal president. A peace agreement was signed in February
allotting to Sandino's demobilized soldiers a vast territory in the
northeast, the Río Coco basin. There he dedicated himself to building an agricultural "commune" along the lines recommended by
the Magnetic-Spiritual School.

At the same time his men were ready to be mobilized on
twenty-four hours' notice. Although Sandino supposedly had
turned over his guns and ammunition to the government in carrying out his part of the peace agreement, he had secretly rearmed his
followers with weapons from neighboring Honduras.[54] Ostensibly,
he would defend the president and the Constitution; actually, he intended to launch a new military offensive should the occasion
arise, an offensive aimed at seizing power and making a revolution
first in Nicaragua and then in the rest of Central America in the
effort to establish a Central American commune.[55]

From February 1933 to February 1934 two powers effectively contended for the new president's allegiance: Somoza's U.S.-
originated, trained, and unconstitutional National Guard; and
Sandino's demobilized Defending Army. During this period Sandino's strategy was to defend the duly-elected constitutional govern-

ment against pressures from Somoza, who eventually deposed the president in a military coup.

By defending both the president and the Constitution, Sandino hoped to give legitimacy to his Defending Army. When his strategy began to bear fruit, Somoza was driven to act. After dining with the president on 23 February 1934, Sandino was seized outside the presidential mansion by soldiers of the National Guard and assassinated with two of his generals. That same night some three hundred followers at his agricultural cooperative in Wiwilí were surrounded by the National Guard and massacred on Somoza's orders.

Thus ended the heroic saga of Nicaragua's rustic philosopher-guerrilla. Sandino's father, who had been seized also, after they had dined with the president, was forcibly detained near the city's outskirts. His life was spared but as he heard the shooting from a distance, he said, "Now they are killing them. Those who are redeemers always die crucified!"[56]

Understanding Sandino

Most studies of Sandino describe him as a political activist without a coherent ideology. They question his importance as an ideologue by disputing the influence of his beliefs and rhetoric and characterize his thought as a half-formed and ill-digested set of ideas that were incidental to his main role of expelling the U.S. Marines from his native soil. Liberals and Communists alike have questioned both the intellectual content of his ideology and the lessons to be learned from its application to Nicaragua.

The Liberal Somoza attempted to discredit Sandino by ridiculing the theosophical foundations of his political program. He exhibited Sandino's correspondence with his fellow theosophists as evidence of a perturbed mind "congested with ideas he did not understand but unthinkingly tried to apply."[57] Luis Sánchez Sancho, general secretary of the mainline communist party calling itself the Nicaraguan Socialist party (PSN), claims that Sandino's liberation struggle was guided by a prescientific ideology without a clear conception of class interests or a coherent political and economic program.[58]

To this unengaging portrait North American social scientists have added a skeleton of their own. Despite Sandino's association with spiritualist and theosophical groups, Macaulay believes that "in the end it was Latin American nationalism that became Sandino's creed."[59] John Booth insists that Sandino "never manifested a doctrinaire ideological strain of any sort," that he "lacked a well-developed ideology," that his "economic thinking . . . did not contain any consistent ideological thread."[60] Other American scholars concur with the opinion that Sandino's ideology was a loose blend of populism and nationalism, but little more.[61]

These characterizations show only a superficial acquaintance with Sandino's thought and with his sources. On close examination Sandino's belief system was extraordinarily complex, because it was designed to appeal to many different groups. At the same time, its ideological foundations remained concealed except to his most ardent supporters. Rather than unassimilated and half-baked notions, what emerges is a core of politically activating beliefs originally formed in Mexico but with different faces that appeared in response to the changing circumstances of his struggle in Nicaragua.

One hurdle to understanding Sandino is the paucity of his writings. His personal letters, circulars, communiqués, manifestos, and short autobiographical sketches cover less than 450 printed pages and leave us guessing about his underlying beliefs. His reported interviews and conversations fill in some of the gaps. But politically cautious as he was, he hesitated to reveal himself even to his most sympathetic biographers. Since they, too, were unable to penetrate the surface of his thought, one must examine his intellectual sources and the revolutionary currents that made an indelible impression on him.

Another obstacle to interpreting Sandino's thought accurately lies in the different weights to be assigned to the competing ideological strands he wove together. For most scholars his theosophical doctrine has proved embarrassing and on certain points incomprehensible. Somoza inflated its importance in an effort to present Sandino's thought as the outpourings of an erratic and uneducated mind; most North American scholars tend to ignore it altogether or to dismiss it as tangential if not irrelevant to his political outlook. To add to the problems of interpretation, Sandino was sometimes deliberately misleading. The clandestine character of his struggle and mounting political pressures made him unusually guarded concerning his ultimate political objectives. These he expressed only in the cryptic and symbolic language of his political theosophy. To those uninitiated in Sandino's sources his most pregnant ideas are not only obscure, but also intellectually suspect because of their inspirational character.

In reading Sandino one must not confuse the successive public statements of his political ideology with the inner development of his thought.[62] Rather than a progression from philosophical liberalism to populist and loosely socialist ideas, and from there to his peculiar brand of anarcho-communism supported by a theosophy of liberation, his ideology evolved from a rudimentary anarcho-communism acquired during his first stay in Mexico into the comparatively sophisticated political theosophy developed during his second visit there from 1929 to 1930.

Although under his father's guidance Sandino began his political apprenticeship as a Nicaraguan Liberal, under the influence of the Mexican Revolution he assimilated the mainstream of populist and socialist ideas crystallized in the 1917 Constitution (which he used to mobilize the miners of San Albino and later incorporated in his bases for an agreement with General Moncada) and the anarchist side-current that went beyond liberalism, populism, and socialism in favoring a classless society administered by the workers. Simultaneously, he came under the influence of Mexican revolutionary Masonry and Spiritualism, which added a spiritual foundation to his anarchism.

Already a flaming revolutionary when he returned to Nicaragua in 1926, Sandino learned to keep his political convictions to himself. From December 1926 to the end of 1928 he couched his ideology in patriotic and liberal phraseology that soon attracted the support of liberals in his own country and abroad. This phase ended when, under the influence of Farabundo Martí and strong Communist backing, he alienated his Liberal supporters by opposing General Moncada's election in November and then refusing to recognize him as president.

The loss of Liberal support led Sandino to present his views in the new garb of populist and loosely socialist ideas, although these represented a change in the mode of mobilizing support for his political convictions rather than in those convictions themselves. Under the cover of this new ideology he turned for military aid and assistance to the Mexican government, and for moral and political support to the Communist International, which had become his principal ally. This phase ended when he ran afoul of both.

It was then that, frustrated by the Mexican government's refusal of material aid and simultaneously fed up with the Communists, who insisted that he cooperate on their terms, Sandino began to look for new allies to invigorate his struggle. Chief among these was the Magnetic-Spiritual School of the Universal Commune. Henceforth, from his second return to Nicaragua in 1930 until his assassination in 1934, he presented his anarchist convictions under the protective covering of his theosophy. This was not just a Machiavellian stratagem, for he sincerely believed in the doctrines of the school.

Unlike his other covers, his theosophy provided the inner strength to carry on his struggle against almost overwhelming odds. Far from signifying a flight from the world, his philosophy of rational austerity helped him to cope with reality. Ramírez notes that it also helped "to deepen his understanding of the real problem of justice and injustice, the real problem of exploitation of some men by others, the real problem of the distribution of wealth."[63] Sandino's theosophical system enabled him to perceive his country's problems in a unique light. His understanding of Nicaragua's political history and of his own struggle for liberation was profoundly indebted to it.

Sandino's ideology was fundamentally eclectic. It combined diverse political currents to suit different purposes and also added to his anarchism a theosophical dimension. In this capacity it became not only a forerunner, but also a model for the ideological pluralism of later Sandinistas.

That an ideology is eclectic does not mean that it is incoherent and unoriginal. In its intellectual sense, eclecticism implies a combination of doctrines based on a variety of sources that may or may not be consistent. The ideas are secondhand but sometimes they are synthesized in novel ways. We have seen that Sandino's ideology combined anarchist and communist ideas with what he had assimilated from Mexican Freemasonry and Spiritualism. The blend was his own, but was it coherent? Owing to its occult elements, Sandino's ideology has come under fire for being either confused, bizarre, or downright irrational.

"Many people hastily try to disencumber themselves of the Sandino problem," writes Sergio Ramírez, "saying that it was all right that Sandino struggled to expel the North Americans from Nicaragua, that it was laudable, but that underneath Sandino was confused, an ignoramus, that he was crammed full of ideologies he had never understood and had hurriedly acquired in Mexico."[64] The welter of ideologies that emerges from Sandino's writings gives the impression that he either subscribed to apparently contradictory theses or could not make up his mind. Such impressions are illfounded because they mistake the public statements of his ideology for what he actually believed. What others take for confusion I interpret as political astuteness and as a strategy for mobilizing support for his struggle from widely divergent sources.

The more compelling criticism is that Sandino's ideology was so strange or idiosyncratic that it lacked mass appeal. If this had been the case, then his immediate followers and sympathizers would have grudgingly tolerated his aberration for the sake of driving the Americans from Nicaragua. But the evidence points to a different conclusion. The members of his Defending Army, according to both Beals and Belausteguigoitia, revered him as a religious teacher and seer. His words of wisdom concerning God, the human spirit, and death were repeated frequently by his soldiers. None of this indicates that Sandino's theosophy fell on deaf ears. On the contrary, the escalation of his armed struggle in 1930 went hand in hand with the first public pronouncements of his theosophy, which is further evidence that it contributed to mobilizing popular support for his cause.

Finally, there is the criticism that Sandino's theosophy, whatever its strategical usefulness, was basically unintelligible. In part this was Somoza's criticism. But the same may be said of other forms of religious commitment. Most Christians find their faith to be intelligible, just as Sandino's followers had apparently few difficulties in comprehending his general message. Belief in the impossible and not just the improbable is a distinguishing facet of social myths.

To be sure, there is an element of truth in most of these criticisms. The difficulty lies in singling out what is true from what is falsely attributed to Sandino. Lacking information concerning his sources, Somoza was completely mystified by his theosophy. His mistake was to conclude that his confusion was caused by Sandino's. There are instances in which Sandino did not thoroughly assimilate what he had learned from the Magnetic-Spiritual School. Some of his ideas were ill-digested, but Somoza was not equipped to identify them.[65] Such mistakes of assimilation may be committed by almost anyone and should not be confused with what Somoza called a disorderly and unbalanced mind.

Sandino's statements are frequently equivocating, since they were intentionally ambiguous and misleading. But equivocation is not reducible to a jumble of ideas. Politically, equivocation is a Machiavellian stratagem designed to keep the enemy off balance.

It is not always possible to decipher Sandino's meaning, because of missing connections and clues. But a statement may be indecipherable without being confused. Sandino was deliberately obscure to keep the enemy in ignorance.

Because of their jarring contrasts and striking incongruities, Sandino's beliefs were unquestionably bizarre. But bizarre does not mean incoherent. Sandino's critics have mistakenly assumed that, because his beliefs were not strung up on a single ideological hanger, they were inconsistent.

What seemed exotic to urbane liberals like Somoza was less than exotic to Sandino's followers. As Sergio Ramírez observes, "Neither Emiliano Zapata, nor Pancho Villa, nor any of the other popular leaders of Latin America was alien to this type of exotic idea."[66] Although Ramírez notes the strangeness of Sandino's ideas from today's perspective, he acknowledges that they were less strange at the time. In Sandino's day the only effective religious protest against the rigid and reactionary theology of the Catholic church took the form of outright rejection of the only form of Christianity familiar to most Latin Americans. Since the historical conditions were absent for developing a theology of liberation within the established church, a religious substitute was found outside it.

To be sure, Sandino denied that Spiritualism, Freemasonry, and theosophy were religious substitutes. To him they were entirely in keeping with the discoveries of modern science. But his commitment to what he called "reason" was not a commitment to the experimental sciences. In the last analysis, what struck Román about Sandino's philosophical ideas was their intuitive character: "Sandino is very romantic, sentimental, and more quixotic than Don Quixote!"[67]

2. Activating Ideologies

In Sandino's artisan's approach to philosophical matters, ideologies are like the mechanic's tools. Just as screwdrivers and wrenches may be used to achieve an effect, so ideologies may be made to complement one another. In Sandino's pragmatic approach to belief systems may be found the basis of his ideological pluralism. The more ideologies the better, as long as they served the purpose for which they were intended—mobilizing people toward a specific goal.

Sandino's ideological interests covered a broad spectrum. Macaulay reports that in Tampico he became a Freemason while associating with Spiritualist groups and also studied theosophy, yoga, and Seventh Day Adventism.[1] Even then Sandino took an active interest in matters that might broadly be described as philosophical. These interests became more pronounced in later years. When Belausteguigoitia asked him about his studies, he replied, "I am interested in the study of Nature and of the fundamental relations among things. That is why I like philosophy!"[2]

As early as his first trip to Mexico he became familiar with different political, moral, and religious philosophies as guides to human conduct. The fundamental concepts on which he based his political philosophy, such as Reason and Justice, were subsequently inflated into cosmic principles governing both nature and history. Some "rights" acquired a "sacred" character for him, and "God" also figured in his philosophical musings. Later, as his seeming obsession with his fatherland began taking second place to his presumed mission of liberating all of Central America and then the world, these concepts would be recast in terms of "Universal Love." By then his earlier political philosophy had mushroomed into a cosmogony and philosophy of universal history in the final version of his philosophy of liberation.

To piece together the puzzle of Sandino's activating ideologies is not easy. His correspondence contains the clues, but his principal interpreters have not followed them up. One explanation lies in the image they have fashioned of Sandino as the "general of free men."[3] Most scholars believe that Sandino's philosophy, if not an aberration, was incidental to his task of driving the marines from Nicaragua.

But challenging Goliath was not his chief concern. However much he loved his country, his patriotism was mainly a vehicle for making a revolution and spiritually redeeming his countrymen. Mexican anarchists had taught him patriotism's political uses. Later, under the influence of the Magnetic-Spiritual School, his patriotism would acquire a spiritual significance.

Sandino had in his possession a copy of Trincado's book "The Five Loves."[4] In ascending order these were love for one's family, one's city, and one's particular region or province leading to love for one's country and to the most important and least egoistic love of all, universal love or fraternity. The priority of this fifth love was basic to the school's "Communist Ethic."[5] While the instrumentality of universal love was an anarchist and communist revolution, its goal was "the complete man: the Communist Spiritist."[6] This was no tangential matter for Sandino; it was the crux of his philosophy of liberation.

The intellectual foundations of Sandino's philosophy may be found in Mexican anarchism, Spiritualism, Freemasonry, and theosophy, and in the Magnetic-Spiritual School of the Universal Commune's custom-made fusion of anarchism and Spiritism. As we shall see, what Sandino assimilated from each of these is crucial to understanding the political role he assigned to his Defending Army.

The Legacy of Mexican Anarchism

Sandino's anarchism had several sources. Some of it derived from Spanish anarcho-syndicalism, but his principal debt was to the father of Mexican anarchism, Ricardo Flores Magón (1873–1922).

As the leader of the extreme revolutionary current opposed to the dictatorship of Porfirio Díaz, Flores Magón escaped persecution only by emigrating to the United States. Ironically, he fell victim to repressive legislation and spent most of his years there in jail. His final conviction came after publishing his inflammatory "Manifesto to the Members of the Liberal Party, to the Anarchists of the World, and to the Workers in General" (16 March 1918).[7] This pamphlet protested U.S. entry into World War I and linked his revolutionary current in the Mexican Revolution with that of the Bolshevik Revolution of October 1917. The American government responded by arresting, trying, and sentencing him to a twenty-year term in Fort Leavenworth. He died in prison on 20 November 1922.

Flores Magón's death in an American prison aroused the Mexican people to such a pitch that it became a major news item for several months. Andrés García Salgado, who with two other Mexicans joined Sandino's Defending Army in 1928, recalled why Sandino adopted the red and black flag: "Because they were the colors [red for communism and black for anarchism] defended by Ricardo Flores Magón who, from his prison cell in Leavenworth in the United States, railed against 'the violators of Nicaragua, the ravishers of Haiti, the vandals who dismembered Colombia, the scourge of Puerto Rico, the butchers of Spain, and the stranglers of the rights of weak peoples.'"[8]

Although Mexico's Chamber of Deputies voted to pay for the return of the hero's body, the Confederation of Railroad Brotherhoods brought it back at its own expense.[9] Attended by tens of thousands of Mexican workers, Flores Magón was buried with state honors in the nation's capital on 16 January 1923. His funeral contributed more to radicalizing the Mexican labor movement than perhaps any prior event in the country's history.[10]

Seldom have anarchists obtained the national renown and recognition that Flores Magón received from the Mexican people. A year before his death the General Confederation of Workers (CGT) was founded in Mexico City under the influence of his ideas—a peculiar blend of anarcho-communism and revolutionary syndicalism. Several months later, workers throughout Mexico went on strike and boycotted all U.S. goods to secure his freedom. The Mexican government not only instructed its embassy in Washington to press for his release, but also voted him a pension as the intellectual father of the revolution.[11]

Because of pressure from the Mexican government, those who had been imprisoned with him were finally freed. On 1 March 1923, his brother Enrique returned home from the United States to embark on a major campaign of disseminating his ideas. In town after town where Enrique addressed the people, thousands stopped work to listen to his propaganda. On 2 October Librado Rivera, Flores Magón's closest collaborator, was released and deported to Mexico. That same month he settled in Villa Cecilia, a suburb of Tampico that is today's Ciudad Madero. There he continued Flores Magón's work by agitating among the oil workers.[12]

When Sandino arrived in Tampico in 1923, it had just been selected as an organizing base for the Magonist campaign of propa-

ganda and agitation among Mexico's industrial workers. In 1924
Rivera began editing the newspaper *Sagittario*, whose incendiary
articles eventually led to his arrest and imprisonment.[13]

To the workers of Tampico, Rivera distributed copies of Flores
Magón's *Semilla libertaria* (*Libertarian Seed*) in an inexpensive
two-volume edition of ten thousand copies subsidized in part by
the Ministry of Education under José Vasconcelos.[14] From the moment it appeared in 1923 it became a kind of political bible, the
single most important source of ideas for the Mexican working
class. An avid reader, Sandino could not have escaped its influence.

Semilla libertaria consisted of a collection of articles from
Flores Magón's weekly journal *Regeneración*, which first appeared
in Mexico in 1900 and continued to be published in the United
States with brief interruptions until his final imprisonment in
1918. The book contained his most important articles, beginning
on the eve of the Mexican Revolution in September 1910, and ending with his provocative manifesto to the workers of the world. It
described the role of anarchism in the revolution, the feasibility of
a classless outcome of the revolutionary struggle, and concluded
by linking together the Mexican and Russian revolutions as heralds
of a world proletarian conflagration. Its publication placed Flores
Magón among the luminaries of international anarchism alongside
the Russian Peter Kropotkin (1842–1921) and the Italian Errico
Malatesta (1853–1932).

Flores Magón owed a major intellectual debt to each. From
Kropotkin he derived the idea of a social revolution that would lead
to a new order called "anarchist communism" or "communist anarchism." This project differed from the collectivist anarchism of
Michael Bakunin in advocating common ownership not only of the
means of production, but also of the collective fruits of human labor. Rather than each worker's being entitled to the proceeds of his
or her own labor, each would be allowed to appropriate what he or
she needed. Malatesta also adopted this program as his own. But
unlike Kropotkin, he came to terms with Marxism by accepting
the materialist interpretation of history and by relying on the
workers to emancipate themselves through their own revolutionary
organizations.[15] So did Flores Magón.

Like his anarchist precursors, Flores Magón tried to combine
the legacies of two different and opposed revolutionary traditions:
the radicalized liberalism and democratism of Rousseau, which
achieved its maximum expression during the French Revolution of
1789; and the communized socialism of Marx and his followers,
which would reach its apogee during the Russian Revolution of

1917. Both legacies, he believed, faced a common enemy in the alliance of Property, State, and Church. He dubbed them the "three thieves" because they lived off the fruits of other people's labors: "He who said, 'This is mine!' He who shouted 'Obey me!' And he who, raising his eyes toward heaven, hypocritically stammered, 'I am the minister of God!'"[16]

Against the first thief Flores Magón called for economic equality; against the second, for political liberty; and against the third, for universal love. Thus the old order would be replaced by "the saving revolution that goes to the bottom of things, that . . . annihilates once and for all the old system and implants the new one of liberty, equality, and fraternity."[17] These were also Sandino's principles.

The principle of fraternity aimed to regenerate people from the corrupting influence of the Roman Catholic church in particular and religion in general. People had been taught to love God and neighbor, but this doctrine had been twisted into a new idolatry that expressed contempt for others, hence the anarchist imperative of establishing a new order based on love. Wrote Flores Magón, "I believe in the abolition of international frontiers; I struggle for the universal fraternity of men."[18] This was not a passing sentiment. Elsewhere he urged the "fraternization of peoples" and the "fraternization of the human races."[19] Lenin in particular, he believed, was responsible for spreading the sentiment of universal fraternity to all the nations of the earth.[20]

During his years in exile Flores Magón never wavered in his dedication to the goals of anarcho-communism. But his particular priorities shifted in response to changing political conditions at home. Before the fall of Porfirio Díaz, he gave priority to the struggle against the authoritarian state, a position in line with classical anarchism.[21] After the fall of Díaz in May 1911, his emphasis shifted to the class struggle between capital and labor. In conformity with Marxism, capital became the fundamental enemy.[22] Several years later, when Emiliano Zapata's forces in the South were under attack from the new government made up of revolutionary moderates, he momentarily returned to the classical anarchist emphasis on the state.[23] Finally, a few years before his death, he abandoned the Marxist theory stressing the importance of economic factors for the primacy most anarchists assign to a moral transformation. "The revolution," he wrote, "does not begin with a forcible or peaceful change in the collective social, economic, and political way of life . . . long before such a change is attempted there has already been a revolution in the collective consciousness."[24]

Similar shifts in emphasis may be found in Sandino's writings. As long as the Conservative Adolfo Díaz remained in power unconstitutionally, Sandino gave precedence to the struggle for justice and right against established political authority. After the Liberal Moncada was elected president in 1928, Sandino made common cause with the Communist International by gradually shifting his focus to the struggle between labor and capital. International capitalism or imperialism thus became the fundamental enemy. Finally, under the influence of the Magnetic-Spiritual School of the Universal Commune, he began insisting that moral regeneration was a precondition of any thoroughgoing economic and political revolution.

Sandino was not an original political thinker. Most of his political theses may be found in Flores Magón's letters, political manifestos, and communiqués. In some instances even the style of expression and choice of words are similar.

All of the bizarre political ideas Sandino articulated in terms of "communism," "communization," "fraternization," and the coming "chaos," "world conflagration," and "proletarian explosion" may be found in the two volumes of *Semilla libertaria*.[25] The meanings Sandino gave them were the meanings given them by Flores Magón. Sandino's development of the doctrine of liberalism, his peculiar concept of patriotism, his advanced social program, and his revolutionary strategy all have their foundations in Flores Magón's writings and the practice of the Mexican Liberal party. Although Sandino also studied the works of Spanish anarchists, what he borrowed from them reinforced what he had already learned from Ricardo Flores Magón.

Basic to Sandino's radicalized version of liberal political philosophy was the opposition of the "force of right" and the "right of force," concepts also fundamental to Flores Magón's liberalism.[26] Like Flores Magón, he counterposed the enlightened trinity of "Liberty, Equality, Fraternity" to what the other called the hydra with three heads: "Authority, Capital, Clergy."[27] In depicting himself as simultaneously a liberal and a "rational communist," Sandino again echoed Flores Magón.[28] Sandino's doctrine of "universal love" and "justice" is also to be found in Flores Magón's writings.[29]

Like most anarchists, Flores Magón claimed that the struggle of labor against capital is a matter not only of human justice, but also of class interest.[30] On the one hand, his moral philosophy based on reason, justice, and universal love was a development of the eighteenth-century liberal doctrine of human rights.[31] On the other, his focus on class struggle was predicated on the Marxist theory of exploitation in *Capital* and on a strategy of emancipation by the workers themselves. Sandino also fused these two themes, the moral justification with the economic and historical basis of the class struggle.[32]

Unlike most anarchists, Flores Magón depicted state authority as the gendarme of capital rather than as an autonomous power.[33] Madero's constitutionalist objective was identified with a bourgeois republic like that in the United States.[34] All of the evils of modern society were traced to the role of capital buttressed by state authority and organized religion. He thus acknowledged the precedence of economic over political and cultural factors in the explanation of human oppression.[35] This specifically Marxist component is also evident, as we shall see, in Sandino's account of capitalism and economic imperialism.

By "communism" Flores Magón meant a social arrangement in which the land, factories, and workshops belong to the producers, who share the products on a fraternal basis.[36] The common ownership of land, he believed, is a condition of the common ownership of industry: "factories, workshops, and foundries can function only with the products taken from the land; therefore . . . the city laborer must unite with the worker in the countryside and all together must begin by expropriating the land."[37] The farms and factories would be managed by peasants' and workers' collectives instead of a centralized bureaucracy. Planning and the regulation of production along with accounting and distribution would be organized by regions rather than nationally. "Everything produced will be sent to the community's general store from which each will have the right to take ACCORDING TO HIS NEEDS, without any other requisite than a signed note testifying that one is working in this or that industry."[38] Such was the system of workers' and peasants' cooperatives without centralized authority that was also basic to Sandino's synthesis of anarchism and communism.

Spiritualist, Freemason, Theosophist

For the philosophical foundation of his anarcho-communism Sandino turned to the study of occult philosophy. Common to both was their covert or underground existence and opposition to the social establishment and intellectual mainstream to which both were marginal. For Sandino, the chief attraction of occult philosophy was its subversion of the ideological status quo.

There were several schools of occult philosophy that interested Sandino in the course of his intellectual development. Spiritualism,

into whose peculiar practices he was introduced during his first
stay in Mexico, was one of them. Revolutionary Freemasonry was
another. But of more lasting influence were his theosophical
studies, also begun in Mexico during his first visit there in 1923.
Later, these would help convince him that "Communist Spiritism"
rather than Spiritualism or Freemasonry was the activating ideology he needed.

In Mexico from 1923 to 1926 Sandino enjoyed the company
of Spiritualists. His early utterances on religious themes indicate
a religious influence. Among his most frequent sayings, Carleton
Beals reported the following: "Death is only a moment of displeasure
not to be taken seriously"; "He who fears death is the first to die";
"God is the one who disposes of our lives"; and "God and the
mountains are our allies."[39] Beals concluded that "[t]here is something religious in the ideology of this man."[40] For us the importance of these aphorisms is their suggestion of a Spiritualist origin.
That death is only a passing moment of sorrow suggests that the
life of the spirit does not end when the body stops functioning. The
belief that the spirit lives a separate existence both before and after
its association with a particular body is a key Spiritualist doctrine.

Mexican Spiritualism may be traced to two principal sources.
Unlike other Latin American countries where Spiritualism
emerged under the influence of the French Society of Spiritual
Studies, founded by Allan Kardec in 1858, in Mexico it was diffused
from centers in the United States, where it had taken root a full
decade earlier, in 1848.[41] The Spiritualist movement originated in
connection with the alleged discovery by Margaret and Kate Fox of
the art of mediumship or communication with disincarnate spirits.
As a dissident movement within American Protestantism convinced that God is not a person but the radiating force of love, it
soon turned into a critique of American society. Both before and
after the Civil War it became associated with schemes for utopian
communities, women's rights, free love, prison reform, and labor
radicalism.[42] It was in the vanguard with regard to abolishing slavery and securing social justice for American Indians. Victoria
Woodhull, president of the American Association of Spiritualists
during the early 1870s, was a notorious socialist who believed that
Spiritualism signified not only religious enlightenment, but also
a cultural, political, and social revolution. In 1872 she published
the first English translation of the *Communist Manifesto* and tried
to persuade Karl Marx that the goals of Spiritualism were the same
as those of the International Workingmen's Association![43]

In addition to this American source, Mexican Spiritualism had an indigenous origin in the teachings of a recalcitrant Roman Catholic priest known as Father Elías (Elijah). Because of its extreme nationalism, anticlericalism, and appeal to Mexico's downtrodden masses, this indigenous brand of Spiritualism easily prevailed over its rivals by establishing temples throughout the interior and also along the United States border.[44]

Founded in 1861 by the enigmatic Father Elías, Mexican Spiritualism began as a countercultural movement against Roman Catholicism during the period when Mexico suffered from extreme internal dissension, civil war, foreign invasion, and the socially disrupting effects of nascent industrialization. The son of an Indian woman and a mestizo of Spanish-Jewish descent, Father Elías claimed to be the incarnation of the Holy Ghost.[45] He also believed that Mexico had been chosen by God to become the New Jerusalem. Thus in several respects his doctrine showed traces of the religious tradition against which he and his followers had revolted.

Much of it derived from Joachim of Floris, the twelfth-century Cistercian monk who rebelled against the church and proclaimed the millennium. Father Elías conceived of human history as periodized into three stages patterned on Joachim's three ages.[46] The first stage of God the Father, or time of the Old Testament, was followed by the stage of the Son, corresponding to the New Testament. The third or final stage is that of the Holy Ghost, or time of spiritual understanding, when the prophet Elijah was supposed to return and even unbelievers would look to God and all creatures would be redeemed. Mexican Spiritualists believe the present or third stage to have been ushered in by Father Elías, a doctrine that was considerably in vogue during the Mexican Revolution.

This Mexican brand of Spiritualism combined elements of the dominant Roman Catholic religious ideology with belief in a continuing revelation based on the testimony of psychic mediums. "Mexican Spiritualists believe in the Trinity—the Father, Jehovah; the Son, Jesus Christ; and Father Elías, the Holy Ghost—and in the Virgin Mary."[47] These Spiritualist deities "irradiate" messages during church services through mediums especially gifted to receive them.[48] Sandino rejected these particular survivals of the Christian religion. Nonetheless, he shared with Mexican Spiritualists the belief in extrasensory communication with other spirits and in the dawn of a New Era corresponding to that of the Holy Spirit.

Mexican Spiritualism was an expression of religious dissent closely tied to political dissidence. The most prominent example of each during the Mexican Revolution was Francisco I. Madero, who replaced Porfirio Díaz as president. He led the main forces of the

revolution that toppled the Díaz dictatorship in 1911. Under the influence of Spiritualist ideas proceeding from the United States, he
believed that "a mystical community of prescient beings, living
and dead, could guide humanity toward new heights."[49] He and his
fellow Spiritualists testified to a noncorporeal presence within all
persons capable of interacting with the material world and of transmitting extrasensory messages to persons properly attuned to receiving them.[50] "Magnetism" was the name given to the power of
thought so transmitted.

The concept of magnetism extended to spiritual affinities or
attractions owes a profound debt to Franz Anton Mesmer (1734–
1815), whose research provided a much needed "scientific" foundation for modern Spiritualism. The father of magnetic or hypnotic
therapy based on the discovery of "animal magnetism," a supposed
magnetic or electricitylike fluid present in all animals, he was also
the founder of a secret Masonic lodge for propagating his ideas—
the Société de l'Harmonie Universelle (Society of Universal Harmony).[51] In France during the decade leading up to the Great Revolution, Mesmerism became transformed into a political movement
aimed at regenerating humanity and overcoming the obstacles to
human fraternity. It hoped to do so "by restoring a 'natural' society
in which physico-moral laws of nature would drown aristocratic
privileges and despotic governments in a sea of mesmeric fluid."[52]
That Mesmerism made inroads into Mexico is testified by the influence it had on Sandino.

Sandino believed that he possessed the psychic powers required
to receive and to transmit spiritual messages. Belausteguigoitia recalled having seen a letter from Sandino's half-brother Sócrates,
noting that Augusto had an enormous telepathic receptacle for receiving extrasensory impressions.[53] Sandino claimed that his ideas
and even his voice could be heard in distant places: "The magnetism of a thought is transmitted. . . . In battle, with the nervous
system in tension, a voice with magnetic quality has an enormous
resonance."[54] Although these statements were made after he had
become an adept of the Magnetic-Spiritual School, his conviction
of belonging to the spiritual elect and of possessing exceptional
spiritual powers preceded by several years his studies in austere rational philosophy.

Masonry was another rival for Sandino's affections. Although
he did not become a Master Mason until 1929, he is believed to
have attended Masonic meetings in Tampico or its vicinity during
his first trip to Mexico in 1923. Freemasonry was then the vogue
but there was more than one kind of Masonry and not all were

revolutionary. For the historian of ideas the task is to identify as nearly as possible Sandino's particular brand.

Radical and revolutionary during the American and French revolutions, Freemasonry had become by the late nineteenth century a society of free-thinking liberals who deliberately shunned political and religious controversy in favor of cementing the bonds of human fellowship through social and philanthropic activities. The Mexican National Rite had become a social club or fraternity stressing self-improvement, knowledge of the natural sciences, and community services. The contrast between this socially acceptable version of Freemasonry and the conspiratorial current could not have been more profound. In view of Sandino's anarchism, it seems likely that it was the conspiratorial current that captured his imagination and that he "drank deeply of the revolutionary ideas being proclaimed in those reunions."[55]

In Mexico Freemasonry became a significant political force when, under the influence of Benito Juárez and his Liberal Reform, it became a politically subversive and anticlerical side-current based on French revolutionary notions of "Liberty, Equality, and Fraternity." Later revived in the heat of the Mexican Revolution, these ideas made an indelible impression on Sandino.

The origins of this revolutionary brand of Masonry go back to the Masonic lodges during the French Revolution. They had become dens of anarchism for the general overturning of government and established religion. In *Proofs of a Conspiracy* (1798), John Robison showed that the political clubs and correspondence committees during the revolution, including the famous Jacobin Club, sprang from these Masonic lodges.[56] In the same work he traced the doctrines of this subversive Masonry to the German Order of the Illuminati founded in Bavaria in 1776 by Dr. Adam Weishaupt, a professor of canon law at the University of Ingolstadt.[57]

Taking the nom de plume of Spartacus, who headed the insurrection of slaves in Pompey's time and kept Rome in an uproar for three years, Weishaupt wrote to his fellow-illuminatus Cato a letter containing the basic elements of the doctrine we have discovered in Sandino. "How can the weak obtain protection? Only by union; but this is rare. Nothing can bring this about but hidden societies. Hidden schools of wisdom are the means which one day will free men from their bonds. . . . Princes and nations shall vanish from the earth. The human race will then become one family, and the world will be the dwelling of rational men. Morality alone can do this. . . . Reason will be the code of laws to all mankind!"[58]

Besides invoking reason, morality, and fraternity, Spartacus made a plea for justice, liberty, and equality. He commended Jesus of Nazareth for teaching people the lessons of reason in the form of parables:

> Let us only take Liberty and Equality as the great aim of his doctrines and Morality as the way to attain it, and everything in the New Testament will be comprehensible; and Jesus will appear as the redeemer of slaves. Man is fallen from the condition of Liberty and Equality, the STATE OF PURE NATURE. He is under subordination and civil bondage arising from the vices of men. This is the FALL and ORIGINAL SIN. The KINGDOM OF GRACE is that restoration which may be brought about by Illumination and a just Morality. . . . By subduing our passions or limiting their cravings, we may recover a great deal of our original worth and live in a state of grace. This is the redemption of man—this is accomplished by Morality; and when this is spread over the world we have THE KINGDOM OF THE JUST.[59]

All these notions are to be found in Sandino's writings, along with belief in illumination based on what he called the "Light and Truth." Wrote Spartacus in another letter to Cato dated 6 February 1778, "The allegory on which I am to found the mysteries of the Higher Orders is *the fire worship of the Magi.* We must have some worship, and none is so apposite. LET THERE BE LIGHT, AND THERE SHALL BE LIGHT. This is my motto and my fundamental principle."[60] Similar allusions to Zoroaster's doctrine may also be found in Sandino's letters and manifestos.

In the summer of 1929 Sandino was also being drawn to the "Light and Truth" doctrines of the Magnetic-Spiritual School. But his confidence in his Masonic brothers remained unshaken. He had entrusted the archives of his Defending Army to the Masonic Grand Lodge at Mérida.[61] There they were to remain even after he had become an adept of Trincado's austere rational philosophy.

Sandino's philosophy of liberation is sometimes referred to as "theosophy." For some scholars what is understood to be his theosophy has proved embarrassing and even incomprehensible. But theosophy is hardly more bizarre than Spiritualism. Actually, they are ideological cousins in claiming special or inside knowledge concerning the workings of the spiritual world.

From the Greek *theos,* god, and *sophia,* wisdom, theosophy tries to establish direct contact with the source of all life through acts of contemplation and meditation. In its reliance on an inner light, it is distinct from theology, whose knowledge of God is derived from external sources. Only when capitalized does the word *theosophy* denote the doctrines of a special sect, Madame

Blavatsky's Theosophical Society, which incorporates elements
of oriental religious worship. The term was first used by the Hel-
lenic philosopher Ammonius Saccus (ca. A.D. 175–242), sometimes
credited with the founding of Neoplatonism, to fit those systems
of thought proceeding from the Orient that stressed extrasensory
perception.

Most theosophists trace their doctrine not to Madame
Blavatsky and the Theosophical Society founded by her and Henry
Olcott in 1875, but to the succession of mahatmas or masters of
wisdom who supposedly guide the evolution of humanity by sharing with ordinary mortals their superior knowledge.[62] Madame
Blavatsky described a mahatma as "a personage who, by special
training and education, has evolved those higher faculties and has
attained that spiritual knowledge which ordinary humanity will
acquire after passing through numberless series of incarnations during the process of cosmic evolution."[63] This description fits the
so-called missionary spirits Sandino described.

It is likely that Sandino was already a theosophist before joining the Magnetic-Spiritual School. From the accounts given to
Belausteguigoitia by both Sandino and his father, "it was there [in
Tampico] where, taking advantage of the free time from his work,
Sandino dedicated himself to reading about social questions and
steeping himself in theosophical ideas."[64] What these ideas were
can only be guessed. Years later Sandino would identify Zoroaster
as the founder of theosophy, and indicate a knowledge of the
Zoroastrian texts, acquired independently of the Magnetic-Spiritual
School.[65] When and where he acquired this knowledge is open
to debate, but there is a strong possibility that he acquired it in
Tampico.

Sandino's assimilation of Zoroastrian doctrines may be traced
to three different but related sources: the Zend-Avesta or Zoroastrian scriptures, the Jewish Gnosticism of the Kabbalah, and Trincado's austere rational philosophy. Published around the turn of
the century was a Barcelona edition of Zoroaster's oracles appended
to the Zend-Avesta, possibly the source referred to in Sandino's
letter to Dr. Barahona (27 May 1933).[66] As for the Kabbalah, there
are Sandino's direct references to it in his letter to Gen. Pedro
Altamirano (3 February 1931): "Sincerely, brother, . . . I tell you
in private that even I did not know that you and brother general
Carlos Salgado are among the missionary spirits who are with me,
and that on many other occasions we have been together. I did not
learn this until I arrived in Mexico. . . . I still cannot tell you who

you were because the Kabbalah does not allow it."⁶⁷ To this he
added that the Atlantic Coast should be fertile ground for General
Altamirano's armed column, because such was the "latest prog-
nosis based on our Kabbalah."⁶⁸

On returning to Mexico in 1929, Sandino resumed his studies
of occult philosophy. But they began to take a different turn. In
Mexico most Spiritualists still believed in some of the core doctrines of the Christian religion. Sandino became impatient with
this religious heritage. Later, he would insist that religions were a
matter of the past, that he had rejected all religious beliefs, and that
he relied entirely on reason.⁶⁹ But we need not take him at his
word, for what he called "reason" was not only the power of logical
reasoning from premises to conclusions, but also an independent
source of knowledge superior to sense perception. Thus a constant
in Sandino's credo was the belief that "Justice, Right, and REASON"
were not just moral principles; they were divine powers that ruled
the world, and he and his Defending Army were their instruments.⁷⁰

In his conversations with Sandino, Belausteguigoitia was impressed by what he correctly interpreted to be Sandino's "theosophical faith."⁷¹ Sandino also used this term in reference to Zoroaster's doctrines. As he wrote to his fellow theosophist Humberto
Barahona, "As a theosophist you have the obligation of acknowledging that every human being has a mission to be fulfilled"—a
doctrine that figured prominently in Zoroaster's teachings.⁷² Sandino then added that Barahona had the further "obligation of knowing the counsels of Zoroaster . . . , the founder of theosophy."⁷³ Although most theosophists trace their doctrines to an Indian origin,
Sandino traced his to a Persian source.

Zoroaster's God was the Spirit of Light and Truth. According to
the Prophet's original cosmogony, God gave birth to two primal
twins, one of whom went astray through a wrong choice or misuse
of reason. Besides the Destructive or Evil Spirit, God created the
Holy Spirit.⁷⁴ This Spirit, which also figures in the Christian doctrine of the Trinity, is the most important of God's Helpers, followed
by the Good Disposition.⁷⁵ The Good Disposition has a daughter
who produces good deeds. That daughter is Love.⁷⁶ Sandino made
much of both but inverted their relationship. In his Light and Truth
Manifesto he declared that Love has a daughter who produces good
deeds, but that daughter is Justice.⁷⁷

Each spirit is destined to fulfill the divine plan but is also responsible for its ultimate fate, which makes Zoroastrianism the religion of free will par excellence—an ethical rather than a cosmo-

logical dualism.[78] Ahriman or Satan is not an evil substance, he is evil by choice.[79] All spirits, whether incarnate or disincarnate, are likewise judged by their works and rewarded or punished accordingly.

For Zoroastrians, the human self is essentially triadic. Man is a composite of body, an internal soul or mind encased within the body but freed from it at death, and a pre-existent external spirit independent of both.[80] In its unredeemed state, this pre-existent spirit is unconscious, asleep, or benumbed by the nonspiritual soul. The awakening or liberation from this state of ignorance depends on "knowing your trinity," Sandino wrote in a letter to Dr. Enoc Aguado (26 October 1930), to which he added that the spirit cannot be redeemed without the "spark of love and justice."[81] This trinity is the composite self and its redeeming "spark" is an emanation of the universal spirit. To know one's trinity in the deepest sense is thus to know God.

Among the later doctrinal accretions consistent with Zoroaster's monotheism was the belief that matter is essentially good, because it was created by God acting through the Holy Spirit.[82] Because spirits are created out of a primal matter or ether, they, too, have a material component. Soul health implies the health of the body and its release from death; soul sickness implies physical ailments and the mortality of the flesh. Here it is worth mentioning that the source of the Christian word *paradise* was the Persian *pairidaeza*, predicated on this Zoroastrian conception of matter. That souls would be reincarnated and that the earth would become a paradise after the Final Judgment were also doctrines dear to Sandino.[83]

Basic to Sandino's theosophy was the struggle between the forces of light and darkness, between good and evil—a doctrine traceable to Zoroaster. The mission of humanity on earth is to escape the limitations of the flesh not by fleeing from the material world, Sandino believed, but by actively working to change it. As exemplars he cited Moses and Simón Bolívar.[84] The guidelines were Zoroaster's, based on the belief that the Good should be sought in what is True, that knowledge of the real world is humanity's supreme obligation in this life.

Zoroaster believed that in the cosmic battle with God, the Evil Spirit is doomed to failure because his intelligence system is defective.[85] Deficient in both data and judgment, he is incapable of assessing accurately his enemy's forces and position at a given moment. Consequently, his legions are again and again taken by surprise. One can well imagine the impression made by this cosmic military imagery on Sandino, and its relevance to his struggle in Nicaragua.

It was under Zoroastrian influence during the Babylonian exile that Jewish prophecy took an apocalyptic turn.[86] Whereas the term "prophetic" denotes a straightforward forecast of impending doom or salvation, the word "apocalyptic" (from the Greek *apokalyptein*, "to uncover, reveal") signifies the cryptic and symbolic forecast central to the Old Testament Book of Daniel and its New Testament counterpart, the Book of Revelation. Written in an idiom like Sandino's, with bizarre fantasies presented against a background of supernatural happenings, it requires a spiritual code to unlock its secrets. Otherwise, the meaning remains sealed (Dan. 12:4).

Just as prophecy was politically dangerous, so were apocalypses announcing the doom of earthly despotism. Their central theme was a message concerning the end time believed to be near at hand, a final holocaust followed by the coming Kingdom of God. Sandino's Light and Truth Manifesto is a classic example of apocalyptic literature indebted to Zoroastrian sources.

Although apocalyptic literature shares the prophetic conviction that God's battle with the forces of evil is a historical one, the flesh-and-blood war against unrighteousness is blown up into a superhistorical military struggle of cosmic proportions. In Zoroastrian doctrine there is the anticipated showdown between the children of light and the children of darkness in this world. But joined to this belief is one in a final battle between the angelic hosts and the legions of Satan, God's archenemy. In the Zoroastrian apocalypse these two struggles are presented as closely interrelated aspects of a single overarching confrontation between the Kingdom of Heaven and the Kingdom of Hell.[87] Finally, this struggle promises to be accompanied by a cosmic catastrophe prior to the final deliverance.[88] These three themes of Zoroastrian eschatology were also central to Sandino's apocalyptic utterances.

Unlike the Christian apocalypse, in which the earth sinks deeper into sin and can only be regenerated by divine intervention, the Zoroastrian apocalypse offers the prospect of continual moral progress and the renovation of the earth at least partially from within. Man is the principal agent in the defeat of Satan and the earth is regenerated by the work of missionary spirits until the final battle between the angelic hosts and the princes of this world brings the cosmic drama to a close. The Final Judgment is an expression of God's love rather than of his wrath. The spirits condemned to hell will be released and their sins purged through submersion in a stream of molten metal.[89] By then all spirits will have learned the lessons of reward and punishment; all will be saved in recognition of their inward transformation. Although Sandino retained the millenarian expectation of a holocaust and believed that some refractory spirits would be banished to other planets to continue with their purgatory, he too affirmed the ultimate redemption of the universe.[90]

In Sandino's theosophy the three stages of the Zoroastrian cosmic drama—creation, the progress of the human spirit, and universal redemption—roughly parallel the three Spiritualist ages.[91] Like Mexican Spiritualists, Sandino believed that the third stage had received its baptism of fire in Mexico. The Mexican Revolution had more importance for Sandino than for most Mexicans because he considered it a prelude to his struggle in Nicaragua. Convinced of the cosmic significance of his struggle, he associated it with the threshold of a New Era.

From this account it is evident that Zoroastrianism was neither an exclusively this-worldly nor other-worldly religion; it was both-worldly.[92] In the Zoroastrian scheme of things the earth would not be abandoned to its fate but transformed by love and good works—the fundamental objective of Sandino's Defending Army spelled out in his Light and Truth Manifesto. If all men are born of one father, as Sandino believed, then they are all brothers and should help each other—another grain of Zoroastrian wisdom.

That Sandino owed an intellectual debt to Zoroastrianism may raise more than a few eyebrows. However, one can say with assurance that he not only knew the principal Zoroastrian doctrines as I have sketched them, but also adopted them as his own. It should not surprise us that there was a Zoroastrian vogue in Mexico during the revolution and the years immediately following. Zoroastrianism shared with revolutionary anarchism and communism a fraternal philosophy committed to the complete transformation of human society. Although the Zoroastrian community in Mexico is today conservative rather than revolutionary, it was not always so.[93]

Sandino was not alone in testifying to the influence of Zoroastrianism on the politics of the Mexican Left. In those days even Communists acknowledged Zoroaster's influence. Valentín Campa notes in his memoirs that in 1922 the monthly journal of the Railway Workers' Alliance contained a series of polemics on political issues written by a worker with the pseudonym "Zarathustra."[94] Julio Antonio Mella, the founder of the Cuban Communist party, had fled to Mexico to escape repression, and also had occasion to mention Zoroaster's contribution. As he said of the professional revolutionary in December 1926, "He understands like Zoroaster the importance of this world. He is a this-worldly saint!"[95]

The Spiritism of the Magnetic-Spiritual School

Zoroaster's teachings were also basic to the thought of the Magnetic-Spiritual School as systematized by Trincado in his *Filosofía austera racional.* Published after the end of World War I, this treatise became the principal source of Sandino's activating ideology, which he acquired in Mexico in 1929 and applied to Nicaragua from 1930 until his death in February 1934. Although but one of a dozen original works published by Trincado, it was the philosophical foundation of his doctrine and the text used by the students of the Magnetic-Spiritual School.

Who was Trincado and how did he happen to enter Sandino's life? Of Basque descent, Joaquín Trincado (1866–1935) emigrated to Argentina in 1906, but retained his Spanish citizenship.[96] Trained as a master electrician, he was the first to introduce the light bulb and electrical heating into Buenos Aires, where he established a small workshop producing electrical equipment. Although educated by priests, he soon acquired a fanatical dislike for all forms of religious indoctrination. He also rejected Spiritualism and Masonry because of their religious holdovers. Anticlericalism was to become, if not an obsession, the pervasive concern of his entire published work.

Trincado first came to public attention when on 30 May 1910 he launched the proclamation summarizing the tenets of his bizarre philosophy.[97] His proclamation, "The Whole World Communized," affirmed first, the solidarity of all creation; second, the advent of world communism; third, the unitary substance and unitary law governing all being; fourth, the unitary origin and unitary end of all things; and fifth, the presence of spiritual magnetism everywhere.[98] Beginning in December 1910 he organized a series of public talks in which he added to his cosmology a sketch of universal history. During these talks he called for the abolition of national frontiers and for the establishment of a universal commune in the interest of world peace. His message warned of a coming geological as well as social cataclysm and held forth the principles of "true communism" as an alternative to the false hopes stirred up by religion.[99]

Appalled by the traces of Christianity among Argentine Spiritualists, Trincado was prompted to organize his own "school"

based on his May 1910 proclamation. He founded the Magnetic-
Spiritual School of the Universal Commune on 20 September 1911.
His "New Era" calendar, replacing the Christian one, dates from
that event. He chose this date on purpose. Symbolic of his school's
anticlericalism, the date commemorated the same day and month
in 1870 when Italian troops freed the former papal states and con-
fined Pope Pius IX to the Vatican. This was the pope responsible for
the Dogma of the Immaculate Conception in 1854, the Syllabus of
Errors in 1864, and the Doctrine of Papal Infallibility in 1870, the
same pope who declared, "Defend and conserve the church even
if it means shedding the blood of all humanity!"[100] To which Trincado retorted, "We will save humanity at the cost of destroying all
religions!"[101]

The school's Declaration of Principles states that religions are
enemies of human liberty, progress, and justice and the cause of all
the wars suffered by humanity.[102] The father and creator is thus
not the god of any religion. The declaration places the Magnetic-
Spiritual School on the side of the people against both the altar and
the throne, the cross and the sword—the two original forms of
despotism.[103] Opposed to the division of society into antagonistic
classes, it calls for a new "communal fraternity with equal rights
and duties to work and to consume, in which each produces what
he can and consumes what he needs."[104] This is to be achieved by
founding agricultural and industrial cooperatives managed by the
workers themselves.

There was a communist as well as anarchist ring to these
statements. Consequently, to protect the school from charges of
subversion, the declaration adds that "The Whole World Communized" should not be equated with what is misunderstood to be
communism or anarchism.[105] On top of that it claims to represent a
moral rather than a political tendency.

Like the Masonic orders, Trincado's school aimed at divulging
his philosophy piecemeal through stages and degrees. There were
three principal degrees, Novice, Sympathizer, and Adherent.[106] To
receive the third degree and with it the credential of membership in
the school, it was necessary to own and to have studied all the
books prescribed by the lower degrees, to accept the Declaration of
Principles, and to make voluntary contributions in money according to one's capacity.[107] In addition, it was necessary to sign and return a pledge of allegiance to the school accompanied by two
personal photographs.

The school was hierarchically organized with directives proceeding from the top down. The highest office was that of director

of the Central Cathedra or school headquarters in Buenos Aires. The director and his counselors constituted the "Government of Spiritism."[108] Next came the *celadores* or trustees of the regional, provincial, and city cathedras where they happen to have been established. The regional trustees were charged with administering the school's affairs within geographical areas corresponding for the most part to national states. These together with the provincial and city trustees were directly responsible to the school's government in Buenos Aires.

The Magnetic-Spiritual School did not become a significant tendency until after World War I, when the Bolshevik Revolution began spreading its own principles. In response to the wave of communist ideas Trincado founded his own International, the Hispano-American Oceanic Union, on 12 October 1920 (Columbus Day). It was intended to implement his project of a universal commune. Only then did the school begin to attract political radicals.

Soon a second cathedra was organized in Mexico City, followed by a third one in the sugar-refining center at Xicoténcatl, Tamaulipas, about one hundred miles northwest of Tampico, in March 1922. When Sandino arrived in Tampico a year later there were already "sympathizers" and "adherents" in the port city. Two years later, on 9 June 1925, following a rash of new cathedras throughout Latin America, a thirteenth cathedra was set up in Tampico itself.

The forty-ninth cathedra was established by Sandino in Nicaragua. Among the official documents at the school's headquarters in Buenos Aires is an album containing the photographs of all the *celadores,* including one of Sandino, the forty-ninth in order of appointment. It is quite likely that this cathedra was established as early as 1931, the year after Sandino returned from his second trip to Mexico.

According to Trincado's report of 12 September 1935 to the Central Cathedra, there were 183 cathedras at that time.[109] This is roughly the number that still survived in 1985, after a noticeable decline from the peak of some 250 reached just before World War II. Today, as in 1935, the year following Sandino's death, the total membership hovers around five thousand. This figure gives some indication of the school's importance as a propaganda vehicle for Sandino's struggle in Nicaragua.

How strong were Sandino's ties to the Magnetic-Spiritual School? Besides assimilating its austere rational philosophy and naming a military camp in its honor, he adopted the flag of the Hispano-American Oceanic Union. The second number of Trincado's fortnightly, *La Balanza* (February 1933), contains a photograph of Sandino standing under the two banners that came to symbolize his cause. On his right is the red and black flag of his Defending Army. On his left is the flag of the Hispano-American Oceanic Union. Its seven bands of rose, green, purple, yellow, red, white, and blue had been designed by Trincado to represent the flags of all the Hispano-American countries.

The photograph was reproduced in connection with an article about a modern Quixote who had traveled from New York to Buenos Aires by foot after arriving in North America from Spain some ten years earlier.[110] After visiting all the states of North America he crossed over into Mexico in July 1930. He entered Nicaragua in February 1931 in the hope of finding Sandino, who welcomed him as a guest of honor in his camp. There, in the traveler's own words, "Sandino spoke to me under the flag of seven bands and seven colors created by a Spaniard for the Hispano-American Union."[111] The photograph was taken during his stay in the camp, the same month that Sandino issued his Light and Truth Manifesto (15 February).

Shortly afterward, Sandino was appointed the school's regional trustee for Nicaragua. In an article in *La Balanza* (February 1935) commemorating the first anniversary of his death, he was remembered as the "general representative of the Magnetic-Spiritual School of the Universal Commune in Nicaragua."[112] And in an editorial in the same issue he was hailed as one of the missionary spirits "who, having received from above the earth a mandate from those who in right and justice sent him here, has at his disposal the invincible forces of the universe."[113]

Trincado's school gave unstinting support to Sandino's struggle in Nicaragua. In a letter from Sandino to Trincado (12 November 1932), reproduced in *La Balanza* but not included in Somoza's biography, Sandino thanked him for the school's diploma and medallion in connection with his appointment as the school's trustee for Nicaragua.[114] In return, Sandino included the credentials that gave Trincado the right to represent the interests of his Defending Army in Argentina, with the same honors and privileges as Dr. Zepeda in Mexico, General Portocarrero in El Salvador, and José Idiáquez in Honduras.

It was as the official representative of the Magnetic-Spiritual School that Sandino undertook the task of establishing an agricultural cooperative in Wiwilí during 1933–1934. This effort was an integral part of his struggle to implement the anarcho-communist objectives of the Universal Commune. As he wrote in a letter to Rafael Ramírez Delgado (16 July 1933), "Here I am dedicated to the founding of a society of mutual aid and universal fraternity. I want to put my grain of sand in favor of the emancipation and social well-being of the working class, which, as you well know, has always been exploited and looked down upon by the bureaucratic bourgeoisie!"[115] The first agricultural cooperative of this kind had been established by the school in Argentina in the province of Tucumán. If it had not been stamped out by the National Guard, Sandino's cooperative in Wiwilí would have been the second continuing experiment of this kind.

Trincado traced the doctrines of the Magnetic-Spiritual School to three principal sources. The first source, the austere rational philosophy of Zoroaster, was the "basis of all the austere schools that . . . reached their zenith in Moses."[116] The second, that of Moses, who supposedly founded the oral tradition behind the Kabbalah, was identified with the "*secret school* of the Essenes."[117] The third source, that of the nineteenth-century Frenchman, the "Apostle Allan Kardec," revealed what the Kabbalah had kept hidden for some thirty-six centuries.[118] Kardec's philosophy of Spiritism, as distinct from Spiritualism, was the immediate predecessor of Trincado's own philosophy.

The Zoroastrian influence is evident in the two basic principles directly taken from the Zend-Avesta: "Seek the Good in the Truth" (virtue is wisdom); and "Good and Evil, Light and Darkness, proceed from the same source."[119] Self-knowledge and the knowledge of the real world, according to Trincado, were both necessary to humanity's redemption. Although this was the extent of his direct indebtedness to Zoroaster, he was indirectly indebted to Persian sources through the Kabbalah, notably its doctrines of a Primordial Light, Divine Emanation, Reincarnation, Missionary Spirits, and a Final Judgment.[120]

The importance of the Kabbalah as a source of Trincado's austere rational philosophy is borne out by his multiple references to it.[121] The Kabbalah supposedly contained the wisdom of the Essenic School concerning how to develop extrasensory perception, the powers of mediums, and the magnetic fluids associated with magic.[122] Mohammed and Jesus were identified as members of this school.[123] These teachings remained hidden until the "century of lights" (nineteenth), when they were revealed because of the imminence of the final judgment of humanity, whose regeneration had begun with the race allegedly founded by Adam and Eve.[124]

The importance of the Kabbalah as a source of Trincado's philosophy is further evidenced in the emblem he chose for his school. Among its salient features is an equilateral triangle containing the scales of justice joined to an anchor, underneath which are the

Emblem of the Magnetic-Spiritual School of the Universal Commune

words "This Is the Law." From the anchor but outside the triangle is suspended the Star of David with "Only Elohim" (the Hebrew word for god) inscribed above it. The triangle and the Star of David occupy the center of a shield having the appearance of certain Kabbalistic drawings.[125]

Of special interest to Trincado was the Kabbalah's application of the doctrine of reincarnation to the stories of the Old Testament. That Adam was a missionary spirit sent to earth for the purpose of redeeming humanity is suggested by the following excerpt from the Kabbalah: "After Adam sinned his soul passed into David, and the latter having also sinned, it passed into the Messiah."[126] With such passages as a model, Trincado began making connections of his own. Thus Adam's spirit became reincarnate in Joseph, the father of Jesus, and Eve's spirit in that of Mary, his mother.[127] Even more startling, Adam's son Seth became successively reincarnated as Jacob, Moses, Confucius, Socrates, and James, the younger brother of Jesus; Isaiah returned to earth as Jesus; and Ignatius Loyola as Giuseppe Garibaldi![128]

These connections did not pass unnoticed by Sandino. In a letter written to Abraham Rivera (February 1931), he likened his wife, Blanca Arauz, to Mary, that is to say, Eve, who came with Adam and other missionary spirits to redeem humanity, "missionary spirits who . . . are among us directed by their own leaders!"[129] The inference should be clear. Sandino's Defending Army was being directed by missionary spirits under the leadership of Adam and

Eve. If Sandino's wife, Blanca, was a reincarnation of Mary's spirit, who was originally incarnate in Eve, then Sandino was a reincarnation of Joseph's spirit, who was the original Adam. One may well imagine how this thought inspired Sandino, whose Defending Army seemed to him destined to complete Adam's original mission on earth.

The immediate source of Trincado's Spiritism was the school founded by Allan Kardec, whose real name was Hippolyte Léon Denizard Rivail (1804–1869). Founded on 1 April 1858, the Parisian Society of Spiritual Studies had for its purpose the investigation of all phenomena covered by what today goes by the name of parapsychology. "Political questions, and controversial religious and socioeconomic questions, were prohibited."[130] Renowned for its seemingly scientific approach, the society soon gained an international following. At the time of his death the number of Kardec's adherents reached several million, and the periodicals disseminating his philosophy numbered over forty.[131] Among the thousands who sought him out were many of high rank in the social, literary, and scientific worlds, including the Emperor Napoleon III, who invited him several times to the Tuileries.[132]

From Kardec's exhaustive study of mediums and their testimonies, Trincado derived what he believed were "irrefutable proofs that everything is spirit," which is to say that the world is made up of spirits.[133] As a master electrician, he was particularly impressed by Kardec's interpretation of Spiritist manifestations as electrical-magnetic phenomena.[134] That all souls are wrapped in an invisible "Ether" or semimaterial electrical substance was another of Kardec's contributions to Trincado's school.[135]

Kardec believed in the existence of different Spirit worlds, some spiritually advanced but others retrograde: "primitive worlds," in which there are only incarnations but no reincarnations; "worlds of purgation," in which evil predominates; "regenerate worlds," in which the souls of the redeemed outnumber those who are fallen; and "celestial or divine worlds," in which good is untarnished by evil.[136] In this cosmology the earth is a place of purgation. Originally a "primitive world," it became populated by exiled spirits from another planet who refused to accept God's law, but were sufficiently advanced to help raise the spiritual level of the savage races that originally populated the earth.[137] Such "exiled spirits" were distinct from the "messenger spirits" sent by God to accelerate the process of redemption.[138] These notions were also fundamental to Trincado's school.

If Trincado had been fully convinced by Kardec's brand of Spir-

itism, there would have been no need for a school of his own. He
was driven to establish one because of fundamental differences
with Kardec's Argentine followers. Trincado's first disenchantment
occurred at a congress organized by the Spiritist Confederation of
Argentina on 29 June 1910.[139] Subsequently, he came to reject several of Kardec's fundamental tenets: first, the belief in the possibility of reconciling the claims of science and religion; second, the
belief that Spiritism was compatible not only with Christianity,
but also with the Christian amalgams of Spiritualism, Freemasonry,
and theosophy.[140]

Spiritualists, according to Trincado, erect a Chinese Wall between matter and spirit, body and soul.[141] He, however, believed
that even disincarnate spirits are wrapped in an ethereal or semimaterial substance. On what he took to be scientific grounds, he
argued that the entire universe, including its creator, consists of a
spiritual refinement of matter or electricity. Although he referred
to the primal Ether of spiritualized matter as an emanation of the
Father and Creator, he did not think of the Creator as a personal
god to be worshipped.[142] Spiritism, as he conceived it, was the
scientific knowledge of incorporeal or spiritual beings, a science
uncompromised by religious worship, articles of faith, belief in
miracles, and so on.[143]

Trincado also rejected Freemasonry. Although recognizing
in the German Illuminati a precursor of his school, he believed
that their philosophy of moral perfectibility, their conviction that
"REASON . . . ought to regulate human actions," had been imper-
fectly assimilated by modern Masonry.[144] Although Masons were
dedicated to the struggle against religious and political absolutism,
they had become involved in immoral conspiracies from having to
operate underground.[145] Trincado also objected to the degrees and
rituals of the Masonic orders, which he associated with religious
survivals. Thus when awarded an honorary thirty-third degree by
Argentine Freemasons, he refused to accept it.[146]

Theosophy fared no better. Despite Trincado's reliance on the
masters of wisdom from Zoroaster to the present, he believed that
the Hindu scriptures had irreparably mystified their fundamental
principles.[147] Theosophists had yet to rid themselves of religious
worship, another feature shared with oriental religions.[148] They had
made a virtue of eclecticism by fusing incompatible elements from
different religions.[149] And they had attempted to reconcile religious
dogma with modern science, "which is impossible."[150] These criticisms were crucial to distinguishing his own school from others in
the theosophical tradition.

What is one to think of Trincado's philosophical contribution? His claim to a science of the spiritual world lacks credibility because it blurs the distinction between knowledge and faith. Spiritism may be rational, but it is not scientific. Its basic theses are deductions from premises that go beyond matters of fact. The notions of an eternal creator, disincarnate spirits, reincarnation, and so forth, are at bottom religious beliefs because they are not subject to ordinary procedures of verification and disconfirmation. Trincado correctly perceived that Spiritualism and theosophy—he might have added Freemasonry—attempt the impossible by trying to pass off religious beliefs as scientific. Yet he did as much while calling it by another name. So did Sandino.

Sandino differed from his mentor in welcoming allies with different and even opposing ideological views. He did not share Trincado's concern with repudiating the allegedly confused doctrines of the school's principal rivals. He felt no need to refute the beliefs of his Spiritualist friends. After joining the Magnetic-Spiritual School he retained his contacts with Freemasonry and his degree of Master Mason. And he continued to subscribe independently to the theosophy and counsels of Zoroaster.[151]

Although Sandino accepted the general outline of Trincado's philosophy, he did not stress the same ingredients. Whereas Socrates and Confucius figure prominently in Trincado's discussion of his intellectual precursors, Sandino does not even mention them.[152] Lacking Trincado's encyclopedic interests, he turned his attention to what was doctrinally familiar to him in Trincado's Spiritism, to the common ground it shared with Mexican Spiritualism, Freemasonry, and theosophy.

Sandino stressed the Zoroastrian legacy of austere rational philosophy. It was the closest to his vital experience as a field commander. The battles he fought were interpreted in terms of Divine Justice, the coming showdown of Armageddon, and a Final Judgment—doctrines ultimately derived from Zoroaster's teachings and the Christian Apocalypse. Their political-military symbolism had a relevance for Sandino that they could not possibly have had for Trincado.

The Anarchism of Austere Rational Philosophy

Among the attractions of the Magnetic-Spiritual School was a fully articulated social and political philosophy, which was lacking in Mexican Spiritualism and the other schools of occult philosophy.

When Sandino began his studies at the school's provincial cathedra in Yucatán, he was already a dedicated anarchist committed to making a social revolution. What attracted him to austere rational philosophy was its project of a universal commune based on the same general principles as his anarcho-communism. That was not all. Trincado's anarchism had the distinct advantage of having a spiritual dimension derived from the legacy of Spanish anarchism.

Sandino came under the influence not only of a variety of interpretations of the spiritual world, but also of more than one form of anarchism. Next in importance to Mexican anarchism in the formation of his political thought was Spanish anarchism. His red and black flag had an anarcho-syndicalist origin, having been introduced into Mexico by Spanish immigrants. Further evidence of this Spanish influence may be found in the books discovered by the National Guard among Sandino's possessions. There was a treatise on revolutionary syndicalism or trade unionism by the Spaniard Francisco Cañadas, published in Barcelona in 1931.[153] Under the influence of Georges Sorel, the original theoretician of anarcho-syndicalism, Cañadas advocated a complete transvaluation of human values with the help of the creative and transforming role of religionlike exaltation and intuition.[154] As evidence of Sandino's subversive ideology, Somoza reproduced two passages from Cañadas's work that the guerrilla had underlined in red.

The first paragraph compared revolutionary syndicalism with the barbarian invasions of Europe and with primitive Christianity. "It resembles the first because it is a sweeping force that will swell and overrun the borders of ancient Right and stale customs, breaking all the dikes and changing completely the contours of society. It resembles the second because it exhibits the same qualities of spiritual concentration, mystic exaltation, and creative intuition. THE SYNDICALIST LEVIATHAN UNDERMINES AND DISRUPTS THE FOUNDATIONS OF BOURGEOIS SOCIETY LIKE THE CATACOMBS PERFORATED THE ENTRAILS OF CEASARIST ROME."[155]

The second paragraph advocated a syndicalist strategy of direct action and class confrontation:

> It seems logical that the weapons that should be used against capitalism should not be exactly the same as those that were used in the past century and that are still current among the socialists. The syndicalist belittles, of course, all social legislation, he repudiates every form of authority whether political or otherwise, he does not accept arbitration. . . . The only acceptable strategy for the syndicalist is

DIRECT STRUGGLE, BODY AGAINST BODY, WITH THE BOUR-
GEOIS, without intermediaries or witnesses, the duel to the death
and without conditions.[156]

This paraphrasing of ideas from Sorel's classic *Reflections on
Violence* highlights Sandino's commitment to armed struggle by an
activating minority.[157] It also brings out other features of his anarchism that were shared with Spanish anarcho-syndicalism. Among
these were moral enthusiasm and a messianic belief in the coming
victory of the world's oppressed, common to certain heretical sects
during the Middle Ages.[158]

Spanish anarchism may be distinguished from other expressions of European anarchism by its charismatic and peculiarly religious qualities, which we have already noticed in Trincado's work.
It developed in response to systematic persecution and a climate
of repression and martyrology unmatched in any other European
country.[159] Spanish anarchists interpreted their struggle against the
bourgeoisie as a means not only of political and moral regeneration,
but also of spiritual redemption. This religious quality has suggested to at least one commentator that Spanish anarchism is the
"last great religious expression of the Spanish people."[160]

This characterization has been confirmed by other observers.
Ilya Ehrenberg notes that the leaders of Spanish anarchism, unlike
those in other parts of Europe, were not coffee-house litterateurs
and bohemians but teetotalers with strict morals, who behaved as
if they belonged to a religious order.[161] George Woodcock says they
shared the "iconoclastic fervor of the radical sects of the Reforma-
tion" in a country that, because of the Inquisition, had stifled any
tendency toward religious dissent.[162] He calls it a "delayed Reforma-
tion movement."[163] And George Brenan believes that the fierce anticlericalism of the Spanish anarchists, which placed them in the
first ranks of the world's church burners (along with the Mexican
anarchists), is to be explained as the "hatred of heretics for the
Church from which they have sprung . . . [a] church [that] occupies
the position of anti-Christ in the Christian world . . . the fountain
of all evil."[164]

These observations are helpful in understanding the extreme
reaches of anticlericalism attained by Trincado's anarchism. That
the Catholic church is the fountain of all evil is assuredly stronger
medicine against organized Christianity than the denunciation of
this or that pope as the anti-Christ. But the fiercest denunciation
was to come from Trincado's pen. No association of Christians, not
even the early Christian church, escaped his wrath. This was tantamount to denying that Jesus and his original band of disciples were

Christians. According to Trincado, the Christian religion founded by St. Paul not only distorted Jesus's teachings, but also became their mortal enemy.[165]

The Roman Catholic church, he believed, had entered into an unholy alliance with the Roman Empire. In return for becoming recognized as the state religion, the church had consecrated the empire.[166] Ecclesiastical authority was thus buttressed by imperial power and vice-versa. Trincado singled out Pope Gregory VII (Hildebrand) for having used the threat of excommunication to establish the preeminence of the spiritual power over the temporal, a sinister device for achieving the church's temporal objectives. He further charged this pope with endangering the human species by imposing on the Catholic clergy the unnatural and perverse vow of celibacy.[167]

Trincado looked for biblical support for his anticlericalism in the Epistle of James and the Book of Revelation. James's Epistle was important to him because it "summarized all the moral principles of all the ages taught by all the prophets, messiahs, and missionaries [missionary spirits]."[168] The fundamental moral principle of the Epistle is to "pay no servile regard to people" (2:1). Trincado interpreted it as meaning that everyone is equal before the Father and Creator, and no one should submit to another. This principle applied not only to priests, but also to the wielders of power and the owners of capital. Neither they nor their gods, for Trincado, were worthy of being worshipped. Another blow at established religion was James's oft-quoted epigram: "For as the body without the spirit is dead, so faith is dead without deeds" (2:26). In effect, there is no redeeming faith other than with good works, which makes both the papacy and the Catholic religion obsolete.[169]

The Apocalypse was crucial to Trincado's argument because it not only portends the end of injustice in this world, but also identifies the material and spiritual causes of injustice. These were identified with the two beasts of Revelation (13:1–18), the first beast interpreted as the Christian religion founded by St. Paul in defiance of the original apostles, and the second as its official state embodiment, the Roman Catholic church, institutionalized in A.D. 325 at the Council of Nicea.[170] The Apocalypse gives the first beast the number 666, which Trincado interpreted as the last in a long series of more than six hundred established religions.

The Dragon of Revelation was singled out as the power behind these leviathans. He is "that old *serpent* called *the Devil* and *Satan*, the seducer of the whole world" (12:9). Since this Dragon *is* Christ, according to Trincado, it follows that Christ *is* Satan.[171]

"Christ is the root and cause of all evil in the world."[172] Thus Trincado blamed early Christianity and its institutionalized expression in the Roman Catholic church for everything vile under the sun.

In this perspective, Christians worship an idol called "Jesus Christ" who is anything but the historical Jesus.[173] This reincarnation of the prophet Isaiah, Trincado claimed, did not found a religion.[174] The early Christians who followed St. Paul "took Jesus as their bastion but nicknamed him Christ Crucified, thus sanctifying the Cross"—a symbol of death, terror, and suffering.[175] This symbol is an affront, Trincado argued, because "the design of the Creator is not the death of men but their life."[176] Jesus became transformed into an odious divinity, his gallows into a sign of salvation. As for the word *Christ*, it means danger, from which we need an "anti-Christ" to deliver us.[177] Trincado identified the Anti-Christ with the author of the Epistle of James: "the true Anti-Christ who swore to the Father on Mount Calvary, on the blood of his brother [Jesus], to free him from the epithet Christ (danger), and through him all humanity from the threat of being crucified."[178]

The figure of Jesus had special significance for Trincado, who considered him to be the original founder of socialism.[179] By the word *socialism* he meant not only the tepid and reformist principles of the social democratic parties in Europe, which no longer considered themselves revolutionary, but also the revolutionary overthrow of the existing social order. "Socialism is the universal protest directed against the exploiters of the workers," he wrote. "In its doctrines socialism has belatedly recognized that the first socialist was *Jesus the revolutionary* and martyr of the priests."[180]

Trincado believed that the original doctrines of socialism, like those of Jesus, had been falsified beyond recognition. He held organized religion responsible for this perversion. The socialist parties had become a haven for religious believers transformed into "hypocritical socialists."[181] Just as the triumph of religion had divided and atomized the human species, so socialism had split into so many contending sects that it had become a Babylon of unintelligibility. Having deprived socialism of its strength, the clergy no longer feared it. Thus even should the various socialist factions overcome their petty jealousies, Trincado concluded, "they will not promulgate socialism anymore but rather communism without frontiers and territorial divisions, because communism disowns all religion."[182]

Nineteenth-century socialism failed, Trincado argued, because of church intrigues and other hostile pressures against the parties of the proletariat representing four-fifths of humanity. "But this will not stop it from completing its mission as a *bridge between bondage and freedom.*"[183] By bondage he meant egoistic, brutal, and parasitic "imperialism" (shades of Lenin's last or highest stage of capitalism), and by freedom the "communism of love."[184] He blamed the socialists for not living up to their ideas. Consequently, what is conventionally called socialism is at most a transitional movement that has yet to establish a new social order. Unlike socialism, bolshevism responded to the terror and ignorance imposed by the Russian state and church with a social explosion, the destruction of the aristocratic state, and the establishment of a revolutionary regime. To its lasting credit it began the redemption of the world proletariat and paved the way toward a universal commune.[185]

It is clear that Trincado sided with the bolsheviks against the social democratic and nominally socialist parties of Western Europe. This further endeared him to Sandino, who likewise preferred the Communists to their populist and socialist rivals. Unlike the socialist parties that stood for compromise, the bolsheviks succeeded in turning Russia upside down. Their example proved contagious. The communist wave cannot be contained, Trincado wrote, but is advancing with giant strides and with the force of electricity throughout the world.[186]

Trincado distinguished two main varieties of communism. "Extremist communism," which he identified with bolshevism, came in response to the violence of religion, to the violence of aristocracy, and to the violence of exploitation.[187] "A social revolution has begun in Russia, the country of the lash and of the massacres of the pontifical Czar. The Russian people's hatred for their tyrants had a dreadful epilogue: the powerful implored their gods for help but the spirit, until then oppressed, destroyed these fantasmal deities."[188] For Trincado, this fateful and earth-shaking event signified the "beginning of the end of the Lie."[189]

But this was not the way to establish the "true commune" based on love, nor did the Russian people really want to meet violence with violence. They had no choice under the conditions determined for them: "The dilemma was frightening: either kill or be killed!"[190] Although the Russian people annihilated their oppressors in self-defense, Trincado believed that those driven to extreme measures usually end by repudiating them. Social peace is the fundamental objective of communists, he observed, but there can be no peace under conditions of civil strife and hatred.[191] In meeting violence with violence, he concluded, bolshevism is ultimately self-defeating.

Bolshevism fell short of the communism of love not only in its methods, but also in the exceptions it made to the principle of fraternity. Although it favored common ownership, distribution would be based initially on differences of skill as well as work. Trincado believed that any honoring of special talents, whether natural or acquired, was unfair to those who lacked them. True communism required a different principle: "Everything in the world belongs to the community."[192] Although special skills are obviously particular to the individuals who acquire them, their benefits should be shared by all. There should be no favoritism or exalted status for the science of our heads over the labor of our bodies. Distribution should be regulated not by how or what each produces, but by a code of love based on human needs.[193]

In this perspective, Trincado's universal commune appears as the higher stage of communism, whereas bolshevism appears as the lower. In his "Critique of the Gotha Program," Marx associated the lower stage of communism with a condition permeated by survivals of bourgeois society, including the bourgeois notion of a "right" to the proceeds of one's own work.[194] In the higher stage this "right" would no longer be recognized and distribution would be based on need. Such a principle already operates within the family, Trincado noted, but has yet to be applied beyond it.[195] When universalized it becomes the principle of fraternal communism— Sandino called it "rational communism"—as distinct from the "retrograde communism" of bolshevism.[196]

For Trincado, the contemporary alternative to bolshevism was his own project of a universal commune. What distinguishes the universal commune from its bolshevik competitor is, among other things, the role it assigns to the individual—the human soul under communism. One objection to bolshevism is that it relies on laws and institutions to make people equal; another is that it sacrifices individual interests to those of society. The "natural commune" would invert this dependence by discovering the law in each person, thus making society dependent on individuals.[197] That law is the law of love, whose one and only mandate is "Love your brother!"[198]

"True communism," according to Trincado, is predicated on the "true commune," which is also the "natural commune."[199] Despite the ownership of everything in common, individuals rather than society would be the final authority. Unlike retrograde communism, this advanced form would "leave the individual sovereign in the bosom of society" and "each individual the *sovereign proprietor of all.*"[200]

To students of the history of political thought, this idea of a natural commune shows the influence of Rousseau rather than Marx. The fundamental social question for Trincado, echoing Rousseau, was to find a form of association that would defend with the public power the person and goods of each associate while each obeyed only himself or herself and remained as free as before.[201] Rousseau's attempt to answer this question has had a traditional appeal for anarchists because it combines freedom with equality.

For Trincado, Rousseau's political philosophy "leads infallibly to communism."[202] He believed this was evident from its guiding principle, "the greatest good of all."[203] "All" does not refer to a majority, which always leaves somebody out. Rousseau's principle should not be confused with the democratic principle of "the greatest good of the greatest number." Unlike the democratic principle, it implies liberty and equality for everybody: "liberty, because all particular dependence means so much force taken from the body of the State, and *equality, because liberty cannot exist without it.*"[204]

In effect, equality has precedence over liberty. Rousseau adds that, "in respect to riches, no citizen shall ever be wealthy enough to buy another, and none poor enough to be forced to sell himself."[205] There can be no servants and no wage laborers under such conditions. Accordingly, Rousseau's ideal society is incompatible with the existence of Marx's two great classes: the bourgeoisie and the proletariat. It is incompatible with exploitation and class antagonisms. Evidently, it implies a classless society.

The thorny issue hinges on how to apply Rousseau's principle to differing historical conditions. Considering the social circumstances with which he was familiar, petty commodity production in a preindustrial age, Rousseau envisioned a classless society based on private property rather than property owned in common. Such a society of independent artisans and farmers is a far cry from communism, and under conditions of industrial civilization it is also hopelessly utopian. Does this mean that Rousseau's principle cannot be adapted to present conditions? Not at all. Trincado astutely observed that where labor is cooperative rather than individual, property tends to be owned cooperatively. If Rousseau's principle leads to communism, it is because social conditions in the twentieth century no longer correspond to those in the eighteenth.

Trincado traced Rousseau's political philosophy to the communards of Castille.[206] In 1520 a revolution by the Spanish communes or townships was headed by Juan Padilla in defense of ancient liberties that were being threatened by Charles V. In the battle of Villalar the *comuneros* (communards) were defeated. But their memory lingered on and their example was later revived by Spanish Free-masons. Under the influence of the French Revolution of 1789 and the Illuminati, Spanish Freemasons organized a secret political society in 1821 known as the Confederation of the Communards.[207] The goals of these new *comuneros* were to promote freedom by any and every means, to defend the people's rights against the abuses and encroachments of royal and priestly power, and to help the needy. The historical importance of this second edition of the Spanish *comuneros* may be adduced from the fact that nearly sixty thousand joined this secret society.[208]

Trincado's project of a universal commune was rooted in the history and struggles of the *comuneros.* The commune, he pointed out, is not an artificial creation but has its sources in Spanish history. Born of the family, the sense of fraternity spreads to the township and to the nation that must live the life of the family if people expect to live in peace. Not until all nations reach this condition and become confederated for the same ends will there be "communism," which is the superlative of "commune."[209] Thus Trincado recommended that his school's adepts call themselves "communards" rather than "communists," until the communes of all the nations have joined together under a single code.

Spanish anarchists also trace their origins to the *comuneros.* Trincado considered their doctrines to be "advanced." The anarchists are right, he says, to protest all abuses of power. But they are "mistaken because they want to destroy society and return to the individual regime of the forest and the cave."[210] This caricature of anarchist philosophy was based on a misunderstanding. Individualistic anarchism, whose heyday was the late eighteenth and early nineteenth centuries as the extreme expression of modern liberalism, had by the early twentieth century given way to collectivistic and communitarian forms of anarchism. On close inspection, Trincado's "true communism," like Sandino's "rational communism," corresponds to what today is called anarcho-communism.

Although Trincado nominally repudiated anarchism, his solution to the social question agreed with Flores Magón's. Trincado understood by "true communism" a social arrangement in which everyone is equal, meaning that "each one produces according to his abilities and receives from the common deposit . . . according to his needs." No one has to worry about how much his brother consumes, because enough is produced to satisfy everybody.[211] About the same time, Flores Magón defined communism as a social arrangement in which the means of production are owned in common and the workers share the products according to their needs. Trincado's "common deposit" corresponds to Flores Magón's "general store."

Like Flores Magón and other anarchists, Trincado depicted communism as a moneyless economy in which there is no buying and selling. Where "the only money is man, tyranny can no longer exist because there is no place for inequality," which is to say, there is no economic basis for it.[212] Thus Trincado railed against "plutocracy," which he associated with "parasitism."[213] Unfamiliar as he was with the writings of Karl Marx, he used the term "plutocracy" for what Marxists call "capitalism." The three fundamental parasites preying on the working class, according to Trincado, are "religion, militarism, and moneylenders or financiers."[214] These correspond to Flores Magón's three-headed hydra—Clergy, Authority, and Capital.

Nonetheless, there are some differences distinguishing Trincado's anarchism from Flores Magón's. Trincado identified the fundamental enemy as the clergy, whose religious domination has been buttressed historically by the political and military power of the state. Economic exploitation by the moneyed class was depicted as dependent on this nefarious alliance. Unlike most of his fellow anarchists, Flores Magón came to believe that capital was the fundamental enemy, in turn supported by political and military authority, whose spiritual ally was organized religion. Whereas the workers' economic struggle against exploitation became Flores Magón's central preoccupation, anticlericalism was the focus of Trincado's anarchism.

Sandino's writings do not reflect Trincado's all-consuming hatred of religion. Rather than the two beasts of Revelation, the fundamental enemies for Sandino were the "Yankee pirates," the "Wall Street bankers," the "White House," and Nicaragua's corrupt political leaders. As we shall see in chapter 4, these remained in the forefront of his thought even after his conversion to the doctrines of the Magnetic-Spiritual School. Although Sandino repeated key passages from Trincado's major work almost verbatim, he did not assign first importance to the struggle against the Catholic clergy.

Sandino's anarchism differed from that of his Spanish mentor in focusing on the political-military struggle as the necessary prelude to establishing a society of workers' and peasants' cooperatives in Nicaragua. Authority was the immediate enemy, whereas the world capitalist system was the fundamental one. Although he subscribed to Trincado's philosophy of universal history, his main concern was the struggle against imperialism interpreted as the highest

stage of capitalism. There was both a Marxist and a Leninist component in his anarchism that was missing in the anarchism of the
Magnetic-Spiritual School.

Sandino's "Rational Communism"

For Sandino the superiority of Trincado's philosophy lay in its fusion of Spiritism and anarchism. This was an unbeatable combination because it gave a spiritual justification to anarchism and an
anarchist dimension to traditional theosophy. Having discovered in
the austere world of spirits an explanation of humanity's material
existence, Sandino also discovered there a rationale for an anarchist
and communist revolution that would destroy privilege and make
austerity binding on all. In effect, his philosophy of austere rationality was a philosophy of rational austerity.

We have seen that the teachings of the Magnetic-Spiritual
School consisted of Trincado's rationally based Spiritism, and its
political project of a universal commune tantamount to "the whole
world communized." This provides a clue to what Sandino meant
by "rational communism." In a letter to Dr. Humberto Barahona
(27 May 1933), he distinguished his peculiar brand of communism
from that of the Comintern. Accused of giving up the struggle for
social justice because of the terms of peace he had accepted with
representatives of the Liberal and Conservative parties, Sandino
gave the reasons for laying down his arms. The elected president,
Dr. Sacasa, chose to come to terms with him "against the will of
the State Department." The latter hoped that the civil war would
continue until Sandino was completely wiped out. But at the same
time, the Nicaraguan Congress was pressuring Sacasa's government
to accept a loan of two million dollars for the purpose of destroying
the Defending Army. This danger had to be averted. Contrary to the
many rumors, Sandino had not renounced his rights as a citizen
and his social program had not been liquidated, as his detractors
believed. "I will die in the open struggle seeking the triumph of our
ideals. . . . While you flee from calling yourself a communist, with
all the strength of my being I declare to the entire universe that I
am a rational communist." [215]

Sandino did not explain his peculiar juxtaposition of "rational"
and "communist." However, we know that his belief in a world
communist revolution was based on his theosophy, which proclaimed itself rational rather than dogmatic. A "rational communist" to Sandino was a communist guided by divine reason. Keeping these two essential components of his theosophy of liberation

in mind, let us examine the rational or Spiritist component and proceed from there to its communist application.

Arguing that theosophy is not religion, Sandino declared, "We are guided by reason."[216] He believed that reason and religion were opposed, that religion rested on faith rather than knowledge, and that theosophy was a rational substitute for faith. Critical of all religion, he claimed that the purpose of his theosophy was to enlighten and instruct the ignorant. Thereby, they might "know, respect, and care for themselves."[217] His theosophy effectively backed up his earlier appeals to the principles of "Reason, Justice, and Right," the same "principles of Justice, Right, and REASON that we have defended for more than two years against Yankee piracy."[218] Reason, his criterion of the Right and the Just, stands out as Sandino's basic principle. It had a theosophical foundation in what he called the "Spirit of Light and Truth."

The first public statement of Sandino's theosophy was his Light and Truth Manifesto, composed within a year of his second return from Mexico. In this document he identified the communist forecast of world revolution with the Final Judgment of the Scriptures. "By the Final Judgment of the World should be understood the destruction of injustice on earth and the reign of the Spirit of Light and Truth, i.e., Love. You must also have heard that this twentieth century, the century of Light [*sic*], is the epoch in which was prophesied the Final Judgment of the World."[219] He predicted that by the year 2000 the holocaust would have occurred. "What will happen is the following. The oppressed peoples will break the chains of humiliation with which the imperialists of the earth have tried to keep us subjugated. The trumpets that will be heard will be the bugles of war intoning the hymns of liberty of the oppressed peoples against the injustice of the oppressors. The only thing that will be submerged forever is injustice; what will remain is the kingdom of perfection or Love with Divine Justice, her favorite daughter."[220] If this had been only Sandino's personal fantasy, then he might have been a little balmy, but as an integral part of his Zoroastrian heritage and the teachings of the Magnetic-Spiritual School, his theosophy had a collective basis.[221]

What Sandino added that was original is the preeminent role assigned to his Defending Army in challenging the forces of evil and deciding the fate of the world. Justice, Sandino believed, was on the side of his heroic soldiers: "We have the honor, brothers, of having been chosen in Nicaragua by Divine Justice to begin the judgment of injustice on earth."[222] In the same context he assured his men that it was not necessary to wait for some divine signal before launching the final battle. Nor was there anything to fear from the coming confrontation with evil. Neither the earth nor all its inhabitants would be destroyed during the final holocaust, Sandino assured them, because victory over the enemy was guaranteed.

With his theosophical doctrines Sandino provided ideological support for his Defending Army. As he wrote to a colonel in his army, he hoped to exert influence over the thoughts as well as the deeds of his fellow citizens: "Possibly we will get the opportunity of having military, civilian, and religious control over our Republic!"[223] Religious control would strengthen his humanitarian program for a free and rational communism. The doctrine of Divine Justice would help instill respect for social justice in the struggle against foreign and domestic oppressors.

Divine Justice, Sandino wrote in an encouraging message to his troops in April 1931, had been responsible for the earthquake that leveled the capital in March. "On the thirty-first of March of this year half of the city of Managua was destroyed when, among other things, the airfield caved in with a great part of the war planes and munitions of the enemy. On the other hand, now that Divine Justice is directly harassing the enemy, we have to finish the job by terrorizing the terrorists."[224]

Sandino's doctrine of Divine Justice culminated in the prophecy of a final judgment that would reinforce the communist expectation of a world revolution. This final episode in divine and human history would be preceded by a world war, the prophesied battle of Armageddon, involving the angelic hosts and legions of the Devil as well as incarnate spirits on earth. In a letter to another of his supporters in April 1931, Sandino indicated that the prophesied battle would be unleashed by the Wall Street bankers in an effort to complete the construction of an interoceanic canal through Nicaragua, an effort doomed to defeat because Divine Justice impelled Nicaraguans to stop them.[225] "You should understand that Nicaragua will be the principal cause of the next world war in which the oppressors of rank and wealth will be destroyed so that the people may cast off their oppression."[226]

Further prophecies and visions of doomsday were brought out in Belausteguigoitia's interview with the philosopher-general. In the struggle between the forces of justice and injustice, Sandino declared, the spiritual world is enmeshed with the material; good and evil spirits in the flesh and without flesh have fought one another since the creation of humanity. The final confrontation set for Central America would be accompanied by a geological and social catastrophe: "I envision something that I have never told before. . . . I see Nicaragua covered in water, a huge depression on the Pacific coast, the volcanoes alone projecting. It is as if one sea emptied itself into the other."[227] Here was the anticipated Yankee canal with a vengeance! Such a catastrophe might fulfill the American dream of linking the Atlantic and Pacific oceans in a great waterway many times the size of the one in Panama, but at the cost of submerging the U.S. Marines as well.

Although Sandino rejected faith in a personal god and denied the divinity of Christ, he acknowledged a predetermined destiny chosen for each person by a supposedly conscious force behind all of natural and human history.[228] The human spirit not only survives the physical body, he believed, but also has the power to receive messages from other spirits directly in the form of visions, premonitions, and prophecies that turn out to be true.[229]

Sandino praised the marvelous imagination of children. "Faith, I believe, is eternally childlike and creative; childlike, because it joins the real world with the marvelous and, although separating us from the doubt of skepticism and old age, transports us into the dream world of those early years in which, as the poet Wordsworth says, men still retain the memory of an incarnation that has not yet been forgotten with the lapse of time and the loss of sensitivity."[230] Here he stressed the personal benefits of professing a religious faith: it helps miserable sharecroppers to feel that their lives are worthwhile and that they will not dissipate like smoke; it raises the peasants' hopes and expectations because they think of themselves as actors in an eternal and ever-renewed drama in which victory favors the just. The common laborer looks forward to the turning of the tables, when the first shall be last and the last shall be first. Although in his own case Sandino professed to have replaced faith by reason, he was not averse to encouraging religion in others. Although he looked on established religion as an opiate of the masses, he believed that faith might also become an impulse to revolution.

It is evident from Sandino's letters that he thought that his theosophical beliefs supported revolutionary actions because they dissipated the fear of death and encouraged the struggle for justice. As he remarked in the first privately recorded testimony of his theosophical faith, matter as electricity is a form of light or spirit, and all spirits are consubstantial with the Father and Creator of the universe.[231] Injustice is self-defeating, Sandino believed, because it comes from ignorance of God, who is Eternal Love. Injustice first appeared during the embryonic stage of humanity and is destined to disappear with knowledge of our spiritual origin and nature.[232] It has no reason for being because it is against the law of love, the only law that governs people who see the light. A new dawn is now at hand: "The earth was a place of expiation where for millions of centuries Divine Justice kept those spirits that disobeyed the divine law; but today the earth is ready for regeneration and those refractory spirits will be hurled out onto other less progressive planets."[233]

But to overcome injustice one must attack it. That, Sandino believed, is our mission on earth. Recalling his interview with General Moncada, who had ridiculed him for his patriotic sentiments, Sandino noted that it was not prudence but vileness to try to live well on the tears and sacrifices of others.[234] For countless centuries everything enjoyable in life had been monopolized by a few parasites, according to his account, while the masses had to grovel and sweat without receiving even what was necessary for survival. Injustice had prevailed because of humanity's egoism based on ignorance. But the rule of oppressors, Sandino prophesied, would soon be overcome by the war of liberators. From that time forward there would be peace and justice on earth.[235] If revolutionaries must have an activating myth, this one seemed better than most.

The picture that emerges from these components of Sandino's theosophy is of a world created by Divine Love and ruled by Divine Reason—tantamount to a law of love. The first substance was the Ether, the primal form of matter. Light as electricity is the spiritual essence of matter. It is consubstantial with love, the will to create combined with the willingness to sacrifice for others. The earth has been a purgatory where divine justice has punished refractory spirits concerned mainly with themselves. But it will be regenerated by the recognition that all men are brothers and by the courage to stand up to injustice and oppression. This regeneration will not happen peacefully. A final holocaust will occur before the end of the twentieth century and the proletariat will rise against the exploiters and defeat forever the forces of darkness. The earth will then be inhabited only by men of light living in perfect harmony.

Although such collective fantasies can hardly qualify as rational, Sandino identified the end time with the reign of reason and love. As he envisioned it, communism was rational because it conformed to Divine Reason.

An important corollary of this doctrine was a belief in the reincarnation of spirits. Since these are consubstantial with God, they never die. For each one of us, life is eternal; our bodily form is transitory. This does not imply that all spirits are incarnate, but only those that are destined to inhabit the earth.

Among the great prophets of humanity who can lead us toward the light, Sandino gave first place to Zoroaster.[236] But other prophets were also important. In his conversations with Belausteguigoitia, Sandino mentioned Adam, Moses, Jesus, and, indirectly, Mahomet, who worshipped the same god under a different name.[237] Thus the elements of four great historical religions were combined in this amalgam: Zoroastrianism, Judaism, Christianity, and Islam.[238] To be precise, their monotheism and eschatological and moral teachings were syncretistically fused with the Oriental doctrine of reincarnation as revived by modern Spiritualism, the free-thinking outlook of modern Freemasonry, and the theosophy of the Magnetic-Spiritual School.

Sandino's theosophy provided the "rational" basis for his anarcho-communism. Liberalism, the progenitor of communism according to Sandino, had its roots in the ages-long controversy between the Roman Catholic priesthood and so-called heretics or freethinkers. For his sketch of the spiritualist prehistory of this controversy I turn to the most obscure letter he ever wrote, without doubt the most politically embarrassing for his many admirers. Addressed to a member of the Conservative party, it provides the best single statement of the political content of his theosophy. Although Ramírez does not include the letter's full text in his anthology, possibly because its fantasies raise doubts concerning Sandino's rationality, it has a respectable source in Trincado's *Filosofía austera racional.*[239]

The letter begins with a brief statement concerning the origins of social injustice. "Man was born of the fifth essence of nature . . . from which the spirits who had received judgment and had been banished from other planets formed the bodies of men. Since all the animal instincts are imprisoned in men, they are antagonistic toward one another as long as they do not recognize their trinity, but prefer to accept what is agreeable to their bodies rather than what is useful to everybody."[240] Thus our unmanageable appetites are the ultimate cause of injustice on earth.

Later, when men became apprehensive about death and dying, Sandino continued, they began to believe in a being superior to themselves and to the world about them. They not only assigned the most intelligent persons the job of investigating such important matters, but also agreed to sustain them by their labors. But those who were thus exempted from ordinary labor established the principle of inheritance, by which their children also became exempt and able to accumulate riches. Privileged classes and private property were the result of this original duplicity: "The first thieves

who existed on earth were those who today are called priests."[241]
Here Sandino was on firmer ground; anticlericalism has a distinguished history.

After priests, Sandino lashed out at the warriors or military caste representing authority and the state. "The second set of thieves were those you today call the military. It was natural that the first person entrusted to make [spiritual] investigations would have need of others to protect his interests in what he might accumulate." But the discovery of gold changed everything. The priests thought this treasure belonged to them, whereas "the soldiers, that is the guardians of the priests, believed that part of this discovery was rightfully theirs."[242] The ensuing conflict between soldiers and priests resulted in the first revolution, according to Sandino.

After this first disastrous conflict, twenty-nine missionary spirits headed by Adam and Eve arrived on earth on a mission of redemption.[243] Adam became incarnate as the son of a priest, and Eve became incarnate as the daughter of a warrior. In telling a different story, according to Sandino, the Old Testament obscures the real one.

By the time of the New Testament a third set of thieves had emerged alongside the priests and soldiers—the bankers. All three classes were challenged by "the revolutionary and communist Jesus of Nazareth in his harangues against the priests, the bankers, and the authorities."[244] As Sandino depicted him, Jesus was the leader of an "army of twenty thousand in open warfare against the bankers of Jerusalem."[245] Whether or not these were the progenitors of the Wall Street bankers, they along with the clergy and the state—the other principal targets of Sandino's wrath—were also Flores Magón's main targets. However, the source of these biblical interpolations was not the Mexican anarchist but the founder of the Magnetic-Spiritual School. They are taken almost verbatim from chapter 2 of Trincado's major work.

To Jesus we owe the notion of "liberty," Sandino continued. Thus the modern representatives of his teachings are called liberals. At the opposite pole are the conservatives, the group opposed to liberty and freedom of thought. In Sandino's account, their origins go back to the priests who persecuted Jesus and to the official Catholic religion, concerned with suppressing ideas it considered dangerous. "Liberals are called heretics because they propose to discover the reality of things through the exercise of free thought."[246] Liberty is anathema to conservatives because they want to keep the masses of humble people ignorant and in a condition of servitude.[247] In this perspective, Jesus was a champion of the poor and oppressed against the conservatives of his time. This portrait of Jesus as the father of modern liberalism owes less to the Magnetic-Spiritual School than to modern Freemasonry.

In any case, Sandino concluded, Nicaragua is an exception to the general tendency of modern societies to split into two parties representing what the names conservative and liberal traditionally stand for. Those who call themselves conservatives do so mistakenly because there has never been a military caste in Nicaragua linked to the privileged aristocratic families of Europe.[248] As for many self-styled liberals, they don't deserve the name because they defend the same stupid causes as their political enemies. Because of ignorance, Sandino reflected, Nicaraguans have been led to deny what they really are. Virtually all Nicaraguans belonged to what he called the "common class" of those who labored for a livelihood. Thus, rather than being liberals or conservatives, "we are more like 'commonists,'" a play on words suggesting that the people's real interests are those of "communists."[249]

The Coming "Proletarian Explosion"

We have seen that Sandino's "rational communism" had two principal components: the rational element referred to his Spiritist theosophy; the communist component, to the coming proletarian upheaval that would replace world capitalism with an international communist order. Specific support for a world communist revolution is evident as early as his Light and Truth Manifesto in February 1931. As he assured his Defending Army, "we shall soon have our definitive triumph in Nicaragua, which will light the fuse of the 'Proletarian Explosion' against the imperialists!"[250] To this he added in a letter to Alemán Bolaños in August of the same year, "It gives me great pleasure to announce that our army will wait for the approaching world conflagration to begin developing its humanitarian program in favor of the world proletariat."[251]

A realistic program must come in response to concrete historical conditions, Sandino indicated, but these were not yet present. Shrewd strategist that he was, he believed in waiting for the right moment to strike. The Defending Army had first taken on the traitors in both parties for having betrayed the nation's sovereignty and the Constitution. Next, it challenged them for failing to provide protective legislation for Nicaragua's workers and peasants and for ignoring the conditions of collective progress and self-defense through a Central American Union. Finally, it turned against the economic and political system that maintained them in power.

Although Sandino had broken with the Mexican Communist party and the Comintern, he had returned to his country in 1930 prepared to escalate his war of liberation and to launch a class struggle against Nicaragua's capitalists. To escape the accusation of communism, he deliberately disguised his class war as a struggle for right and justice. But his commitment to communism was evident in his new policy toward the rich. That policy was sketched in a communiqué to his armed forces in October 1931, followed by his Manifesto to the Capitalists in November.

In his communiqué Sandino notified Nicaragua and the world of his army's new policy toward property owners. When one of our columns arrives at an hacienda or large estate within our national territory, Sandino noted, it will often seize the owner's goods and provisions and it may even take his shoes and clothes: "Well, our brother soldiers need them more than he does, and . . . it is not right that the men who are building the foundations of liberty in Nicaragua should go about dressed in rags." For such acts Sandino's soldiers had been decried as bandits. But "history will show the justice of our acts, mainly when it is understood that the capitalists despoiled of their property are the ones most directly responsible for what has happened in Nicaragua, because they are the ones who brought the Yankee mercenaries into our national territory."[252]

Sandino's Manifesto to the Capitalists came in response to news from Jinotega of efforts by businessmen to organize a Chamber of Commerce, whose purpose was to get the central government and the U.S. Marines to protect their interests. Sandino replied, "As long as foreign intervention exists in Nicaragua there will be no protection for people's lives and interests. . . . Liberty is not conquered with flowers but with bullets, and that is why we have had to use the VEST CUT, GOURD CUT, and BLOOMERS CUT."[253] These "cuts" were references to the three forms of extreme retribution meted out to the marines and their collaborators. In the "vest cut" the offender's head was lopped off with a machete and his arms severed at the shoulders; in the "gourd cut" the top of the victim's skull was sliced off; in the "bloomers cut" the traitor's legs were hacked off at the knees and he was left to bleed to death.

Horrified by such tactics, Belausteguigoitia searched for an explanation consistent with his impressions of Sandino as a hypernervous and anguished individual who loathed violence and practiced yoga to quiet his nerves. "Once the struggle became generalized, the Americans became crazed with the idea of annihilating the region where they perceived in each cabin a center of hostile life and in each inhabitant a guerrilla or spy." One has to imagine the state of mind of Sandino's soldiers to appreciate their exaggerated response to the invaders, whose "aim was to terrorize and desolate rebel territory and to make the enemy's life impossible."[254] Persecuted and killed like wild animals or "bandits" who did not qualify as prisoners of war, their families driven from their homes and hunted down as informers, Sandino's men began replying in kind. "It seems that the famous 'vest cut' was first applied by an American officer against Sandino's soldiers or alleged spies or sympathizers of the cause [a reference to the marine who beheaded a Sandinista and was then proudly photographed with his victim's head], after which it was copied by General Altamirano to save on ammunition."[255] After suffering a lifetime of persecution by the civil authorities for a mistake of his youth, this formidable guerrilla of almost seventy years was Sandino's principal and most loyal supporter. Against incredible odds, he had managed to carry on the war when Sandino and his general staff left Nicaragua for Mexico. While Sandino did his utmost to discipline his men, in this instance he repaid a personal debt by excusing his general's atrocities.

Sandino made no attempt to justify the atrocities committed by his soldiers, but he did make some crucial distinctions. Whereas both sides decapitated and castrated their enemies, they did so from different motives. "The principal difference is that the marines did it to subjugate us, whereas we did it to liberate ourselves." This was not the only difference. "They attacked indiscriminately the rural population, including old people, women, and children who were completely apart from the struggle, whereas we attacked only the invading army." Finally, when they could not conceal their atrocities, the marines tried to justify them. "I have the courage and dignity to confess the brutality of our actions, for which, although there is no justification, there is an explanation. They try to cover up and deny the truth about their war crimes and, even in those cases in which the evidence is undeniable, try to justify what they have done as a means of saving Nicaragua from banditry."[256]

Sandino's partiality to communism is evident in his letters alerting his soldiers to the danger of the war spreading throughout Central America. Should the Honduran government do the Yankees' bidding by sending troops across the border to fight us, Sandino wrote, "we will proclaim the Union of Central America under the name of Central American Communards led by workers and peasants . . . , taking as our field of operations the entire Central American territory."[257] The class content of this threat was reinforced by a clear perception not only of the foreign but also of the domestic enemy. "Our movement for a Central American Union should be disentangled from bourgeois elements, which have always obliged us to accept the Yankee humiliations agreeable to their interests."[258] Since the Isthmus had been unified before as the United Provinces of Central America (1823–1840), it was not a matter of achieving something heretofore unobtainable but of restoring the past in a substantially changed form.

Sandino's projected union envisioned a government of workers and peasants. Beyond that, he anticipated that it would become a step toward Latin American unification, better still toward the Hispano-American Oceanic Union of Hispano-American communards that would include all Spanish-speaking peoples.[259] It would also involve the establishment in Central America of "our first government of the Universal Commune," the prelude to worldwide communization.[260]

Elsewhere, Sandino denounced the nominally liberal government of Nicaragua and the government of Honduras, "because both are agents of the Yankee bankers and our two peoples expect nothing from such human refuse."[261] In the event these governments should go to war over their disputed boundaries, Sandino declared, it would be in conformity to the interests of Wall Street and the White House's policy of divide and conquer. What would be his response? Sandino promised to take advantage of the situation to attack whichever army happened to be defeated. He also promised to establish a new and free republic for all the peoples of the earth—an allusion to his projected Central American Commune.

When the Defending Army was finally demobilized in February 1933 its place was taken by the token Emergency Force of one hundred men ultimately responsible to Sandino. This new force represented the core of the Defending Army's successor, the secretly projected Autonomist Army of Central America. Specifically committed to the doctrine of "universal fraternity"—Sandino's euphemism for "communization"—his army's statutes declared that the Bryan-Chamorro Treaty was henceforth abrogated.[262] The statutes further declared any Latin American government to be illegitimate that might refuse to recognize the Central American Union proclaimed and defended by the Autonomist Army. Sandino's "Plan for Realizing Bolívar's Supreme Dream," originally formulated in March 1929 but held in abeyance, was put in effect on 18 August 1933, when the statutes were presented to his general staff for approval. His new army's flag was to be the symbolic red and black banner, and all official communication among his soldiers was to begin with the salutation, "My very dear brother" and to close with the words "Ever onward!"—the motto of the Magnetic-Spiritual School of the Universal Commune.[263]

Two days earlier, in the name of the Autonomist Army, Sandino had drawn up a parallel document entitled the "Supreme Proclamation of the Central American Union." Without justification, Sandino noted, all of the original Central American countries except Honduras had one by one seceded from the Central American Federation, which made Honduras an appropriate symbol of his proclaimed Central American Union and the appropriate site for its future capital.[264] After describing the projected government of the Central American Union, Sandino lashed out at the main obstacles in its way. One obstacle was U.S. imperialism. Another was Central America's political leaders, who "have surrendered and are surrendering huge tracts of our lovely Central American land to avaricious and exploiting Yankee companies, such as the maritime ports, customs offices, railways, mineral and oil deposits, and other major sources of Central American revenue, [thus] converting Central Americans into slaves and our lands into gardens of exploitation from which to extract still greater resources for exploiting other fraternal peoples."[265]

This grotesque Yankee imperialism and the sellout policies of our governments, the document continued, "have incensed our people and launched them into the redemptive war undertaken by the Autonomist Army of Central America."[266] Evidently, the revolutionary civil war was about to resume on a scale that included not just Nicaragua but virtually the entire Isthmus. "Even though the military, political, and economic expulsion from our soil of the ailing Wall Street bankers may require that we leave our dead bodies facing the sun . . . , the racial dignity of the Indo-Hispanic race hinges at this moment on the Autonomist Army of Central America!"[267]

What kind of documents were these? Did they in fact include the statutes of a secret army organized as the successor of the Defending Army? Had they in fact proclaimed a Central American union on behalf of which a new revolutionary war had already begun? Even Somoza, who ridiculed Sandino for his eccentric, inflated, and demagogical but impractical ideas, conceded that they were only guidelines for subversion. The statutes of the Autonomist Army were actually presented by Sandino not as the statutes of an existing army but as "The Model of the Autonomist Army of Central America, by which all its Members are Irrevocably

Governed."[268] The Proclamation of Central American Union was characterized in no uncertain terms as "only an abridgement of the ideality of the Autonomist Army of Central America, not its code of doctrinaire rules, which would be revealed to the world when the cherished Central American Federation became a reality."[269] Although the above documents tell us very little about the prospects of Sandino's Central American Commune, they do provide a clue to his revolutionary ideology.

When the marines evacuated Nicaragua in January 1933, they took with them the files of the National Guard for the period 1927–1932, when it had been under marine command. Among those documents in the Naval Records Section of the National Archives in Washington are many of Sandino's papers and other sources of information about him. An unidentified newspaper clipping from those files acknowledges that Sandino had been visited in his camp by the Quixotic traveler from Spain, Ramiro Molla Sanz, in whose book of recollections the general had written, "Spain and America will communize the earth!"[270]

In his conversations with Belausteguigoitia, Sandino spoke of Spain as a nation predestined to achieve the "universal communization of mankind."[271] Why Spain? Because Spain, for the Magnetic-Spiritual School, had been selected by the Father and Creator for the special "mission of bringing light to the world and unifying mankind . . . in a single race with a single language."[272] Because Spain had been destined to become the "mother of nations" through its discovery of America; because it was the birthplace of the Society of Jesus, which had always been a thorn in the side of the Vatican; because it had become the seat of the Anti-Christ; because it had been chosen by Jesus's younger brother, James, and by his mother, Mary, as the most appropriate terrain for disseminating the pure teachings of the new fraternal order founded by Jesus.[273]

Asked by Belausteguigoitia to clarify what he meant by "communization," Sandino explained that it meant association on brotherly terms. Political nationalism was only part of the solution to Nicaragua's status of dependency and Balkanization: "Above the nation is the federation: first, continental; and afterward a broader union eventually including all."[274] Sandino's point was that there could be no genuine fraternization among peoples that was not based on mutual respect and equality among nations. Sandino did not spell out to his guest all that this implied. A convinced liberal, Belausteguigoitia still believed in the future of capitalism and of the so-called middle class. He had no inkling of Sandino's predilection for an international proletarian revolution.

What Sandino understood by fraternization may be gleaned from his correspondence concerning the agricultural cooperative he founded in Wiwilí, a port on the Coco River. This community was a refuge, he writes, for the disinherited and for families afflicted by misery and that could not find work or adapt to city life.[275] It was a society for mutual aid in which "fraternization" stood for the sharing and cultivation of property in common.

It was not the Comintern but Sandinismo that was turning Nicaragua upside down with this doctrine of fraternity. For the Liberal government of President Moncada it was imperative to halt the spread of such ideas. Suspecting Sandino's ulterior motives, Moncada declared at the end of his presidential term, "For some time there have been sproutings of Sandinismo in the interior. . . . We all know that the present government cannot and must not tolerate Sandinista and Communist writings, meetings, or financial support, in order that we may deal with the author of the ruin of the Segovias."[276] The American occupation forces and the National Guard were also aware of the danger of Sandinista subversion. By 1932 the contagion had spread from the countryside to Nicaragua's cities and ports: "particular attention was paid to the University of León, a virtual hotbed of Sandinismo."[277]

The focus on exploitation and the struggle against capitalism help to distinguish communists from other social reformers. But Sandino was no ordinary communist. For him communism was a way of life, not just a social movement or novel mode of production and distribution. Because he couched his ideology in religious phraseology, he presented a more attractive figure to Nicaraguan peasants, workers, and university students than did the agents of the Communist International, with their harsh materialism and appeals to scientific knowledge. Sandino successfully challenged not only the Comintern's claim to a monopoly of revolution, but also as the sole representative of communism in the hemisphere. It would not be the only instance of an indigenous communist movement—the FSLN is the most notorious example—proving to be more viable than an established Marxist-Leninist party in Central America.

3. Strategy for Subversion

Sandino had a peculiar affinity for occult ideas and secret societies. After absorbing the esoteric forms of wisdom associated with Mexican Spiritualism, Freemasonry, and theosophy, he became an adept of the even more exotic Magnetic-Spiritual School of the Universal Commune. His initiation into secret and semi-clandestine fraternal organizations made him familiar with the behavior of psychic mediums, grand lodges, bizarre schools that in Mexico still operated underground, and with the inner sanctum of the Mexican Communist party's Central Committee. In Mexico he also consorted with anarchists and evidently knew of the ideas of Ricardo Flores Magón and of the duplicity of the Mexican Liberal party.

From doctrines and associations repugnant to most citizens, Sandino learned the political value of secrecy and the imperative of couching his real intentions and beliefs in inoffensive language that appealed to the masses. A master of political camouflage, his subversive designs for Nicaragua took the form of occult wisdom.[1]

Protected from hostile outsiders by a screen, Sandino began to build a political movement of his own. It appeared successively as a tendency within the Nicaraguan Liberal party, as a Liberal party split-off supported by patriots from other parties, and as a populist and nationalist movement for implementing the social reforms of the Mexican Revolution. His principal allies consisted of Nicaraguan Liberals and their supporters abroad, native populists inspired by the example of the Mexican Revolution and the prospect of support from that country's revolutionary government, and the Communist International. Few of his political allies ever really fathomed the extent of his political objectives. His underlying commitment to anarchism remained concealed not only from them, but also from most of his own followers, including members of his inner circle.

By keeping his objectives secret, Sandino was in a favorable position to build the broadest possible alliance for implementing his ideals. Historically, he was a progenitor of the policies of a "popular front" subsequently adopted by the Comintern and later by Fidel Castro and by the FSLN. It was a Machiavellian strategy culled from the practices of secret societies and, as we have seen, from his initial political mistakes in dealing with General Moncada. Although this policy was only one facet of his total strategy, it was among the most crucial. Sandino's other major contribution to the strategy and tactics of guerrilla warfare has been dealt with exhaustively by Macaulay and need not concern us here.[2]

Appeals to Patriotism

From the beginning Sandino mobilized support for his cause by appealing to his people's moral and religious beliefs. His political manifestos served a dual purpose: they informed his countrymen of the intentions of his Defending Army, and they enlisted the active support of Nicaragua's workers and peasants by responding to their needs and aspirations in a language they could understand. An authentic folk hero, he assiduously cultivated the image of himself as a new Bolívar. With this image he tried to capture the public eye and strike a sympathetic chord in the people.[3] He wanted them to know that the cause of his Defending Army was a patriotic one.

Sandino continually waged a campaign against the government's false portrayal of him as a bandit surrounded by criminal and predatory elements.[4] Although publicly he called for social change, he always presented himself as a defender of law, justice, and morality, never as a revolutionary or subverter of the existing constitutional order. Revolutionary he was, but it was through appeals to patriotism that he led his followers from liberalism through populism and socialism to his own blend of communism and anarchism reinforced by a theosophy of liberation.

Patriotism is central to understanding Sandino's mass appeal. His first political manifesto (1 July 1927) began with the lines, "The man who does not ask from his country even a few inches of earth for his burial deserves to be heard, and not only heard but also believed. I am a Nicaraguan and I feel proud that Indian blood, more than any other, circulates through my veins, which because of atavism encloses the mystery of my being a loyal and sincere patriot."[5] Owing to such statements, most of his supporters were encouraged to believe that the liberation movement he led was guided by the single overriding concern of expelling the Yankee invaders from Nicaragua.[6]

The concept of patriotism is usually equated with defense of the homeland, a belief all patriots share. But as we shall see, the word *patriotism* covers a broad spectrum of political meanings conditioned by opposing political ideologies. Aware of the different dimensions of patriotism, Sandino took full advantage of each in seeking the widest possible support for his Defending Army of National Sovereignty.

Sandino equated the most elementary form of patriotism with nationalism or defense of the "national honor." An oath taken by a Sandinista column on 7 September 1927 included a promise to defend the homeland against hostile domestic and foreign enemies: "Do you swear by your military honor to defend with loyalty and discipline the national honor against the invaders of our country until they are expelled, and also to refuse to obey any directive from the traitor Adolfo Díaz and all those who collaborate with him?"[7]

After the swearing in, the statutes of his military collective were read to the assembled troops. The official name of his collective was the Military Institution of the Defenders of the National Honor, otherwise known as the Defending Forces of the National Honor or more often as the Defending Army of Nicaragua's National Sovereignty. Although this last was the name that ultimately prevailed, it is worth noting that the term "sovereignty" was interpreted by Sandino as interchangeable with national honor. Thus a patriot was someone who defended his nation's honor, meaning what was right and just for his country.

A nation's right to sovereignty or independence, Sandino believed, was a "sacred" or inviolable right. Since patriotism meant defending this right, it became a "sacred" duty. But not all rights are equally sacred: "the right of the weak is more sacred than that of the strong and, should the strong in their pride fail to recognize this maxim, then their violation of it should be sealed in blood to punish their audacity."[8] These bold words were directed against the so-called assassins of weak peoples.

What few of Sandino's supporters understood at the time was that this doctrine might also be used to defend the rights of the poor against those of the rich, and to punish the audacity of General Moncada and the wealthy class in Nicaragua. In effect, Sandino acknowledged two dimensions to his elementary patriotism: the liberation of Nicaragua could be viewed "from the perspective of Latin American nationality . . . relative to the canal and the construction of the naval base in Nicaraguan territory projected by North American piracy; and second, relative to the country's internal politics."[9]

Patriotism, even in its most elementary sense, meant for Sandino defending the constitution against domestic usurpers. Although he separated himself from the Liberal party because its leaders had betrayed the Constitutionalist cause in 1927, he continued to defend the party's rights. The Defending Army was committed, according to article three of its statutes, to "the defense of our sovereignty and the rights of the Liberal party."[10] Sandino interpreted this commitment to mean the recognition of Dr. Sacasa as the nation's constitutional president, unless or until he should publicly and formally resign from this highest office.[11] As late as August 1928, he continued to regard his Defending Army as representing "the honorable men who have remained faithful to the principles of the Liberal party" as opposed to those who had betrayed it from within.[12]

After breaking with General Moncada, Sandino explained to Carleton Beals in February 1928, his primary objective had been to expel the marines from Nicaragua. Once that struggle was over he would go back, if necessary, to his occupation as a mechanic. "I will not take up arms against the Liberals, nor against the Conservatives, nor in civil struggles except in the event of a foreign invasion. We have had to fight because the other leaders betrayed us, sold out to the enemy, or bent their necks in cowardice. We are fighting in our own country for our inalienable rights. . . . Is that or is that not patriotism?"[13] But this was only Sandino's immediate objective. Contrary to what he told the American journalist, his final objective was to make a social revolution that was tantamount to civil war.

Although his first manifesto was an appeal to patriotism in the most elementary sense, it also contained allusions to other, more advanced objectives. Its racial symbolism pointed toward the eventual political unification of the Indo-Hispanic peoples, and its class symbolism aimed at mobilizing workers and peasants in their struggle against poverty and exploitation. Sandino bragged about the Indian blood surging through his veins and his past occupation as a manual laborer. The two symbols were closely connected, as in his declaration that "my greatest honor is to have arisen from among the oppressed, who are the soul and nerve of the race."[14] Ostensibly, his manifesto was a call to begin fighting against the marines and to continue fighting for Liberal and Constitutionalist principles against both the Conservative party and that sector of the Liberal party that had chosen to accept the U.S.-imposed conditions for ending the civil war. Actually, his racial and class symbolism went beyond the Liberals' political horizons.

Sandino acknowledged the "authentic" character of elemen-

tary patriotism in opposition to the "fake" patriotism of General
Moncada, but nonetheless considered it to be "short-sighted."[15]
The expulsion of the marines and the abrogation of the Bryan-
Chamorro Treaty might restore his country's political sovereignty,
but they would leave untouched Nicaragua's economic dependence
on the United States. So Sandino peeled off the top layer of his patriotism to reveal its populist content. When Sacasa from exile gave
a last-minute endorsement to Moncada as the Liberal party candidate in the 1928 presidential elections, Sandino could no longer
count on Liberal support. Certainly, he could no longer claim to be
defending the rights of Dr. Sacasa as the constitutional president.
To continue his struggle he would have to mobilize the people behind a new ideology distinct from liberalism.

Henceforth, Sandino fought to oust not just the marines but
also the new Liberal government, which was collaborating with the
invaders. Since Liberalism had lost its claim to patriotism with
Dr. Sacasa's endorsement of Moncada, Sandino began to focus his
appeals on Nicaragua's workers and peasants and on far-sighted patriots in other Central American republics. Thus he demanded that
the peasants be free to cultivate and export tobacco for their own as
well as their country's benefit, that workers be paid in money instead of coupons redeemable at the company store, and that the
government take steps toward establishing a Union of Central
American Republics.[16]

It was a matter of changing his public image from that of a defender of the Liberal party to that of a champion of the people's
right to well-being. As a former officer in the Defending Army reported in a document dated 6 November 1928, "Sandino's one slogan is 'The Welfare of the Fatherland,' always stressing his interest
in the peasant class." The document also presented a glimpse of
what Sandino meant by well-being: "He has frequently said that
if he or one of his close friends ever gets control of the government . . . the isolated sections of the Republic will benefit the
most."[17] In this interpretation of patriotism the needs of the lowest
sectors and most backward sections of society would be given priority over the demands of the highest and most advanced.

In the pursuit of his country's well-being, Sandino sent letters
to the presidents of Guatemala, Honduras, Costa Rica, and El Salvador appealing for help in his efforts to expel the marines and to
unify Central America. A union of the Central American republics,
he wrote to the president of El Salvador, is indispensable both to
their progress and to their collective self-defense against present
and future acts of aggression by the United States.[18] A Central

American union would be a step toward a still broader union of all the Indo-Hispanic or Latin American countries motivated by collective self-interest. "I am a son of Bolívar," Sandino said in a June 1928 interview with Max Grillo.[19] (Bolívar was his favorite hero, but he also admired the other great liberators of the Latin American people: Hidalgo, the father of Mexican independence, and San Martín, the liberator of Argentina and then of Chile and Peru.)[20] Because Bolívar had worked for a formal union of the Latin American republics, this made his patriotism truly exceptional. Since Sandino had made that goal his own, he was hailed throughout the hemisphere as following in the Liberator's footsteps.

Inspired by Bolívar's example, Sandino wrote a letter to President Yrigoyen of Argentina in March 1929, proposing a conference of the Hispano-American nations with the aim of discussing his project for achieving Bolívar's supreme dream.[21] Aimed at unifying all of Latin America, his project would have contributed to ousting both the marines and the quisling government in his own country.

Although Bolívar's patriotism was neither superficial nor short-sighted, it had its limitations. In its most profound sense, Sandino believed, a concern for the national honor includes the well-being of each citizen. Patriotism would give all an equal stake in the nation. We have here the germs of his definition of patriotism, in which the "sacred" right of the weak includes individuals, not just sovereign peoples. Thus, as he became bolder, Sandino peeled off another layer of his patriotism to reveal its communist content.

Sandino thought of the people as his flock and he relied on his manifestos to guide them. But for that purpose he had first to understand their state of mind. As he wrote in a letter to the Nicaraguan journalist Gustavo Alemán Bolaños (8 September 1929) concerning a document he had just released, "I believe the manifesto will produce the desired effect. Truly, you understand our people's psychology and we agree with your understanding of it."[22] He then added that his goal of national redemption depended on coming to grips with the people's actual sentiments and convictions.

The political manifesto was the literary form Sandino chose to arouse in his fellow Nicaraguans the will to fight for their country. From the moment he refused to lay down his arms in May 1927 to the withdrawal of the marines in January 1933, he put his hand to twelve manifestos—an average of two a year. In 1927, when he began his war of resistance, he issued three manifestos, and during the escalation of his armed struggle in 1931 he signed as many as five. His last two manifestos appeared in March and June 1933—

bringing the total to fourteen—which is evidence that Sandino attached special importance to this vehicle of propaganda and agitation aimed at awakening the people.

The manifesto (6 September 1929) was designed to bolster the morale of his followers in Nicaragua during the months he had to spend abroad negotiating with the Mexican government the conditions of political and military aid for his Defending Army. It was not an easy task. In a follow-up letter to Alemán (9 September 1929) he reiterated the importance of mass psychology, of keeping step and not losing contact with those who are mistaken, disoriented, confused, or short-sighted in their patriotism. Referring to his manifesto of 6 September 1929, he said it should help guide those people and eventually redeem them. Toward that end, "our orientation will be presented with prudence down to the last detail."[23]

In a manifesto issued in February 1930, Sandino claimed that Nicaragua's workers and peasants were in the front line of resistance against Yankee imperialism and that this struggle was in their class interests.[24] He called on them to join the only trade union defending those interests, the Communist-controlled Confederation of Latin American Trade Unions. With the intensification of the struggle against imperialism, he observed, the ranks of Nicaraguan patriots were thinning. He complained that the rich were more concerned with defending their property than with the rights of their fellow citizens and were deserting him because their patriotism was only skin deep.

It was after returning from Mexico the second time in June 1930 that Sandino became acutely aware of the need for a new activating ideology. We have a glimpse of his frustrations as the people's guide and mentor in a candid letter to José Idiáquez (26 April 1931): "It is very difficult to continue arousing emotions in sleeping people."[25] But he evidently succeeded in this task. In a letter to Alemán Bolaños three months later he noted that the general conditions of his army were completely different from what they had been, "now that we have been able to raise the people's consciousness."[26]

How had he accomplished this tour de force? By means of patriotic symbolism, to which had been added a spiritual dimension. Shortly after his return from Mexico, Sandino replied to a letter from Moncada's vice-president, the Liberal Enoc Aguado, explaining some of the symbolism of his movement. "Dear Brother in the Homeland," the official salutation in correspondence between members of his Defending Army, was chosen to "maintain alive in our people the concept that the Homeland is our Mother, that all of us are brothers in her; thus it is our duty to come to her defense because by defending her we defend ourselves."[27] If, as Sandino believed, our country is somehow our mother, then all Nicaraguans are brothers and sisters united by a blood relationship. Consequently, whoever loves his country must also love his countrymen as members of the same family.

To encourage all Nicaraguans to support his cause, Sandino reinterpreted the symbolism of his flag to suit the circumstances. To revolutionaries it was clear that black was the banner of anarchism and that red stood for both socialism and communism. But to liberals Sandino offered a different explanation: "The burning colors of our flag, the red and black, symbolize 'Liberty or Death!'"[28] It was during the final stage of his struggle that he gave to these colors a theosophical significance: black came to signify death, red resurrection after death.[29] There was thus a spiritual dimension to Sandino's patriotism, behind his image as a new Bolívar.

Where did the national honor fit into this symbolism? Justice, Sandino claimed in his Light and Truth Manifesto, favors oppressed peoples in the war against oppressors.[30] It is also on the side of an oppressed class, the proletarians, in their struggle against the capitalists or "imperialists of the earth."[31] Since defending the national honor was a matter of justice, it meant striking at the roots of class antagonism and the division of society into a minority of privileged individuals and a multitude of defenseless and exploited workers. Sandino's patriotic objective was to prepare his political-military vanguard for the coming proletarian revolution that he hoped would transform the world.

Couched in theosophical symbolism, this objective was based on the expectation of a future brotherhood and reign of universal love. By condemning egoism in all its forms, his theosophy aimed to create a new man as the principal agency for bringing about the new society. It strengthened his nationalism, upgraded his populism, and made his independent brand of communism halfway respectable.

Unquestionably, Sandino was a nationalist. But he was also committed to internationalism and beyond it to the spiritual union of humanity. Nationalism should not be confused with chauvinism or vile efforts to boost the fortunes of one nation at the expense of others. The payoffs of imperialism must be weighed against the human costs, Sandino noted, for a chauvinistic policy can backfire.[32] Because chauvinism exaggerates the benefits and underestimates the costs of an expansionist policy, "the force of right can accomplish more than the right of brute force."[33]

Sandino believed that patriotism means nationalism, that nationalism contains the elements of populism, and that populism can lead people to communism. In Marxist terminology, he defended three separate social programs: an elementary nationalism for the short-sighted; a transitional or people's nationalism based on protective legislation for workers and peasants with a union of Central American republics for their collective progress and self-defense; and an advanced revolutionary nationalism buttressed by a theosophy of liberation in anticipation of the coming world proletarian revolution. Although these programs were successively revealed to his immediate followers and supporters, they were present in germ from the beginning of his struggle and, once revealed, were applied simultaneously in an effort to reach as many sectors as possible of the Nicaraguan people. If we may liken Sandino's moral faith to an onion, we can say that he never exposed more than one layer at a time. In this way he kept pace with the people's growth in social awareness as he worked his way down to his faith's inner core.

Sandino's Liberalism

The label that characterizes Sandino's early political struggles in Nicaragua is "liberalism." Beginning with the Liberal government of José Santos Zelaya (1893–1909), Nicaraguan Liberals rather than Conservatives distinguished themselves by their patriotism and opposition to U.S. intervention in their country's affairs. The Mexican Revolution further encouraged the development of strong sentiments of nationalism and anti-imperialism among Nicaraguan Liberals. Under its influence, Gen. Benjamín Zeledón launched a Liberal insurrection in 1912 aimed at driving the Conservatives from power and the marines from Nicaraguan territory. Its successor, the Liberal insurrection of 1926–1927, in which Sandino distinguished himself as a Liberal general, was not the last in the series of Liberal revolutions inspired by the Mexican example.

The last of the insurrections under a Liberal banner was that under Sandino's leadership in May 1927, after General Moncada and the Liberal forces under his command had decided to capitulate before the threat of an armed confrontation with the United States. Sandino's decision to continue the so-called Liberal revolution had the support of a radicalized sector within the Liberal party concentrated in the geographical area under his military control. This sector reconstituted itself under the name of the Liberal Party of the Segovias.[34]

Sandino's first political manifesto in July 1927 called for a resumption of the "Liberal revolution."[35] Simultaneously, he announced that its program was to open an interoceanic canal through Nicaragua, to promote the country's industrial development with Latin American rather than U.S. capital, and to educate the Nicaraguan people under conditions of "effective democracy."[36] Although these nationalist objectives did not go beyond those of President Zelaya at the turn of the century, they were to be fought for under a new political banner—the red and black flag that had inspired his soldiers during his earlier campaign as a Liberal general.[37]

There is no doubt about Sandino's profound love for his country. But what is seldom appreciated is that his patriotism had an anarchist source in its debt to Ricardo Flores Magón. A unique feature of Flores Magón's anarchism, which had a strong effect on Sandino, was the role it assigned to patriotism. Flores Magón recognized in the ties of loyalty and kinship binding together fellow nationals a major source of human solidarity. The War of Independence, he observed, made Mexicans out of the common people who fought against Spanish colonialism; the War of Reform under Juárez and the adoption of the liberal constitution of 1857 made them citizens; the next step, the struggle for economic liberty or emancipation from human exploitation, would make them comrades.[38] Sandino anticipated a similar outcome to his struggle in Nicaragua.

Flores Magón distinguished a natural from a conventional patriotism, as did Sandino.[39] Only natural patriotism, he believed, could qualify as rational. Against conventional patriotism or loyalty to a particular government or state he counterposed the natural sentiment of affection for one's birthplace and the special feelings of sympathy for those who speak the same language, share the same customs, hold the same values, and confront the same problems. So did Sandino. Like his Mexican precursor, he defined patriotism as love for one's homeland rather than loyalty to the state.[40] His political slogans, "Homeland and Liberty!" and "Free Homeland or Death!" were but minor variations on Flores Magón's "Land and Liberty!" and "Land and Liberty or Death!"—slogans also adopted by Emiliano Zapata and his Army of the South.[41]

Flores Magón believed that the bourgeois exhibit a false or inauthentic patriotism.[42] They pretend to be patriotic but exploit their fellow nationals; they care more for their possessions than for their compatriots and are loyal to any government that protects their property. In contrast, authentic patriots struggle to rescue the land from private owners and to defend their compatriots against those who prefer profits to people. Sandino also developed this distinction between authentic and inauthentic patriotism.

There are some interesting parallels between Flores Magón's political career and Sandino's. The former began as an ardent liberal under the tutelage of his father, who had joined Benito Juárez's forces during the War of the Reform and continued fighting for liberal principles against the French intervention and the Empire of Maximilian during the 1860s. In 1901 he played a key role in reviving Juárez's Liberal party, which he linked to the earlier movement of liberal reform and to the defense of the 1857 liberal constitution. This party suffered the wrath of the dictator Porfirio Díaz until in 1904 its leaders, already converted to anarchism, had to flee into exile to escape imprisonment and death.

In the United States Flores Magón and the decimated Liberal leadership adopted a change of line. Calling themselves the Organizing Junta of the Mexican Liberal Party (PLM), they issued a new party program in July 1906. The new program committed the party not only to overthrowing the dictator and restoring the constitution, but also to major constitutional reforms.[43] The proposed changes governing land tenure and the relations between capital and labor were later incorporated into Mexico's 1917 Constitution.[44]

As long as Díaz remained in power, Flores Magón was careful not to reveal his anarchist ideas to the public. His strategy of revolution precluded any action that might risk losing the support of broad sectors of the population. Only when the head of the Constitutionalist forces, Francisco Madero, betrayed his Liberal allies in favor of a negotiated settlement with Díaz in March 1911, did the Liberal party issue a new program aimed at pushing the revolution toward a higher stage. Flores Magón's manifestos of 3 April and 23 September 1911 proclaimed to a surprised Mexican public that the Mexican Liberal party was in fact committed to revolutionary anarchism.[45]

Just as Flores Magón had concealed his revolutionary anarchism behind the façade of the Mexican Liberal party, so Sandino hid his subversive intentions under the cover of the Nicaraguan Liberal party. We have seen how he was indebted to the ideological legacy of the Mexican Liberal party. It remains to consider how he copied its strategy.

Like Flores Magón, Sandino publicly stressed the importance of liberal principles. Among these were the defense of the Constitution, a government of law rather than of people, and the right of nations to self-determination. Subsequently, he radicalized his program so that it corresponded more closely to the populist reforms proposed by the Mexican Liberal party in its 1906 program. Sandino's open letter to President Hoover in March 1929, in which he

publicly upheld the principles of "Reason, Justice, and Right," reads
like the September 1906 proclamation of the PLM's goals of "Reform, Liberty, and Justice."[46] Not until his Light and Truth Manifesto of February 1931, which corresponds roughly to Flores
Magón's manifesto of 23 September 1911, did his revolutionary political line completely overshadow his earlier commitment to
liberalism.

Mexican workers knew that Flores Magón was an anarchist,
but they did not know that he had become one as early as 1903.[47]
He retained his Liberal party affiliation, as did Sandino. In 1905 he
attended the meetings of Russian anarchists in the United States
and continued to defend liberal principles in which he no longer believed. Only in 1911 did he begin to collaborate publicly with the
Industrial Workers of the World (IWW), the anarcho-syndicalist
successor of the defunct International Workingmen's Association
founded by Karl Marx in cooperation with European anarchists in
1864.[48] When the Bolshevik Revolution was successful in October 1917, he embraced it with enthusiasm, defended it before the
world, but continued to advocate a government of workers' and
peasants' communes instead of a communist dictatorship by a vanguard party.[49] Sandino adopted virtually the same position toward
international communism.

Although Sandino acknowledged a debt to other heroes of the
Mexican Revolution, notably Pancho Villa and Emiliano Zapata, he
did not travel their path but that of Flores Magón.[50] The latter's revolutionary strategy and propaganda, like Sandino's, evolved through
three clearly delineated stages.[51] The first, from 1901 to 1905, stayed
within the boundaries of traditional liberalism by upholding the
constitution against the dictatorship of Porfirio Díaz. The second,
from 1905 to 1911, stood for a populist or democratic revolution
against the Díaz regime, the overthrow of the landed oligarchy, an
extensive agrarian reform, and social legislation for Mexico's workers. The third, from 1911 until Flores Magón's imprisonment in Fort
Leavenworth in 1918, called for a total revolution against both capitalism and the state.

The strategy Flores Magón adopted went beyond the conventional anarchist reliance on the spontaneity of the masses. "What
is necessary is an activating minority," he wrote, a "courageous minority of libertarians . . . who will move the masses to take possession of the land and machinery of production, despite the doubts of
the incredulous, the prophecies of the pessimists, and the alarm of
the sensible, coldly calculating, and cowardly."[52] Such an activating
minority was tantamount to the central committee of a vanguard

party—a vanguard within the vanguard. It was restricted to a revolutionary elite, to professional revolutionaries in the strict sense. As we have seen, Sandino also believed in the catalyzing role of an activating minority in enlightening and leading the masses. Although he believed in the transformation of societies by the action of the state, he insisted that little might be expected from the state without a prior transformation of human consciousness.[53]

Flores Magón believed that an activating minority must rely on secrecy, including deception, to achieve its goals. From the moment of his entrance into the United States, he came under surveillance by the authorities, who intercepted several of his letters (now part of the records of the Department of Justice). In one of them he wrote,

> Everything reduces to a mere question of tactics. If from the start we had called ourselves anarchists, only a few would have listened to us. Without calling ourselves anarchists we have influenced minds. . . . No liberal party in the world has our anticapitalist tendencies. . . . In order not to have everybody against us, we will continue with the same tactics that we have already used with so much success; we will continue to call ourselves liberals during the course of the revolution, but in reality we will go on propagating anarchy and carrying out anarchist deeds.[54]

Sandino subscribed to these same tactics and applied them to Nicaragua.

The rationale behind this strategy of duplicity was spelled out in Flores Magón's essay on the duty of the revolutionary.[55] That duty is to make the revolution, not to wait for it to begin but to precipitate and direct it toward a communist or classless outcome. The masses will adopt a communist goal during the revolution, he argued, only after it begins, not before. That is why anarchists must participate in all movements that may lead to revolution, regardless of a movement's ideology or immediate objective, and must work in order that events do not take a course the anarchists do not want.

This is why, according to Flores Magón, the PLM did everything it could to arouse the Mexican people against the Díaz dictatorship by initiating the insurrectional movements of September 1906 and June 1908, and by preparing the conditions for the great insurrection of November 1910.[56] As Librado Rivera noted, "To propagate anarchist ideas in their fullness during that epoch, when people's brains were filled with prejudices, would have led our revolutionary agitation to strengthen the tyranny instead of precipitating its fall."[57] In short, liberal doctrine became a vehicle for radi-

calizing the masses and disseminating anarchism under a respectable cover—as it would also become for Sandino in Nicaragua.
Whatever Sandino knew about the Mexican Liberal party it is safe
to say that he learned a lesson in tactics: to launch a successful
revolution, one must avoid the anarchist and communist labels.

The Turn toward Populism

In an effort to acquaint the outside world with the issues underlying the struggle of his Defending Army, Sandino chose as his first
personal representative abroad the Honduran Liberal, Froylán Turcios. A poet, journalist, and the editor of the influential journal
Ariel, Turcios stood in the mainstream of Latin American cultural
resistance to U.S. imperialism and also served as a mentor to the
federations of Latin American students.

Turcios defended Sandino's interests abroad from September 1927 until his official break with Sandino in January 1929.
He named his journal after Uruguayan José Enrique Rodó's book
Ariel, for many years among the most widely read and influential
philosophical-political treatises in Latin America. The book's central theme was the superiority of Latin American to Anglo-Saxon
culture, of traditional humanistic and spiritual values to the crass
utilitarianism, positivism, materialism, and social egalitarianism
of the Yankees. A vaguely disguised contempt for leveling medi-
ocrity inclined Rodó to espouse a form of cultural elitism. Precisely
because of his overriding concern with resisting the penetration of
Anglo-Saxon ideas into Latin America, he proposed an association
or front of the Latin American republics against U.S. cultural imperialism. Economic and political imperialism were for him only secondary concerns.

Turcios broke with Sandino over the issue of what he perceived
to be a "new ideology." This showed itself in Sandino's refusal to
support the Liberal party candidate for president in 1928, followed
by his refusal to accept the Liberal party's victory at the polls, and
his decision to establish a rival government.[58] Turcios interpreted
Sandino's new strategy as the transformation of what had been a
purely patriotic war against U.S. imperialism into a fratricidal civil
war that he, Turcios, could not accept. To counter what he believed
to be a totally disastrous policy, Turcios proposed to Sandino an alternative strategy. He urged him not to form a rival government but
to put pressure on the existing one to achieve the withdrawal of
the marines.[59]

Turcios also objected to Sandino's project for a Central American union against U.S. imperialism, a union to be achieved by the people of Central America, presumably under Sandino's leadership rather than their respective governments. As a Honduran patriot, Turcios had committed himself to defend what he believed to be his country's interests in the threatening war with Guatemala over a petty border dispute. Sandino had rebuked him for this stance.[60] The patriotism of Latin Americans, Sandino replied, recognizes no such artificial frontiers, because loyalty to the greater Latin American nationality has precedence over loyalty to any Latin American state. Since the Central American governments had reversed this order of loyalties, one could not look to them to establish a Central American union unless it should happen to promote U.S. interests in the region. Sandino's reply created quite a stir among intellectuals in Central and South America.

Sandino planned to involve the other Central American countries in Nicaragua's struggle for liberation and to extend the battle for Nicaragua to a battle for all of Central America. In February 1928 he had expected that the war in Nicaragua would be shouldered by Central American patriots, because its liberation had become their moral duty as well as their common interest.[61] Central Americans are obliged to unite against the common aggressor, he argued, for tomorrow the other republics of the Isthmus will be waging similar struggles of their own.

In a letter to the presidents of the Latin American republics in August 1928, Sandino urged them to oppose collectively all U.S.-imposed governments propped up by American bayonets.[62] He said the people had a right to replace them with governments representing their own interests. In the conviction that liberty is not conquered with flowers, he called for drastic action against Latin American tyrants who were openly supported by the U.S. government. Patriots must begin by putting their own houses in order, he argued, by getting rid of bloodthirsty and degenerate dictators like Gómez of Venezuela, Machado of Cuba, and the Peruvian Leguía. In this ingenuous letter, which reminds one of his earlier mistaken trust in General Moncada, Sandino alienated his potential supporters among the governments of Latin America by impertinently meddling in their affairs.

When a rupture seemed imminent, Turcios reminded Sandino that he had devoted his "best energies to making the general shine forth as the new Bolívar under the American sky."[63] But there was more to Bolívar than the liberator of South America. Besides his military struggle against Spanish occupation, he had dreamed of a

Latin American confederation that might stand on a par with the United States of North America. Not just independence but the well-being of the several Latin American peoples came to preoccupy him, as it did Sandino. Thus in Max Grillo's interview in June of the same year, Sandino was reported as saying, "My country, for which I struggle, has Spanish America for its frontiers. At the beginning of my campaign I thought only of Nicaragua. Afterward . . . my ambition grew. I thought of the Central American Republic whose coat of arms has been sketched by one of my comrades. . . . Tell Hispano-America that as long as Sandino breathes, the independence of Central America will have a defender. I shall never betray my cause. That is why I am the son of Bolívar."[64]

Bolívar's two causes were here presented as one. But Liberals like Turcios gave only lip-service to the image of Bolívar as the unifier of Spanish America. For Turcios patriotism was primarily the defense of his country and Latin America against foreign aggression. There was to be no abolition of national frontiers. Consequently, there was already cause for friction when Sandino, in a letter written in June 1928, instructed Turcios in the "obligation of making the people of Latin America understand that among us there ought not to exist frontiers!"[65]

Why this sudden change in Sandino? The answer is to be found in the American government's policies involving Nicaragua. The November elections in Nicaragua were approaching and the candidates of both the major political parties had already launched their pre-electoral campaigns. As early as February Sandino had protested in a letter to Rear Adm. D. F. Sellers that the elections should be supervised by Latin American representatives rather than by the U.S. Marines.[66] Sandino was especially concerned that the elementary patriotic and nationalist pretext for his struggle might suddenly disappear. The Liberal Moncada promised to be a sure victor in the coming elections, after which the U.S. government had promised to withdraw the marines. Without the unconstitutional government of Adolfo Díaz or the marines to defend that government, nothing would be left of Sandino's cause. It is in this historical context that Sandino's ambition to unify all of Central America began to overshadow his earlier, more pedestrian, concern for Nicaragua. At that particular political conjuncture in the summer of 1928 he had only one alternative if he hoped to keep his movement alive. Thus his Liberal cult of Bolívar gave way to a populist one.

Sandino's new strategy no longer limited him to defending the Constitution and to fighting the marines. The social transformation of Nicaragua also became a ranking concern. This is evident in a letter to Froylán Turcios in November 1928, outlining his plan for countering Moncada's election as president.[67] A rival people's government would be formed, presided over by Dr. Pedro José Zepeda, who had formerly served as Dr. Sacasa's personal representative in Mexico. Backed by Sandino's Defending Army, it would be supported politically by a Patriotic Front of the major political groups independent of the established Liberal and Conservative parties and would be noteworthy for having actively resisted the American occupation.

Among the marginal political parties and pressure groups supporting Sandino's populist program in 1928 were the Republican Liberal party, with its seat in Managua, and the Labor party, under Dr. Escolástico Lara, with its stronghold in León.[68] By far the most important successor to Sandino's Liberal Party of the Segovias, the Labor party was strong enough by the end of 1930 to win a political majority in León, Nicaragua's second largest city. There it defeated the Liberal party in the elections for mayor.[69]

What did the Labor party want? Its representative in Costa Rica, Norberto Salinas de Aguilar, identified its principal objective with the collective well-being based on the interests of the impoverished majority.[70] This majority consisted of the "working classes oppressed by capital": wage earners, peasants, and self-employed artisans.[71] Although the proletariat of wage earners was considered the leading force in this alliance, its objectives were so loosely formulated that Nicaraguan laborism became synonymous with populism.

For Turcios this alliance was tantamount to defiling Sandino's struggle for national liberation with a cheap political ingredient that promised to transform a great and noble cause into a personal bid for the presidency. Such a policy, Turcios insisted, was unworthy of his support and effectively undermined all his previous efforts to present Sandino as a twentieth-century Bolívar.[72] For this reason he opposed the general's anticipated mission to Mexico to obtain military aid from its government.

As Turcios spelled out his disenchantment, "On the basis of the new ideology that you present to me, you are fast marching toward certain failure. . . . I see that we are not in agreement concerning the finality of the struggle; that you no longer heed my advice of limiting yourself to the single objective of sovereignty in your action against the pirates; and that you endeavor now to find means for changing a domestic political regime by resorting to civil war."[73]

If he persisted in this new strategy, Turcios warned, they would have to separate as brothers. Evidently, Turcios believed that the defense of the constitution was no longer a vital issue. Since Moncada's election had returned the Liberal party to power after a lapse of fully two decades, Turcios saw no need for Sandino's "new ideology."

As the representative of the Defending Army in Tegucigalpa, the Honduran capital, Turcios had received periodic dispatches by courier direct from Sandino's headquarters in El Chipote. These he published together with Sandino's letters and manifestos in *Ariel*. When the two finally split in January 1929, the loss of the journal represented a severe setback for Sandino and must have been a bitter disappointment as well.

Sandino had begun his struggle against the marines by enlisting the support of short-sighted patriots who saw no farther than the wisdom of expelling the invaders. Although he had simultaneously repudiated most of Nicaragua's political leaders, he had remained within the confines of his country's two-party system. His so-called new ideology broke with that tradition. For Turcios this signified a betrayal of Nicaraguan liberalism. Turcios never got beyond what Sandino called an authentic but short-sighted patriotism, which meant he could not accept Sandino's new "ism."

Gregorio Gilbert, a member of Sandino's general staff, has given an inside account of Sandino's change of strategy.[74] Sandino had called a meeting of his general staff to decide what policy to adopt should the marines withdraw from Nicaragua as promised. The day set for the withdrawal was 1 January 1929, when the president-elect, General Moncada, was due to take over the presidency. Sandino posed three major questions for discussion: Was it likely that the Yankees would withdraw as promised? What should the Defending Army do in that event? and What kind of civilian organization should it promote for carrying on the struggle?

Since Sandino was the first to give his opinion, there really was no discussion. With the exception of Gilbert, his advisers unanimously supported their chief. The first question having been answered in the affirmative, Sandino gave his answer to the second question: "Continue the war!"[75] Gilbert then gave Sandino's response to the third question:

Sandino indicated that Dr. Pedro J. Zepeda, a Nicaraguan residing in Mexico City, was a prestigious man in the Aztec Republic, which had made it easy for him to secure arms from that country for the 1927 revolution against the government of Adolfo Díaz. Dr. Zepeda also organized and presided over the Nicaraguan revolutionary junta that recognized Dr. J. B. Sacasa as the *de jure* president of Nicaragua. For these reasons . . . Sandino proposed that he be invited to the headquarters of the Defending Army so that he might be proclaimed president of insurgent Nicaragua, organize a government, and try to obtain recognition from the other nations of the world.[76]

Gilbert had dissented on the first question and refused to give an opinion on the second. Asked why, he replied, "Because when the last Yankee leaves Nicaragua by one door, I shall return to my country by the other!"[77] Afterward, he explained to Sandino that he made this decision because he believed the purpose of Sandino's struggle was to expel the invader. That was its officially declared purpose as presented in the statutes of the Defending Army. Should the Yankees withdraw, it would be pointless, therefore, to continue the war.

Sandino's reply was unexpected. True, if that had been the only goal of his movement, but it was not: "In addition, we propose to carry the peace achieved in Nicaragua, whether peacefully or militarily, to all the countries of Latin America with the goal of creating a single, strong, and respected nation with a single flag, without frontiers that divide it."[78]

Gilbert disagreed with Sandino's "new ideal." He considered all of its points to be unfeasible, especially for Sandino's meager forces, which were not even strong enough to drive the marines from Nicaragua.[79] Even should the marines be expelled, Gilbert argued, who could bring about the miracle of unifying an entire continent as divided politically and racially as Latin America? Bolívar failed because he set himself an impossible task. Francisco Morazán, who tried to hold together the newly born Central American Union, also failed. Gilbert believed that Sandino's project was unjust as well as impractical. The Latin American countries were proud of their independence and had their own ideals, which disagreed with Sandino's. To apply force to them would be criminal, Gilbert insisted, so let those unite who wanted to but leave the rest to follow their own course. Force should be used only in defense of one's ideals, he concluded, never for the purpose of imposing them on someone else.

These were also Turcios's reasons for rejecting Sandino's new ideal. But the ideal was not new. It was only being revealed for the first time. Turcios and Gilbert had retained their faith in the political principles of liberalism, which they believed General Moncada had betrayed; thus, when Sandino revealed his true colors, which they mistook for a new ideology, they parted company with him.

Sandino was caught in a dilemma. On the one hand, the clear

victory of the Liberal party in the November 1928 elections had put an end to his army's pretext of unseating the unconstitutional government in power. On the other hand, a policy of continuing the war against a Liberal government was bound to erode Sandino's support for what could no longer be described as a Liberal cause. Both horns were unacceptable on practical grounds. Thus according to a U.S. intelligence report a week after the elections, the "opinion that Sandino is finished is absolutely general amongst the natives."[80] The political conditions were so adverse to Sandino's struggle that even his father expected him to lay down his arms.

What was Sandino to do? His liberalism had never been more than skin deep and a cover for a far more ambitious project aimed at an economic, social, and political revolution in Nicaragua. His only hope was to radicalize his movement by direct appeals to the country's workers and peasants. He was compelled to adopt a new strategy that would no longer focus only on expelling the marines, but also on a new deal for the Nicaraguan people.

He called this new deal "effective democracy."[81] Elected governments were not enough; they had to correspond to the people's aspirations. The Liberal Porfirio Díaz had been Mexico's elected president from 1884 until 1911, when the people took other than electoral means to remove him. Madero had called for "effective suffrage, no re-election!" but Sandino hoped for something more. By "effective democracy" he meant not only effective suffrage, but also the populist "right to be represented by virile men . . . and not by useless, domineering persons without moral courage and patriotism."[82] By effective democracy he meant what the people wanted: "the restoration of their rights lost since 1909. The Nicaraguan people will not recognize any government as legal, *much less the present one,* if it continues being a handmaiden of the United States government!"[83]

Pressured from all sides, Sandino nominally tried to reach an agreement with President Moncada in January 1929. Since Moncada's election took place under conditions of a people in arms against a foreign invader, Sandino argued, the only way to legitimize it would be for the new government to acquire the votes of patriots by accepting an agreement with his Defending Army. With that purpose he presented his army's terms for what he regarded as a compromise.

Those terms were of two kinds.[84] There were those aimed at ridding the country of U.S. intervention whether direct or indirect, and there were others covering purely domestic reforms. One set called for applying armed force against the marines, establishing a

Central American union as a step toward a Latin American confederation, rejecting all American loans, declaring null and void the
Bryan-Chamorro Treaty, abrogating all other pacts and agreements
signed with the United States since the first official American
intervention in 1909, and denouncing U.S. efforts to supervise
Nicaragua's elections. The other demands included such domestic
reforms as the eight-hour workday, additional pay for overtime,
money wages instead of coupons redeemable in company stores,
the responsibility of employers to provide schools for the children
of workers in all enterprises with more than fifteen employees,
equal pay for equal work for men and women, child labor laws, the
right to organize trade unions, and the establishment of a Department of Labor.

Sandino must have known that Moncada would have difficulty
accepting proposals that bordered on a Nicaraguan edition of the
Mexican Revolution. However, a flat rejection might embarrass the
new government. In any case, Sandino believed that failure to come
to terms with his Defending Army would mean that responsibility
for continued armed resistance would rest squarely on Moncada's
shoulders.

Sandino's promotion of a populist domestic program went hand
in hand with his "Plan for Realizing Bolívar's Supreme Dream."
He completed this plan in March 1929 with the intention of presenting it at the international conference of representatives of the
twenty-one Latin American governments he hoped would take
place in Buenos Aires. As the delegate of the Defending Army,
Sandino expected to represent his country's interests at the proposed conference. "A first mistake was committed in relation to
our Indo-Hispanic America in not having consulted it in opening
the Panama Canal," he wrote, "but we can still prevent a second
mistake in connection with the Nicaraguan Canal."[85] If the conference had materialized, Sandino would have pushed his plan for a
Latin American military, political, and economic union with juris-
diction over both the Panama Canal and the proposed Nicaraguan
waterway.

In his plan Sandino proposed a Latin American alliance rather
than a confederation of states, and Latin American possession rather
than internationalization of the Panama Canal.[86] The Monroe Doctrine would be declared null and void. A Latin American Court of
Justice would replace it, preferably on Nicaraguan soil, as the sole
arbiter of the conflicting interests among the Latin American states
and as a warning to the United States not to proceed with its designs against Nicaraguan territory.[87] A token military force would

be organized from contingents supplied by each of the Latin American republics. The president of the Court of Justice would serve as the supreme commander and his general staff would consist of one member each from the general staffs of the participating governments. Against actual or potential foreign intervention, the members of the alliance would apply the collective threat of a unanimous and simultaneous rupture in diplomatic relations followed, if necessary, by the automatic confiscation of the aggressor's foreign holdings and investments in Latin America. These would be used to finance an ensuing war of liberation.

In other less-grave instances of intervention by a foreign power, a total boycott of that country's trade would follow. Sandino also proposed that a committee of Latin American bankers should be organized to finance the projected Nicaraguan Canal and to negotiate the purchase of the Panama Canal. The Court of Justice would have the responsibility of securing the immediate withdrawal of all U.S. troops from military bases in the hemisphere. A common customs union would be established covering foreign imports into Latin America, and a 25 percent reduction in duties would be arranged for imports from member states for the purpose of facilitating trade. The alliance would forbid any direct or indirect U.S. investments in Latin America and, as in the case of the Panama Canal, would buy out all U.S. interests. This would put an end to American designs ostensibly concerned with protecting the lives and property of U.S. citizens. North Americans would be protected under Latin American laws, but they would be forbidden to own property other than personal articles of consumption. Such was Sandino's response, elaborated in the form of a populist ideology, to continued American interventionism in collaboration with the unpopular governments of Central and South America.

Sandino and the Comintern

With the Liberals back in power, Sandino returned to Mexico in 1929 in search of new sources of support. There he came under pressure from the moderates in his movement, who hoped for a second edition of the Mexican Revolution in Nicaragua, and from extremists, who wanted a new edition of the Russian Revolution. Sandino tried to satisfy both. On the one hand, he paid lip service to the moderates: "Neither extreme right nor extreme left but a United Front—that is our motto. Accordingly, in our struggle it is not unreasonable for us to seek the cooperation of all social classes that are free of 'isms.'" On the other hand, he encouraged the support of extremists: "I consider it very reasonable that we are joined by the organizations of the extreme left, such as those that would have some people believe that we favor a particular social doctrine or 'ism.'"[88] Evidently, he felt no compunction in using short-sighted patriots to achieve his immediate objectives, and the organizations of the extreme Left to achieve his final objectives. While the Communists were endeavoring to manipulate Sandino to achieve their strategic goals, Sandino was astutely manipulating the Communists.

In his biography of the Nicaraguan guerrilla, Anastasio Somoza painted a portrait of Sandino as a fanatical Communist intent on dismembering Nicaragua and establishing a separate Communist republic in the Segovias. Although he twisted the facts, there was a grain of truth in this characterization. Sandino refused to take orders from the Communists and disagreed with their strategy; but, like them, he wanted to abolish exploitation and the capitalist system through a worldwide proletarian revolution. He also believed in cooperating with the Communists to the point of joining and working through Communist-controlled organizations, from which he hoped to recruit support for his struggle in Nicaragua. Like them he relied on the vanguard role of the working class and the supporting role of backward peasants. The timid will desert our cause, he declared in February 1930, but "the workers and peasants will persevere to the end," to which he added that "only their organized force is capable of victory."[89]

Although heavily indebted to Flores Magón, Sandino's anarchism differed from that of his Mexican precursor by incorporating elements from other political philosophies that came to his attention. Macaulay tells us that in Mexico in 1929–1930, three principal forces fought for the mind of General Sandino in an effort to implement their particular schemes for revolution in Central America.[90] Besides the current represented by Mexico's revolutionary government, both the Mexican-based American Popular Revolutionary Alliance (APRA) and the Communist International (Comintern) wrangled over Sandino's allegiance.

Nicaraguan physician Pedro José Zepeda, the general's personal representative in Mexico City, advocated a populist program of effective democracy patterned on that of Mexico's revolutionary mainstream. It would be implemented through a patriotic broad front representing all social classes. Peruvian exile Esteban Pavletich, who represented the APRA at Sandino's headquarters in Mérida, advocated a similar program, but as a transitional measure toward the more ambitious objective of a Socialist United States

of Indo-America based on the mestizo race.[91] The third rival for
Sandino's affections, the Salvadoran Agustín Farabundo Martí, who
served as the general's personal secretary and represented the interests of the Comintern on his general staff, advocated a strategy of
class confrontation aimed at replacing Sandino's original broad
front against imperialism with a more militant but narrower-based
worker-peasant alliance. "Sandino, who did not want to alienate
any of his supporters," writes Macaulay, "realized the advantage of
the broad united front advocated by the Nicaraguan physician, but
the radicals on his staff in Mérida, Pavletich and Martí, were closer
to the General ideologically than was Dr. Zepeda."[92]

This was not a three-way contest among equals. The principal
contestants were Dr. Zepeda, who had been on close terms with
the Mexican government since serving as Dr. Sacasa's personal liai-
son with it in 1926–1927, and Farabundo Martí who, as Sandino's
personal secretary, soon became his principal adviser. Although by
1929 the APRA had established the organizational nucleus of nationally based social democratic parties in Guatemala, Cuba, Haiti,
Puerto Rico, Costa Rica, Argentina, Chile, Bolivia, and Peru, it
could not compete on equal terms with the international assistance given to Sandino's movement by the Comintern and its front
organizations. Nor was it a match for the Mexican government as a
source of material and moral aid such as that provided to the Constitutionalist forces in Nicaragua in 1926–1927. Thus it is understandable that even before Sandino arrived in Mexico in 1929, his
principal overtures were to the Mexican government and to the
Comintern as the institutional representatives of, respectively, the
Mexican and Russian revolutions—the two great cataclysmic
movements of the twentieth century with an affinity to his own
struggle in Nicaragua.

Sandino had additional reasons for being skeptical of the
APRA. Founded in Mexico City in May 1924 by Peruvian exile
Víctor Raúl Haya de la Torre (1895–1979), the APRA represented a
third force straddling the Mexican and Russian revolutions but
without the institutional supports of either one. Because of the
collision between the Comintern and the APRA at the Anti-
Imperialist World Congress in Brussels in 1927 and the exclusion
of the APRA's delegates from the Communist-controlled International Anti-Imperialist Congress in Frankfurt in 1928, Sandino
was virtually compelled to choose between them. He could have
chosen Pavletich for his personal secretary, but instead he chose
Martí. As we shall see, he was closer both pragmatically and ideologically to the Communists.

Although the APRA had launched a fund-raising campaign in Mexico to provide men and arms for Sandino's fighting forces, nothing ever came of it.[93] In March 1928 the Mexican daily *Excélsior* announced that an APRA legion—the first in a series of "Caribbean legions" dedicated to freeing the Caribbean and Central American republics from repressive and unconstitutional dictatorships—was prepared to go to Nicaragua to fight alongside the soldiers of Sandino.[94] Late that summer Haya arrived in the Nicaraguan port of Corinto, but his plan to join Sandino was frustrated by the National Guard. In the end his only support was of a moral nature, in a tribute to Sandino's "noble guarantee of Central American greatness . . . a spirit whose memory will be revered by a hundred million men if he knows how to die as we expect him to die, by giving with his life and sacrifice the best of victories!"[95] Small consolation this must have been for Sandino.

Obliged to continue his journey, Haya stopped over in San José, Costa Rica, where he was joined by Pavletich.[96] After hearing of Haya's difficulties in linking up with Sandino, Pavletich had left Nicaragua to confer with his chief in Costa Rica. That Pavletich had managed to reach Sandino but Haya had not suggests that Haya's voyage to Nicaragua was more of a publicity stunt on behalf of the APRA than a genuine effort to help in the national liberation of that country. Although in 1929 Pavletich would rejoin Sandino in Mexico, by then Sandino had begun cooperating mainly with the Comintern.

During the years when the APRA made a bid for Sandino's allegiance, it was outmaneuvered by the Comintern acting through its front organizations, the Anti-Imperialist League of the Americas and the Mexican-based Hands Off Nicaragua Committee. Initiated at the Fifth Congress of the Comintern in June 1924, the league took shape at the beginning of 1925. Its headquarters were in Mexico City and it included a Continental Organizing Committee charged with setting up national sections throughout the hemisphere. The league was responsible for organizing the Hands Off Nicaragua Committee in conjunction with the Mexican Communist party.[97] In 1927 this committee was authorized to raise funds for Sandino's struggle. The league's New York affiliate cooperated in this effort by conducting a major propaganda campaign against U.S. intervention in Nicaragua. One of its most effective spokesmen was Sandino's half-brother Sócrates, who had been working as a mechanic in Brooklyn since 1926.

The league had been quick to recognize Sandino's importance

in the continental struggle against imperialism. It first denounced
U.S. interference in Nicaragua during the Constitutionalist War.
Then, when Sandino resolved to carry on the struggle as the leader
of the most important liberation movement in the Americas since
Benito Juárez's, he was given all the support the league could muster.

Leading the campaign from Mexico in support of Sandino was
the head of the league's Continental Organizing Committee, the
exiled founder of the Cuban Communist party, Julio Antonio Mella
(1903–1929). What Haya de la Torre was to the APRA, Mella was to
the league. In April 1928 he published his most important work,
"¿Qué es el ARPA?" which denounced Moncada as a traitor and defended Sandino as an authentic Nicaraguan patriot.[98] Because of his
systematic criticism of Haya de la Torre and the role of the APRA
in Central America, he soon earned their lasting hostility. Presumably, his pamphlet was brought to Sandino's attention by Farabundo
Martí and played a key role in cementing the general's sympathies
for the league and the Comintern.

The league successfully brought Sandino's cause to international attention at the first International Anti-Imperialist Congress in Frankfurt in September 1928. The Sandinista delegates in
attendance were drawn from the general's supporters in Mexico
and their passage to Germany was paid by the Comintern acting through either the Mexican Communist party or the league.
Sandino hoped to obtain worldwide support at the Congress. To one
of the organizers, the French Communist Henri Barbusse, Sandino
wrote, "Although at the present historical moment our struggle is
national and racial, it will become international."[99] On the podium
at the Congress a Sandinista delegate unfurled the captured American flag that had been sent by Sandino to his supporters in Mexico
City and afterward exhibited by the Communist Hernán Laborde in
the Mexican Chamber of Deputies.

The league was represented at Sandino's headquarters by
Agustín Farabundo Martí (1893–1932). Having become involved
in the league's activities during the spring of 1928, Martí joined
Sandino's forces with three other Salvadoran volunteers in June of
that year.[100] He rose to the rank of colonel and also served as the
representative of the Mexican Communist party on Sandino's general staff.[101] Martí had gone to Nicaragua to fight the marines and
to get others to volunteer for the same purpose. His mission was
both to provide international support for Sandino's struggle and to
win Sandino over to the Communist cause.

Martí's role at Sandino's headquarters must be understood in

the light of Lenin's theses on the national and colonial question
adopted at the Second Congress of the Communist International in
June 1920:

> The Comintern should support bourgeois-democratic movements of
> national liberation in backward and colonial countries only on condi-
> tion that the elements of future proletarian parties, which will be
> communist not only in name, are brought together and trained to
> understand their special task of combatting the bourgeois-democratic
> movements within their own countries. The Comintern should join
> in a temporary alliance with bourgeois democracy in the backward
> and colonial countries, but should not merge with it. It should uncon-
> ditionally defend the independence of the proletarian movement even
> in its most embryonic form.[102]

This policy applied by the league to Nicaragua helps to clarify
Martí's task of persuading Sandino to support the Comintern.

Sandino's refusal to accept a detailed social program and to
carry out Martí's recommendations, however, became a source of ir-
ritation to the Communists. He was never fully persuaded to adopt
the same program as the Comintern's. Later, when he broke with
Martí, the Mexican Communist party stopped raising money for
his army and denounced him as a traitor to the working class and
the anti-imperialist movement. It even questioned his patriotism.

Martí returned to El Salvador to found and lead the Communist party in that country. On 1 February 1932, he was executed by
a firing squad for crimes of sedition and rebellion against the state.
During the brief time between his conviction and execution, he recalled the circumstances of his break with Sandino. There was no
doubt, he said, about Sandino's moral principles or patriotism.[103]
Martí had refused to return to the Segovias because Sandino did not
want to embrace Communist principles. He had broken with the
guerrilla leader because Sandino had collaborated with the out-
going Mexican president, Emilio Portes Gil, whom Martí characterized as an agent of imperialism. The league had given Sandino the
opportunity to travel to Europe with all expenses paid for the purpose of publicizing the role of imperialism in Latin America and
Nicaragua in particular. But Sandino had refused the offer because
he was waiting for Mexican arms to resume a struggle that, for
Martí, was tainted by bourgeois-democratic principles.

Sandino told a different story. Martí had been expelled from
his general staff and the Defending Army because of his efforts
to enmesh Sandino in the intrigues of the Comintern. He had
been expelled because of differences over strategy combined with
insubordination. "Actually, I never disagreed with him ideologi-

cally," Sandino confided to one of his biographers, "but because of his rebelliousness he was unable to appreciate the limits imposed on my mission to Mexico or his role as a subordinate."[104]

Martí took for granted that there could be only one source of communist ideas, namely, the Comintern. But we have seen that Sandino's communism had an anarchist component derived from Mexican sources that antedated the founding of the Comintern in 1919. Although he agreed with the Comintern's earlier strategy of a broad anti-imperialist front, he could not accept the new strategy adopted at its Sixth Congress in September 1928. Confronted with the imminent destabilization of world capitalism on the eve of the Great Depression, the Comintern opted for a hard line directed against its former allies.

Because of the failure of its earlier policy of collaboration with the Chinese Kuomintang, the Comintern shelved the strategy of supporting noncommunist movements of national liberation. Henceforth, multiclass patriotic fronts, such as the Kuomintang and Sandino's own Defending Army of National Sovereignty, would be fought if Communists were not in a position to dominate and control them. This strategy was to prove disastrous wherever it was applied, and Sandino did well to repudiate it. For that matter, Mao and the Chinese Communists also rejected it in deeds, if not in words. A corresponding strategy was applied in Western Europe with regard to the socialist and social democratic parties, which were likened to a Trojan Horse within the workers' movement. For refusing to unite with the Communists, they were denounced as "social fascists."

It is true that Sandino's banner was mainly one of national independence. But this was a strategical move in the interest of uniting a wide variety of forces toward a single concrete and attainable goal. Realism demanded that Sandino's social program be kept in abeyance until after national liberation or at least until his movement had caught fire among the masses on a national scale. For years he closed his correspondence with the slogan, "Homeland and Liberty!" Although other anarchists had joined forces with the Communists, Sandino maintained his independence on grounds of ideology as well as expedience, for he was aware of the alien character of the ideas professed by the established Communist parties— ideas that had been popularly discredited because of their "atheism" and "materialism."

The Congress of Latin American Communist Parties was held in Buenos Aires in June 1929, where the new hard line was adapted to Latin American conditions.[105] The proceedings described the workers and peasants as an emerging independent force no longer pushing for revolutionary change with but against the middle strata that were everywhere capitulating to the bourgeoisie. The proceedings affirmed further that in all Latin American countries, the petite bourgeoisie and the nascent industrial bourgeoisie were directly linked to imperialist interests. In view of the new balance of social forces allegedly favorable to radicalization, a call was made for the creation of rival people's governments on the basis of soviets of workers, peasants, and soldiers. This was the policy Martí carried out in 1932 with dire consequences for himself and some thirty thousand workers and peasants who were massacred by government troops. There was also a proposal to establish separate Indian republics in countries with large Indian populations. It is in the context of the Comintern's mistaken assessment of the world situation and its adoption of an ultraleft strategy of class confrontation that the breach between Sandino and Martí must be understood.

Before this new policy had taken effect, Sandino invited Venezuelan Communist Gustavo Machado to become his personal representative abroad.[106] In exile in Mexico City and working through the Hands Off Nicaragua Committee, Machado had taken the initiative in raising one thousand dollars for Sandino's Defending Army. Faulty communications between Nicaragua and Mexico may explain why he neither accepted nor rejected Sandino's offer. Although he did accept another responsibility, preparing a pamphlet to let the world know about Sandino's struggle in Nicaragua, he refused to do it for nothing. So the pamphlet was never written and Machado was not asked a second time to become Sandino's personal representative. In October 1929 Nicaraguan physician Dr. Pedro José Zepeda was chosen in his place.

Shortly after learning of this decision, Machado launched a smear campaign against Zepeda for having encouraged Sandino to accept aid from the Mexican government. He then attacked Sandino, charging him with having accepted money from the Mexican Communists to carry on the struggle in Nicaragua and a $60,000 bribe from the United States to exile himself in Mexico.[107] Indignant, Sandino wrote to Laborde, the secretary of the Mexican Communist party, categorically denying having accepted such a bribe while reaffirming his intentions of maintaining cordial relations with the Mexican Communists.[108] He explained that of the $1,000 raised by the Mexican Communist party and given to Machado to deliver in person to him in Nicaragua, all that remained after deducting Machado's round-trip expenses was a mere

$250. Surely the acceptance of such a paltry sum did not commit him to follow the Communist party line. An investigation ordered by Laborde exonerated Sandino of the bribe-taking charge. But the party never clarified why it had allowed Machado to make such a damaging accusation.

These events took place in Mexico, where Sandino had transported his general staff during the summer of 1929. The Mexican Communists did not raise the money for this trip; Sandino obtained it from the Mexican government. In a letter to Dr. Zepeda (25 January 1930) he explained that Captain Paredes, a Mexican volunteer in his army, had arranged with Mexican authorities to pay the passage and expenses of staying in the country preliminary to his anticipated interview with the president.[109] Sandino had accepted on paper a loan of ten thousand dollars required to cover travel expenses and the cost of continuing the armed struggle in Nicaragua during his absence. He claimed to have received only half this amount, which raised all sorts of difficulties in defraying the most basic expenses of food, clothing, and lodging for those of his men who arrived in Mexico. As matters turned out, they lacked even the funds requisite to return to their country, so Dr. Zepeda was instructed to raise an additional sum to provide for the emergency.

The Communist attack on Sandino was triggered by his efforts to reach an understanding with the Mexican government. It was known that Sandino's visit to Mexico in June 1929 had been preceded by other contacts with the Mexican authorities involving, according to rumors, a treaty signed with President Calles in January 1928. Sandino would be provided with a million rounds of ammunition and official recognition of his government when the marines withdrew; in compensation Mexico would have a controlling voice with Japan over the construction of a new interoceanic canal through Nicaragua.[110] In May 1929 Captain Paredes returned to Nicaragua from Mexico with the news that President Portes Gil would furnish Sandino with arms and ammunition. But this promise, like the aforementioned treaty, turned out to be an illusion.

At this point the Mexican Communist party withdrew its support from the Mexican government. The near success of a 1929 right-wing military rebellion, which was not crushed until May and only after two months of fighting, signaled to the party the approaching disintegration of the Mexican political order. It was already in difficulty because of the world economic crisis and its effects on the Mexican economy. In defending the revolutionary government and the Constitution, the party had armed the peasants and launched a guerrilla war of resistance. But for this act of patriotism the Mexican government had rewarded it with the court martial and execution of the leader of the resistance along with his entire general staff.[111] It is no wonder, then, that the party opted for open opposition to the government and criticized those participating in the resistance for not organizing soviets of workers and peasants where the enemy had been defeated. A series of expulsions of party cadres followed this internal criticism. In this heated political context in which the Mexican Communist party had decided to resist the Mexican government, Sandino's appeal to the Mexican president could easily have been confused with betrayal.

Although cleared of the charge of having taken money from the United States, Sandino was accused on his return to Nicaragua of having accepted money elsewhere. In a news report from Mexico City in the *New York Times* (30 May 1930) we read, "General Augusto Sandino, Nicaraguan leader, was charged by Mexican Communists today with having turned traitor to the cause of world anti-imperialism and with having gone back to Nicaragua 'to sell out to the highest bidder.' A Communist Party statement said that Sandino, after accepting Communist money and agreeing to a world tour against imperialism, obtained funds from other sources and returned to his homeland to renew the fight with small bourgeois groups for control of the country."[112] The Mexican Communist party had painted Sandino in such a distorted light that he appeared a traitor no matter what he did: a sellout to bourgeois interests for having given up the struggle against the marines, and a sellout for having returned to his country to resume the struggle. In fact, the Mexican Communists believed that the United States had consented to Sandino's return, according to the same article in the *New York Times*, to maintain the menace of a Sandino victory over the Moncada government.

Sandino's relations with the Mexican Communist party were described in an article in the party's newspaper, *El Machete* (June 1930). On "The Treason of Augusto C. Sandino," it purported to show that between February and April 1930 Sandino formally committed himself and his Defending Army to the general line of the Communist International, but that afterward he reneged on this agreement. The article documented a secret meeting Sandino and his general staff held with members of the party's Central Committee and representatives of the Anti-Imperialist League on 3 February in Mexico City. There an agreement was reached whose fundamental paragraph reads,

> Given the necessity of elucidating the theoretical and practical principles that should govern the anti-imperialist struggle . . . [we] arrived

at the conclusion that anti-imperialist action on the continent can only be effective and efficient when waged on the basis of . . . the internationalization of the revolutionary struggle and the harmonious linking of armed actions against imperialist military aggressions with the political and trade-union movement of the oppressed masses, workers and peasants.[113]

By implication, Sandino's struggle in Nicaragua was to be coordinated with Communist activities throughout Central and South America.

Sandino delayed his return to Mérida to participate in a series of secret interviews with Communist party representatives. During these, said the article in *El Machete,* he agreed to cooperate with the Comintern and the league in making a propaganda tour of Europe and Latin America. On the basis of this agreement the party then outlined what it expected of Sandino. A Central Committee resolution on 22 February called on Sandino to denounce the counterrevolutionary government in Mexico for luring him from the battlefield with false promises of military aid, for trying to keep him silent, inactive, and marginalized from anti-imperialist activities during his stay in Mexico, for repressing the Mexican workers' and peasants' movement, for becoming an instrument of U.S. foreign policy, and for joining the anti-Soviet bloc in the Americas and breaking off diplomatic relations with the Soviet Union.[114]

This resolution was sent to Sandino in Mérida in a letter dated 27 February. On 7 March he replied, expressing his complete agreement with it.[115] This was followed by a new letter on 12 March in which he added, "We are preparing the declarations that we should make on Mexico's present international policy. We are relying, as you can understand, on the documentation that will make them irrefutable. It has always been our policy to assess matters carefully so that at any moment we can say things with clarity; and the moment has come, although it may appear that we are being ingenuous, to unmask with irrefutable evidence those who have sold themselves to Yankee imperialism."[116]

The article in *El Machete* then criticized Sandino for changing his mind. In April Sandino had his second interview with Emilio Portes Gil—the first was in January when Portes Gil was still provisional president. He received permission to leave Mexico and also a gift from the former president of two machine guns with four thousand rounds of ammunition and two thousand pesos to cover his return trip to Nicaragua.[117] "In exchange for this 'aid' Sandino effectively backed off from his agreement with us, shelved the declarations he was preparing against the Mexican government, and left the country without replying to our letters or saying a single word about his new intentions."[118] The party had reason to feel betrayed. But Sandino also had reason for breaking with the party that was pushing him into making rash and hostile declarations that might be injurious to his cause. In any case, the Communists were mistaken concerning Sandino's motives.

The matter did not end there. Three years later, in February 1933, when Sandino agreed to a truce and laid down his arms after the departure of the marines from Nicaragua, the Comintern again accused him of betraying the struggle for national liberation.[119] This charge was repeated the year after his assassination in an article entitled "Struggles of the Communist Parties of South and Caribbean America" in the principal organ of the Comintern, *The Communist International* (20 May 1935): "In Nicaragua, where the rebel bands of Sandino had since 1927 carried on the struggle against military intervention by the United States, the struggle ended with Sandino's capitulation in 1933 and his passage over to the side of the counterrevolutionary government of Sacasa."[120]

The irony in this defamation is that the Comintern, by adopting a new strategy similar to Sandino's, had already abandoned the old ultraleft policies it had pursued since its Sixth Congress in 1928. The article affirms that the bourgeois and petit bourgeois parties had been erroneously lumped together in a single reactionary front against any and all efforts aimed at national liberation. As a result, "the Communist parties underestimated the special importance of bourgeois national reformism, which has great influence over the petty bourgeoisie, the peasantry, and even the working class in Latin America."[121] One mistake led to another, until the Communist parties "fell into a passive attitude and isolated themselves from the masses of toilers at times when big political events took place."[122] We have here a complete, albeit belated, affirmation of the strategy Sandino had been pursuing since his first armed action in November 1926, but without giving any credit to Sandino or rectifying the Comintern's previously mistaken assessment of his actions.

At its Seventh Congress in August 1935 the Comintern officially rejected the strategy of class confrontation in favor of the new strategy of a popular front. Efforts were made to reestablish united action with the mass movements against fascism and imperialism. In fact, the Comintern made a turnabout of 180 degrees that converted it into an ardent fan of nationalism throughout the Third World. In China Mao had been successful in forging a broadly based bloc of four classes against the Japanese occupation. His patriotic front included not only workers and peasants, but also patriotic representatives of the petite bourgeoisie and national bourgeoisie. Mao followed the same strategy that Sandino had applied in Nicaragua against the American intervention. Whether or not he had studied Sandino's strategy is immaterial, but he must have known something about it, since the Comintern had rallied to Sandino's defense in 1928 prior to applying its strategy of class confrontation.[123] Sandino had become a familiar figure in China both to the Communists and to the Kuomintang, which had named one of its units the "Sandino Division."[124] In any case, the new strategy of national liberation based on a bloc of four classes was adopted by the Comintern partly in response to Mao's demonstrated success in applying it.

Sandino realized that the Comintern and its mass organizations, the International Anti-Imperialist League and the affiliated Anti-Imperialist League of the Americas, were the principal outside supports of his struggle. Thus he tried to remain on friendly terms with them. It was they who broke off relations with Sandino, but only because he refused to bend completely to Communist demands. While Machado and the Mexican Communist party were defaming him, Sandino was urging Nicaraguan workers to organize in trade unions and to join the Communist-sponsored Confederation of Latin American Trade Unions. As he described this confederation in his manifesto of 26 February 1930, it was "the only labor organization defending the interests of the working class."[125] In this manifesto he also agreed with the Communists that the bourgeoisie had become unreliable and that only a united front of workers and peasants could be expected to persevere to the end in the struggle against the marines. The petite bourgeoisie and intellectuals were not even mentioned, although he would later include students among his principal allies. And there would be no compromise with imperialism.

Half a dozen years earlier Enrique Flores Magón, Ricardo's brother, had provided an example for anarchists throughout Latin America by joining the Mexican Communist party and representing the Comintern at the founding of new Communist parties in the Caribbean area.[126] When he joined the Mexican party, other anarchists followed suit. They did so because the bolsheviks shared with anarcho-communists the same ultimate objective of abolishing capitalism and establishing a classless society. But Sandino did not follow Enrique's example.

Although for two years Sandino worked on close terms with the Comintern (1928–1930), he never completely trusted it. He could agree to carry on the struggle against imperialism without help from leaders of the Liberal party, but he could not accept a strategy that would drive their followers into the arms of his enemy from fear of the consequences of the Communists' new hard line. Thus Sandino rejected the Comintern's sectarian policies, the foundations of which had been laid at the Sixth Congress. He stuck to his own immediate strategy of marshaling a broad front of Nicaraguan patriots to fight the marines. That is how he viewed the problem of an effective strategy for national liberation as a prelude to the anticipated social revolution that would follow.

4. The War in Nicaragua

Besides downplaying Sandino's importance as an ideologue, most studies show little if any appreciation of his political assessments. Those who question whether he had a fully developed and consistent ideology also question whether he had a theoretical understanding of the historical circumstances, the balance of social forces in Nicaragua, and the prospects of the struggle he had undertaken against the marines. Selser says "he was not exactly an intellectual."[1] Macaulay adds that, although the philosopher-general was one of the great strategists of guerrilla warfare, he "lacked the political sophistication of the leaders of the post–World War II liberation movements."[2]

Did Sandino have a revolutionary theory, at least a rudimentary one? To be specific, did he have an intellectual grasp of the American presence in Nicaragua and of the historical connections between his country's past and the events that unfolded beginning with the Liberal revolution of 1926? A close examination of his writings reveals that he had a fairly elaborate conceptual apparatus derived from anarchist and Marxist sources. He also had a coherent explanation of his country's predicament as a pawn of the United States based on his understanding of Nicaragua's political history. His anti-imperialism, as we shall see, was more than a visceral reaction.

Sandino's political assessments had as their primary focus the war in Nicaragua. Among the principal enemies of his country he included not only the Wall Street bankers and the U.S. government, but also the American people, personified by Gen. William Walker. To these he added most of Nicaragua's political leaders, both Liberal and Conservative, who were seeking an accommodation with the United States. Against these enemies of the people stood his Defending Army of National Sovereignty. Like his contemporary

Mao Tse-tung, Sandino asked the same fundamental questions: "Who are our enemies? Who are our friends?" and "Who are the people?"[3] If Mao had a revolutionary theory predicated on his answers to those questions, so did Sandino.

In the effort to make his views attractive to ignorant and illiterate peasants, Sandino gave them a dramatic cast. The American people were "pirates," "freebooters," "blond beasts," and "machos." The Wall Street bankers worshipped the "golden calf." The White House appeared as a "whited sepulcher," clean on the outside but rotten within. The political leaders of Nicaragua were "traitors" and Judases who sold out their country for a few pieces of silver. In contrast, his Defending Army was presented as God's instrument for regenerating not only Nicaragua, but also all of Central and South America. In short, he gave to his political thought an ideological coating. This has misled most students of Sandino into believing that he did not have a theory worthy of the name.

The Yankee "Machos"

Sandino's account of his struggle begins with a description of the strategic importance of his country in the history of the New World. "Because of its natural resources this region of the earth has been coveted by foreign powers since the discovery of America. Proceeding from the Atlantic coast, the Spaniards always sought the slenderest part of the continent to communicate with the Pacific."[4] After establishing their first settlements in the Americas, they thought of building a canal through Nicaragua.

But there was a crucial difference for Sandino between the Spanish conquest and settlement of Central America and the Anglo-Saxon invasions that followed. Concerning Spanish colonization of the New World he said, "I used to look with resentment on the colonizing work of Spain, but today I have profound admiration for it. . . . Spain gave us its language, its civilization, and its blood. We consider ourselves to be the Spanish Indians of America."[5] Unlike the Spaniards, the Anglo-Saxons in Central America did not mix their blood with the Indians but remained racially aloof and alien to the native culture. Whereas Sandino favored eventual union with Spain, union was simply unthinkable with the "Barbarian Colossus of the North."

Under the influence of the Mexican Revolution, Sandino had acquired a genuine hatred for the Spanish colonial legacy. His changed assessment of Spain may be attributed to the teachings of

the Magnetic-Spiritual School. Its founder, an ardent Spanish nationalist, believed that Spain had been chosen by the Father and
Creator to regenerate the world.[6]

In a bitter and partly fanciful sketch of the role of the Anglo-
Saxons in the New World, Sandino noted how North America was
settled by "pirates." "Resentful because of Spain's discovery of
America, the English dedicated themselves to piracy along with
other European nations. Instead of returning home, the English pirates sought a sanctuary in North America, principally in what
today is called New York—settled by descendants of the golden
calf."[7] Determined to deprive Spain of its possessions in the New
World, the English and later the American "pirates" tried to establish a foothold in Nicaragua.[8]

When the Spanish colonies in Central America achieved independence in 1821, England seized control of the entire east coast of
Nicaragua. On 23 April 1825, Sandino relates, an Indian was picked
by the British to become emperor of the Mosquitos (Miskitos)—the
Carib people named after this mosquito-infested region.[9] "And
since that time Great Britain exercised dominion over our Atlantic
littoral until the beginning of this century [actually 1894], when
the Liberal president of Nicaragua, Gen. José Santos Zelaya, recovered for Nicaragua that portion of our territory that the English
had illegitimately exploited."[10]

The Yankees, according to Sandino, had even greater ambitions.
"On 4 May 1855 an expedition of North American pirates headed
by William Walker sailed from San Francisco for Nicaragua with
the aim of taking over Central America. Walker succeeded in becoming president of Nicaragua. But afterward he was defeated by
the Central American armies, which, at the initiative of Pres.
Rafael Mora of Costa Rica, were able to unite and defend themselves against the common enemy."[11] Without filling in the details
or even mentioning Walker's second armed expedition to Central
America, Sandino added that Walker was finally executed by a firing squad in Trujillo, Honduras, in September 1860.[12]

With the failure to take Cuba from the Spaniards, American
freebooters turned toward comparatively defenseless Central America. The principal figure in this expansionist effort, the most talked
about American and the hottest news personality since the Mexican War, was William Walker (1824–1860)—Sandino's key to understanding Nicaraguan history and his own patriotic war more than
half a century later. Walker's ruthless exploits are vividly remembered in Nicaragua. Schoolbooks still describe how the conquest

of that country by American filibusters during the Filibuster War of 1855–1857 was finally overcome only by the combined forces of five Central American republics. Walker was important to Sandino's account of the events leading to his patriotic war because Walker personified the American people.

The term "filibuster" in a strict sense means a soldier of fortune, a freebooter or land pirate seeking to enrich himself in unauthorized warfare against countries with which his own government is at peace.[13] However, Sandino used it in a figurative sense, as well, for the "avalanche of Walker's descendants" who had designs on Nicaragua, and for the "North American filibuster forces," the "thousands of North American pirates" or U.S. troops dispatched to Nicaragua in the role of "hired thugs of the Wall Street bankers."[14] In this loose sense the term included a significant portion of other Americans.

Walker was both a filibuster and an incarnation of Manifest Destiny. Believing in the predestined right of the Anglo-Saxon race to expand the boundaries of its civilization at the expense of the mongrel Indo-Americans, he aimed to open Central America to white settlers and to replace the Indo-Hispanic cultural heritage with Anglo-Saxon freedom and progress.[15] His objectives included seizing control of the Nicaraguan government, taking possession of the country's inland waterways, and building the promised canal that would link the two great oceans and make Nicaragua a bustling commercial metropolis like the United States. Because Walker did not look on his freebooters as "pirates," his account of this first American intervention in Nicaragua was completely at variance with Sandino's.

In *The War in Nicaragua* (1860), Walker justified his filibustering assault with an appeal to white supremacy. White North Americans, he believed, were morally as well as genetically superior to the mestizos of Mexico and Central America.[16] "They are but drivellers who speak of establishing fixed relations between the pure white American race, as it exists in the United States, and the mixed Hispano-Indian race, as it exists in Mexico and Central America, without the employment of force."[17] In the struggle between these two races Walker predicted the victory of the superior one, because the white race represented the side that he believed was right and just.[18] Thus Walker hoped to use his influence to lift up and regenerate what he perceived as a miserable, unenlightened, and undisciplined race that had shown itself unfit for self-government. As he declared in a speech in New Orleans, where he received a hero's welcome, "I call upon you . . . to regenerate the amalgamated race . . . , to assist in carrying out and perfecting the Americanization of Central America."[19]

Walker's presidential decree of 22 September 1856 was the pivotal act of his entire brief administration.[20] It shifted the ownership of land from mestizos into the hands of white settlers and paved the way toward modernizing Nicaragua. In a concession to the economic interpretation of history, he wrote, "The military force of the state might, for a time, secure the Americans in the government of the Republic, but in order that their possession of the government might be permanent, it was requisite for them to hold the land."[21]

Paradoxical as it may sound, Walker labored to promote industrial growth and capitalism through the reintroduction of slavery into Nicaragua.[22] The secret of Anglo-Saxon power, progress, and prosperity, he argued, was that the British colonies in North America had retained the institution of slavery while the Spanish crown had allowed it to lapse through miscegenation. "Instead of maintaining the purity of the races as did the English in their settlements, the Spaniards had cursed their continental possessions with a mixed race."[23] Consequently, it would have been little less than miraculous at the moment of independence, if the new Spanish American republics had decided to keep instead of abolish slavery. The preachers of the new gospel of equality and fraternity, Walker remonstrated, had yielded to the mad rhapsodies of Rousseau and to the wild errors of the French Revolution, when they should have been content with the place assigned by divine providence to the black race in the order of creation.[24]

These views on slavery and on the role of the white race in Central America stand out as the complete antithesis of Sandino's. Walker defended his land-grabbing freebooters, capitalism in the free-labor states of the North, slavery in the American South, and Anglo-Saxon racial supremacy with its corollary, the reestablishment of slavery in Central America, on economic, political, moral, and religious grounds. Sandino denounced Walker's freebooters for as many different reasons, along with the efforts of Wall Street bankers and southern slave-owners to impose their will on Nicaragua. Against the Walker doctrine of white supremacy, Sandino countered with his own doctrine of the superior culture of the Indo-Hispanic or mestizo race. At issue was a question of partisanship rather than truth, a choice of sides in the continuing battle for Nicaragua. What is important for our purposes is that, thanks to his countermorality of the oppressed, Sandino saw complicity on the part of the American people in these events.

Yankee imperialism represented the interests not only of an aggressive and privileged class of capitalists, Sandino insisted, but also of the American people—it was a folk or people's imperialism. Despite the loss of American lives, the seizure of half of Mexico in the Mexican-American War of 1846–1848 had transformed the emerging American nation from a comparative weakling into a giant. Even though Americans might be duped by their government into supporting wars of expansion and intervention against their best interests, they still took pride in America's growing power. The "Barbarian Colossus of the North" was the creation not only of the magnates of Wall Street and the White House, Sandino believed, but also of millions of ordinary Americans.[25] This interpretation held the American people responsible for the actions of their elected representatives and ran counter to established Communist doctrine, which completely exonerated them from any responsibility.

In the successive interventions in his country after 1855, Sandino discovered what seemed to him a clue to the American national character. Because the marines were not conscripts but volunteers, like the soldiers in his Defending Army, there was no reason to believe they were basically different from other Americans. The American people and not just the White House, Sandino concluded, had hypocritically justified expansion under cover of the Monroe Doctrine. In Sandino's eyes, this made them the willing accomplices of their leaders. Certainly, William Walker's invasion was not instigated by Washington. It was a grass-roots expression, according to Sandino, of American piracy.

In his first political manifesto Sandino proudly defended the Indo-Hispanic race against the "claws of the monstrous eagle with curved beak that feeds on the blood of Nicaraguans, while in Managua flies the flag representing the assassination of weak peoples."[26] There lay the proof of the "hostility toward our race" on the part of the "blond invader."[27] In a series of letters written shortly afterward, we find the same diametrical opposition between the Anglo-American and the Indo-Hispanic races. On 20 September 1927, Sandino wrote, "My obsession is to reject with the dignity and pride of our race whatever imposition is being cynically prepared in our country by the assassins of weak peoples."[28]

Several months later, without alluding to either Wall Street or the White House, Sandino reiterated that the "blond beasts" bordering on the northern extremity of Latin America were poised to take advantage of the least weakness exhibited by their neighbors to the south. For that reason, the "Yankees are the worst enemies of our peoples."[29] As Sandino commented in a letter to the manager of the La Luz and Los Angeles Mining Co., after having dynamited the mines and reduced them to ashes, "In the beginning I had confidence in the thought that the American people would not condone the abuses committed in Nicaragua by the government of Calvin Coolidge, but I have been convinced that North Americans in general uphold the attitude of Coolidge; . . . for that reason . . . everything North American that falls into our hands is sure to meet its end."[30]

Two years later he affirmed a similar conviction. "In Nicaragua, too, we once believed in the famous democracy of the Yankee people, just as some still believe that the abuses committed by governments in the White House were looked on askance by the North American people. However, later we became convinced of the contrary."[31] The "avalanche of Walker's descendants" had fallen on his country while upholding their natural-born right to do as they pleased: "Although my . . . imputation to the North American people of the same imperialist attitude of their leaders will provoke explanations counter to what I sustain, I am completely convinced that the North American people support and will always support the expansionist policy of their immoral governments."[32] Although such a low opinion of Americans was unlikely to find wide acceptance in the United States, I presume Sandino had in mind an effective majority of the American people and not some dissident minority.

An early biographical study of Sandino by the Mexican jurist Isidro Fabela relates a curious example of his allegedly "uncontrollable Yankeephobia."[33] During his return visit to Mexico in 1929, the general had been invited to Fabela's home for dinner together with George Moreno, the manager of an American firm in Mexico but also an admirer of Sandino's exploits against the marines. Near the end of the meal and after praising Sandino to the skies for his tremendous courage and many victories, Moreno is reported as saying, "You must not believe, General, that in my country we are all against you. On the contrary, you have many admirers in the United States who understand your noble cause and the unjust conduct of my government."[34] But Sandino brusquely and angrily retorted, "I do not believe in your admiration for me because you are a gringo and all gringos are enemies of liberty!"[35] Surprised by this personal attack, Moreno courteously insisted that Sandino was mistaken. But after an avalanche of invective hurled at the American and at the United States, Sandino asked to be excused and departed.

Sandino may have perceived some hypocrisy in these protestations from a representative of U.S. business interests in Mexico. Moreno was there not as a tourist but to take home profits for his company. But as Fabela interprets Sandino's outburst, "feeling in his guts the foreign aggression that was mercilessly killing his compatriots and destroying his country's independence, he was suddenly overcome by a violent loathing that extended without reason to all North Americans."[36] In any case, Sandino called on his race to expel not only North American capital but also North American citizens from the Indo-Hispanic homeland.[37] Although the oppression suffered by indigenous peoples under the Spanish conquistadores was by most accounts far more brutal than that under the U.S. Marines, Spain was no longer the enemy but America. That was what mattered to Sandino.

The theme of the centuries-old struggle between the Anglo-Saxon and Indo-Hispanic peoples is present in several of Sandino's political tracts and letters. He thought of it as a racial conflict compounded by the opposition between the multistate Hispanic-American nation and the multinational but federated North American state.[38] By "race" he meant mainly ethnic and national traits, to which he attached far more importance than to physiological characteristics. In his portrayal of the Anglo-Saxon "blond beasts," it was their behavior that counted, not the color of their skin or hair.

Sandino had a virtual arsenal of epithets for the American people. Besides castigating them for being "pirates" and "filibusters," he denounced them for being "beasts" and "assassins of weak peoples."[39] These expressions contained an indictment of the American racial and national character as both acquisitive and aggressive. In addition to these clearly pejorative descriptions, he described the Americans as "machos."[40] Although the word *macho* in Central America is commonly used to mean "blond" and "fair-skinned," this was not Sandino's usage. He used it not as a neutral substitute for "blond" but as the equivalent of "blond pirate" or "blond beast."[41] In this sense it stood for the aggressive and domineering character traits of the Americans. From the verbs *machar*, *machacar* (to pound, break, crush, hammer, beat, bruise, screw), "macho" in Mexican usage refers to any agent or implement that overpowers or invades another. Sandino returned from Mexico with a street vocabulary that included the Mexican use of "macho" and "gringo," alike pejorative and associated with rape—the rape of the Mexican people as a result of the Mexican-American War.[42]

The Americans were not only bullies, Sandino believed, but also cowards. Because they were powerful, because there were 120

million of them united against 90 million Indo-Americans divided
into twenty Balkanized republics, they could flex their muscles
with impunity. In Latin America they could do as they pleased,
which is why Sandino characterized them as the assassins of weak
peoples. But collectively even the weak can clip the eagle's claws
and put it to flight. Behind his towering appearance the American
was a chicken at heart, "the chicken in the form of the eagle that
serves as the Yankee emblem!"[43]

There was a popular basis for the Anglo-Saxon conquest of
North America, for the expansion westward from the Appalachians
to California. The traditional dynastic empires of Europe expanded
in ways that seldom coincided with the objective interests of their
peoples. This was not true of American expansionism. It directly
benefited the frontiersmen, who reached out for new and better
lands. The movement westward and southward into Mexico was a
mass movement of settlers rather than a mercenary force like that
of the Spanish conquistadores. Even Walker's filibusters came to
Nicaragua as settlers. The Spaniards conquered Mexico through a
series of alliances with Indian princes, but the land so conquered
belonged to the crown. The Americans who expanded westward did
most of the fighting but they took the land for themselves. Thus
American imperialism had a folk basis that European imperialism
lacked. This supports Sandino's thesis that the American people
and not just the U.S. government and the Wall Street bankers were
behind American policy in Nicaragua.

Sandino would have agreed with the conclusion of a work by a
Cuban patriot that "in no case did the governments responsible for
those violations lack popular support nor, in the final instance, ret-
rospective approval by the American people . . . , not once have the
American people failed to take advantage of the conquests unjustly
made, not one of which has yet been repudiated."[44] This conception
of American imperialism was neither Lenin's nor Flores Magón's. It
derived from the popular literature of Yankeephobia and its intellectual sources familiar to Sandino in the works of socialists like
Manuel Ugarte and Luis Araquistaín.[45]

Even so, this was not Sandino's last word. Occasionally, he
qualified his strictures against the American people by acknowledging that not all were to be blamed for the actions of their rulers.
After all, they had not always taken sides with the strong against
the weak. Sandino recalled that the Americans, too, had fought a
long, drawn-out war for independence.[46] He also made evident his
sympathies for the fathers, sons, and brothers of the marines who

were being ordered about like robots by the White House and sent
to their deaths in Nicaragua.[47] The Americans' acquisitive and aggressive national character had been used to advantage by the U.S.
government: "The true and legitimate brigands are in the dark re-
cesses of the White House in Washington from where they direct
the pillage and the assassination of our Spanish America."[48]

Although I have stressed the passages in Sandino's writings
that express his loathing for the Americans and his desire to expel
every last one from Nicaragua, there are others that show a con-
ciliatory tone. In one of his letters, he acknowledged that "the
Yankees may only come to our Latin America as guests, never as
lords and masters."[49] At least some were welcome. And in a 1933
interview with Belausteguigoitia he welcomed the benefits from
foreign immigration: "There are many lands here to distribute.
They [the immigrants] can teach us much, but on condition that
they respect our rights and treat our people as equals."[50] Although
Sandino continued to hold the Americans partly responsible for the
actions of their government, he did not blame them for the role of
the Wall Street bankers in Nicaragua.

The Bankers of Wall Street

In his *Manifesto to the Peoples of the Earth,* Sandino continued his
sketch of the principal events leading to his involvement in the war
in Nicaragua. After more than three decades of Conservative rule
following Walker's expulsion in 1857, the Liberals who had returned to power in 1893 not only ended British control over the
Mosquito Coast, but also became a major obstacle to U.S. interests
in the area.[51] In commending Pres. José Santos Zelaya for refusing to
bow before U.S. pressures on his government (1893–1909), Sandino
alluded to the imposition of severe restrictions on foreign investment that finally persuaded the United States to begin construction of a canal through Panama, despite its preference for the Nicaraguan route.[52] Later, when Zelaya tried to build a rival canal through
Nicaragua after a treaty with the emerging naval powers of Germany and Japan, the U.S. government joined the British and displaced Conservatives to topple his regime. "Convinced of his high
patriotism and the impossibility of using him to promote its own
interests at the expense of Nicaragua's sovereignty, the United
States fomented the 1909 rebellion in Bluefields."[53]

The rebellion was headed by three generals, Juan Estrada,
Emiliano Chamorro, and José María Moncada (who in those days

was a Conservative), and by the civilian Adolfo Díaz. Two U.S. citizens hired by the rebels to mine ships transporting government troops down the San Juan River were caught and summarily executed. This was the pretext, according to Sandino, for the United States to demand Zelaya's resignation. He complied but that was not enough. "The U.S. government tried to capture him, but the Mexican government under Porfirio Díaz came to his rescue with a Mexican warship that saved him from the ferocity of Uncle Sam."[54]

Behind the interventionist policy of the U.S. government, Sandino believed, were the interests of American capital "juggled by the bankers of Wall Street."[55] The same theme recurs in a number of works.[56] Wall Street had a major stake in the construction of a Nicaraguan canal and the financing of a naval base to guard its approaches on the Pacific. Both were needed as guarantees of North American power.[57] Both had been projected by northern bankers.[58]

The 1909 intervention was set in motion when "Wall Street bankers lent Adolfo Díaz $800,000 [actually $600,000] to overthrow the government of Gen. José Santos Zelaya."[59] In October 1929 Sandino wrote that twenty years earlier North American "imperialism" had introduced into his beloved country the perverse influence of money, which had been used to buy Díaz and to induce further betrayals.[60] For Sandino the presence of the marines represented only the surface of the imperialist iceberg. To say that North American imperialism was responsible for bribing his country's political leaders meant that the bankers were responsible. As Sandino pointed out in his open letter to President Herbert Hoover, "Nicaragua doesn't owe a cent to the United States but the United States owes us the loss of our country's peace since 1909, when the Wall Street bankers introduced the corrupting influence of the dollar into Nicaragua."[61]

Sandino's longest and strongest indictment of Wall Street appeared in this same open letter:

> For every thousand dollars invested in my country by the Yankee bankers a Nicaraguan has died. . . . Adolfo Díaz was induced to become the instrument of the Wall Street bankers in Nicaragua. They pushed him into the rebellion. . . . Díaz and other corrupt Nicaraguans were used as instruments of the bankers to get Nicaragua to accept loans we didn't need. The bankers chose those denationalized persons for the purpose of signing pacts and treaties that would give the appearance of legality to the appropriation of Nicaragua for themselves. . . . In that epoch the bankers of Wall Street considered themselves the owners and lords of Nicaragua. On bended knees in front of

their strongboxes filled with metal, with their hands and eyes lifted up to heaven, they thanked their Gilded God for the great miracle He had bestowed on them. Oh, fiendish dollar! You are the death rattle that undermines the foundations of Yankee imperialism.[62]

The Wall Street bankers had disguised their imperialist ambitions, Sandino contended, behind the cover of the U.S. government. "Dollar diplomacy" in Central America was the apt designation for the foreign policy of Wall Street and the imposition of loans that Nicaragua would have done better without. Through international treaties and pacts of friendship, lopsided and extortionate business dealings acquired the status of law. The Nicaraguan government was induced to accept loans from Wall Street bankers for the purpose of paying off its debts to foreign interests and improving its public services. Since North American capital required guarantees, the U.S. government arranged for the payment of interest and the amortization of the principal to be covered by Nicaraguan customs duties and taxes. To add insult to injury, a U.S. citizen was appointed tax collector by the Nicaraguan government at the recommendation of American bankers.[63]

Because the bankers personified American business interests, Sandino believed, they were also the personification of American capital. Consequently, he considered it imperative "to expel completely North American capital and U.S. citizens from his country's soil."[64] Only in that way, it seemed, might Nicaraguans defend themselves from the voracity of American business interests.

As instances of dollar imperialism Sandino cited the U.S. interventions not only in Nicaragua, but also in Panama, Puerto Rico, Cuba, Haiti, and the Dominican Republic where "those who reach the presidency, supported by the magnates of Wall Street, defend the interests of the North American bankers."[65] Underlying official American political and economic policy toward those countries, according to Sandino, could be discerned this economic basis and essence of U.S. imperialism.

Rather than representing the people's interests, Sandino noted, "the government of the United States [was] . . . the docile servant of the Wall Street bankers."[66] In the last analysis, the bankers were responsible for sending to Nicaragua American troops, the thousands of North American pirates Sandino had denounced as the hired ruffians of Wall Street.[67] If the American government was the meek instrument of the bankers and the U.S. Marines were the bayonets of the government, then the marines were indirectly the bankers' own bayonets. Thus resistance to the U.S.-imposed governments in Nicaragua meant facing up to the "Yankee soldiers in the service of Wall Street."[68]

It is worth noting that Sandino made all of the foregoing references to American bankers during the latter part of 1928 and through the early months of 1930. It was at this time that he came under the influence of Farabundo Martí, the Mexican Communist party, and the Comintern. Even after breaking with each, he retained the substance of their conception of imperialism. As late as March 1933, he acknowledged that the border squabbles and territorial litigations among the Central American states obeyed the designs and the expansionist policy of the United States, as did the fratricidal war between Bolivia and Paraguay. "All played into the hands of the bankers of Wall Street." Even some of the projects for bringing about Central American unification, he noted, showed signs of "the imperialist tendency favored by the North American bankers."[69] Far from having a merely visceral and populist content for Sandino, this concept of imperialism had its roots in the Marxist intellectual tradition. Its original source was Lenin rather than Ricardo Flores Magón.[70]

That Sandino's critique of the Wall Street bankers was not entirely off target is apparent from the hearings before a congressional committee in 1934 headed by Brig. Gen. Smedley Butler, the highest-ranking officer in the Marine Corps. On that occasion he testified that Wall Street interests had offered him three million dollars to stage a mass march on Washington with the expectation of toppling the Roosevelt government and putting an end to the New Deal. Characterizing the marines as the hirelings of Wall Street, he declared, "I spent thirty-three years [in the marines] . . . most of my time being a high-class muscle man for Big Business, for Wall Street and the bankers. In short, I was a racketeer for capitalism."[71] This was the same Smedley Butler who had helped make Nicaragua safe for democracy between 1909 and 1912 and a decent place for the international banking house of Brown Brothers to do business. According to his testimony, the fundamental enemy of Nicaraguan independence was not the Marine Corps, which he characterized in the same terms as Sandino did, but American imperialism personified by Wall Street.

Such sentiments as Butler's were widely entertained in the United States both immediately before and during the Great Depression. Wall Street became the butt of criticism not only for socialists and communists, but also for a broad spectrum of liberals in the United States. Wrote Samuel Guy Inman, "The bitter com-

plaints heard in Latin America against Wall Street are matched by
the constant attacks without quarter made by liberals . . . and published daily in the many radical newspapers in our country. If it
were not for them, by now the TRUSTS would have swallowed up
completely the life in Latin America."[72]

The Wall Street bankers made their influence felt on the U.S.
government, Sandino believed, through the State Department. It
was Philander C. Knox, the secretary of state during President Taft's
administration (1910–1913), who coined the term "dollar diplomacy" to describe the government's reliance on American business
leaders to represent U.S. foreign policy and on the State Department to represent American business interests.[73] Knox was a prime
example of the interlocking of the U.S. government and the interests personified by the American bankers. As the legal representative of the Fletcher family, owners of the La Luz and Los Angeles
Mining Co. in Pis Pis near the eastern coast of Nicaragua, Knox
clashed directly with President Zelaya when the company refused
to submit to Nicaraguan law.[74] Besides being legal counsel for the
company, Knox was reputed to be a major shareholder.[75] In a communiqué dated February 1928, Sandino related how his soldiers had
dynamited and completely destroyed the company's mines "which
belonged in part to former Secretary of State Knox"—as punishment for his insolence.[76]

The Wall Street bankers were also ably represented, according
to Sandino, by Frank B. Kellogg, President Coolidge's secretary of
state (1925–1929). Both were castigated by Sandino for sending the
marines back to Nicaragua. Instead of recognizing the Constitutionalist forces, the State Department pressured Emiliano Chamorro to resign in favor of his fellow Conservative and former
bookkeeper of the Fletcher mines, Adolfo Díaz. In his message to
Congress on 10 January 1927, President Coolidge justified the presence of U.S. troops in Nicaragua for the same reason they had been
sent there in 1912—to quell revolution and to protect the investments of American capital.[77] Sandino was incensed: "Feigning a political morality before the civilized world, the United States did not
recognize Chamorro; but it recognized his accomplice Adolfo Díaz.
Undoubtedly, all this was the work of Coolidge and Kellogg at the
mandate of Wall Street."[78]

Besides his role in Nicaragua, Kellogg became involved in a
plot with the U.S. ambassador in Mexico and the representatives of
the oil companies to overthrow the government of President Calles.
When the oil companies refused to submit to Mexican legislation,
Kellogg came to their defense. Apparently, he threatened to inter-

vene with force unless the properties of American citizens in Mexico were fully respected by the Mexican government. A similar
pretext was used for intervening in Nicaragua's civil war against
the threat of "Mexican bolshevism."[79] For the bankers of Wall
Street the official Mexican recognition of Vice-President Sacasa's
provisional government raised fears concerning the export of the
Mexican Revolution and the specter of the expropriation of American properties in Nicaragua.[80]

The third secretary of state singled out by Sandino in connection with Wall Street interests in his country was Henry L. Stimson. After having served as President Coolidge's personal representative in Nicaragua in 1927, he became President Hoover's secretary
of state (1929–1933). As Sandino portrayed him, Stimson was a
"natural agent of the Wall Street bankers."[81] By this Sandino may
have meant that the secretary of state represented their interests
without having any banking connections of his own to defend. Although a lawyer rather than a businessman, Stimson, in Sandino's
judgment, upheld the policies of Wall Street during the most crucial period of American intervention, from 1927 to 1933, when liberals in both countries concealed their intentions behind a mask of
hypocrisy.

The "Whited Sepulcher"

The White House was a perfect symbol, according to Sandino, of
what he considered to be the hypocritical policies of the United
States toward Latin America. "In reality it is not a White House but
rather one of those whited sepulchers referred to by Jesus, white
and pretty on the outside but putrid and fetid within."[82] He relied
on the same metaphor in an earlier letter, adding that the White
House was being counseled by "Black Spirits" whereas his Defending Army was protected by the "Spirits of Light."[83] In the case of
the White House, force was being applied by the strong to take advantage of the weak, in conformity with what Sandino called the
"immoral morality of present day societies."[84]

The White House was directly responsible, Sandino believed,
for the crimes committed by the marines in Nicaragua. Among
the American soldiers there were many ignorant ones pushed
like machines by their leaders in the White House.[85] As Sandino
commented sympathetically in his manifesto of May 1931, the
Americans killed by his forces in Nicaragua had President Hoover
and his advisers to blame. They were the assassins: "May the American people . . . and the fathers, sons, and brothers of the marines

who have fallen in the fields of Segovia curse today and forever
those funereal rulers!"[86] Elsewhere, referring to the "criminal international policy" of the White House toward Nicaragua, Sandino acknowledged that it was "injurious even to the Yankee people."[87]

Fearful of appearing unjust before its own people and the
world, Sandino noted, the White House concealed its real intentions. It hid behind the Monroe Doctrine and feigned a moral posture it did not have: "The immoral governments of the United
States have been able to cover up their policy in Nicaragua with a
hypocritical mask that gives them the appearance of legality before
the world, disguising in this way their intervention in our internal
affairs"—intervention on behalf of American business interests.[88]

Yankee hypocrisy, Sandino maintained, went to assuring the
American people that the White House's intentions were honorable, decent, and just. In May 1927, his failure to comply with the
U.S. peace proposals was made to appear arbitrary and irresponsible—he even appeared so to the leaders of Nicaraguan liberalism.
Unlike earlier Spanish intervention in the Americas, which hinged
on narrowly dynastic interests, U.S. intervention depended on
popular support. Before and after intervening in Nicaragua, the U.S.
government tried to persuade the American people of the rightness
of its actions.

The reasons justifying intervention were varied. Sandino was
familiar with several White House pretexts. A favorite stratagem
was to portray a nationalist regime unfriendly to the United States
as unpopular and its leaders as virtual dictators and tyrants. This
was the policy applied against Colombia in 1903, by which the U.S.
liberated Panama and acquired exclusive rights for building a canal
through what had been Colombian territory, and it was the policy
applied against the Liberal government of Nicaragua in 1909. President Zelaya was depicted as a tyrant, but the real purpose of American intervention was concealed from the public. A second stratagem
was to persuade an unpopular but friendly government to invite the
United States to intervene against a popular movement threatening
to overthrow it. Such was the policy applied in Cuba as a pretext
for the Spanish-American War, and again in Nicaragua both in 1912
and in 1926 with the collaboration of Adolfo Díaz.

"The Yankees," wrote former Guatemalan president Juan José
Arévalo, "are masters of pretext."[89] To this he added that if one pretext is found wanting, they will invent another; and they will be
sure to believe it because they are also masters of self-deceit. By the
"Yankees" Arévalo had in mind mainly their official representative,

the U.S. government. He took one of his key examples from official U.S. intervention in Nicaragua.

Sandino attributed this hypocritical morality, which guaranteed that whatever the American government did was right, to the superior power of the Americans as a nation, to their role as the Colossus of the North. As he indicated in his manifesto of July 1931, the moral basis of U.S. policy was the right of force rather than the force of right.[90] To employ Sandino's emotion-laden symbolism, it was the self-justification of the American eagle that feeds on the blood of its prey.[91]

In his sketches of Nicaraguan history Sandino focused on official U.S. intervention in his country's domestic affairs. His *Manifesto to the Peoples of the Earth* explains that the Conservatives were pushed into power in 1909 so that the U.S. government might obtain control over Nicaragua's inland waterways. Toward that end the Conservatives were used by the White House to consummate the "criminal Bryan-Chamorro Treaty."[92] Once construction began on the Panama Canal, the U.S. government did everything it could to prevent the construction of a rival canal financed by some foreign power. Preparatory negotiations for a treaty dealing with this matter were begun as early as 1909 and designed to guarantee to the United States exclusive rights to an alternate route through Nicaragua. But not until several years later, when the Panama Canal was completed in 1914, was the treaty finally signed by representatives of the two governments: William Jennings Bryan, the U.S. secretary of state under President Wilson, and Emiliano Chamorro, the Nicaraguan ambassador to Washington.

In response to those negotiations, Sandino wrote in his manifesto, "There was the 1912 revolution as a sign of protest, which culminated in the assassination of the invincible and glorious Gen. Benjamín Zeledón."[93] A Liberal like President Zelaya, Zeledón upheld his nation's dignity by refusing to countenance the proposed treaty that would have made Nicaragua a U.S. dependency. When he failed to surrender to a contingent of nearly three thousand marines sent by President Taft to restore law and order, his army was pursued and finally crushed in November 1912.

Sandino summarized U.S. intervention between 1909 and 1927 in his letter to the Anti-Imperialist Congress at Frankfurt: "The entire civilized world knows that since 1909, the year in which the United States revealed its project for constructing an interoceanic canal . . . through Nicaraguan territory and for establishing a naval base in the Gulf of Fonseca in waters belonging to the republics of

El Salvador, Honduras, and Nicaragua, there has been a situation of unalterable struggle to maintain our territorial integrity against the menace of U.S. imperialism."[94] The letter contained a chronology of the principal U.S. violations of Nicaragua's sovereignty.

In 1912, when the United States announced the terms of the proposed treaty, a bloody rebellion was the result. The United States intervened militarily to quash it.[95] In 1923 the United States arranged a conference of the Central American governments—Panama was not invited—which resulted in a treaty stipulating that the signatories would refuse diplomatic recognition to any Central American government that might arise from a military rebellion.[96] The United States also bound itself to this agreement. As Sandino recalled in his open letter to President Hoover, the purpose of the treaty was to maintain the status quo and to preserve in power those who had made Nicaragua a pawn of U.S. interests.[97] Although he did not say so, this Treaty of Peace and Friendship was directed against the contagion of revolutionary nationalism in Central America emanating from the Mexican Revolution.

In October 1925 Emiliano Chamorro's coup against the legitimate government had the support of leading members of the Conservative party.[98] In his open letter to the American president, Sandino filled in some of the details. "They obliged the president to resign and declared him to be crazy. They denied the legality of the vice-president, they persecuted him, and he emigrated."[99] But the terms of the 1923 treaty interfered with U.S. recognition of the new regime. So the United States turned to its old and trusted ally, thus making Adolfo Díaz again the guardian of U.S. interests in Nicaragua.

In May 1926 the Nicaraguan people rose up in arms to repudiate the unconstitutional government of Emiliano Chamorro.[100] The response of the United States was to send back the marines. Sandino's account of their return in December 1926—they had withdrawn in August 1924 in the conviction that the Liberals had been tamed—was based on direct knowledge of the events. "On 24 December 1926 the Yankees declared Puerto Cabezas to be a neutral zone, ordering Dr. Sacasa to evacuate the Constitutionalist army and all its equipment from the port in 48 hours."[101] In its hurry to leave, the army abandoned guns and ammunition, which the marines seized and threw into the sea.

Finally, in May 1927 the victory of the Constitutionalist forces in the civil war was thwarted by another blatant act of intervention. "When our Constitutionalist army was at the gates of Managua already triumphant, it received from the government of the

United States through Henry L. Stimson, the personal representative of President Coolidge and now the secretary of state, the
most insulting and unprecedented suggestion, that our army of liberation should lay down its arms with which we had the right to
achieve our country's freedom." [102] To add to this humiliation, Sandino added, the Liberal generals complied with Stimson's request.

Sandino recalled that the Constitutionalist army had made it a
fundamental principle to abrogate all treaties imposed on Nicaragua by Yankee bayonets. [103] These included the Bryan-Chamorro
Treaty signed in 1914 and ratified by the U.S. Senate in 1916, and
the Treaty of Peace and Friendship signed and ratified in 1923. Presumably, that was why the United States had intervened—to ensure that those treaties would be respected.

All these acts of intervention in Nicaragua's affairs were perpetrated, according to Sandino, under the umbrella of the Monroe
Doctrine. [104] As the basis of America's spread-eagle concept of Manifest Destiny, the Monroe Doctrine had legitimized its expansion
westward. Without mentioning the annexation of Texas in 1845 or
the immense territories seized from Mexico after the Mexican-
American War of 1846–1848, Sandino indicated that America's expansion to the Pacific was a prelude to a second wave of expansion
southward through Central America and the Caribbean. [105] The ambitions of the White House were seemingly insatiable, Sandino believed, and its policy of divide and conquer fed on the tensions
among the Central American republics.

Sandino agreed with the nominal objective of the Monroe Doctrine: America for Americans. But he interpreted it to mean that
everyone born in the Americas was *ipso facto* an American. That
was not the White House's interpretation: "The misunderstanding
arises from the interpretation of the Monroe Doctrine as America
for the Yankees." To clear up this misunderstanding, Sandino proposed to reformulate the doctrine: "The United States of North
America for the Yankees; Latin America for the Indo-Latins!" [106]

Sandino looked to Mexico for support. Mexico, he argued, had
a vested interest in halting the U.S. advance southward and in aid-
ing his resistance forces in Nicaragua: "What would happen to
Mexico if the Yankees succeeded in their dastardly designs to colo-
nize Central America? . . . The celebrated Carranza Doctrine states
that Mexico's geographical position requires that Mexico be—
and in fact it is—the advance sentinel of Hispanic interests in
America." [107] He had in mind Mexico's intervention in the Nicaraguan civil war on the side of the Constitutionalist forces. The
American intervention was ostensibly in response to Mexican de-

signs on Nicaragua. President Coolidge had tried to hold the Mexican government responsible for Nicaragua's civil war.[108] President Calles was charged with having directed Mexican officials to collaborate with Dr. Sacasa in providing arms and military training for the Constitutionalist forces, and also in permitting Mexican soldiers to serve in the Constitutionalist army.[109] A Mexican general who fought in the Constitutionalist army testified that President Calles sent two expeditions to aid Dr. Sacasa with several ships loaded with soldiers, arms, and munitions. One of those ships had been bombarded by the U.S. Air Force.[110] Thus Sandino looked to Mexico to put a brake on the White House's designs on Central America.

On the presumption that the United States could not remain in Nicaragua forever and in anticipation of the moment when the marines would withdraw, the White House proceeded with its plan to organize the National Guard. Formally established by an executive agreement between the U.S. and Nicaraguan governments in December 1927, the National Guard was granted legal status by the Nicaraguan Congress in February 1929. From 1927 until 1933, when the U.S. occupation formally ended, the Guard was under U.S. command. All of its officers were American marines. From its inception its purpose was both to preserve the status quo and to defend U.S. interests in the area. That purpose did not change after it came under Nicaraguan control. In continuing to care for U.S. interests, the Guard became another instance of what Sandino called the hypocritical mask of the White House.

Nicaragua's Political Leaders

Direct U.S. intervention in Nicaragua occurred in almost every instance with the cooperation of leaders of one or both of Nicaragua's major political parties. From 1909 to 1929 the Conservative party was the chief domestic ally of the White House and the Wall Street bankers. After 1929 the Liberal party performed this role. The Americans could not have accomplished their criminal objectives, to use Sandino's language, without the collusion of local traitors.[111]

Sandino did not mince words concerning the treasonable conduct of Nicaragua's political leaders. "When I left Mexico for these privileged lands my spirit had no idea of the terrible and heavy task that lay ahead: the events were giving me the key to the attitude I should take as a legitimate son of Nicaragua . . . confronted by the betrayal and cowardice of our political leaders."[112] Having shed his illusions concerning the Conservative party, he still believed that the Liberal party represented the people's interests. "However, in the actual theater of events we discovered that Nicaragua's political leaders, both Liberals and Conservatives, were a gang of scoundrels, cowards, and traitors . . . who were allies of the invaders."[113] Next to the invaders, Sandino was saying, these traitors were the major source of Nicaragua's ills. Since they depended on each other, he usually lumped them together.[114]

The political leaders of both parties, Sandino maintained, had become the instruments of American imperialism. The only friends the Americans had in Nicaragua consisted of this "small group of immoral men who do not represent the real sentiments of the Nicaraguan people."[115] Besides being an agent of the White House, according to Sandino, the Nicaraguan government was an "agent of the Yankee bankers."[116]

Aware of the decisive role of Nicaragua's political leaders, Sandino highlighted the Conservative and Liberal betrayals of his country's interests. "As in the other countries of our racial America, Yankee imperialism in Nicaragua gave form to a small and corrupt oligarchy made up of submissive men. . . . Headed by Adolfo Díaz, Emiliano Chamorro, and José María Moncada, this oligarchy was used by Yankee imperialism to uphold the shameful treaties prejudicial to our fundamental rights as a free people."[117] Elsewhere, he referred to the members of this oligarchy as the "bandits who controlled the government with the aid of Washington"—bandits because they were corrupt politicians who had sold out what did not belong to them.[118]

As early as his first political manifesto (1 July 1927), Sandino denounced the leaders of both political parties. Of the Conservatives he wrote, "It is seventeen years since Adolfo Díaz and Emiliano Chamorro ceased to be Nicaraguans, because ambition killed the right to their nationality." And of the Liberals he said, "The traitor Moncada failed in his duties as a military man and as a patriot . . . [because of] his unbridled ambition."[119] His last political manifesto (13 March 1933) reaffirmed his original judgment. In May 1927 "General Moncada strangled Nicaraguan Liberalism just as General Emiliano Chamorro had killed the Conservative party in signing the Bryan-Chamorro Treaty."[120] Sandino concluded that there were no longer authentic political parties representing national interests in Nicaragua, but only *camarillas* serving personal ambitions at the country's expense.

In his open letter to the governors of the Americas (4 August 1928), Sandino probed into the nature of the Conservative and Liberal betrayals.[121] Political ambition was one aspect of treason; the payoff by a foreign power was another. Treason did not go unrewarded; in Latin America, Sandino explained, its reward was political office.[122]

In examining Nicaragua's history, Sandino noticed the correlation between acts of national betrayal by domestic traitors and U.S. pressures on Nicaragua. Among the instances of domestic treason, he singled out the most notorious: Adolfo Díaz's acceptance of a bribe to finance the Conservative rebellion in 1909; President Díaz's invitation to the marines to intervene in 1912; Emiliano Chamorro's negotiation of the Bryan-Chamorro Treaty in 1914; and Díaz's invitation to the U.S. government to intervene a second time in 1926. The leaders of the Conservative party, headed by Díaz and Chamorro, had been responsible for these violations of Nicaraguan sovereignty. But the Conservatives were not the sole offenders. To the above examples Sandino added the betrayals by the Liberal party under General Moncada. Three events stand out in Sandino's account of how the Liberals, too, betrayed the interests of their country: Moncada's acceptance of the U.S.-negotiated Peace of Tipitapa in May 1927; his refusal to negotiate an end to the civil war when he became president in January 1929; and the refusal by Anastasio Somoza, as head of the National Guard, to accept the authority of President Sacasa, installed as Moncada's successor in January 1933.

In considering Díaz's first act of treason, Sandino observed that the bribe in the form of a loan was financially unwarranted, since Díaz had no collateral of his own. As a mere bookkeeper for the La Luz and Los Angeles Mining Co., Díaz received the meager wage of 2.65 pesos daily. The borrowed money was used to finance the military takeover of the Department of Bluefields by Gen. Juan José Estrada, the military governor of Bluefields, who with the support of Emiliano Chamorro then went on to seize the capital in Managua.[123] Estrada was encouraged to revolt not only by the money offered to him by Díaz, but also by the promise of the presidency.[124] On 9 September 1912, he explained to the *New York Times* how his rebellion had been financed: besides the $600,000 contributed by Díaz, he had received $1 million from U.S. companies in Nicaragua, $250,000 from the firm of Joseph Beers, and $150,000 from Samuel Weil.[125]

Although Sandino fell short on dates, the Conservative rebellion launched in October 1909 lasted almost a year, ending in August 1910. Sandino held the Conservatives responsible for the civil war that followed from July to October 1912 and also for the civil war of 1926–1927. During the twenty years from 1909 to 1929, he claimed, "the American government and the *camarilla* of corrupt politicians headed by Adolfo Díaz, Emiliano Chamorro, and José María Moncada was responsible for the assassination of 50,000 Nicaraguan citizens of both sexes and for the destruction of national wealth valued at one hundred million dollars."[126] In 1931 Sandino reported that the costs of the civil war had escalated to 150,000 lives plus the destruction of more than two-thirds of Nicaragua's national patrimony.[127] Although these figures were partly guesswork, it is fair to say that the Liberals outdid the Conservatives in bringing unnecessary disaster to their country.

The Bryan-Chamorro Treaty was another Conservative betrayal of Nicaragua's national interests. Negotiated by Emiliano Chamorro during the presidency of Adolfo Díaz, it made the Conservative party directly responsible for authorizing the continued presence in Nicaragua of the U.S. Marines. For an insignificant sum the U.S. purchased exclusive rights to construct a canal through Nicaragua. As Carleton Beals reported in his February 1928 interview with Sandino, it was a token payment: "'The Yankees have stolen our rights to the canal. Theoretically, they paid us three million dollars . . . , which distributed among all Nicaraguan citizens would not even have bought a soda cracker and sardine for each one.'" The discussions concerning the sale, Sandino added, took place within a spurious congress, behind closed doors guarded by Conservative soldiers, and supported by Yankee bayonets.[128]

In his "Bases for an Agreement with General Moncada," Sandino claimed that all those who had climbed the presidential ladder since 1909 had done so, save in one instance, with the help of American bayonets. The sole exception occurred during the November 1924 election of a compromise ticket headed by a Conservative candidate for president, Carlos Solórzano, and Juan B. Sacasa as his Liberal running mate.[129] But the new government that took office in January 1925 was unacceptable to Emiliano Chamorro and the traditional leadership of the Conservative party. The resulting coup of October 1925, Sandino mistakenly believed, was made with the connivance of Adolfo Díaz and with the tacit support of the State Department, which had been instrumental in reaching a compromise among the moderates in both parties.[130]

It is true that after the coup and President Solórzano's involuntary retirement, the White House refused to support Vice-President Sacasa's constitutional claim to the presidency. Because Washington also refused to recognize Chamorro's unconstitutional government, however, it could hardly have instigated the coup. In any case, the leaders of the Conservative party betrayed their country's interests in soliciting and obtaining Washington's recognition of Adolfo Díaz as the new president. The outcome was a bloody civil war that was all for nothing, since in the end the Liberals triumphed. In retrospect, the war was self-defeating for the Conservatives and destructive to the Nicaraguan nation. This major betrayal of the country's interests in 1925–1926 should be blamed mainly on the Conservatives, Sandino believed, although the United States bore part of the responsibility for having supported Chamorro's Conservative successor.

Sandino's account of Moncada's betrayal appears in his autobiographical sketches covering the events of May 1927, and in his circular letters issued that same month. His first rude awakening came after returning to his country in 1926. Although he found enough people among Moncada's sympathizers to organize his own column of volunteers, he had reason to question the leaders of the Constitutionalist movement. He observed that many were motivated by personal ambition and the prospect of acquiring military honors that might later advance their political careers.[131] While hanging around Moncada's camp he unearthed a scandal concerning one of the general's supporters: "I learned that an expedition to the Segovias was being organized under the command of Gen. Adrián Espinosa, who on another occasion had rubbed shoulders with the North American invaders; and it was even proposed that I should accompany him, provided I agreed to campaign politically for whomever the army high command should choose as its candidate!"[132]

The decisive blow to Sandino's faith in Nicaraguan Liberalism came in May 1927 when he arrived at army headquarters and General Moncada tried to persuade him to surrender.[133] Among the reasons Moncada gave for accepting peace was that the United States wanted to end the civil war. With that purpose the White House had accepted the invitation of Adolfo Díaz to supervise the presidential election scheduled for November 1928 and to act as custodian of the arms of both the Liberal and Conservative armies.[134] In return for the surrender of arms to the marines, the U.S. government would pay ten dollars for the rifle of each soldier who surrendered one. Those who refused to surrender would be disarmed by force. The leaders of the Liberal party would be compensated by receiving control of six of the country's departments. (Sandino had been chosen to be political head of the Department of Jinotega.) In addition, Díaz's government would pay for all the horses and mules at the disposal of the Constitutionalist forces. As interpreted by Moncada, this meant that the commanding officers, including Sandino, were free to appropriate as many animals as they could.

Sandino asked Moncada if the other Liberal generals were agreeable to these terms. "'They have to be,'" he answered, "'since to each one would be paid the salary due him . . . during the period he had served under arms.'"[135] To Sandino corresponded ten dollars per diem in back pay—a sizable sum. Moncada then invited him to attend a meeting of the Constitutionalist officers in Boaco on 8 May to ratify the peace terms formally. Stimson had given them eight days to reply.

For Sandino these terms amounted to shameless bribery. Moncada had already declared 4 May a holiday, the day on which the armistice had been signed, thereby showing his contempt for the opinions of his fellow officers. What mattered to him, said Sandino, was the promise of the presidency he carried in his pocket. "The so-called Constitutionalist revolution came to an end when Moncada realized he could achieve his old ambition of becoming president without troubling about the means that should be observed, without considering that the country was being surrendered anew to the interventionists, and without heeding Dr. Sacasa's delegates . . . who, once they had arrived in the capital, published a manifesto making known Moncada's intentions, which violated Dr. Sacasa's instructions."[136] Sandino was convinced that on the threshold of a Liberal victory, Moncada had betrayed the Constitutionalist cause in return for U.S. support of his own presidential aspirations. How else explain that Moncada, rather than Dr. Sacasa, would become the Liberal party's candidate for president in 1928? A secret pact with the invading forces was one way to account for this anomaly.[137] Sandino believed the surrender of the Constitutionalist Army was based on a personal agreement between two men; he referred to it as the "Moncada-Stimson Pact."[138]

Sandino told Moncada that he would oppose the treaty. "Moncada then said that it would be madness to fight the United States because it is a powerful nation of 120 million people; that I could do nothing with the 300 men under my command; that we could expect the same treatment as prey in the claws of a tiger."[139] But Sandino was not to be dissuaded, saying that it was his duty to liberate his country or die. With that objective he had unfurled his red and black flag symbolizing liberty or death. Again, Moncada scornfully replied, "No, man, . . . how are you going to sacrifice yourself for the people? The people are ungrateful. . . . I tell you this from experience. . . . Life will be over and the people will remain. . . . The duty of every human being is to enjoy himself and to live well without concerning himself too much for others."[140]

In the first of his circulars concerning Moncada's treason, Sandino stressed the imminent victory of the Constitutionalist Army at the moment Moncada opted to surrender. "The decisive moment had arrived; the last bell had tolled for the Conservatives. The Liberal Army had seven thousand well-armed men bursting with enthusiasm, whereas the Conservatives could count on only one thousand or so, who would rather desert than fight. Victory was ours in every respect."[141] According to Sandino, the Liberals had already won the civil war. They were preparing for a final assault on the capital "when the Barbarian Colossus of the North . . . , seeing that the government forces were surrendering their positions and having arrived at an agreement with Adolfo Díaz, proposed to General Moncada an armistice of forty-eight hours in an effort to make peace."[142]

Besides the terms already mentioned, Sandino continued, the United States proposed that two ministries be assigned to the Liberals in Díaz's Conservative government, the Ministry of the Interior and the Ministry of War. The latter was offered to General Moncada, but he refused to accept it as long as Díaz remained president. A majority of Liberal generals also refused to have anything to do with Díaz. But they eventually came to terms because of the U.S. assurance of fair elections in 1928, which they expected to win.[143]

In the second of his two circulars, Sandino claimed that Moncada, in the course of serving his personal ambitions, deliberately undermined the morale of his troops:

> On returning from Managua, Moncada demoralized the army in the following manner: he withdrew the troops that were in Las Banderas and Boaco, the military train that was in Teustepe, along with the other forces that remained under our command; he did so without the general consent of the army while inviting his chiefs to a conference in Boaco to decide whether to accept or reject the Yankees' terms; and at the same time he announced his own readiness to accept what the machos had proposed.[144]

He had not only made up his own mind, Sandino concluded, but also intended to make the other generals agree with him.

Moncada was not the only traitor on the Liberal side. Sandino believed that most of the generals feared a confrontation with the American government in May 1927 and were willing to stop fighting in return for their promised sinecures. Financially, they stood to benefit from the peace; politically, they could count on moving up to a ministerial post after the 1928 elections. The entire leadership of the Liberal party had disappointed Sandino's expectations. "The flaccidity of our political leaders became downright ridiculous; it was then that I understood that the sons of the people were without leaders and that we had need of new men."[145]

Sacasa had stood almost alone in opposing the American peace terms. But Sandino remembered that when the United States occupied Puerto Cabezas in December 1926 and demanded the withdrawal of the Liberal forces, "Sacasa thought only of saving his own skin."[146] He and the members of his cabinet had been of minimal help to Sandino. In Prinzapolca Sandino had become aware of the personal ambitions and disorganization that surrounded Sacasa, a situation that would be repeated in 1933–1934. Sacasa became president and Sandino was assassinated by one of Sacasa's fellow Liberals.

Together the leaders of the Liberal and Conservative parties had collaborated with the United States in giving birth to the National Guard. Organized, equipped, and trained by the United States, its purpose was to do the job of the marines so that the American forces of occupation might leave the country in peace. But it was also designed by the U.S. government to forestall a Mexican-type revolution in Nicaragua. That Sandino had to wage a civil war against his own countrymen was the responsibility of Nicaragua's political leaders, who also feared the contagion of Mexico's social upheaval.

The legal recognition of the National Guard by these political leaders, Sandino argued, did not make the Guard constitutional. He repeatedly questioned the constitutionality of an armed force recognized by the Nicaraguan Congress under conditions of U.S. military occupation. Although most of his battles from May 1927 until he left for Mexico in May 1929 involved confrontations with the marines, when he returned in June 1930 the Guards had become the principal force of repression in the countryside.[147] By 1932 the National Guard almost completely overshadowed the marines in Sandino's reports of enemy casualties.[148] Nicaragua's political leaders were partly responsible for this predicament. Consequently, not only the National Guard, but also the Nicaraguan government could be said to be "serving as a pawn in the game of chess played at the convenience of the U.S. State Department."[149]

Without support from Nicaragua's political leaders, Liberals as well as Conservatives, the National Guard could never have played a major role in Nicaraguan politics. To compound their betrayal of Nicaragua's national interests, these political leaders had financed the National Guard out of vital tax revenues needed for other purposes: "The customs duties and other taxes that provide for the people are to pay for a guard of vile Nicaraguans under the direction

of a numerous as well as inept Yankee officialdom. The railway
tracks and roads that Moncada has giddily ordered to be built are
with a view to his ridiculous strategy. . . . Moncada, Díaz, and
Chamorro constitute the *evil trinity* among the wretched traitors
of our country."[150] Because of this "evil trinity," the patriots in
Sandino's army had been obliged to confront a "deluge of pirates by
land and more than twelve thousand national traitors"—a reference
to the National Guard.[151] Furthermore, even after the marines departed in 1933, the guards went on serving the same political interests "under the thumb of the North American ambassador in
Nicaragua."[152]

The Defending Army of National Sovereignty

Sandino's assessments of the principal "enemies" of the Nicaraguan
people were coupled with comparable assessments of the ways and
means of combatting them. For this purpose the primary vehicle
was his Defending Army of National Sovereignty, formally constituted in September 1927. Its original liberal objectives were to carry
on the Constitutionalist War betrayed by Moncada and the other
Liberal generals and to expel the Yankee invaders invited to Nicaragua by Adolfo Díaz and his fellow Conservatives. The statutes of
the Defending Army specifically disavowed the treasonable government of Nicaragua imposed by the interventionists and committed
itself to "the defense of our national sovereignty and of the rights of
liberty violated by the turncoat and traitor, José María Moncada."[153]

The Defending Army of National Sovereignty was the natural
successor to the Liberal column Sandino had officered during the
Constitutionalist War of 1926–1927. From the beginning his soldiers had differed markedly from those enrolled in the other Liberal
columns. Sandino had professed a revolutionary nationalist mystique symbolized by his red and black flag, a curiosity behind
which General Moncada sensed something sinister and malevolent.
Having renounced the principle of forcible recruitment, he had relied exclusively on persons who believed it was their duty to defend
Nicaragua's freedom. It was part of Sandino's strategy to build an
army on which he could completely rely and that might serve as a
springboard to the revolution he contemplated.

As the leader of a war of resistance against the superior military might of a foreign army of invasion, Sandino depended heavily
on the local population for support. The result was a strategy conditioned as much by political as by military considerations. Mili-

tarily, he relied on a war of movement based on highly mobile columns of approximately one hundred men, on ambushes rather than frontal attacks, on striking only when the odds were clearly in his favor, on hit-and-run tactics rather than efforts to defend a given region, on surprise actions that penetrated deep into enemy territory, and on constant communication by couriers between the supreme command and the other columns. Politically, he tried to win over the population within his zone of operations, to establish an extensive intelligence network with its help, to recruit part-time as well as full-time guerrillas from among the peasants, to boost the morale of his impoverished soldiers through the absence of privileges based on rank, to develop a spirit of comradeship among them, to cement a worker-peasant alliance on a national scale, and to mobilize international support with the help of revolutionaries in other countries. The principal elements of this strategy were subsequently adopted by Fidel Castro and Che Guevara in the first successful example of a Sandinista-type revolution in Latin America.

From the beginning there was an international dimension to Sandino's Defending Army. When he resolved to stand up to the United States and to resist U.S. military intervention in his country, patriots from all over Latin America flocked to his cause because they saw in his Defending Army a vindication of their own opposition to imperialism. Historically, this international brigade became the progenitor of the self-styled "Caribbean Legions" of liberals, radicals, and revolutionaries dedicated to toppling Caribbean and Central American dictators after World War II. Sandino called it his Latin American Legion.[154]

Because its members were assigned to different columns operating in different geographical regions, the legion never constituted a coherent body. But as Sandino describes it, it was big enough to constitute a regiment. Among the officers assigned to different fronts were a Guatemalan general who had studied at the Potsdam Military Academy in Germany and a lieutenant-colonel from Venezuela. The officers included Capt. Alfonso Alexander and Lt. Rubén Ardila Gómez of Colombia, Capt. Gregorio Gilbert of the Dominican Republic, Capt. José de Paredes of Mexico, Capt. Agustín Farabundo Martí of El Salvador, and Esteban Pavletich of Peru, who acted as one of Sandino's advisers. Most of them joined Sandino's forces fairly early. Paredes and his entire Mexican squadron, which had fought under General Moncada, went over to Sandino in May 1927, Pavletich signed up in May 1928, and Martí in June of the same year.[155] These three personages in particular played a key role in Sandino's strategy of establishing alliances with, respectively, the Mexican government, the Comintern, and the APRA.[156]

Sandino sought national support for the Defending Army in the patriotic traditions of his country. He believed that the struggle by the Liberal party, from the time of President Zelaya's overthrow to the outbreak of the Constitutionalist War, had for its objective the restoration of constitutional government and the repudiation of U.S. intervention. His war of liberation was conceived as reviving the earlier struggle by the Liberal general Benjamín Zeledón: "Thus we consider the war we are undertaking to be a continuation of his own."[157]

Sandino recalled that when he left Mexico for Nicaragua in May 1926, he did so "in the understanding that Nicaraguan liberalism struggled for the restoration of our national independence gravely threatened by the illegal Bryan-Chamorro Treaty."[158] Opposition to this treaty is the thread tying together his participation in the Constitutionalist War, his defense of Nicaraguan sovereignty against the American intervention, and his final escalation of military actions with virtually no help from abroad. This framework of three stages, sketched in his *Manifesto to the Peoples of the Earth*, is decisive for understanding his Defending Army, from its early Liberal origins to its later peacetime role.

The first stage covered the initial recruitment and organization of the Liberal column he led during the Constitutionalist War, ending with its partial demobilization in May 1927. During this phase Sandino actively supported the Liberal party, of which he represented the left wing.[159] Opposite him was General Moncada, the leader of the party's right wing.

The origins of Sandino's Defending Army may be traced to his efforts, after arriving in Nicaragua from Mexico, to raise a military force consisting of patriots like himself. Emigdio Maraboto relates how Sandino went about his self-appointed task: "By chance he encountered a group of workers on their way from León to the San Albino Mine, where they were going to work. He joined them as someone who needed work, but with the secret hope of disseminating among the miners his revolutionary propaganda."[160] After working in the mine, he became aware of the onerous conditions under which the miners labored. Indignant at their having to wait months before receiving their wages in money, Sandino told them about the Mexican Revolution, "that Mexico had advanced legislation, that the government had a labor department charged with protecting workers from exploitation, with assuring their payment in money, with providing medical attention, schools, an eight-hour day, and other advantages the Nicaraguan pariahs were compelled to do without."[161] As Maraboto tells the story, Sandino organized the miners with a double purpose: to get them to join the Constitutionalist cause and to prepare them for making a social revolution.

Other biographers add to this account some interesting details. As the assistant bookkeeper in the mine, Sandino discovered the full extent to which the workers were being exploited for the benefit of Charles Butler, the American owner. "They labored fifteen hours a day, were poorly fed, slept on the ground in barracks, and exchanged their coupons at the company store, where everything was more expensive."[162]

Sandino tried to get them to resist. "In the four months he worked in the mine, Sandino clandestinely organized a labor union, informed the workers about the trade-union struggles in Mexico, . . . incited them to strike, and then to join the struggle against the hosts of Adolfo Díaz."[163] From legal methods of resistance he turned to armed resistance:

> The fact is that in less than five months Sandino had indoctrinated, recruited, and trained twenty-nine revolutionaries, had organized a systematic pillage of the dynamite deposits in the mine, and had taught his companions how to make hand grenades with tin cans filled with spikes, nuts, pieces of glass, stones, and dynamite—weapons that were frequently as lethal for the user as for the victim. When his clandestine organization was discovered, Sandino and his men blew up the mine and disappeared in the jungle toward Honduras with three hundred dollars to buy their first arms.[164]

This account is based in part on a 1979 interview with Camilo Guillén, a veteran Sandinista and the son of a former Liberal party leader in the Segovias. His recollections of the origins of Sandino's red and black flag are also revealing: "'Passing by the hacienda of El Conejo, the property of Jacinto Sosa, the group that left San Albino entered the house. The workers ransacked it and discovered two strips of cloth, one red and the other black, with which they put together the first flag used by the column commanded by General Sandino.'"[165] It was a worker's flag symbolizing their struggle for liberation. It was this flag rather than the official blue and white one that inspired Sandino's fledgling forces during his first efforts at armed resistance.

Shortly after blowing up the mine at San Albino in October 1926, his original band of twenty-nine had expanded into a force of some one hundred volunteers.[166] In early November he led this force in an attack on the government garrison at El Jícaro but was re-pelled. Demoralized by defeat, most of his followers returned to their homes. Dividing up the remaining ones, Sandino then traveled down the Coco River to the Atlantic coast in search of arms and reinforcements from Dr. Sacasa's provisional government in Puerto Cabezas. When he returned to El Jícaro in February 1927, his reorganized army had close to 180 men.[167]

Within weeks Sandino succeeded in driving off the Conservative forces in the Segovias and in liberating its four departments. By April, after barely three months of fighting, his original group of twenty-nine workers had mushroomed into a cavalry force of eight hundred—if we are to believe his own account.[168] The size and popularity of his column soon roused the ire of General Moncada. "Moncada ordered a decree read to the reunited Constitutionalist Army prohibiting the transfer of soldiers from one column to another—because a large number wanted to belong to my Segovian column," recalled Sandino.[169] Once again, Moncada sensed that there was more behind Sandino's Liberal veneer than met the eye.

The second stage of Sandino's struggle began in May 1927 with his denunciation of both the Liberal and Conservative parties for agreeing with the peace terms that effectively sanctioned the American occupation. He reorganized his fighting forces, founded the Defending Army of National Sovereignty in September, launched a guerrilla war of attrition against the U.S. Marines and the U.S.-trained National Guard, and assiduously cultivated international support for his cause.

Sandino officially rejected the peace terms on 12 May 1927 from a village in the Segovias. In his first published document, a circular to local authorities of all the departments of Nicaragua, he announced, "I will not surrender my arms in the event all the others do. I will die with the few who accompany me because it is better to die as rebels than to live as slaves."[170] In a follow-up circular to the authorities of the Segovias on 19 May, he explained that he no longer spoke for the Liberal party but for an independent offshoot of it, the Liberal Party of the Segovias.[171] About the same time, he directed his main efforts toward recruiting Liberals who had already served in the Constitutionalist cause: "The Liberal revolution is in march. There are those who have not betrayed it, who did not surrender or sell their rifles to satisfy Moncada's ambition. The revolution goes on and is today stronger than ever, because the only elements that remain are those with courage and self-abnegation."[172]

In August 1927 Sandino reaffirmed his partiality for the Liberal party. Although he claimed his Defending Army was nonpartisan, he promised to turn over his arms to a Liberal government, provided the marines withdrew. Under no circumstances, he declared, would he "permit the division of the party in the coming elections because that would allow the Conservatives to win—an outcome that all patriots seek to avoid."[173]

Beginning in February 1928, there was a perceptible shift in Sandino's strategy. The split in the Liberal party no longer concerned him. When the American journalist Carleton Beals left San Rafael del Norte for Managua after having interviewed Sandino, he carried with him Sandino's reply to a letter from Admiral Sellers. The letter, dated 3 February 1928, cautioned the admiral not to misinterpret the nature of the resistance: "Don't believe that the present struggle has for an origin or base the [Liberal] revolution just passed. Today this is a struggle of the Nicaraguan people in general to expel the foreign invasion of my country. . . . The only way to put an end to this struggle is the immediate withdrawal of the invading forces from our territory, at the same time replacing the actual president with a Nicaraguan citizen who is not running as a candidate for the presidency, and supervising the coming elections with representatives of Latin America instead of American marines."[174] A noteworthy feature of this reply was its undisguised contempt for the politicians of both parties when the price of obtaining the presidency was subservience to U.S. interests.

Sandino's special emphasis on the nonpartisan character of his Defending Army was brought out in Carleton Beals's interview. After repeating the section of his army's statutes stating that its purpose was to defend the interests not just of Liberals but of all Nicaraguans, Sandino noted, "As you can see, we are working for all Nicaraguans, both Conservatives and Liberals. This colonel, for example, is a Conservative but he is convinced of the reasonableness of our cause. We only want to throw out the foreign invader."[175]

Sandino's new policy led him to boycott the November 1928 elections. From his army's headquarters he urged Nicaraguans who loved their country to remain firm against the electoral blandishments of the Americans. Specifically, he warned against the electoral imposition of either a Liberal or a Conservative, arguing that the Liberal candidate, General Moncada, was as much a traitor to his country, a *vende-patria,* as his Conservative opponent. "If Moncada is imposed, we men of honor who have remained faithful to the principles of the Liberal party must fight until we remove him from office, because he betrayed our party by entering into secret pacts with the invaders. If a Conservative is imposed, our duty will be to struggle against him for the same reason that we rose up in arms against the sell-out party headed by Chamorro and Díaz, because of its coup against the military fortress of La Loma in Managua."[176] The election of either one of these pro-American candidates would be contrary to the nation's interests, Sandino concluded, and no matter which party won, the other would try to displace it by force. In either case the result would be civil war.

This new policy of his Defending Army, enunciated in August 1928, aimed at taking advantage of the revolutionary situation engendered by the anticipated breakdown of law and order, the absence of legitimacy, and the inability of the ruling class to agree on which party should represent it in the government. "We shall make the most of that struggle between Conservatives and Moncada's followers, since it will be the hour to proclaim and establish the National Government, which must be presided over by an honorable and patriotic person who is not a big shot and who has never before held political office."[177]

With the election of Moncada on 4 November 1928, Sandino began taking concrete measures to establish a national government over the liberated areas controlled by his Defending Army. A pact was agreed on with the marginal Labor party and dissenting groups that supported him. Late in November they agreed to organize a governing junta.[178] They also empowered a delegate of the Defending Army to cooperate with the Hands Off Nicaragua Committee in the Mexican capital "to obtain the armaments needed to organize the expedition that, when the hour arrives, will disembark in one of the Nicaraguan ports . . . to fortify the government that will be installed in a part of the Segovias or in some other opportune place."[179]

The hour of the promised departure of the U.S. Marines from Nicaragua, to take effect after the inauguration of President Moncada in January 1929, was to be the signal for implementing the terms of the agreement and preparing the military expedition from Mexico. Since Dr. Zepeda had been instrumental in arranging Mexican aid for the military expeditions in support of the Constitutionalist cause in 1926, it appears that Sandino expected from him a repeat performance. To ensure that the Defending Army would be the real power in the patriotic front and the governing junta, Sandino stipulated that the junta's president would be assisted by a special delegate of the army as his private secretary.

But Moncada stood firm against Sandino's "bandits," the U.S. Marines did not withdraw from Nicaragua, and the proposed revolutionary government never materialized. Because of the election of

a Liberal president, the Defending Army suffered a political setback. How strong was it? Of its eight hundred volunteers in April
1927, Sandino was left with only sixty full-time soldiers when he
attacked the marine garrison at Ocotal in July of the same year.[180]
Although by November 1927 it was again at eight hundred—a level
maintained with minor fluctuations throughout most of 1928 and
the beginning of 1929—Sandino believed he could succeed in his
objectives only with Mexican military aid.[181] With that purpose in
mind, he left Nicaragua for Mexico in May 1929.

The third stage of Sandino's struggle began with his return in
1930. Disillusioned by the cooling-off of the Mexican Revolution
and of the new hot-headed policies of the Comintern and the Mexican Communist party, Sandino had to rely on his own resources.
Even so, he was able to escalate the armed struggle with the support of Nicaragua's workers and peasants: "From that moment our
military operations redoubled in brilliance without expecting
hardly anything from anybody."[182] This phase, during which "nobody helped us, neither with munitions nor with economic aid,"
lasted until the United States abandoned Nicaragua in 1933.[183]

When Sandino returned from Mexico, he found the people ready
for action. Apparently, the armed struggle had not de-escalated during
his absence.[184] At the height of the resistance the Defending Army
consisted not of eight hundred volunteers but, according to one estimate, of more than two thousand.[185]

One military encounter followed another until in his manifesto of 28 July 1931 Sandino could boast of eight separate columns
in the field, covering more than half of the departments in the
country.[186] The growing popular support for his movement encouraged him to radicalize his appeals to the masses, to lead them beyond a mere war of resistance to a struggle for social liberation. The
radicalization was such that Sacasa felt pressured to campaign for
the presidency in 1932 on a platform committed to domestic reforms and a complete withdrawal of the marines. It was the mounting strength and radicalization of the liberation movement that
explains Sandino's recourse to Communist slogans, despite having
been abandoned by the Comintern.

What accounts for this tremendous surge in the growth of the
Defending Army? It may be explained in part by the world depression, falling prices, labor unrest, and popular discontent with President Moncada's inability to end the foreign occupation. But these
were not the only causes. The public's familiarity with Sandino's
program of domestic reforms presented to General Moncada in

January 1929 may have contributed to his growing popular support, along with the rash of manifestos periodically issued from his head-quarters.[187] But the most intensive work of consciousness-raising was within his Defending Army. Sandino gave special attention to the task of indoctrinating his own men.

In the summer of 1930 Sandino decreed that all the soldiers in the Defending Army should address one another as "Brother,"[188] and went to elaborate lengths to explain why they should be so ad-dressed. On 15 February 1931, he issued the most startling procla-mation of his career, his notorious Light and Truth Manifesto, which was read aloud to his mostly illiterate troops. Intent on in-stilling what was tantamount to a theosophy of liberation, he set forth his version of the creation, nature, and destiny of humanity, the continuing struggle between the forces of justice and injustice, the fundamental unity of all peoples, the impending Final Judg-ment, and the relevance of all this to Nicaragua.[189]

The Defending Army had gone beyond being a merely political and military organization to become a moral and religious one. Be-sides its earlier objectives of political sovereignty, economic in-dependence, and social justice, it began to herald the moral and spiritual redemption of Nicaragua as part of a coming world pro-letarian revolution. More important than Mexican arms had be-come the conscientization and mobilization of Nicaragua's workers and peasants. Convinced that faith and confidence in a divine providence were required to hold out against superior odds, Sandino instructed his generals to "inject" his soldiers with the new gospel and to make it part of the air they breathed.[190] This is what the philosopher-general meant by relying on his own resources. It is against this background that one must understand both the escala-tion and the radicalization of Sandino's resistance, clearly the turn-ing point in his career.

In response to the new situation and the Defending Army's growing popularity, Sandino issued instructions in December 1931 for the organization of a provisional government under Gen. Horacio Portocarrero. Although General Moncada was not a willing puppet, like Adolfo Díaz, he appeared helpless before the combined pres-sures of the American embassy, the U.S. officers in command of the National Guard, the U.S.-appointed commissioner of customs, and the U.S.-controlled National Bank, not to mention the marines. Moreover, there was little reason to believe that Dr. Sacasa, the Lib-eral party candidate in the November 1932 elections, would be able to achieve what Moncada had failed to. Although leaders of the

Liberal party openly criticized the continued presence of foreign troops in Nicaragua, they collaborated with American business interests and resigned themselves to their country's economic dependence on the United States. The Liberals had made it clear that, with or without the military occupation, there would be no real break with U.S. domination.

The call for a provisional government, a tactic that had also been used on the occasion of the 1928 elections, was combined with a call to Nicaraguan citizens to stay away from the polls. In his January 1932 manifesto, Sandino urged them not to vote because that would be to render homage to the Yankee bayonets that were there to supervise the elections: "Do not obey a single order of the marines in the electoral farce. . . . Let those affiliated with the Liberal party not fear a victory of the Conservative platform, because that platform will not last longer than the people take to nullify it with their Defending Army of National Sovereignty. Let the Conservatives not fear a victory of the Liberal platform, because over it, too, is suspended the admonishing hand of this army."[191]

Later in 1932, Sandino reminded his fellow citizens that the political leaders of both parties were untrustworthy. In complete disgust and repudiation of the Liberal candidate and his Conservative opponent, Sandino wrote to one of his supporters, "[These] political incompetents continue to vie for the invader's whip, the most disgusting aspect of which is that they are fighting like cats and dogs in the same bag to reach the presidency under a foreign watchman—which we will not permit."[192] The point of this indictment was to prepare the country for a third political party of workers and peasants backed by the Defending Army.

Sandino's attempt to form a provisional government never got off the ground. In a letter to Gen. Pedro Altamirano (9 November 1932), he noted that his army had become strong enough for one of his generals, Juan Gregorio Colindres, to proclaim himself provisional president of Nicaragua on the basis of the still nonexistent provisional government projected almost a year earlier.[193] For this act of political foolishness and personal vanity, Sandino promised to have him court-martialed. Meanwhile, he advised that, if the elections were won by the Conservatives, the Defending Army would settle the issue with bullets. But if the Liberals won, they would be pressured to make the following concessions: "To Sacasa we will propose military control of the republic by our army, for which the minister of war must be one of the members of our army; also the minister of finance and the minister of foreign affairs must be designated by our army, for which we designate respectively Dr. Es-colástico Lara and Calderón Ramírez."[194] Thus the plan to form a provisional government was not Sandino's only political option.

A related letter to Gens. Juan Pablo Umanzor and Juan Santos Morales (18 November 1932) notes that General Colindres had been deprived of his command and that all diplomatic affairs had been placed in the hands of General Portocarrero and Dr. Zepeda. Not yet knowing who had won the election, Sandino added that there would be time enough in January "*either* to reach an honorable settlement so that our army can retain military control of the Re-public and the ministries of war, finance, and foreign affairs *or* to obtain arms in sufficient quantity to confront the enemy in pitched battles."[195]

Sandino had become overly confident. Of the officially regis-tered electorate, slightly more than one-third had abstained from voting.[196] But he took too much credit for the abstentions and attached too much weight to the electoral strike called by the Nicaraguan workers' organizations that supported him. He falsely believed that his Defending Army had replaced the Conservative party as the second most powerful political force in the country. This explains the letter he sent in December to the foreign minis-ter of El Salvador, requesting recognition of his provisional govern-ment in the Segovias.[197] The elections, he explained, were nullified by having been controlled and administered by a foreign power. Meanwhile, his Defending Army had assumed control of a sub-stantial part of Nicaragua, more than half, in his overly sanguine estimate. But the would-be provisional government was never rec-ognized and died before it could take form.

The most that can be said for Sandino's estimate of the existing balance of forces is that the Defending Army had become strong enough to obtain a negotiated peace. For Sandino, three events helped to bring the civil war to a close. The first was the official and complete withdrawal of the marines—from then on the Na-tional Guard was on its own, even though it remained an instru-ment of U.S. policy. The second was Dr. Sacasa's assumption of the presidency and his efforts to come to terms with the Defending Army. And finally, there were the articles of peace worked out be-tween Dr. Sacasa's and Sandino's personal representatives, which effectively acknowledged the Defending Army to be the president's only safeguard against the National Guard and Anastasio Somoza's political ambitions.

The terms of peace were reproduced in the *Manifesto to the*

Peoples of the Earth.[198] The first point recognized that Sandino's struggle had been waged out of purely patriotic motives, without regard for any present or foreseeable political advantage. The second point committed the subscribing parties to respect the constitution and to maintain by all reasonable means the political and economic independence of Nicaragua. The third point specified the measures for guaranteeing the political security and economic livelihood of the soldiers to be demobilized from the Defending Army. It also provided for an emergency force of one hundred men under one of its generals to preserve law and order for a period of at least one year in the huge uncultivated lands to be allotted to the peasants who supported Sandino. The fourth point covered the formal cessation of hostilities. The fifth and last point made Sandino the temporary political and military authority in charge of San Rafael del Norte, a major guerrilla center and area of support for his Defending Army.

There was nothing humiliating about this agreement. Sandino would still have some troops at his disposal for the coming year. Since the second point obliged the government to maintain its economic distance from the United States, Sandino was in a position to resume the armed struggle and had a pretext for doing so should the government cave in to foreign pressure. It is noteworthy that he closed the discussion of the peace terms by indicating that they would be obeyed only as long as the government lived up to its part of the agreement.[199]

The peace terms were signed for lack of a feasible alternative. For years Sandino had told his fellow Nicaraguans that he would cease hostilities as soon as the marines withdrew. To continue the armed struggle after they withdrew would bring his credibility into question. If he did not lay down his arms, his countrymen would have strong reasons for blaming the Defending Army rather than the Liberals should the marines return to restore order. As he explained in a letter to one of his supporters, the peace was signed to prevent a new armed intervention that was barely behind the door, ready to return within less than a year in the expectation that Nicaraguans would continue fighting among themselves.[200]

That was far from his sole reason. In a letter the next day he defended himself against the charge of having abandoned the struggle without a fight.[201] There was no other alternative, explained Sandino. The popular will to continue the struggle had exhausted itself; the people were tired of continual warfare and needed a chance to recuperate. Moreover, the government was prepared to receive a loan of several million dollars to destroy his movement, at the price of submerging the country even deeper in political and economic dependency. Since the new government had been elected mainly by Liberals bordering on liberated territory, Sandino continued, his own support was being eroded. On top of this, he had exhausted his economic and military resources. The Defending Army was faced with the prospect of defeat at a moment when its troops could no longer seek asylum in neighboring Honduras and El Salvador owing to the imposition of reactionary political dictatorships in both countries. Thus his people needed a respite in the armed struggle, whatever they might decide to do afterward.

There are contradictory assessments of Sandino's decision to abandon the armed struggle. In Fabela's judgment, "a man who had always been untrusting, alert to every surprise, careful of his life and the lives of his men, became possessed by a patriotic mystique to interpret the historical occasion with the most gullible confidence."[202] Believing that he should honor his word, Sandino placed himself at the mercy of those who refused to honor theirs. This judgment is shared by Selser, who interprets Sandino's decision as a great error:

> His good faith or ingenuousness, which in political matters is inexcusable, placed him at the mercy of his enemies. He surrendered himself defenseless in the conviction that his own honesty was shared by others. . . . But he surrendered not only his own life but also the lives of those who had accompanied him during the years of hazardous and continuing struggle: back in their homes or about to return, they were beaten, persecuted, jailed, tortured, and finally murdered in a rash of sadism that disgracefully fills the history of the Central American peoples.[203]

Contemporary Sandinistas have a very different assessment of Sandino's decision. Jaime Wheelock argues that both the domestic and the international situation in 1933 were unfavorable to armed resistance.[204] The anti-imperialist and antioligarchical character of Sandino's struggle ceased to be convincing once the invaders withdrew and Nicaragua's presumed traitors had been voted out of the government. The nominal assumption of political power by Dr. Sacasa, a far more popular figure than Moncada, undermined the possibilities of prolonging the armed conflict. To this unfavorable internal situation, Wheelock adds the growing fear of a second world war. Because the focus of the political Left had shifted to a worldwide struggle against fascism as a condition of preserving peace, the Defending Army's war of liberation could no longer count on widespread popular sympathy abroad. Humberto Ortega offers a similar argument, adding that Sandino's escalation of the armed struggle had so depleted the Defending Army's resources that he was compelled to make a strategic retreat.[205]

If Sandino was as honest and sincere as Fabela and Selser claim, then they should have believed his own explanation, that the Defending Army needed to recover and build up strength. Wheelock and Ortega rely on facts rather than conjecture. Both Fabela and Selser underestimated the relevance of objective conditions and exaggerated the importance of personal factors in shaping Sandino's decision. They construed his signing of the peace terms as a sign of momentary weakness rather than as a response to political and military realities.

Sandino concluded his *Manifesto to the Peoples of the Earth* with a brief discussion entitled "The Present Moment." There he presaged the beginning of a fourth stage of his struggle. Meanwhile, he would remain in the Segovias, where he planned to provide moral support for Dr. Sacasa's government, although he would continue acting independently of it. What would he do there? "I will take advantage of the time to organize agricultural cooperatives in these attractive regions that statesmen have neglected for centuries."[206] But considering his revolutionary ideology and commitment to the social transformation of Nicaragua, there is little reason to believe he had abandoned his political and military objectives. Humberto Ortega for one concludes that "Sandino opted for a flexible political-military policy to achieve through unarmed political struggle the accumulation of human, political, material, and military forces . . . that would permit at a later moment the unleashing of a revolutionary civil war for the seizure of power, and at the same time better conditions for confronting a new armed intervention by the Yankees."[207]

Sandino boasted that some thirty-six thousand square kilometers of uncultivated lands were made available to his soldiers. Located in the Coco River basin, the area comprised roughly one-fourth of the national territory. "We consider this region to be the Federal District of Central America," Sandino wrote in his manifesto, the capital of a projected union of the five original Central American nations. To this new capital, he added, "the entire Central American proletariat should come along with proletarians from whatever other part of the globe."[208] For what purpose? Ostensibly, to make this Central American union a reality and the basis of a still broader anti-imperialist Latin American alliance. By such measures Sandino hoped to implement the March 1929 project of the

Defending Army, his as yet unpublished plan for realizing Bolívar's supreme dream.[209] But that was not his only dream. His Central American union had a revolutionary purpose: to become a center of proletarian power in the region. It amounted to a revival of his Defending Army's earlier plan for establishing a Central American commune, a workers' and peasants' government that would subvert the established order.[210]

After the peace terms were accepted, Sandino's strategy was to convince the new government that the National Guard was unconstitutional and that resistance to it was a continuation of the Defending Army's struggle against direct intervention by the United States. As Sandino described the situation in Nicaragua to a member of his general staff in May 1933, "The National Guard is the enemy of the government and of ourselves, because it is an institution contrary to the laws and the constitution of the republic; it was created by an agreement between the Liberal and Conservative parties at the instigation of the North American interventionists; this Guard tacitly considers itself to be superior to the government, and this is why in many instances the orders of the president are not obeyed."[211]

In his last manifesto, "Timid Nicaragua" (10 June 1933), Sandino further clarified the new situation in which he hoped to use the peace to demonstrate the disloyalty and unconstitutionality of the National Guard.[212] The Constitution, Sandino declared, was a product of the U.S. armed intervention, because it was elaborated in 1911 and signed by Adolfo Díaz, whom the Yankees had imposed as their choice for president. Even so, it was the only constitution Nicaraguans had, and at that moment it was better than any alternative Congress might propose. It would be replaced when his plan to organize a third Autonomist party, the political counterpart of his Defending Army, got under way: "Only the nascent Autonomist party is capable of elaborating by means of a plebiscite the constitution of Nicaragua for the Nicaraguans."[213] Sandino aimed to show that, in peace as well as war, he would continue to uphold the constitution and to support the government of President Sacasa, which had acquired legitimacy by virtue of its agreement with the Defending Army: "The popularity of Dr. Sacasa in the recent elections gave me reason not to fight him but . . . to unite his popularity with the energies of our army, so that the Nicaraguan people might understand our motives"—the defense of the constitution against the unconstitutional National Guard.[214]

Sandino observed that no government since 1909 had the opportunity that the present one had to assert as a matter of national policy Nicaragua's political and economic independence, provided the country's traditional timidity were overcome. The Defending Army had long been an example of courage and was now an example of national unity for having announced that all Nicaraguans were brothers with an obligation to work for the national interest. At the same time, Sandino acknowledged the vulnerability of his demobilized army in the face of the aggressive and misnamed National Guard, which was not a signatory to the peace and had yet to be legitimized by Sacasa's government. The government, too, was on trial, since it had become obliged by its agreement with the Defending Army to uphold Nicaragua's political and economic independence.

The purpose of "Timid Nicaragua" was to impress on the people their right to disobey the National Guard, as long as it remained outside the constitution. Since it was the only viable military authority rivaling his demobilized Defending Army, Sandino launched a war of propaganda aimed at undermining it. He publicly suggested reorganizing his Defending Army as a popular militia: "In any case, our president has the obligation of arming the civilian population of the republic and of ordering any renegade to surrender his arms. It is unbefitting for men who consider themselves free to kneel before an army that is unconstitutional . . . an army of irresponsibles, irresponsible because it exists outside the law."[215]

We have seen that Sandino planned to organize an Autonomist party as the political vehicle of his demobilized army. But it never materialized because of his continuing preoccupation with the National Guard, which threatened to become the real power in the country. The only match for it was what remained of his Defending Army.

Within six months of signing the peace agreement, Sandino resolved to mobilize his troops to defend the legally constituted government against the threat of a military coup. He mobilized them after receiving news that sabotage had destroyed the stock of munitions at the war arsenal in Managua. Suspecting foul play from elements of the Guard, he notified President Sacasa that he had mobilized more than six hundred men to march wherever the president might direct. As he wrote to the president (7 August 1933),

> We have taken up arms again and have sent forth simultaneous orders to all our people who are now ready to march forth wherever duty calls. . . . I take this opportunity to inform you that the arms received, about which you gave notice in the past, came to five hundred pieces that belonged to the Honduran revolution. However, if you are willing, we will accept in these camps of yours any number of Springfields,

Thompsons, and Lewises that you want us to have in the confidence that, if these weapons should ever be fired, it will be into the ribs of our enemies.[216]

Was this the chance Sandino had been waiting for? In a letter to Dr. Escolástico Lara and Norberto Salinas de Aguilar (6 October 1933), he mentioned the dangers involved in leaving his headquarters in the Segovias, but said he would continue to take such minor risks "as long as events do not come to a head."[217] He acknowledged the inconvenience of continuing to work toward the organization of a third political party. Instead, he proposed to limit his activities to maintaining his moral authority, in order that his movement might become "the decisive factor in the nation's destiny at the first opportunity that presents itself."[218] This was tantamount to preparing his men for a new trial by arms.

Somoza in particular was apprehensive that Sandino was secretly preparing for a confrontation with the National Guard. Besides the weapons turned over to him by Honduran revolutionaries, Sandino had retained most of his own by subtly evading the terms of the peace treaty, surrendering to the government only tokens that were mostly in need of repair—the best of which he received back as arms for his emergency force.[219] Far from being total, as the president's delegate Sofonías Salvatierra described the disarming of Sandino's soldiers, Somoza claimed the disarmament had been a farce and a cause for laughter among the officers of the National Guard who witnessed it. As Sandino acknowledged in an interview published in the Nicaraguan daily *La Prensa* (18 February 1934), "The National Guard is not a legally constituted body; therefore I am not obliged to surrender arms to it."[220] Asked by reporters if he was still in possession of arms other than those of his special armed guards and emergency force of one hundred, commanded by Gen. Francisco Estrada, Sandino replied, "You can't ask me to fulfill the terms of the peace agreement if the other side has not abided by them. . . . The letter of the text says that I shall gradually surrender arms to the legitimate authorities. . . . It also stipulated that we would be given guarantees and this has not been fulfilled."[221] Asked whether he believed the National Guard would prevent the emergence of a separate state within the state, he replied, "But the situation here is that there are not two but three states: that of the president of the republic, that of the National Guard, and my own. The Guard does not obey the president; we do not obey the Guard because it is illegal; and that is the way matters stand."[222]

Sandino concluded the interview by stressing his desire for peace under protection of the law. But the National Guard lay outside the law. Consequently, he would surrender his arms only if the National Guard also surrendered its arms to the president. Meanwhile, there would have to be two contending military forces superficially at peace but ready for war.

The politics and strategy of the Defending Army had responded not only to Sandino's assessments of Nicaragua's history, but also to what Sandino called the "theater of events," or concrete issues surfacing at different stages of his struggle. To each stage corresponded a different policy. As the struggle intensified, his enunciated political objectives became more radical and his strategy more diversified. As he grew stronger militarily, he became more preoccupied with the struggle on the political front. The extension of his military control from the Segovias eastward to the Atlantic coast raised his Defending Army to the status of a third power alongside the Nicaraguan government and the National Guard. Even after it was demobilized in February 1933, Sandino gave the impression that it was still tantamount to a state within the state.

In December 1932 the American ambassador in Managua had asked retiring president Moncada to appoint Anastasio Somoza as head of the National Guard. A Liberal of Moncada's stripe, Somoza was considered by the United States to be one of its faithful servants. Since incoming president Sacasa was of dubious value to the United States because of his willingness to negotiate with Sandino, Somoza was installed as the head of a virtual government of his own. Even when the United States withdrew the marines, their presence was still felt in the form of a watchdog. Thus the National Guard watched carefully over the duly elected government and disputed Sandino's independent base of power in the Segovias.

The crisis of Nicaraguan liberalism that came to a head in May 1927 was not a passing phase in the history of the Liberal party, a minor ailment from which it later recovered. Unlike General Moncada, President Sacasa sought Sandino's help in governing the country and in containing the growing power of the National Guard. But the Liberal Somoza was more than a match for both.

In February 1934 Somoza ordered the National Guard to kill Sandino and then to massacre the bulk of Sandino's armed followers in the agricultural cooperative of Wiwilí. Two years later he directed a successful military coup against President Sacasa. In June 1936 he had himself nominated as the Liberal party's candidate in the elections scheduled for November. After triumphing over his Conservative opponent, he became president in 1937. Then began the drift toward a virtual dictatorship by the Somoza family, a dynasty that fell only with the Sandinista revolution of July 1979.

The Liberal party, which had recovered political power under President Moncada in 1928, held onto it tenaciously for fully half a century. In retrospect, what defined the Liberal party was not men of Sacasa's stature but untrustworthy leaders like Moncada and Somoza, the Liberal counterparts of Díaz and Chamorro.

Stimson or Sandino?

How astute politically were Sandino's assessments? That U.S. intervention in Nicaragua violated both the real interests of his people and the country's formal right to sovereignty was a fundamental premise of his struggle. But was U.S. intervention really an attempt to dominate the country? Not in the view of the State Department, which believed that the United States had intervened to protect Nicaragua's political and economic independence.

In his *American Policy in Nicaragua* (1927), Henry Stimson explicitly denied that the Monroe Doctrine was being used to extend the influence of his government over Central America. That doctrine was directed against the encroachment of European nations in the Western Hemisphere, he claimed, and should not be confused with his government's Isthmian policy of maintaining exclusive control over the interoceanic waterways through Central America while upholding those republics' claims to independence.[223] For a century, he recalled, the United States had defended those republics against some of their own leaders who were convinced annexation would be beneficial. "On more than one occasion has one or the other of them come to us with proposals for annexation or for a cession to us of portions of their territory and we have declined the offer."[224] If the United States had been guilty of imperialist designs on these smaller countries, it would have promoted quarrels and divisions among them. Instead, he assured, "our influence has uniformly been used for peace."[225] What was mistakenly believed to have been a violation of Nicaragua's sovereignty had come in response to earnest requests by the Nicaraguan government or by the party in opposition, Stimson insisted, to restore law and order in that strife-ridden land. He maintained that "the history of our recent action in Nicaragua . . . makes it clear that in no way have we transgressed upon the sovereignty and independence of our sister nation."[226]

Contrary to Sandino's assessment, Stimson denied that his government had been involved in the rebellion that placed the Conservatives back in power in 1910. It had sent its naval forces to Nicaragua to protect American life and property. Not until 1912

were the marines "twice drawn into serious combat with revolutionary bodies." And after 1912 only a token force of one hundred
marines remained in the capital at the request of the Nicaraguan
government.[227] For Stimson, this was not a military occupation,
much less the imposition of an imperialist power on a defenseless
banana republic.

That the marines were necessary to maintain law and order in
Nicaragua, Stimson believed, was evident from what happened
after they returned home in August 1925. Two months later General Chamorro seized the fortress dominating Managua, following
which both the Conservative president and Liberal vice-president
fled the country. With the backing of the extreme Conservative faction in Congress, the membership of that body was reconstituted
by the expulsion of eighteen Liberals and moderate Conservatives.
Chamorro was then elected substitute president in January 1926,
"over the protest of the American government, and against its
warning that under the policy of the Washington conferences of
1907 and 1923 Chamorro could not expect to be recognized as a legitimate government either by us or by the other four Central
American republics."[228] Since U.S. opposition effectively prevented
Chamorro from obtaining the foreign loans he needed, he was compelled to abdicate in October 1926.

The thorny question was how to find a legitimate replacement.
Contrary to Sandino's interpretation of the constitution, Stimson
argued that Vice-President Sacasa had no rightful claim to the
presidency. The deposed president was in California and Sacasa was
in Guatemala, having been out of the country for almost a year.
Citing article 106 of Nicaragua's constitution, Stimson noted that
in the event of the temporary lack of a president, the office of chief
executive devolved on the vice-president, but that in default of the
latter, Congress was constitutionally obligated to elect a substitute.
An extraordinary session of Congress was accordingly convoked
that included the eighteen expelled members. On 10 November
1925, of the sixty-seven members of Congress, forty-four voted for
Díaz, two for the deposed president, seven abstained, and fourteen
were absent.[229] Thus Díaz was elected by an overwhelming majority. The action of the Congress, Stimson contended, "could not be
rightfully claimed to be tainted by the coup d'etat of Chamorro,
nor could it be rightfully said that Díaz was disqualified in any
other way."[230]

Yet it was precisely at that point that Mexico recognized
Sacasa's revolutionary government. Even before this provocative act,
Stimson contended, arms and munitions had been sent from Mex-

ico to the Liberal forces in four shipments, the first as early as August 1926.[231] In contrast to U.S. policy, which was committed to peace and stability in Nicaragua, the Mexican government was fomenting and spreading a climate of violence. That was why the marines returned, "in response to the warning of the Nicaraguan government itself that it could not protect . . . [foreign] lives and property."[232] Far from violating Nicaragua's sovereignty, Stimson concluded, the United States did not take the side of the Conservative government in the civil war that ensued, nor did it interfere with the operations of the revolutionaries by preventing them from taking cities where they enjoyed military superiority.[233]

In an effort to promote peace and prevent bloodshed, Stimson continued, the United States imposed an embargo on arms shipments to both of the contending parties. At the same time it called on Mexico and the other Central American countries to join in the embargo. But Mexico refused, an action Stimson interpreted as a provocation.[234] Mexico was the first to grant recognition to Sacasa's revolutionary regime and it was also attempting to export a revolution of its own. Unlike Sandino, who believed that Nicaragua desperately needed a Mexican-type revolution, Stimson tried to forestall this potential threat to U.S. interests.

Stimson also disputed Sandino's assessment of some of Nicaragua's top political leaders. On leaving that country, he recalled, "There remained with me . . . the memory of two patriotic men, one a Conservative and one a Liberal, each willing to sacrifice personal ambition and party interest to the higher welfare of his country and each willing to trust in the honor and good will of the United States—Adolfo Díaz and José María Moncada."[235]

In former days Díaz had been a political friend of Chamorro, wrote Stimson, "but as I was reliably informed in Managua, he had advised against Chamorro's coup d'etat."[236] Whereas Sandino conjectured that Díaz had been party to the conspiracy, Stimson showed a remarkable gullibility in accepting the word of Díaz's fellow Conservatives. As yet, nobody knows what Díaz's role was during those eventful days in August 1924.

Stimson was ready to believe the best of Díaz, who had expressed his readiness to give up the presidency should that become necessary for achieving peace. Since Díaz was ineligible to succeed himself in 1928, it seemed to Stimson that he could not have been motivated by personal ambition in this apparent gesture of generosity. "He was so convinced of the necessity of American supervision for that election that in order to make it entirely fair he was ready to surrender all the traditional power of the presidency which

had been heretofore used to influence and control election results."[237] In addition, he was willing to disband the army and to establish in its place an impartial constabulary or national police
force under American officers. Stimson praised Díaz's selflessness
in such matters indispensable to peace, his intelligent approval of
U.S. proposals, and his cooperation in securing them. His past
record in dealings with the United States showed that he could be
relied on.

Would the proper course have been to persuade both Díaz and
Sacasa to retire in favor of some neutral candidate? Stimson recalled that for days he sat listening to suggestions of substitutes for
Díaz, but discovered behind every candidate the expectation of political gain.[238] Magnanimous toward his political opponents, Díaz
had been criticized by his fellow Conservatives for being too toler-
ant. This was the quality of character Stimson was looking for:
"Liberal leaders told me over and over again that Díaz was the Conservative most acceptable to their party."[239] In short, he appeared to
Stimson to be the most patriotic and qualified man for the job.

He found similar qualities of character in General Moncada.
"Though a Liberal, he had not hesitated to oppose the Liberal tyrant Zelaya in 1909."[240] This was his first recommendation, that
Moncada placed the interests of his country above party loyalties.
"He had been a friend to U.S. influence in Central America."[241]
This was his second recommendation, that his nationalism was
consistent with an intelligent assessment of U.S. support for Nicaragua's political independence and economic development. "I also
felt that having personally shared the sufferings and losses caused
by the revolution, he might be less technical in approving a substantially just compromise than the civilian leaders of his party."[242]
Stimson would not be disappointed. When the two met at Tipitapa
on 4 May 1927, Moncada insisted that the Constitutionalist forces
would not fight the United States, even though he opposed the continuation of Adolfo Díaz as president. His concern for his country's
welfare was beyond reproach: "He said he did not wish a single life
to be lost on that issue between us."[243] He asked only for a letter
from Stimson outlining the U.S. conditions for peace, which he
would use to persuade his followers to lay down their arms. It is
reasonable to assume that this was the letter Moncada carried in
his pocket when he returned to his troops and that, contrary to
Sandino's conjecture, it did not contain assurances that Moncada
would become the next president. If Moncada had presidential ambitions at the time, he had carefully concealed them from Stimson.

Contrary to Sandino's account of the peace conference, Stimson reported that Moncada consulted Sacasa's delegates and they did not oppose the peace terms. It was they who suggested that General Moncada be invited to the conference.[244] When the rendezvous was arranged for 4 May, Stimson and the delegates drove together to Tipitapa. As Stimson recalled, "I turned over to him the three Sacasa delegates and told him that I should be glad to have a conference with him myself after he had finished with them."[245] Afterward, Stimson met privately with Moncada and then, on the general's recommendation, the Sacasa delegates were called in and informed of the proposed settlement. "After a few moments consultation, they told me that Sacasa would not resist the action of the United States."[246] The alleged conflict between Sacasa's delegates and General Moncada either did not exist at all or Sandino so exaggerated it that it did not correspond to what happened. If anything, Stimson's account confirms Sandino's doubts about Sacasa's patriotism.

Peace is what the people wanted, Stimson believed, and Díaz and Moncada were responsible for giving them peace. Although some Sacasa extremists thought Moncada a traitor, Moncada had consulted with Sacasa's delegates, had come to an agreement with them, and was willing to retire as the head of the Constitutionalist forces to end the civil war.

But was Moncada really trustworthy? He kept his word but was he telling Stimson the truth? "Moncada told me [that], having promised to join in the settlement, [Sandino] afterward broke his word and with about 150 followers, most of whom he said were Honduranean mercenaries, had secretly left his army and started northward toward the Honduran border."[247] Sandino acknowledged that he broke his word to Moncada, but the issue of the Honduran mercenaries was an irresponsible fabrication on Moncada's part. This report was followed by another: "I was told that Sandino had lived in Mexico for twenty-two years, where he served under Pancho Villa, and only came back to Nicaragua on the outbreak of the revolution in order to enjoy the opportunities for violence and pillage which it offered."[248] In effect, Moncada painted Sandino as a bandit and soldier of fortune without any moral scruples. Moncada lied or he was misinformed. Pancho Villa dissolved his surviving forces in 1920, for which he was rewarded with a fat government pension. And Sandino did not leave Nicaragua until 1920, much less arrive in Mexico before 1923.

Moncada deceived not only Stimson but also his own officers. When he returned to his troops he persuaded them to surrender, saying that otherwise they would have to fight the U.S. Marines in addition to the government's troops. As Stimson acknowledged in another work, the letter he gave to Moncada took the form of a "threat that if Moncada did not accept, the United States would forcibly support the Díaz government." However, the letter was only a means of assisting what Stimson called Moncada's states-manlike labors. Stimson would have been extremely embarrassed if Moncada had failed to persuade his fellow generals to surrender, for, as he also acknowledged, "he had no authority to pledge his Government to virtual war in Nicaragua!"[249]

The goal of peace supposedly justified the hoax that both Stimson and Moncada perpetrated on the unsuspecting Constitu-tionalist generals. Only Sandino was not deceived by it. It is true that, not being privy to the settlement, he misinterpreted some of its points. But because the peace settlement meant that all the treaties with the United States remained in force, he had reasons for believing that it was not in the national interest. The Bryan-Chamorro Treaty had been the most damaging, he believed, an interpretation that was shared by some American officials and belatedly by Gen. Emiliano Chamorro himself.

Elihu Root, secretary of state during Teddy Roosevelt's second administration, opposed adoption of the controversial treaty. As he wrote in a private letter subsequently published in the *Congres-sional Record* (13 January 1927), he felt disturbed by the thought that, because the treaty was negotiated under conditions of a U.S. military presence in Nicaragua, it might not really have repre-sented the country's national interests.[250] He noted that this doubt was shared by many Nicaraguans and other Central American peoples. He had been especially dismayed by the reports from the chief of the U.S. Marines in Nicaragua, who claimed that the Nica-raguan government was not freely elected, that the elections for Congress were for the most part fraudulent, and that the Liberal party in opposition represented a majority of the voters. In view of those reports, Root concluded that the Nicaraguan government with which the United States was making the treaty retained power only because of the presence of the marines.

In a telegram to Pres. Franklin Delano Roosevelt in December 1938, General Chamorro implicitly acknowledged his mistake in signing the treaty. Besides violating Nicaragua's sovereignty, he ar-gued, the treaty infringed on the rights of other Central American countries, it interfered with hemispheric security, and it belied the newly adopted Good Neighbor Policy.[251] In Cuba the comparable Platt Amendment had been abrogated in May 1934 in return for Cuban commercial concessions to the United States, but the Good

Neighbor Policy had not altered the terms of the Nicaraguan treaty. Actually, the United States never used its rights to construct a naval base in the Gulf of Fonseca or the Corn Islands. Even so, it was not until 1970 that the treaty was finally abrogated, and then only when the tonnage of international freight liners had so increased that navigation up the San Juan River had ceased to be economically feasible.

Basic to Sandino's conception of U.S. imperialism in Nicaragua were the policies of the White House backed by a majority of the American people, the role of the Wall Street bankers, and the assistance given to both by Nicaragua's corrupt political leaders. His language was abusive and his ideological bias was evident. But despite his errors concerning the details of U.S. intervention, he was among the few Nicaraguans who grasped the extent of his country's political and economic subordination to the United States. Although his Defending Army had contributed to the withdrawal of the "invaders" and to discrediting the "traitors," he predicted that the war in Nicaragua was not yet over. A half century later his predictions were confirmed. In retrospect, it is evident that Stimson's account of U.S. involvement was mistaken and that Sandino's political assessments were for the most part accurate.

PART TWO. *The Sandinistas*

5. From Sandino to Sandinismo

To this point we have been considering the thought of one man, the original philosopher of the Nicaraguan Revolution and founder of its Defending Army. We now shift our focus to the collective leadership of the movement he helped to spawn, the Sandinista Front of National Liberation (FSLN). Although Sandino's movement was so persecuted and decimated that it was eventually wiped out, it re-emerged more than a quarter century later with the founding of the FSLN. Unlike the Defending Army, this new organization was conceived and nurtured by a political-military collective consisting of past and present members of its National Directorate.

The FSLN owes a debt to Sandino for his political assessments of Nicaraguan reality, revolutionary strategy, and ideology of liberation. At the same time it is indebted to the new Marxism that emerged from the Cuban Revolution in the works of Fidel Castro and Che Guevara. Unlike original Sandinismo, contemporary Sandinismo has shed Sandino's anarchism and rational communism for this new Third World variant of Marxism-Leninism.

Recovering Sandino's Thought

The story begins with Carlos Fonseca Amador's recovery of Sandino's political thought.[1] Gen. Abraham Rivera surrendered in March 1934, and the remnants of Sandino's army under Gen. Pedro Altamirano were forced to disband in November 1937.[2] Sandino's movement completely disappeared from the political scene. He was remembered as a bandit—little more. In a November 1970 interview in Havana, Fonseca recalled the quarter century during which Sandino passed into oblivion. Before 1958 his name was heard only in whispers: "In an ambience of terror, obscurantism, domination by the reactionary parties, and conservatism among Nicaragua's intellectuals, the name of Sandino was a murmur."[3]

A bastard like Sandino, with a prosperous father and a servant girl for a mother, Fonseca launched his political career in 1955 by joining the Nicaraguan Socialist party (PSN), the established communist party in Nicaragua.[4] That same year he began the task of compiling and cataloguing Sandino's writings.[5] His short life (1936–1976) straddled the Cuban Revolution in much the same way that Sandino's had straddled the Mexican. Indeed, the triumph of the Cuban Revolution in 1959 contributed to the second turning point in his life, when Fonseca quit the PSN to become a professional revolutionary of a new type.[6] Henceforth, he would dedicate himself not only to rescuing Sandino's political legacy, but also to building a new revolutionary movement independent of the PSN.

Fonseca's life reads like a travelogue across national boundaries, involving Communist party and guerrilla activities interrupted by a series of imprisonments and deportations.[7] In and out of jail in 1956, he was imprisoned a second time on his return from the Soviet Union in 1957, and was again arrested in 1958 and deported to Guatemala. From there he made his way to Mexico, then to Cuba early in 1959. Shortly afterward he was flown to a secret base in Honduras for guerrilla training toward a planned invasion of Nicaragua. He was severely wounded when the camp was attacked and dismantled by the Honduran army. When he recovered he severed his relations with the PSN and returned to Cuba. Thus ended the first phase of his political career.

The second phase began with his clandestine return to Nicaragua in 1960. He was again imprisoned, deported to Guatemala, and reimprisoned in that country. He escaped and once more made his way to Havana, returning to Nicaragua via Costa Rica in 1961. That same year in Honduras, together with representatives of other youth and student movements, he founded the FSLN. After participating in the FSLN's first armed struggle in 1962–1963, he was captured in 1964, imprisoned for six months, and again deported to Guatemala. He returned to Nicaragua in 1966 to participate in the FSLN's second armed struggle. Imprisoned in Costa Rica in 1968, he was released in an exchange of hostages and flown to Havana in 1970. There he represented the FSLN until he returned to his country to engage in another major guerrilla campaign in 1975. He was killed in a National Guard ambush in November 1976.

The movement Fonseca founded had international connections and support far beyond that of Sandino's Defending Army. The philosophy of the FSLN was shaped not only by Sandino's thought, but also by these international connections.

Fonseca had already acquired an appreciation of Sandino's

struggle when, under the influence of the Cuban Revolution, he realized that the continuation of that struggle might accomplish for Nicaragua what the July 26 movement had achieved through Fidel Castro's rediscovery of José Martí. He came to understand that the making of a successful revolution requires more than the standard revolutionary repertoire of Marxist-Leninist theory and strategy. Without native roots and a popular and nationally based revolutionary ideology, he believed, Marxism-Leninism in Nicaragua was destined to remain the thought of a political sect.[8] The task he set himself was to rework Sandino's thought so that it might become the national vehicle, the carrier of Marxism-Leninism in Nicaragua.

In notes he scribbled in prison, Tomás Borge recalls that he, Fonseca, and Silvio Mayorga were recruited into the PSN in 1955 and together began the task of recovering Sandino's written legacy. Fonseca, who had organized a party cell at the National University in León along with a Marxist-Leninist study group focusing on Sandino's thought, conceived this project. From the start there was resistance from other members of the PSN. To this day the party considers Sandino to have been the ideologue of self-employed artisans and small shopkeepers, who struggled against the American occupation rather than against imperialism and never clearly articulated the peasants' need for land. Writes Borge, "Carlos expressed his doubts concerning those arguments. He proposed an in-depth investigation of Sandino's thought."[9]

Fonseca relied on Borge, whose father had supported Sandino and considered himself a Sandinista. Interviewed by a Mexican journalist in April 1979, Borge recalled his father's contribution: "My father had been linked by family ties to Sandino and had several books . . . [on Sandino] that he gave me to read. Among them was a volume by Sofonías Salvatierra, who was my uncle. . . . I also read a book by Alemán Bolaños and several others, including the book supposedly written by Somoza to defame Sandino—which boomeranged because for us it was one of the principal sources on Sandino's struggle."[10]

The first book Fonseca's study group tackled was in fact Somoza's biography of Sandino.[11] Ironically, the dictator's effort to document Sandino's links to the Mexican Communist party was the best argument he could have given for rescuing Sandino's legacy. By presenting evidence of Sandino's "bolshevism," Somoza's book strongly recommended itself to the youth of the PSN interested in the history of their country. By emphasizing the subversive content of Sandino's political philosophy and his efforts to make a communist revolution in Nicaragua up until the day he was assassinated, Somoza made Sandino appear reprehensible to respectable readers, but made him a hero to Fonseca's group.

After assimilating Somoza's biography, Fonseca's group turned to Salvatierra's *Sandino o la tragedia de un pueblo* (Madrid, 1934), followed by Ramón de Belausteguigoitia's *Con Sandino en Nicaragua* (Madrid, 1934). The next books on the list included Salvador Calderón Ramírez's *Ultimos días de Sandino* (Mexico, 1934) and finally Gregorio Selser's works, originally published in Buenos Aires in 1958–1959. As Borge recalls, "With exactness and perseverance, Carlos wrote notes and sifted out passages from Sandino's rich and varied epistles. These he organized in his *Ideario sandinista*, a primer of the first concepts that circulated among the FSLN's militants."[12]

To help diffuse Sandino's ideas, Fonseca founded a review called *Nueva Nicaragua* and a modest publishing outfit with the same name. Launched in 1957, both provided ideological support for the New Nicaragua movement he organized in 1960—the first youth movement inspired and guided by Sandino's ideas. The Cuban Revolution was one of its major sources of inspiration. Says Borge, "Fidel was for us the resurrection of Sandino!"[13]

The bibliographical list Borge provides leaves out a substantial part of the works actually studied. From September 1956 to March 1959 he was in prison and could no longer participate in the work of recovering Sandino's thought. Guillermo Rothschuh Tablada, director of the Central National Institute "Miguel Ramírez Goyena" in Managua, where Fonseca began working as a librarian in May 1955 before going on to the university to study law, adds to Borge's list Emigdio Maraboto's *Sandino ante el coloso* (originally published in Veracruz, 1929), Carleton Beals's *Banana Gold* (New York, 1932), and Gustavo Alemán Bolaños's *Sandino el libertador* (Mexico, 1951).[14] Included in the *Ideario sandinista* are numerous passages from Sandino's writings taken from Alemán Bolaños's work.

Víctor Tirado López, a former militant in the Mexican Communist party, has analyzed the elements of Fonseca's political thought. He traveled to Nicaragua in the early sixties to join the FSLN and, after years of fighting in the mountains, rose to become a member of its nine-man National Directorate. In a speech delivered on the third anniversary of Fonseca's death (8 November 1979), Tirado ranked Fonseca next to Sandino as Nicaragua's second greatest revolutionary thinker.[15] Fonseca rescued Sandino's ideas from oblivion, reedited them, and trained a new revolutionary vanguard on their foundations. "I am convinced that in converting Sandino's thought into the doctrine of the Front of National Liberation, Carlos provided the key to the Nicaraguan Revolution." That key, Tirado believes, was a body of national rather than foreign ideas: Fonseca provided a patriotic basis for the revolution of July 1979 in "the opinions, projects, plans, programs, conceptions, and actions of Sandino."[16]

As a vehicle for diffusing and applying Sandino's ideas, Fonseca's New Nicaragua movement became the impulse behind two other youth organizations. In 1959 the Nicaraguan Patriotic Youth (JPN) had been organized clandestinely and independently of Fonseca's former study group, but the following year he convinced its leaders to adopt Sandino's philosophy as a guide.[17] Silvio Mayorga became its new general secretary. And in 1960 Borge founded another youth movement, the Nicaraguan Revolutionary Youth (JRN), among Nicaraguan exiles in Costa Rica.[18] The presence of a large number of young exiles not only in Costa Rica but also in Honduras, Guatemala, and Venezuela convinced him of the need for a second clandestine youth group to carry on revolutionary propaganda outside the country.

A year later, in July 1961, the leaders of these three youth movements met in Tegucigalpa, where they fused their respective organizations into a single unitary front.[19] Yet it was not until 1963, according to Borge, that Fonseca succeeded in imposing Sandino's intellectual legacy and the name "Sandinista" on the newly formed front.[20]

It was not an easy task. In his prison notes Borge mentions a fourth founder of the FSLN, Noël Guerrero, who had participated with Fonseca in the planned invasion of Nicaragua from Cuba via Honduras in 1959.[21] The senior member of the founding group, he resisted the imposition of Sandino's legacy. Several years later he broke with Fonseca in the Honduran jungles, where a second expedition was being prepared at the juncture of the Coco and Bocay rivers.[22]

In Mexico, Guerrero had organized an exile group of his own, the Nicaraguan Unitary Front (FUN).[23] According to Germán Ordóñez Pomares, an FSLN commander and one of the first to join up with Fonseca in 1961, "Carlos proposed to call the new revolutionary movement the Sandinista Front. But Noël Guerrero, who was . . . one of the most prepared politically, wanted to call it the Nicaraguan Unitary Front to bring together all of the regime's opponents."[24] Until Fonseca succeeded in imposing the name he wanted on the Front, it was directed militarily by a surviving veteran of Sandino's campaigns, Col. Santos López, and politically by Guerrero.[25]

Fonseca insisted on linking the contemporary struggle by Marxist-Leninists, who had come under the influence of the Cuban Revolution, with Sandino's earlier struggle against imperialism and dictatorship. He was the first Communist in Nicaragua to steep himself in his country's national history and Sandino's struggle in particular, which he took as a model for a new generation of Nicaraguan revolutionaries. He wanted the people to understand that the new struggle being launched in Nicaragua was "the continuation of a still unfinished war started by patriots and revolutionaries of former times under conditions peculiar to their epoch."[26]

The rescue of Sandino's political legacy took two forms. The first and most urgent was Fonseca's compilation of a basic anthology of Sandino's political ideas, his *Ideario político del General Augusto César Sandino,* referred to by Borge as the *Ideario sandinista.* The principal document for instructing FSLN cadres in Sandino's thought, it began to circulate when the parent organization was founded in 1961. Fonseca organized Sandino's thought under six basic headings pertaining to people's war, social program, revolutionary politics, internationalism, imperialism, and moral integrity.[27] There is considerable overlapping and the reasons for this ordering are unclear, although there is an apparent progression from Sandino's discussion of Nicaragua's immediate problems to more abstract concerns. Patriotism emerges as the thread tying all these ideas together.

In addition to this anthology, Fonseca wrote a brief biography of his hero entitled *Sandino, guerrillero proletario,* completed shortly before the FSLN launched its second armed operation in 1966. It was the first biography to stress the combined proletarian and revolutionary character of Sandino's war of national liberation. Sandino is presented as a skilled worker, a mechanic by trade, whose original guerrilla contingent consisted of workers—the miners of San Albino.[28] But to survive in the countryside required a thorough knowledge of the terrain and the assistance of the peasant population, so Sandino expanded his original proletarian nucleus to include peasants. Although these came to predominate in determining the social composition of the guerrillas, Fonseca believed that the original proletarian component continued to shape Sandino's social program.[29] Here we have the intellectual thrust of the pamphlet and his own justification for reviving Sandino's struggle for national and social liberation in connection with the Marxism of Lenin, Castro, Guevara, and Ho Chi Minh.[30]

Another noteworthy feature of Fonseca's biography is its stress on the revolutionary content of Sandino's struggle from the moment he returned to Nicaragua in 1926. "Throughout the years of his struggle, from the very beginning until the end of the resistance, one becomes aware of the program of social transformation that Sandino championed."[31] Fonseca also makes a point of Sandino's having been influenced by the Russian as well as the Mexican revolutions. His only criticism of Sandino is that the objective conditions of the nascent anti-imperialist struggle in the Third World "did not permit him to complement his correct military strategy with a correct political strategy that would guarantee the continuity of the revolutionary process."[32] Fonseca believed that the proletarian thrust of Sandino's struggle lacked a scientific basis in a Marxist-Leninist understanding of contemporary society.

How accurate was Fonseca's portrayal of the hero of the Segovias? Actually, he and the FSLN recovered only those aspects of Sandino's thought they considered useful in activating ideologically the movement of national liberation bearing Sandino's name. The anarcho-communist foundations of his political philosophy were passed over along with his bizarre and politically embarrassing theosophical ideas. Hence the complaint of the Magnetic-Spiritual School in Buenos Aires is not unfounded, namely, that the FSLN has disseminated a distorted image of the real Sandino. Only now, with the recent foundation of the Institute of the Study of Sandinismo in Managua, are Sandino's anarchist and theosophical views finally beginning to receive the attention they deserve.

Transmitting Sandino's Example

Fonseca was Sandino's single most influential successor, but he was not the only transmitter of Sandino's legacy.[33] Sandino's political-military strategy survived from 1934 to 1958 thanks to the efforts of Col. Alberto Bayo, who engraved it on Fidel Castro's July 26 movement. Although Bayo did not help to recover Sandino's written legacy, he was influential in perpetuating his example and revolutionary strategy along with his red and black flag—the emblem of both the Cuban and the Nicaraguan revolutions.

Bayo belonged to an earlier generation. He was born of Spanish parents in Cuba in 1892. He became an officer in the Spanish air force until he was forced into exile after the collapse of the Spanish

Republic in 1939.[34] His revolutionary career dates from 1948, when he became the principal military adviser to the various armed groups of liberal and radical revolutionaries collectively known as the Caribbean Legion. Dedicated to overthrowing Central American and Caribbean dictators, the legion relied on Colonel Bayo to train the expeditionary forces against Nicaragua's Somoza in 1948 and the Dominican Republic's Trujillo in 1949. It was Bayo who transmitted the oral tradition of Sandino's struggle, the stories told by the survivors of the Defending Army who had escaped to Costa Rica, where the legionnaires were being trained. Two of those veteran Sandinistas, Gen. Ramón Raudales and Gen. Heriberto Reyes, were to lead an invasion of Nicaragua from bases in Honduras in 1958.

What Bayo learned from the Nicaraguan exiles he trained in Costa Rica he incorporated into his manual of guerrilla warfare, *150 Questions for a Guerrilla*. It became the manual for later legionnaires and for Fidel Castro's Cuban exiles Bayo trained in Mexico in 1956.[35] The manual is dedicated to all those who have resisted the Central American dictatorships, to the "glorious guerrillas of the immortal school of Sandino, hero of the world."[36] For Bayo only patriots were fit to become guerrillas, and Sandino was the greatest of them all. He adopted Sandino's strategy of guerrilla warfare and got others to adopt it. There is a sketch of this strategy in his manual.[37]

Without Fonseca's work it is unlikely that Nicaragua's Front of National Liberation would have taken its cue from Sandino. Without Bayo's manual for guerrillas, Sandino's revolutionary example might never have caught fire. These two lines of Sandino's legacy developed independently of each other, but in 1959 they coalesced when a new invasion of Nicaragua was prepared in Cuba with the help of Che Guevara. The Argentine revolutionary became the link between Bayo and Fonseca, between the successful Cuban Revolution and a second revised edition in Nicaragua.

Cuban exile sources in Miami claim that Bayo, who had returned to Cuba to train special units of the Rebel Army in guerrilla warfare, also trained the expeditionaries preparing for the invasion of Nicaragua in 1959.[38] The Nicaraguan legion known as the September 21 movement, after the date of the assassination of the first Somoza in 1956, included Carlos Fonseca. A guerrilla training camp was set up with Cuban funds at El Chaparral, Honduras, near the border with Nicaragua. Although the camp was attacked and the group was dissolved by Honduran military units in June, it was the first in a series of attempts to liberate Nicaragua in which

Sandino's oral legacy as preserved by Bayo converged on the written legacy recovered by Fonseca.[39]

The interlocking of these two traditions took on a definitive form in 1961 with the creation of the FSLN. Its political cadres had come under Fonseca's influence; its military cadres included survivors of both the September 21 movement and General Raudales's abortive campaign in the fall of 1958.[40] That Fonseca became the general secretary and supreme commander of the FSLN, which was equipped with Cuban arms and trained by another veteran Sandinista, Col. Santos López, shows the extent to which the written and oral legacies finally came together. As Tomás Borge comments on this convergence,

> The relation between Carlos and Col. Santos López was not accidental. The old and the new generations of Sandinistas searched for each other amid the darkness until they discovered one another at the right political and economic moment. The old Sandinistas transmitted their experiences, which fell on a terrain hungry for seeds and new perspectives. Actually, what happened was a displacement of the written knowledge of Sandino's struggle onto the flesh and bones and words of the survivors.[41]

During the first stage of military operations, from 1962 to 1967, the FSLN's strategy followed the lines sketched by Che Guevara in *La guerra de guerrillas* (*Guerrilla Warfare*) (1960). Since this work was indebted to Bayo's manual, which in turn reflected the influence of Sandino, it too became a conductor and transmitter of Sandino's legacy.[42]

The sources of Guevara's knowledge of Sandino were varied. Besides Bayo, he became familiar with veteran Sandinistas including Gen. Ramón Raudales and Gen. Heriberto Reyes in San José, Costa Rica, in 1953.[43] From this experience he acquired his first understanding of Sandino's movement and the factors contributing to its success, mainly the inspirational quality of Sandino's leadership and Sandino's strategy of guerrilla warfare.

That Guevara assimilated these valuable lessons of Sandino's struggle is evident from the testimony of his first wife, Hilda Gadea. In her memoir of him, she recalls his response to the CIA-supported military invasion of Guatemala in 1954 aimed at overthrowing the progressive government of Pres. Jacobo Arbenz. Besides agitating among students to defend the government, Guevara wanted to launch a guerrilla war of resistance from the mountains.[44] Under no circumstances, he believed, should the country be abandoned to the reactionaries without organizing a popular-based defending army patterned on Sandino's.

After Arbenz chose exile and all hope of resistance vanished, Guevara sought political asylum in Mexico. Obsessed with the struggle against Latin American dictators, he joined the Cuban exiles in Mexico City who were plotting to overthrow Batista. In Fidel Castro, according to Macaulay, he recognized the charismatic qualities of leadership that had distinguished Sandino.[45] Charisma was the first ingredient indispensable to the success of the July 26 movement.

The second ingredient was the training received from Bayo based on Sandino's guerrilla strategy. Although Guevara's manual of guerrilla warfare presents his own strategy for liberation, he and his companions applied Sandino's strategy of guerrilla warfare to Cuba based on the lessons they had learned from Bayo.[46]

Fidel Castro's July 26 movement was not the last of the Caribbean legions. The guerrillas who took part in the planned invasions of Nicaragua and the Dominican Republic in 1959 were trained by Bayo but were under the general direction of Che Guevara.[47] He instigated and aided the organization of legionnaires throughout Latin America. The Bolivian legion he personally commanded came to a tragic end in October 1967, when he was captured and assassinated by U.S.-trained special forces of the Bolivian army.

Che Guevara's and Fidel Castro's assimilation of the lessons of Sandino's military campaigns is examined in detail in the last chapter of Macaulay's work. Before Bayo's services were sought, Castro became familiar with Nicaraguan legionnaires of the Sandino Brigade on Confetti Key, the Cuban island where Caribbean and Central American revolutionaries organized the first expeditionary force in 1947 to overthrow the dictatorship in the Dominican Republic.[48] But according to Macaulay, Castro's July 1953 attack on the Moncada barracks, the second largest in the country, showed that he had learned little from Sandino's example.[49] In Mexico, he seldom attended Bayo's classes and was prone to disregard his professional advice.[50] Despite Bayo's criticism of the assault on the barracks, Castro remained true to his own strategy of mass insurrection. Only as a last resort did he turn to guerrilla warfare, when local forces commanded by Frank País failed to take over Santiago de Cuba in conjunction with the anticipated landing of the expeditionaries in December 1956.[51]

Guevara rather than Castro became the principal transmitter of Bayo's lessons on guerrilla warfare. Bayo singled out the Argentine as his "star pupil."[52] Following the lessons he had learned from Bayo, Guevara sought to restrain Castro from broadcasting to the Cuban people news of their planned "invasion." The latter's action alerted the enemy and resulted in the near annihilation of the entire expeditionary force. In a tribute to the author of the *150 Questions*, Guevara testified that "General Bayo . . . was one of my two teachers."[53] The other was the Cuban Revolution.

Guevara took on Bayo's job of disseminating and internationalizing Sandino's example. His role in organizing and arming the September 21 movement in El Chaparral, and the assistance he gave to the FSLN's invading forces from Honduras in 1962–1963, may be considered the repayment of a debt.[54] What he had learned from Sandino through Colonel Bayo and other sources he also disseminated in his manual on guerrilla warfare to the new generation of Nicaraguan revolutionaries commanded by Fonseca.

Guevara's three basic principles of guerrilla warfare were not unique to Cuba's revolutionary experience. He had already learned some of them from Bayo. He presented them in the opening chapter of his manual. First, the popular forces can win a war against the regular army, provided the government is unconstitutional and the people recognize the impossibility of defending their rights through legal channels. Second, it is not necessary to wait for all the conditions of a revolution to be present because some of them can be created through the impulse given by the guerrillas. And third, in underdeveloped Latin America the most suitable terrain for armed struggle is the countryside.[55]

The first principle may also be discerned in Bayo's work. In answer to his first question, Bayo recalls Sandino's experience: "It is necessary to be on the side of the oppressed masses in their struggle against foreign invasion, the imposition of a vile dictatorship, etc. If this prerequisite is not met, the guerrillas will always be defeated."[56] The repressive forces, Bayo argues, are not invincible: "Always remember Sandino, who fought and evaded the Americans for seven years even though his opponents used thousands of well-trained men, motorized units, dozens of radios, which formed concentric circles around the Sierra of Segovia, where our hero was hiding. After seven years of fruitless hunting, they had to make peace with Sandino under the conditions that he dictated."[57]

There is nothing in Bayo's manual corresponding to Guevara's second principle. His third principle, though, has a counterpart in Bayo's guerrillas, who fight only in the countryside. Those engaged in open rebellion are full-time guerrillas; those involved in clandestine fighting are part-time. The first live and fight in the mountains; the second make their living from agriculture. The part-time guerrilla appears to be harmless, but periodically "he takes his arms out of hiding for a night, fights, and returns them to hiding

. . . he returns to his normal routine, pretending he knows and has seen nothing."[58] Bayo's distinction recalls Sandino's reliance on part-time and full-time guerrillas, a strategy first used with success in the attack on the town of Ocotal in July 1927.[59]

These were not the only elements of guerrilla warfare Guevara borrowed from Sandino through Colonel Bayo. Chapter 1 of *La guerra de guerrillas* advocates the application of so-called minuet tactics—advancing when the enemy withdraws and retreating when the enemy advances—so that the guerrilla never fights on the enemy's terms but always relies on surprise.[60] The word *minuet* is taken from Bayo's manual, where these tactics are described in detail.[61]

Guevara's interest in Sandino was more than casual. Rafael Somarriba, a former National Guardsman, had been chosen by Guevara to head the expeditionary forces at El Chaparral. In Havana Somarriba attended the wedding of Guevara and Aleyda March, after which Guevara said he planned to participate directly in the guerrilla struggle.[62] First, he had to complete a mission to Jakarta. Afterward, he would travel to Nicaragua and link up with the guerrillas there. Although it is difficult to substantiate Somarriba's claim, we have Guevara's parting words for the Nicaraguan commandos who left Cuba for El Chaparral in June 1959: "I love the land of Sandino and I want to fight there, too."[63]

The matter did not end there. Three years later, when Guevara began thinking of where he might lead a guerrilla movement and establish a second liberated territory in the Americas, his attention once more shifted to Nicaragua. According to the testimony of a Nicaraguan exile experienced in guerrilla warfare, "In 1962 there were Cuban elements in Mexico. I attended a meeting where I came to know Fonseca. . . . They asked me if I was disposed to organize guerrillas in Finlandé, Chachaua, and Chipote commanded by Che Guevara."[64] These were the FSLN guerrillas who crossed the Honduran border into Nicaragua in June 1963, led by veteran Sandinista Col. Santos López.

It is also worth noting that Guevara read Selser's books on Sandino and had them republished in Cuba. That Selser's two-volume biography of Sandino was the first work to be published by Cuba's revolutionary press has more than passing significance. The year that it appeared, 1960, also saw the Cuban publication of Selser's companion work on Sandino's "crazy little army"—again on Guevara's recommendation.

Carlos Fonseca acknowledged Sandino and Che Guevara as the two most important influences on his political thought.[65] Although

Guevara's Marxism found adherents in virtually every Latin American country, only in Nicaragua did it become rooted in an indigenous movement capable of making a successful revolution. Nicaragua was the first country in which the written and unwritten legacies of a great folk hero and national redeemer became impregnated with the new Marxism, the first instance of the confluence of two different generations of revolutionaries: the surviving veterans of Sandino's army and the new Marxists of the FSLN.

The Marxist Influence

Fonseca assimilated not only Sandino's thought but also, as a militant of the PSN, the legacy of Marxism-Leninism. As early as 1957 he was selected as a delegate to the Fourth World Congress of Democratic Youth in Kiev and to the Sixth World Youth Festival in Moscow. He arrived in the Soviet Union during the first week in August and remained there as a guest until November, with side trips to some of the other socialist countries. The result of his observations of life under socialism he incorporated in his pamphlet, *Un nicaragüense en Moscú.*[66] Although he was expelled from the PSN for refusing to obey a party directive to return to Nicaragua in 1959, his differences with the party were mainly strategical. He preferred the Cuban development of Marxism-Leninism to the doctrinaire version of the Nicaraguan party, because the Cubans had also assimilated and transmitted Sandino's example. This new Marxism was also a new style of Leninism.

Contemporary Sandinismo represents the fusion of Marxist revolutionary thought and Sandino's intellectual heritage. But what precisely were the elements of Marxism that Fonseca combined with his country's revolutionary legacy?

Fonseca identified the Marxist component of Sandinismo with Marx's and Lenin's guidelines to revolution. In a proclamation broadcast on a Nicaraguan radio station in 1970, he declared that the Sandinista popular revolution had a dual objective: whereas one of its tasks was to overthrow the dictatorship, the other was to establish socialism.[67] As he explained in an interview in Havana in November that same year, "We recognize that socialism is the people's only hope of achieving a profound change in their conditions of life . . . the fundamental guide must be the principles of scientific socialism."[68]

The classic exposition of those principles was by Frederick Engels in the first popular manual of Marxism, *Socialism: Utopian and Scientific.* Socialism became a science, according to Engels, with Karl Marx's two major intellectual contributions: the materialist or economic interpretation of history; and the discovery of the secret of capitalist accumulation through surplus value, or how the capitalist exploitation of the worker takes place.[69] The task of socialists was no longer to criticize capitalism as unjust or irrational, but to explain the historico-economic succession of events, in particular class struggles, and to discover in economic conditions the means by which the proletariat might achieve mastery over society and thereby end the conflict.

Fonseca was undoubtedly familiar with Engels's essay and with Lenin's reformulation of the task of scientific socialism. There is only one way to smash the power of a ruling class, wrote Lenin, "and that is to find, in the very society which surrounds us, the forces which can—and, owing to their social position, *must*—constitute the power capable of sweeping away the old and creating the new."[70] After that the task would be to enlighten and organize those social forces for the struggle that lay ahead.

But was Marx's theory and Lenin's reformulation of it Marxism's only contribution to Sandinismo? In his Havana interview, Fonseca acknowledged another major component in the thought of Che Guevara: "In planning to continue the revolutionary struggle we are guided by the most advanced principles, by Marxist ideology [actually, scientific socialism], by Comandante Che Guevara, and by Augusto César Sandino."[71] Guevara was important because he represented the new Marxism diffused by the Cuban Revolution. For the PSN the new Marxism was a virtual heresy, because practice received precedence over theory and Guevara's cult of the new man got more attention than dialectical materialism, the Marxist worldview. Thus to the theoretical component of Sandinismo derived from Marx's and Engels's science of socialism, Fonseca added an ideological or activating component derived from Cuban Marxism and the writings of Guevara in particular.

The new Cuban Marxism was distinguished by its novel conviction that it is not always necessary to know the conditions of revolution in order to make one. Two sentences summarize the new Marxism of Che Guevara and Fidel Castro: "The duty of every revolutionary is to make the revolution"; and "Many times practice comes first and then theory."[72] These two fundamentally pragmatic statements supposedly distinguished authentic from inauthentic Marxists.[73] For Castro, a Marxist is not somebody trying to apply a set of revolutionary guidelines, somebody for whom practice is a test of Marx's revolutionary theory. As Guevara first articulated this novel reinterpretation of Marxism, "the revolution can be made if the historical realities are interpreted correctly and if the forces involved are utilized correctly, even if the theory is not known."[74]

It is a mistake to counterpose Castro's thought and that of Guevara. During the sixties, when the latter was still alive, they shared the same fundamental premises. Together they shifted the emphasis from Marxist theorizing to revolutionary practice, from the conditions of revolution that are independent of human volition to those dependent on our choices. The first imperative was to become a revolutionary; Marxist theory could come afterward. Thus they reversed the traditional Marxist conception of the relation between revolutionary theory and action.

In the case of a vanguard party, they believed, practice grows out of theory and becomes an extension of it. In contrast, for most of the people who make a revolution, theory emerges from actions and reflects on a concrete practice. As Castro commented in a speech on 13 March 1967, "The immense majority of those who today proudly call themselves Marxist-Leninists arrived at Marxism-Leninism by way of the revolutionary struggle."[75] Consequently, for self-styled Marxists to exclude them from their revolutionary organizations is both sectarian and self-defeating. The established communist parties dedicate their energies to making Marxists as a prior condition of making the revolution. Castro reversed the priorities by making revolution the best way of making Marxists. So did Che Guevara. In one of the many aphorisms that showed up in his conversations, "We walk by walking," he indicated that one learns to make a revolution by making one.[76]

Together Che Guevara and Fidel Castro shifted the emphasis from the principles of scientific socialism to revolutionary feeling and attitude. In a 1963 prologue to a manual used for preparing revolutionary cadres, Guevara defended the subjective character of their new Marxism with a citation from one of Castro's speeches:

Who has said that Marxism is the renunciation of human sentiments, of comradeship, of brotherly love, of respect for others, of consideration for one's neighbor? Who has said that Marxism means not to have a soul, not to have sentiments? It was precisely love for man that engendered Marxism. It was love for man, for humanity, the desire to combat the misfortune of the proletariat, the desire to combat the misery, injustice, tribulations, and exploitation suffered by the proletariat that enabled Marxism to surge forth from the mind of Karl Marx precisely when there was a real possibility and, more than a real possibility, the historic necessity of the social revolution of which he was the interpreter. But what made him be this interpreter if not the stock of human sentiments of men like himself, like Engels, like Lenin?[77]

Guevara counseled the party's militants to engrave these words on their memory, because the ideological dimension of Marxism was fundamental to their formation as revolutionaries. He claimed that it was also their most effective weapon against all deviations from authentic Marxism. Extravagant praise for an alleged component of Marxism that was overlooked by Marx and Engels, and also by Lenin in his strategy for revolution.

This ideological or activating dimension of the new Marxism was basic to Guevara's doctrine of the "new man." To be successful, the guerrilla must become a model human being; he "must exhibit a moral conduct that certifies him to be a real priest of the reform he espouses"; he must exercise self-control and practice self-abnegation under the most taxing circumstances; he "must be an ascetic."[78] Similar traits of character were required in the grueling task of building a communist society after the seizure of political power. "To build communism one has to make the new man simultaneously with the material base"—not afterward, according to Soviet Marxists.[79]

During the sixties this ideologically enriched Marxism was adopted by the Cuban leadership, by Fonseca, and by the FSLN. Castro succinctly summarized its components in a speech on 19 April 1965: "Marxism-Leninism is an explanation of historical events; Marxism-Leninism is a guide to action; Marxism-Leninism is the ideology of the proletariat."[80] Besides its theory and practice, it contains a set of nonrational inducements to action. That the duty of the revolutionary is to make the revolution is one example of a nonrational motivating force, such as we have seen in Sandino's ideology of "rational communism." Surely, it has little in common with the traditional Marxist emphasis on rationally based behavior in which the revolutionary makes the revolution in his or her self-interest—as a member of an exploited class.

The conviction that the principles of scientific socialism were not enough to get people to sacrifice themselves in a revolution led the founders of the new Marxism to stress the importance of other motives. As Castro commented in his speech of 26 July 1966,

> We would have been in a real pickle if, to make a socialist revolution, we had been obliged to spend all our time catechizing everybody in socialism and Marxism, and only then undertaking the revolution. . . .
> If a revolutionary happens to be one who arms himself with a revolutionary theory but doesn't feel it, he has a mental relation to revolutionary theory but not an affective one—not an emotionl relation. He doesn't have a really revolutionary attitude and sees the problem of revolutionary theory as something cold.[81]

In making a revolution, he added, those versed in Marx's science of society are less important than revolutionaries of conviction who feel a cause deeply.[82] Although this was an exaggeration, Castro had in mind those Marxists who are so preoccupied with intellectual problems and with formulating a correct strategy that, if one listens to them, one will wait forever before risking a life and death struggle. Thus the revolutionary ideology that takes hold of the proletariat is an asset of no small consequence for revolutionary practice.

Elsewhere, Castro equated Marxism with revolutionary thought and practice.[83] But there are two kinds of revolutionary thought: scientific and ideological. Political action is characterized by being one or the other. If one uses the term "praxis" for the unity of thought and action, then there is both a scientific praxis and an ideological one. In scientifically based praxis, theory comes first and then action. This is how the established communist parties interpret Marxism in the course of giving priority to scientific socialism, but their interpretation is not the only one. Actually, most militants in the FSLN as well as Cuba's July 26 movement were ideologically motivated, having arrived at Marxist theory by way of revolutionary struggle.

In this perspective a pro attitude toward revolution is as necessary as theory in guiding a revolutionary movement. As Castro points out in the same context, Marxism is not a science or theory of revolution only: "Those who do not possess a truly revolutionary spirit cannot be called communists."[84] As revolutionary action, Marxism includes a set of attitudes. "What defines a communist is his attitude toward the oligarchies, his attitude toward exploitation, his attitude toward imperialism; and on this continent, his attitude toward the armed revolutionary movements."[85]

Science and ideology are not incompatible. The mistake of the established communist parties, Castro believed, was to reduce the moral dimension of Marxism to an insignificant or marginal role. For the new Marxism, it is more than that. A sense of duty is needed to give vitality to Marxist theory. If the Marxism of books is by itself impotent, then ideology in addition to self-interest may be required to give it force.[86]

Admittedly, the new Marxism bore the marks of improvisation. As Guevara wrote in a letter to the Argentine writer Ernesto Sábato (12 April 1960), "A Communist leader who visited us in the Sierra Maestra, impressed by so much improvisation and by the way in which all the means that functioned on their own account adjusted themselves to a central organization, said it was the most perfectly

organized chaos in the world."[87] His explanation for this theater of
the absurd was that the Cuban Revolution had moved ahead at a
faster pace than the ideology motivating it and than the theory that
came still later. Castro was a member of a bourgeois party aspiring
to a congressional seat in a bourgeois government, and those who
followed him had little political preparation.[88]

It was the armed struggle against dictatorship that revolu-
tionized them. "There is no more profound experience for a revolutionary than the act of war," Guevara wrote in the same letter, "the
knowledge that an armed man is the equal of any other armed man
and no longer must fear other armed men."[89] Freedom from fear
was tantamount to having courage. An armed peasant represented a
threat not only to the dictatorship in Cuba, but also to the system
of land tenure that excluded poor peasants from having a plot of
their own. Arming the peasants was the first step toward a nationwide agrarian reform. This was not learned from textbooks. Taken
to heart by Fonseca and the FSLN, Guevara's message was that a
revolution *can* be improvised. This was not the accepted practice of
the Nicaraguan Socialist party.

The independent character of Guevara's Marxism earned him
the animosity of the communist parties in Latin America. Directly
based on his experience of the Cuban Revolution, his Marxism did
not conform to the Soviet manuals.

With the same independence, Castro insisted that revolutionaries should learn their Marxism not by rote but should acquire a
critical understanding of it. On more than one occasion he derided
the Soviet manuals for disseminating a petrified, decayed, and
stagnant version of Marxism.[90] Along with encouraging mental
laziness, he noted, they helped to foment intellectual dependence.
Because papal infallibility is the most foreign of all attitudes in
Marxist thought, "we want our masses to acquire an awareness that
does not consist of clichés."[91]

Those who depart from the manuals, Castro continued, are severely censured by the learned and wise doctors of Marxism—but
those doctors are not infallible. "In our own country, in our own
ranks, there are, disgracefully, those who find it scandalous to hear
a word, an argument, a reason that is not exactly how it appears
textually in some little book."[92] The literal interpretation of those
books has cost revolutionaries dearly. Therefore, Castro urged them
to read Marx's own writings and to use their heads in interpreting
them: "Whoever does not want to be misled by another's head
should become capable of thinking with his own."[93] Although
Marxism is the theory, practice, and ideology of socialist revo-

lution, it should be interpreted critically in view of what is happening in the world. Such was Fonseca's Marxism and his legacy to the FSLN.

Promoting the New Marxism

The job of promoting the new Marxism that began in Cuba in the sixties was also taken up in Nicaragua after its victorious revolution. As in Cuba, revolutionaries began combing the works of contemporary Marxists in search of intellectual support for what Soviet Marxists judged to be heresy. By the middle sixties East Europeans were ridiculing the new Marxism as an expression of "tropical communism," a communism of the passions instead of scientific thought.[94] It was in response to these charges that efforts were made to give the new philosophy a modicum of intellectual respectability by an appeal to Marxist authority.

There were few Marxist authorities who could serve in this capacity. In Nicaragua as well as Cuba intellectual support was reduced to two principal sources: the works of the Peruvian Communist, José Carlos Mariátegui (1895–1930), and of his contemporary Antonio Gramsci (1891–1937), founder of the Italian Communist party. Mariátegui is considered by both Cuban and Nicaraguan revolutionaries to have been the most original Marxist thinker in Latin America; Gramsci is honored as the single most important Marxist theoretician since Lenin.[95] Common to both was their emphasis on revolutionary action, on the importance of subjective factors in making a revolution, and on the role of ideology as well as theory in motivating the masses.

In Cuba, Guevara took the initiative of having Mariátegui's major work, *7 ensayos de interpretación de la realidad peruana*, republished by the national press. In her memoir of Guevara, Hilda Gadea recalled that the two of them had discussed this work along with Mariátegui's *El alma matinal*, the principal intellectual source and progenitor of Guevara's new Marxism.[96] Several years later, when Guevara became bogged down with his guerrilla fighters in Bolivia, Mariátegui's seminal essay on ethics and socialism was considered important enough to reproduce in the first issue of the magazine *Tricontinental* (summer 1967), published in Havana.

What Guevara incorporated from Mariátegui in developing his new Marxism also rubbed off on Fonseca and the FSLN. More important than this indirect debt, however, has been the FSLN's direct use of Mariátegui to promote the new Marxism. For example, during the celebration of the fiftieth anniversary of Mariátegui's death in December 1980, the weekly cultural supplement of the Managua daily, *El Nuevo Diario,* ran a front page editorial along with a series of essays from influential international contributors on Mariátegui's unique version of Marxism. The editorial credited the Peruvian Communist with having "launched the revolution in Latin American thought," with having been "the first to investigate the origins, effects and functions, development . . . and role of diverse social phenomena including ideologies."[97] Because of his critique of dogmatic Marxism, the editors noted, Mariátegui had run afoul of the pundits of the Communist International, who cast doubts concerning his Marxism. As a result, his complete works were not published in his native Peru until after the Cuban Revolution, when his name became exonerated. Thereafter, the editorial concluded, his works were translated into English, German, French, and Italian, and in Latin America they gained increasing acceptance with the passage of time.

Basic to Mariátegui's political thought was his effort to provide Marxism with an ideological dimension grounded in human passion. What traditional Marxism lacked, he believed, was a sense of duty to the revolution combined with an epic and heroic sense of life required to inspire people and to encourage them to sacrifice themselves for a great cause. A revolutionary morality, he wrote, "does not mechanically arise from economic interest: it is formed in class struggles waged with heroic fervor and a passionate will. . . . For the proletariat to fulfill its historic mission it must first acquire an awareness of its class interest; but class interest by itself is not enough."[98]

Besides class interest, Mariátegui argued, the workers had need of a "revolutionary myth."[99] Although the messianic millennium will never arrive, revolutionaries cannot do without the belief in a final struggle that will redeem humanity. The illusion of a final struggle becomes a major motivating factor, the "motor of all progress . . . [toward] a new human reality."[100] What the revolutionary needs is a pessimistic vision of reality combined with an optimistic faith in an ideal—an adage of the Mexican philosopher Vasconcelos—to which Mariátegui adds "a mystical courage and a religious passion to create a new world."[101] The authentic revolutionary is like the early Christian, according to Mariátegui: he never gives up; he cannot be discouraged because of the firm conviction that his cause is just and must ultimately prevail.[102] Paradoxically, the Marxist philosophy that teaches the need for revolution has been incapable of understanding the need for a revolutionary faith in the twentieth century.[103]

Mariátegui derived his belief in the regenerating role of social myths from Sorel. Unlike a utopia or intellectual blueprint of an ideal society, a revolutionary myth is a body of images evoking the impulse to fight.[104] Although the workers' emancipation depends on themselves, one cannot rely on their spontaneity to do the job. They need to be inspired, which means that they must be galvanized into action by a revolutionary myth.[105] For Mariátegui, following in Sorel's footsteps, the workers need enthusiasm as well as science.

Mariátegui commended Sorel not only for recovering the revolutionary substance of Marxism, but also for "transcending the rationalist and positivist bases of socialism . . . [and] invigorating socialist thought with the ideas of Bergson and the pragmatists."[106] By this he meant that Sorel had enriched Marxism with a nonrational motivating force under the influence of Henri Bergson's "creative intuition" and William James's "will to believe."[107] Marxism aspires to be realistic, Mariátegui noted, yet shows a remarkable lack of psychological and sociological realism in failing to have appreciated Sorel's theory of social myths based on the experience of religious movements.[108]

Finally, Mariátegui credited Sorel with developing a revolutionary morality. And like Sorel, he advocated an "ethics of the producers," which would be created in the process of the class struggle as an expression of the workers' revolutionary aspirations and as an assertion of their defiance of the prevailing morality. If they were not to continue in slavish subjection, they must adopt the morality of Nietzsche's "superman," tantamount to a complete transvaluation of values and the creation of a new man.[109] Thus Mariátegui commended Sorel for "clarifying the historic role of violence . . . in a period of social democratic parliamentarism . . . [and] psychological and intellectual resistance by the workers' leaders to the seizure of power."[110]

In transmitting Sorel's thought, Mariátegui equated Lenin's vanguard of professional revolutionaries with Sorel's "activating minority." These were "the best spirits, the best minds of the new generation," who in effect followed Lenin's example.[111] The founder of Russian bolshevism, Mariátegui believed, had been decisively influenced by Sorel.[112] The new leaders of the masses, Sorel had written, are not men of knowledge but men of struggle, the charismatic few who, because they are sensitive to the moods of the people, are capable of transforming feelings into action.[113] Intellectual achievements do not make a tribune of the people. Unlike the flaccid leaders of the Socialist or Second International, according to Sorel, the new revolutionary leaders are motivated by moral rather than material incentives. They do not aspire to political office: "The men who devote themselves to the revolutionary cause know that they must always remain poor."[114] For Mariátegui, too, the revolutionary was basically an ascetic.[115]

Under Mariátegui's influence the new Marxism supports all popularly held myths with a known potential for revolution. Besides the social myths of Christianity, these include the moral faith in an immanent justice for humanity and the scientifically disguised Marxist faith in a classless society without capitalist exploitation or exploitation of any kind. Until recently, Marxism-Leninism was supposedly free of any nonrational elements. But the new Marxism has increasingly acknowledged that a proletarian explosion followed by communism, as Marx defined it, has yet to occur. Since the belief persists regardless of the facts, it resembles a Sorelian myth.

The other bastion of the new Marxism was Antonio Gramsci. In Cuba during the sixties he was the only Marxist theoretician who ranked in importance with the classical trinity of Marx, Engels, Lenin. At the University of Havana his works occupied a prominent place next to theirs in the divulgation of Marxist philosophy. The two-volume *Lecturas de filosofía*, prepared by the Philosophy Department as the text for the university's required course in Marxist philosophy, included more selections from his major works than from any other European Marxist after Lenin.[116] A second edition appeared in 1968 and continued to be used until the seventies, when Soviet manuals on Marxism-Leninism began replacing the Cuban texts.

What Gramsci was to the new brand of Cuban Marxists in the sixties he also became to Nicaragua's new Marxists in the eighties. Why was he so important? Because of his overriding concern both with explaining and legitimizing revolution by recourse to ideological or nonrational appeals, sentiments, and beliefs. As Sergio Ramírez commented during a political-educational seminar at Managua's Central American University in August 1980, it is the meaning Gramsci gave to the word *ideology*, as "philosophical vulgarizations that lead the masses to concrete action, to the transformation of reality,"[117] that helps to clarify Sandino's bizarre and seemingly crazy metaphysical and theosophical ideas.[118] Although contemporary Sandinistas no longer have any use for Sandino's theosophy, "no ideologue, no Nicaraguan revolutionary, can explain his own thought without the origins of Sandinista thought . . .

[because] the entire wheel of revolution in Nicaragua was propelled by this motor."[119]

Gramsci's interpretation of Marxism, like Guevara's and Castro's, appealed to Nicaraguan revolutionaries because of its strong voluntarist and activist bent, aimed at conquering the hearts and minds of the working class. Like Mariátegui, Gramsci provided a justification for the FSLN's emphasis on the subjective conditions of revolution and for its reliance on a specifically Christian as well as Marxism-based ideology.

Gramsci owed a major intellectual debt to Sorel. His assessment of the French theoretician of anarcho-syndicalism, although less positive than Mariátegui's, was certainly favorable: "Sorel is, in the field of historical research, an 'inventor.' He cannot be imitated. He does not place at the service of his aspiring disciples a method that can be applied mechanically."[120] Sorel possessed, according to Gramsci, "the virtues of his two masters: the harsh logic of Marx and the restless, plebeian eloquence of Proudhon. . . . Sorel has truly remained what Proudhon made him, that is, a disinterested friend of the proletariat." Most important of all for Gramsci was Sorel's insistence on the ideological autonomy of the workers' movement, his insistence that "the proletarian movement express itself in its own forms, give life to its own institutions."[121]

Gramsci's philosophy of praxis, a word to which he gave currency, helped to legitimize the new Marxism by emphasising the unity of theory and practice, and also by raising the struggle on the ideological front to the status of political and economic struggles. To smash the bourgeois state, he believed, it was necessary simultaneously to change people's attitudes. His model, like Sorel's, was the victory of early Christianity over Greco-Roman culture.[122] The same methods would be used as those used by the early Christians: ideological proselytism and a war of positions or strategy of wearing down the enemy's ideological defenses. Christianity triumphed not because of a monopoly of brute force but by virtue of its moral superiority and inducements to imitate Christ as the "new man."[123] Although economic factors prevail in the long run, Gramsci claimed, the immediate driving force of history is ideological. As one Italian Communist has summarized his contribution, "For Gramsci, Marxism is not just a social and political revolution, it is also (and above all) a *cultural* revolution that will succeed where Christianity has failed: in the formation of a new humanity."[124]

Obsessed with the problem of conquering civil society and not just the state, Gramsci focused on the ideological apparatuses of church, school, and party, on the methods used to legitimize domination by ruling classes, and on the conditions undermining the dominant ideology at a given time. Among his major contributions was the thesis that the power of a dominant class derives less from its control of the coercive apparatuses of the state than from its control of the ideological apparatuses, from its "hegemony" (from the Greek *hēgeisthai*, "to be a guide") or ability to secure the active consent of the governed.[125] This being the case, the conquest of political power requires a long preparatory process of questioning the rules and changing people's values and beliefs.

Like his teacher Benedetto Croce, Gramsci looked on Marx as the "Machiavelli of the proletariat."[126] In a novel adaptation of the lessons of Machiavelli's *The Prince,* Gramsci conceived of the vanguard party as a "modern prince" using whatever means necessary to establish the hegemony of Marxist ideology and the new communist counterculture. What could be more Machiavellian than his insistence that "it was necessary for Marxism to ally itself to alien tendencies in order to combat capitalist hangovers, especially in the field of religion"?[127] For him this meant combatting the "spontaneous philosophy" of the masses, the legacy of popular religion and its secularized expression as "common sense," with a vulgarized edition of Marxism-Leninism in the form not of the principles of scientific socialism but of a Sorelian myth.[128]

In his "Notes on Machiavelli's Politics," Gramsci wrote,

> The fundamental characteristic of *The Prince* is that it is not a systematic treatment, but a "living" book, in which political ideology and political science are fused in the dramatic form of a "myth". . . .
> *The Prince* of Machiavelli could be studied as an historical example of the Sorelian "myth," that is, of a political ideology which is not presented as a cold utopia or as a rational doctrine, but as a creation of concrete fantasy which works on a dispersed and pulverized people in order to arouse and organize their collective will.[129]

For Nicaraguan intellectuals such as Sergio Ramírez and the editors of *El Nuevo Diario,* such passages justify the FSLN's accommodation with not only Sandino's revolutionary legacy, but also grassroots Christianity and its theology of liberation.

What Is Sandinismo?

On a Sunday afternoon in December 1980 I watched the changing sunlight on the giant red and black portrait of Sandino hanging from the cathedral in Managua's Plaza de la Revolución. Next to me was a man who had lost both of his sons in the struggle against

Somoza. "Poor little ones," he sobbed, "but we got rid of the sonofabitch!" Then his tone abruptly changed: "But I am a Sandinista, I am *not* a Communist."

His position was shared by others. Nicaraguans felt attracted to the figure of Sandino but considered communism to be something alien. Many of them denied that Sandino had any affiliation with Marxism. For the present most people rightly believe that, unlike Cuba, Nicaragua is not a communist country—although it may be on the road to becoming one.

As Tomás Borge, the minister of the interior, noted in a May 1981 interview, "The bourgeoisie accuses us of falling into totalitarianism. But it forgets that here in Nicaragua we have freedom of the press; that we do not use torture; that there is no *paredón* [wall against which prisoners are executed by firing squads]; and that an opposition exists. . . . We do not owe imperialism any explanation. But we will say to Latin Americans that we are not going to become another Cuba." Although Cuba was the crucible of the Nicaraguan Revolution, the latter differed from Cuba's revolution in many ways: it recognized a plurality of political parties; it tolerated ideological diversity; it had not officially executed anyone; it had a collective leadership; and it favored a mixed economy. Borge also commented on the differences in foreign policy, noting that "the Nicaraguan Revolution has its own opinions about Afghanistan and Poland."[130]

Although Sandinismo has been favorably received in Cuba, it has been openly criticized by Soviet Marxists. They would like to see it displaced by the more orthodox Marxism of the Nicaraguan Socialist party (PSN). Ironically, the Soviet Union recognizes both the FSLN and the PSN as legitimate representatives of the Nicaraguan Revolution, whereas Cuba recognizes only the FSLN.

In Nicaragua I talked to Sandinistas who were not Marxist-Leninists and to Marxist-Leninists who were not Sandinistas. But the leaders of the Nicaraguan Revolution claim to be following both Marx and Sandino. They are the ones who say that "Sandinismo is Marxism-Leninism applied in Nicaragua." They add that "Sandinismo is Christianity applied in Nicaragua."[131] What they mean to convey is that Sandinismo is a composite of several revolutionary ideologies.

Paradoxically, there are Sandinistas who subscribe to the new Marxism and there are Sandinistas who do not. Actually, Sandinismo developed in two quite different ways, both under FSLN sponsorship. One was popular and folkloric, the other intellectual and systematic. The first consisted of Sandino's political legacy as recovered and transmitted by the FSLN, the "projects, attitudes and beliefs, mode of behavior and concrete actions of Sandino."[132] The result was a collective memory and heroic image of Sandino as a man of the people. Originally, his objectives and the reasons behind them were "transmitted from father to son among the peasant families that had become involved directly or indirectly in the Sandinista campaign."[133] Later, the FSLN disseminated these stories among other Nicaraguan families, stories transmitting a desire for social change and opposition to imperialism and dictatorship. Commitment to this popular version of Sandinismo required neither an acceptance of communism nor a knowledge of Marxism-Leninism.

The second form of Sandinismo reinterpreted and reformulated its popular content in light of the new Marxism. In legitimizing Sandino's thought, Fonseca transformed it into the ideological axis for adapting Marxism-Leninism to Nicaragua. Consequently, commitment to this advanced form of Sandinismo also signified an acceptance of communism.

For the FSLN the first or undeveloped version of Sandinismo served as a stepping-stone to the second or developed version. If we recall how Sandino's precommunist ideology helped prepare his Defending Army to accept the principles of communism, we have reason to believe that the FSLN deliberately adopted a similar policy. Not until after the victory over Somoza and the ensuing consolidation of revolutionary power did the FSLN embark on a massive campaign to raise the political consciousness of Sandinistas to a higher level.

In response to the U.S.-backed counterrevolutionary offensive in March 1982 and the declaration of a wartime national state of emergency, Sandinista leaders and the FSLN's official organ, *Barricada*, began stressing the obsolescence of folkloric Sandinismo and its supersession by Fonseca's intellectual version of Sandinismo.[134] They paid special attention to the vanguard role of Nicaragua's agricultural and industrial proletariat in carrying forward the revolution begun by Sandino. They also recognized the lessons Marx and Lenin drew from history as fundamental to the emancipation of this new social force, which had acquired historical importance only after World War II.[135] Because of the threat from abroad and the workers' increasing demands for socialism, the FSLN's leaders began saying that to be a fully developed Sandinista one also had to be a Marxist-Leninist.

By Marxism-Leninism they meant the new Marxism rather than the old. Unlike the Marxism of the PSN, the new Marxism allowed for a residue of Sandinismo that was not an extension of scientific socialism; it was a residue of revolutionary myths, the moral values of Christianity, the liberal commitment to human rights, and the patriotic values of Sandino. The ideology of this new Marxism or new-style Leninism, although at variance with scientific socialism, was one of the keys to making the revolution.[136]

There is general agreement that the revival of Sandino's movement dates from the efforts by Nicaraguan Marxists to rescue his political legacy from oblivion and to infuse it with a Marxist understanding of Nicaraguan reality. The three principal founders of the FSLN—Fonseca, Borge, and Mayorga—each learned his Marxism from the Nicaraguan Socialist party.[137] They turned to Sandino's writings in an effort to root their Marxism in a nationally based tradition.

But that is not the whole story. In speeches and writings by current members of the National Directorate, Sandinismo is presented in more than one light. Sometimes the Marxist components are stressed; on other occasions Sandino's contribution stands out. Two approaches are necessary because initially the revolutionary vanguard was motivated to act by one set of considerations and the masses by another. For the vanguard there could be no revolutionary movement and no intelligent strategy without a revolutionary theory; but neither could there be a revolutionary movement without Sandino's patriotic values and example. Thus concessions were made to the popular current within Sandinismo.

Fonseca's 1964 statement of the nature of Sandinismo, *Desde la cárcel yo acuso a la dictadura* (*From prison I accuse the dictatorship*), was an open appeal to the Nicaraguan people to join ranks against Somoza. It consisted of two parts: an indictment of the crimes and other illegal acts by the effective head of state, Anastasio Somoza Debayle; and the sketch of a program for united popular action combining the principles of scientific socialism and a call to make ideological concessions for the sake of political unity.[138]

In an effort to broaden his popular support, Fonseca rejected a one-sided commitment to Marxism-Leninism. Publicly, he even denied being a Marxist-Leninist: "I am not a Marxist-Leninist and I didn't cease to be one at this moment!"[139] He could have been telling the truth, considering the ambivalence of "Marxism-Leninism," identified by the media with the alien doctrines emanating from the Soviet Union. As far back as 1961, he recalled, he had written a letter to the leader of Nicaragua's Conservative party setting forth his revolutionary, popular, and anti-imperialist views, views that should not be confused with Marxism.[140] Acknowledging that his pamphlet *Un nicaragüense en Moscú* had stressed the positive and humanitarian achievements of the Soviet regime, he claimed that this admission was not tantamount to accepting communism. He disagreed with the Communists, he explained, in holding that private property still had an important role to play in the future development of his country.

In his prison statement Fonseca urged Nicaraguans to embrace an ideology that would bring about their effective liberation. Such an ideology would not be exclusive. Declaring himself an open-minded Sandinista, he said, "In my thought I welcome the popular essence of the distinct ideologies of Marxism, of Liberalism, of Social Christianity."[141] He then described the popular essence and utility of each. Marxism is valuable not only for its approach to social problems, but also for its capacity to organize people's lives with a view to changing the world. Liberalism is valuable for its defense of individual rights, for its power to move the rich to resist the government's corruption, and because the bourgeois-democratic revolution is based on a historic process that in Nicaragua is not yet finished. Social Christianity is valuable for its progressive uses of Christian doctrine and for saving Christianity from becoming a monopoly of conservative and counterrevolutionary forces. Fonseca concluded his review of the principal appeals for social change by calling for a broad front of Nicaragua's youth based on a common commitment, a national revolutionary ideology that must be the work of Marxists, Liberals, and Social Christians alike—an ideology like Sandino's.

Fonseca also envisioned the creation of a Sandinista party that would encompass most of the new generation. In the interest of common action against the dictatorship, this party would avoid quarreling with other opposition parties, such as the Nicaraguan Socialist party, the Independent Liberal party, and the Social Christian party.[142] Although one ought to criticize their errors, he observed, this should be done in a constructive spirit without resentment. The most urgent task, Fonseca indicated, was to build a united movement in which the various parties might maintain their independence and respective moral commitments. In effect, he anticipated two different kinds of political pluralism: that of a Sandinista movement combining the revolutionary features of Marxism, Liberalism, and Social Christianity; and that of a patriotic front including the corresponding political parties.

Both varieties of political pluralism were unacceptable to Nicaragua's textbook Marxists and sectarians of the PSN. In practice, Fonseca agreed with Mariátegui that more than a scientifically based theory is needed to mobilize the masses for revolution, that revolutionaries must appeal to nonrational as well as rational motives, to the will to believe and to basic human sentiments. A revolutionary must learn to make concessions to the people's lack of political awareness—that is the message of his prison statement.

But there was a limit, Fonseca believed, to the number and kinds of concessions that should be made. Five years later he criticized the Sandinista movement and himself for having temporarily succumbed to ideological opportunism. "Although the Sandinista Front of National Liberation raised an anti-imperialist banner, including that of the emancipation of the exploited classes, it vacillated in presenting a clearly Marxist-Leninist ideology."[143] As a result, the public was not given an opportunity to choose between the "real Marxists" of the FSLN and the "false Marxists" of the PSN. The FSLN could not resist the temptation to cater to the political backwardness of the masses; it underestimated the people's capacity to accept Marxism because of the bad name given to it by the PSN. These were the factors that had "led to vacillation and to the adoption of an ideology that on the national plane was founded on a compromise."[144] The mistake lay in presenting Marxism on a par with Liberalism and Social Christianity, Fonseca concluded, when it was precisely Marxism that had motivated the search for a form of ideological pluralism capable of overcoming differences and cementing the unity of the revolutionary forces.

This position was reaffirmed in Fonseca's November 1970 interview in Havana. In outlining the sources of Sandinista thought, he began by stressing the contribution of Marxism and its reinterpretation by Che Guevara. Marxist socialism rather than radical populism was taken as the guide to solving Nicaragua's pressing problems. Fonseca's only concession to political pluralism was the following: "Although we believe that the principles of scientific socialism must be the fundamental guide, we are willing to march together with persons who have the most diverse beliefs and are interested in overthrowing the tyranny and in liberating our country."[145]

This interview was a candid account of what Fonseca really believed. Among the principal influences on his thought he acknowledged the deep impression created by the overthrow of Jacobo Arbenz's popular government in Guatemala (1954), the assassination of the first Somoza by the revolutionary poet Rigoberto López Pérez (1956), and the example of the Cuban guerrillas fighting in the Sierra Maestra against the Batista dictatorship (1958).[146] The Cuban influence, he acknowledged, was the decisive one for Nicaraguan revolutionaries like himself. Inspired by the Cuban example, the veteran Sandinista general Ramón Raudales had dedicated himself in 1958 to the task of reviving the armed struggle that had been brutally interrupted in 1934. "One may say that Marxism catches fire in a broad sector of the people and of the Nicaraguan youth with the triumph of the Cuban Revolution."[147]

In his other political writings we find Fonseca acknowledging a major debt to Che Guevara—except that Sandino's name invariably precedes that of the Argentine guerrilla. I interpret this to have been a concession to Nicaraguan nationalism. In any case, Guevara's influence was paramount in the observations made in Fonseca's 1970 broadcast during the temporary takeover of a Managua radio station: "Socialist and national emancipation are united in the Sandinista People's Revolution. We identify with socialism but we are not uncritical of the socialist experience. For the most part, socialism has fulfilled the expectations placed on it by history and humanity. The frustrations are not the rule but the exception."[148]

However, for the FSLN to have imposed a socialist ideology on rank-and-file Sandinistas would have undermined its credibility while duplicating the work of the Nicaraguan Socialist party. Disagreements over long-range political goals and principles as well as philosophical differences concerning the nature of man and the meaning of human existence were expected to persist during the foreseeable future. Although a house divided cannot stand, ideological differences were minimized in the effort to reach agreement on immediate and more pressing objectives.

This point was reiterated in a 1972 interview with Ricardo Morales Avilés, a member of the National Directorate who died in combat a year later. Published as a pamphlet by the FSLN, the interview concluded with a series of questions and answers concerning political and strategical issues. Asked whether the unity of the revolutionary forces requires a single ideology, Morales replied that ideological contradictions exist not only between but also within revolutionary organizations, differences that can be eradicated only at the cost of internal disruption.[149] There are fundamental philosophical differences between Marxists and Christians; but that does not prevent them from studying national problems with the aim of establishing socialism in Nicaragua, from working together and agreeing on the same strategical objectives and tactics. Although a Marxist approach to politics is fundamental to Sandinismo, Morales concluded, a Marxist worldview is not.[150]

The latter is essential to Marxism, but is it a necessary prerequisite for revolution? In a major address in December 1979,

Humberto Ortega indicated that it was superfluous.[151] Essential to the Nicaraguan Revolution were national values and the patriotic example of Sandino: "We found political, military, doctrinal, and moral elements in our people and in our history, not in foreign texts or theories of any kind."[152] Even the FSLN's theory was said to be Sandino's creation: "Sandinismo survived because it was the product of the concrete conditions of our country, because Sandino . . . made the people's needs his own, interpreted them, and with his struggle and actions created the theory we have recovered!"[153] Such statements reinforced the popular tendency in Sandinismo, which was alien to classical Marxism, while simultaneously deterring this current from becoming hostile to the FSLN's Marxist leadership.

Víctor Tirado also urged concessions to national values and traditions. He assimilated Marxist theory from the Communist party of his native country but learned to adapt it to the conditions of struggle in Nicaragua. In an interview in April 1979, he declared, "Some forces classify us as a Marxist tendency, as communist. We have never affirmed that we are Marxists. We are a revolutionary front. Although among us are Marxists, there are also Christians. We take positions that are revolutionary and Sandinista." Asked to clarify what he meant by "Sandinista," he replied, "This is equivalent to nationalist. For to be able to give the anti-Somoza process a popular content we have to adopt national values. We shall not fail, since we raise the flag of Augusto César Sandino; we shall complete the work he was unable to consummate . . . with national values. That is why Sandinismo has popular appeal. To adopt international values would be something distinct because the people have no information about them." What concerned the FSLN, Tirado contended, was not whether its militants came from a Marxist party or had assimilated Marxist theory: "What interests us is that they are fully aware of *national values,* of Sandinista values."[154]

The program and objectives of the FSLN were certainly not Marxist, Tirado continued, nor was the struggle in Nicaragua over the question of capitalism versus communism. The issue was whether the people wanted dictatorship or democracy. The FSLN's objectives were democratic: overthrow of the tyrant; installation of a provisional government representative of all social classes; creation of a people's army in place of the elitist National Guard; formulation of an independent and nonaligned foreign policy; support for popular causes in Central America and the Caribbean; expropriation of the properties of Somoza and his inner circle; and application of a program of economic reconstruction.[155]

Tirado's statements recall Fonseca's earlier ones from prison in 1964. Only after victory, in his November 1979 speech on the third anniversary of Fonseca's death, did he affirm the Marxist dimension of Sandinismo. "Neo-Sandinismo"—Tirado's term for Sandino's political thought as refashioned by Fonseca and the FSLN—had its roots in the ideology, theory, and practice of Sandino as developed in the light of the Russian, Cuban, and Vietnamese revolutions.[156] Thanks to the Marxism of Lenin and Che Guevara, contemporary Sandinismo represented a unique blend of Nicaraguan nationalism and the contributions of revolutionary movements in other countries. "The original source of our revolutionary theory is national but never, listen well, never have we failed to take into account the experiences of Cuba, of the Soviet Union, of Vietnam, and of other peoples who struggled against oppression and exploitation. We take Sandino's thought as our starting point, but we have never ceased to consider the thought of Marx, of Lenin, of Che Guevara."[157]

Although an ally of the FSLN, the Nicaraguan Socialist party bitterly rejects the FSLN's concessions to popular ideology. In its judgment, the figure of the heroic general stands in the way of a consistent struggle for socialism in Nicaragua, because his ideas represent a conception of the world incompatible with Marxism-Leninism.[158] Behind the scenes the PSN criticizes the Sandinista leaders for *not* being good Leninists. Guevara's brand of Marxism is also judged to be defective. Formally speaking, the PSN is right in claiming that the new Marxism diverges at various points from Leninist orthodoxy. But orthodoxy does not always lead to revolutionary effectiveness, and where it does not, as in Nicaragua, it rather than Sandinismo is incompatible with the revolutionary essence of Marxism-Leninism.

Fonseca's reformulation of Sandino's thought provided Marxism with a popular vehicle, which the PSN lacked, for making its influence felt on a national scale. The FSLN took to heart the maxim that there can be no leaders without followers, no revolutionary vanguard without significant concessions to the masses. Since Marxism-Leninism in Nicaragua had to retreat before a virulent and widespread anticommunism, an ideology that contradicted the premises of scientific socialism was required to mobilize the people. In rejecting the PSN's supervision, according to Tirado, Fonseca saved the FSLN from becoming a dogmatic sect alien to the history and experience of the Nicaraguan people: "Deeds have demonstrated the uselessness of the PSN's counsels."[159]

The PSN's distrust of Sandinismo is rooted in the anti-ideological strain of classical Marxism. Marx and Engels had resisted efforts to confuse their scientific outlook with the moral sentiments and prejudices of the workers. Idealistic, mystifying, and conventional appeals to morality were only grudgingly accepted, and then only under pressure from representatives of the workers' movement.[160] Wrote Marx in March 1875, "What a crime it is to . . . force on our party again . . . obsolete rubbishy phrases, while . . . perverting the realistic outlook . . . by means of ideological nonsense about 'right' and other trash common among the democrats and French Socialists!"[161] Fonseca and the FSLN were not so cavalier. Under the influence of Che Guevara they developed their own revolutionary ethics, and Marxism was redefined as both a science and an unscientific postscript for waging the class struggle.

The history of contemporary revolutions, beginning with the October Revolution of 1917, had shown that Marx's grudging concessions to the ideological currents among the masses were far from sufficient. The Marxism of the Communist or Third International did not make up for this deficiency. Lenin's advocacy of a specifically communist morality dissolved on analysis into a pseudoethics based exclusively on class interest and the worker's own self-interest.[162] Obligation, duty, self-sacrifice—the nonrational components of morality—were conspicuously absent. For Leninism, as for classical Marxism, the only rationale for risking human life in a revolutionary upheaval was that workers have only their chains to lose, because their lives are not worth living under the old system, and they have a world to win.

The new Marxism spawned by the Cuban Revolution challenged this preconception. In Nicaragua the FSLN made concessions to the people's prejudices and nonrational convictions from the beginning. The cult of Sandino performed an indispensable role in mobilizing the masses for a general insurrection, as did the FSLN's moral commitment to human rights and the concessions it made to the revolutionary current in Christianity (to be considered in the final chapter). The unique contribution of the Cuban and Nicaraguan revolutions was not only to adapt Marxism to the peculiar conditions of each country, but also to remold it as part of an indigenous movement independent of the local Communist parties. What Fidel Castro's revival of José Martí did for the July 26 movement in Cuba, Fonseca's recovery of Sandino's political legacy did for the struggle against imperialism and dictatorship in Nicaragua.

In its development of the new Marxism, the FSLN has shown political, strategical, and ideological flexibility. Its nonsectarian and pragmatic approach to making a revolution appears in its leaders' refusal to adhere rigidly to a supposedly "correct line," whether to a unitary assessment of political and historical events, or to a narrow and exclusive political-military strategy, or to a monolithic ideology. Although Marxist-Leninist parties also try to be flexible, their flexibility does not extend to matters of ideology.

Political flexibility should not be mistaken for lack of principle. Nonetheless, some Marxist-Leninist parties, including the PSN, have charged the FSLN with "opportunism." In their public statements the Sandinista leaders do in fact give the impression of having rejected "communism," howsoever one interprets this emotionally charged and ambivalent term. As Bayardo Arce, the effective general secretary of the FSLN, said in a recent interview, "If you find a political project such as ours where 70 percent of the economy is in private hands, where you have 12 legally existing political parties, where all religion is freely operating, where you have radios and newspapers that freely operate pro and con . . . , that is Sandinismo, and that type of project certainly does not attract communists!"[163] After the revolution triumphed, he added, all sorts of people began calling themselves Sandinistas. That is why Sandinismo has become a synthesis of different and even opposed political and ideological currents not only of applied Marxism and Christianity: "I can also tell you that it is liberalism applied in Nicaragua!"[164]

Such statements are meant not only to be witty, but also to undercut hostile criticism of the FSLN. Actually, they are based on an esoteric or secret political line that is a distinguishing characteristic of revolutionary vanguards. Although the FSLN's propaganda has shifted in response to changing events and political pressures, its commitment to an economic, political, and cultural revolution in Nicaragua has remained unchanged. And because the FSLN's fundamental line continues firm, what is believed to be opportunism is not political flabbiness but revolutionary shrewdness aimed at winning political friends and neutralizing potential enemies. Despite Arce's disclaimers, the Sandinista project of political pluralism and a mixed economy *does* attract "communists."

Another and fundamentally different image of Sandinismo is widespread among supporters of the Nicaraguan Revolution in the United States. Several eminent scholars, including specialists on Central America, have so stressed the peculiar national characteristics of the Nicaraguan Revolution that it appears to offer a third path promising the best of both the capitalist and socialist worlds. Conservative ideologues are mistaken, they claim, in believing that the presence of Marxists in the FSLN's leadership indicates that the revolutionary government will follow the pattern set by the Cuban Revolution. On the contrary, "although they logically felt [and feel] a bond of friendship and found [find] much in common with the only real revolutionary government in Latin America, the Nicaraguan revolutionaries, above all, were [and are] nationalists."[165] A similar portrait could be painted of Sandino.

Given this populist image of Sandinismo, the supposed perils of communism represented by the FSLN are dismissed because of their "patently bogus nature." Rather than an application of Marxism-Leninism to Nicaragua, the FSLN's Sandinismo is associated with a "cluster of highly nationalistic and political-economic reformist symbols with deep roots in the Nicaraguan psyche." Thus the impression is created that Sandinista ideology has a purely "populist origin and framework."[166] Such statements mistake the FSLN's appearance for reality.

Although the Sandinista leaders no longer disclaim their Marxism, as they once did, they present to the public an innocent version of what they mean by it. Said Humberto Ortega in an address on 1 September 1980, "In Nicaragua the revolution triumphed with a clearly Marxist leadership, but not with a Marxistoid and bookish one that advertised itself as being 'Marxist-Leninist' and that understood by Marxism-Leninism something completely deformed and rigid. We did not understand Marxism in that way but as something else, as simply an instrument of analysis. . . . One has to study history and to find in history . . . the elements of this revolution."[167]

In characterizing Marxism as a mere instrument of analysis, Ortega sought to emphasize its scientific contribution. Who would object to that? Or to his professed concern for social justice? "I should have no fear in saying that we are in search of a just society, a society without exploiters and exploited. . . . If there are Christians like Gaspar García Laviana who gave their blood to make this revolution, then that is what counts!"[168] In short, the FSLN stands for an ideological revision of Marxism-Leninism fortified by Sandino's revolutionary legacy.

What, then, *is* Sandinismo? It is an amalgam of Marxist theory and Sandino's revolutionary legacy under the auspices of the new Marxism. Like the new Marxism, Sandinismo has three principal dimensions: it offers an explanation of historical events; it arouses people to act with emotional appeals; and it serves as a guide to action. Marx's principles of scientific socialism hold sway in the area of historical explanation. Sandino's patriotic ideas and example prevail in matters of ideology. Sandinista practice is shaped by both of these components. In effect, Sandinismo is Sandino's revolutionary legacy impregnated with the new Marxism.

6. Political Assessments

The FSLN began its armed actions with a set of theoretical guide-lines—the principles of scientific socialism—for interpreting what was happening in Nicaragua and the world. The Nicaraguan So-cialist party shared the same guidelines with strikingly diverse results. Differences emerged concerning how to apply Marxism-Leninism to the concrete conditions of Nicaragua's history and socioeconomic reality. Further differences arose within the FSLN, which developed several contradictory interpretations of the ex-isting political situation as seen through the prism of the new Marxism. Some were less realistic than others, and most had to be revised and in part rejected because of the mistakes to which they led.

Initially, the FSLN relied on Fonseca's efforts to update San-dino's account of the war in Nicaragua. This interpretation was based on Che Guevara's version of neocolonialism as the final stage of imperialism. Subsequently, Ricardo Morales Avilés was respon-sible for an alternative assessment based on Gramsci's concept of political hegemony and Mao's analysis of class contradictions. This interpretation was challenged by Jaime Wheelock's application of neo-Marxist dependency theory to Nicaragua. Finally, Humberto Ortega presented a composite picture of Nicaraguan reality influ-enced by Fidel Castro's perception of the revolutionary process in Latin America.

At issue was whether the fundamental opposition between Nicaragua's bourgeoisie and the rest of society was active or latent, focal or peripheral to the problems that had actually surfaced. Dif-ferences arose concerning how to characterize the struggles that were daily occurring. Were the bourgeoisie and big landowners im-mediately pitted against workers and peasants (Fonseca); were capi-talists quarreling mainly over the division of the spoils (Morales); was there a direct confrontation between capitalists and workers (Wheelock); or were the issues too complex to be reduced to any one of these formulations (Ortega)? In any case, the picture that emerged was of a bourgeoisie reluctant to defend the country's interests because of dependence on the U.S. multinationals and the State Department. This common perception of the changed role even of that sector of the bourgeoisie producing for the domestic market—the misnamed "national bourgeoisie"—was part of the intellectual legacy of the Cuban Revolution.[1]

Nicaragua's Neocolonial Status

Sandino's sketch of Anglo-Saxon interventions in Nicaragua covered the period from his country's independence from Spain in 1821 to the final withdrawal of the U.S. Marines in 1933. In *Nicaragua: hora cero*, Fonseca took up the story where Sandino left off, adding to the traditional role of U.S. imperialism in Nicaragua the altered structure of neoimperialism or neocolonialism and the new forms taken by the struggle for national liberation in the wake of the Cuban Revolution.

The key to Nicaragua's history since Sandino's death, Fonseca contended, lay in its neocolonial status in relation to the United States. The withdrawal of the marines in 1933 did not substantially alter Nicaragua's victimization by U.S. business interests: "The Nicaraguan people have been suffering under the yoke of a reactionary *camarilla* imposed by Yankee imperialism practically since 1932, the year when Anastasio Somoza was designated commander-in-chief of the so-called National Guard—a post previously held by Yankee officials. This *camarilla* has reduced Nicaragua to the status of a neocolony exploited by both the Yankee monopolies and the native capitalist class."[2] From having directly occupied and dominated the country for more than two decades, the United States entered a new phase in which its intervention in Nicaragua's affairs took place indirectly through economic concessions to the government and to the Somoza family's business ventures. In return, Somoza collaborated with U.S. designs for overthrowing popular regimes and containing national liberation movements in the Caribbean area.

The extent of the Somoza dynasty's betrayal of national interests was highlighted by Fonseca's discussion of Nicaragua as a base of military aggression.[3] In 1948 Anastasio Somoza García intervened in Costa Rica's civil war. The war culminated in the repression of the labor movement in that country. In 1954 his government supported the CIA-financed Guatemalan mercenaries who overthrew the democratic government of Jacobo Arbenz. In 1961 his son Luis Somoza offered Nicaragua as a base for training the anti-Castro forces that embarked from Puerto Cabezas but were defeated at the Bay of Pigs. In 1965 troops of the National Guard captained by U.S. Marines occupied Santo Domingo and crushed the Constitutionalist movement in the Dominican Republic. And in 1967 Anastasio Somoza Debayle announced his decision to send contingents of the National Guard to participate alongside the U.S. forces in Vietnam. Here we perceive traces of Sandino's interpretation of Nicaragua's history as a function of the "Wall Street bankers" in conjunction with the "White House" and Nicaragua's corrupt political leaders.

For Sandino the United States was both the fundamental enemy of the Nicaraguan people and the immediate or visible enemy. But with the transformation of old-style imperialism into neo-imperialism, according to Fonseca's analysis, the immediate enemy became the reactionary Somoza *camarilla* representing U.S. interests. Although conceding the existence of rival sectors among Nicaragua's capitalists, Fonseca stressed the hegemonic role of the sector in control of the government. The government "manipulates the funds of the state banks as if these were personal funds . . . , the Somoza family, which on assuming power disposed of very limited economic resources, now has a vast fiefdom whose dominions extend beyond Nicaragua's frontiers to the other Central American countries."[4]

Despite economic and political differences between the Nicaraguan capitalists in power and those in opposition, they have much in common. "Although the capitalist government sector represents the part of the capitalist class that dominates, one should note that the capitalist sector referring to itself as the 'opposition' also participates in the exploitation of the Nicaraguan people. In many instances the government sector and the 'opposition' jointly exploit important lines of business in the national economy, as in the case of sugar, milk, the press, the banks, liquor distilleries, etc."[5] This means that the fundamental opposition was not between Nicaragua's capitalists, but between the exploited classes of workers and peasants and the entire capitalist class in association with the U.S. monopolies and the State Department.

Fonseca believed that this conflict, which until then had simmered beneath the surface, had become the focus of class struggles in Nicaragua. "The FSLN thinks that during the present and for some time to come, Nicaragua will be passing through a stage in which a radical political force will continue taking shape. Thus at the present moment it is necessary for us to emphasize that our great objective is a socialist revolution."[6] Besides a struggle for national liberation against imperialism and the Somoza dictatorship, Fonseca foresaw a parallel and simultaneous struggle aimed at preventing the "false opposition" from acquiring political power and the "false revolutionaries"—a slap at the PSN—from deceiving the masses concerning the issues at stake.[7]

This was not the PSN's assessment. In agreement with the other communist parties in the hemisphere, it claimed that the two most urgent problems in Central and South America were the struggle against imperialist exploitation, and semifeudal conditions in the countryside. Together imperialism and the landed oligarchy were held responsible for obstructing Nicaragua's economic development. Nicaragua's cosmopolitan bourgeoisie and the multinationals were blamed for siphoning off more capital in the form of profits than they had invested in the country, and the landed oligarchs were blamed for relying on labor-intensive instead of capital-intensive methods in agriculture. Opposed to imperialism and the landed oligarchy were the so-called people, consisting of four principal classes: the "workers," or class of wage earners in industry, commerce, and agriculture; the "peasants," who barely subsisted whether as sharecroppers or cultivators of their own small plots; the misnamed "petite bourgeoisie" of small shopkeepers and petty manufacturers, whose small capital was only a secondary source of their livelihood; and the "national bourgeoisie" of small, medium, and big capitalists producing mainly for the domestic market. Since the people's struggle against imperialism and the landed oligarchy had become the focus of the class struggle in Nicaragua, the PSN concluded, the confrontation between the workers and the national bourgeoisie would have to wait until these more urgent problems had been settled.

In opposition to the theses of the PSN, Fonseca took his guidelines from Che Guevara, who differed from the Soviet manuals on two crucial issues. One concerned the interpretation of economic "underdevelopment," and the other the role of the "national bourgeoisie."

"Underdevelopment," Guevara believed, was the most urgent economic problem confronting the Latin American republics. But its causes were not simply a function of the decapitalization of industry and the undercapitalization of agriculture. He likened "underdevelopment" to a dwarf with an enormous head and a swollen chest, but with spindle legs and short arms that do not match the rest of the torso.[8] It is the product of a malfunction. "Ours are countries with distorted economies because of imperialist policy that has abnormally developed the industrial or agricultural branches to complement the imperialists' own complex economies. 'Underdevelopment' or distorted development carries with it a dangerous specialization in raw materials that holds over our peoples the threat of hunger. . . . We are also countries of monoculture, of a single product . . . , the uncertain sale of which depends on a single market."[9] Thus to imperialism conceived as exploitation by foreign capital he added the phenomenon of economic dependency and, on top of that, what he called HUNGER OF THE PEOPLE: "weariness from being oppressed, abused, and exploited to the maximum; weariness from selling one's labor day after day from fear of becoming a part of the great mass of unemployed."[10] In short, workers and peasants were hungry for a revolutionary change, a "true revolution against the owners of capital."[11]

In this perspective, the "national bourgeoisie" was not part of the "people." "The national bourgeoisie . . . fears popular revolution even more than the oppression and despotic dominion of imperialism . . . and since the beginning has not hesitated to ally itself with imperialism and the landowners to fight against the people and to close the road to revolution."[12] Guevara used the word *oligarchy* for this reactionary alliance between all sectors of the bourgeoisie and the landlord class in Latin America. Their combined rule even within a legal system of representative government he characterized as an "oligarchical dictatorship," because their acceptance of legality was only skin deep and because they violated both the laws and the constitution when it was in their interest to do so—as in Nicaragua.[13] Even the modernizing sector of the bourgeoisie producing for the domestic market had betrayed the national interest for the benefits of working on close terms with foreign capitalists and subsidiaries of the multinationals:

> The national bourgeoisies have, in the majority, banded together with U.S. imperialism; thus their fate and that of imperialism will be the same in each country. Even when . . . a contradiction develops with U.S. imperialism, this occurs within the boundaries of a more fundamental conflict . . . [involving] *all the exploited* and *all the exploiters*. This polarization of classes into antagonistic forces has so far been more rapid than the development of contradictions over the division of the spoils.[14]

Underlying the political differences between Fonseca and the PSN were their differing assessments of Nicaragua's neocolonial status. The PSN believed that the national bourgeoisie had a progressive role to play because neoimperialism—the principal enemy of autonomous economic development—functioned as a force external to Nicaragua's economy. By nationalizing foreign enterprises and stopping the drain of capital abroad, the national bourgeoisie could presumably develop an independent form of capitalism like that in Western Europe and the United States. But if, as Guevara believed, economic dependence was somehow internalized through the integration of the satellite economy into the world capitalist market, which precluded the national bourgeoisie's acting independently, then there could be no hope for an autonomous road to development.[15] By implication, the struggle for socialism was not premature when the anti-imperialist and antifeudal struggle had to be waged against the national bourgeoisie instead of with it.[16]

Against the thesis of Latin American Communists that revolutions develop through clearly demarcated stages, Guevara revived the early Leninist doctrine of a continuing revolution. Instead of the two stages of the coming revolution, a bourgeois-democratic stage followed by a socialist stage, he envisioned a single revolutionary process dominated from the beginning by a coalition of workers and peasants led by a revolutionary vanguard. Whereas most Communist parties allowed for the leading role of bourgeois nationalists during the initial stage of struggle against imperialism and feudalism, Guevara agreed with Lenin's famous passage and applied it to Latin America: "We know that owing to their class position they are incapable of waging a decisive struggle against tsarism. . . . The only force capable of gaining 'a decisive victory over tsarism' is the *people*, i.e., the proletariat and the peasantry, if we take the main big forces, and distribute the rural and urban petty bourgeoisie (also part of 'the people') between the two."[17]

Fonseca agreed with Guevara that throughout Latin America U.S. monopoly capital holds sway. Regional integration of Nicaragua's economy, he observed, was part of an economic plan to submit the entire Central American market to the U.S.-based multinationals. The scandal had reached such proportions that even Somoza felt pressured to declare publicly that the industries established as a result of integration had not contributed to Nicaragua's economic growth.[18] Economic dependence was being reinforced by Nicaragua's status as a political satellite; an informal alliance of the Central American puppet governments with the United States was becoming the political force behind regional integration. As Guevara wrote in his message to the *Tricontinental*, "The puppet governments or, in the best of cases, the weak or fearful ones cannot disobey orders from the Yankee boss."[19]

As for the national bourgeoisie, its policy of modernization had been taken up by Somoza's Liberal party in opposition to the

politically reactionary Conservative party.[20] Thus it would have
been self-defeating to ally with the Liberals. The PSN's mistake,
Fonseca noted, was to have supported the Liberal party against the
Conservative opposition because it believed that the national bourgeoisie was still basically opposed to imperialism.[21] From 1959 to
1962, the FSLN harbored the illusion that it could succeed in changing the PSN's opportunist line. The course of events showed not
only that this was impossible, but also that it was hopeless to expect any kind of working agreement with the party's leaders.[22]

Fonseca's work provided the foundation for a series of more detailed studies of Nicaragua's socioeconomic and political conditions. These addressed themselves to two central issues: the nature
and causes of the political crisis in Nicaragua under the Somoza
dynasty; and the class character and social composition of the
Somoza dictatorship.

The Rise of a Bourgeois Opposition

One of the earliest studies of this kind was by Ricardo Morales
Avilés. Consisting of a 1973 taped lecture and reply to questions, it
was later issued by the FSLN as *La dominación imperialista en
Nicaragua*.

Morales viewed the correlation of class forces in Nicaragua as a
function of the contradiction between the local bourgeoisie allied
to foreign capitalists, and the working class in conjunction with
the rest of the people.[23] Given this fundamental premise, his task
was to investigate the "structure of domination" involving foreign
interests, and the "crisis of domination" or "crisis of political
hegemony" of the Nicaraguan bourgeoisie.[24] As we shall see,
Morales's interpretation of Nicaragua's politico-economic situation
in the seventies supported the FSLN's changed strategy of "armed
struggle developed in the form of prolonged people's war," a strategy based on Mao Tse-tung's analysis of class contradictions.[25]

Morales contended that in Nicaragua the structure of domination had taken a different form from that in the more developed
countries of Latin America, where the traditional landed oligarchy
had been replaced by a new national bourgeoisie producing for the
local market. "On the contrary, in our country there is no crisis of
the oligarchy, of its political hegemony, but rather . . . a fusion of
the traditional oligarchy with the new bourgeois force, the new elements of the bourgeoisie; in other words, the oligarchy becomes
bourgeoisified, it becomes modernized, and it participates in the

modernization of the forms of domination."[26] There was a "crisis of political hegemony," to use Gramsci's expression, but it was not a crisis of the traditional oligarchy.

In Nicaragua the crisis of political hegemony emerged from this new structure of domination, not from the old. As a crisis of the bourgeoisie in its totality and of the related structure of imperialist penetration, it showed itself "as the incapacity of the bourgeois class to get its particular class interests accepted as the general interests of society."[27] It was a crisis of legitimacy because the working class, the peasantry, and the middle sectors rejected the values that the bourgeoisie wanted to impose on the nation.[28]

According to Morales, with the development of cotton production during the fifties and the accompanying industrialization process, Nicaragua managed to bypass a Mexican-type confrontation with the traditional landowners. The result was an interlocking of the interests of the old Conservative cattle and coffee oligarchy with those of the Liberal modernizing bourgeoisie. The capitalization of agricultural production from above rather than below closed the door on agrarian reform, with the effect of shutting out small and medium enterprises from sharing in the expanding surplus created by the new agribusinesses.[29] The oligarchy's monopolization of financial credits excluded the bulk of the bourgeoisie from investing in these new industries. At the same time, the accumulation of the surplus in a few hands and the lack of effective demand by the country's workers and peasants contributed to stifling the internal market.[30] This meant that alongside the promotion of capitalist agriculture for export, production for domestic consumption continued to be dominated by precapitalist forms. In short, the only dynamic sector of the economy was the capitalist export sector and the specific industries serving it. The crisis of the traditional oligarchies had been avoided, but at the price of a crisis in the new structure of domination.

Since the dynamic sector of the economy was the export sector penetrated by foreign capital, the structure of native bourgeois domination was inextricably linked to the structure of imperialist domination. The monopoly of credit by Nicaragua's old and new robber barons depended directly on the monopoly of financial resources by the American banks.[31] The fortunes of Nicaragua's big bourgeoisie depended on both the extent of foreign investment opportunities in Nicaragua and on their profitability. Morales listed three principal sources of the profits on which the structure of domination depended: financial profits or interest from loans to the handful of local capitalists directly or indirectly producing for export; commercial profits from the marketing of those products abroad; and industrial profits from the sale of agricultural implements and related manufactured imports indispensable to agribusiness.[32]

Within this new structure of domination by the monopoly bourgeoisie, Morales distinguished two primary sectors: a Liberal sector consisting of political and military bureaucrats who had used the state power to modernize the economy and to transform themselves into big capitalists; and a Conservative sector consisting of the established landholding families who had become "bourgeoisified" by adapting to the process of modernization.[33] Together they made up the newly integrated Liberal-Conservative oligarchy. But they were not the whole bourgeoisie. In addition to these sectors, Morales distinguished a third sector of small and medium capitalists excluded from a privileged share of the spoils.

Morales further showed that within this structure of bourgeois domination not all elements of the bourgeoisie had access to political power. The structure of domination was hierarchically organized into three main tiers: first, the top layer of the modernizing bourgeoisie consisting of the Somoza clique in control of the Liberal party; second, the Conservative bourgeoisie excluded from political power but otherwise benefiting economically from its ties to the dictatorship; and third, the bottom layer of small and medium capitalists linked to the Conservative and Independent Liberal parties legally recognized as the "political opposition."[34] It was within this structure of political domination that Morales located the causes of Nicaragua's crisis of legitimacy.

The issue of legitimacy arose, Morales argued, whenever the differences between the state bourgeoisie and the opposition bourgeoisie came to a head. The structure of domination tended to collapse because the Conservative sector of the oligarchy then joined forces with the bourgeois opposition. Why? To defend the common interest of the capitalist class against the destabilizing effects of dictatorship and the threat posed by the popular forces.[35] This polarization of the bourgeoisie into two camps, Morales concluded, was responsible for the nationwide political crisis.

Morales characterized the political crisis of domination as a crisis within the ruling class resulting from its lopsided sharing or monopolization of the economic surplus.[36] As perceived by the bourgeois opposition, these so-called inequities were the fault of the monopoly bourgeoisie and of the Somoza clique in paticular. Through its privileged access to the flow of U.S. capital, credit, and government aid, the state bourgeoisie had not only lined its own pockets, but also provided privileges for other big capitalists in their role as associates of American business.

At the same time, there were rifts within the monopoly bourgeoisie because the Somoza clique had access to most of the foreign credit and shared in the economic surplus disproportionately to its assets.[37] Through its control of the national bank and its role as the political representative of American business interests in Nicaragua, it collaborated with foreign banks in regulating the flow of credit to the comparative disadvantage of some big and most medium and small capitalists.

This analysis led Morales to characterize the Somoza regime as bourgeois despotic, as a bourgeois military dictatorship whose political hegemony was the fundamental source of its economic privileges. The dictatorship was not the armed power of the bourgeoisie, but rather "the armed bourgeoisie in power."[38] By this Morales meant that the state was not simply an executive organ for managing the common affairs of the bourgeoisie, but rather a monopoly of bureaucrats who had become capitalists through their abuse of political power. Since most of the bourgeoisie was excluded from this Liberal party monopoly controlled by the state bourgeoisie, the Somoza regime was basically unstable.

It followed from this account that intrabourgeois antagonisms were more important than the struggle between the bourgeoisie and the popular forces in explaining the crisis of political hegemony. Because the middle and lower strata of the bourgeoisie were excluded from participation in the expanding surplus, the tendency toward united action with its upper stratum was overshadowed by the tendency toward divergence and antagonism. In addition, Morales noted, this division within the capitalist class had generated a corresponding division within the popular forces. The split within the Left, between the PSN in favor of supporting the bourgeois opposition and the FSLN in favor of an independent alternative, was a reflection of this division. As long as an influential segment of the Left continued to wag the tail of the democratic wing of the business class, the focus of class antagonisms would continue unchanged: "on the one hand, the bourgeois in possession of concentrated political power, surplus value, and wealth; on the other hand, the sectors of the reformist bourgeois opposition disaffected with Somoza's mode of governing, looking for a way out, for an alternative to his mode of class domination and for a way of controlling the popular movement."[39]

This assessment of the correlation of social forces in Nicaragua departed significantly from the FSLN's earlier model. First, it established that socialism could not be on the immediate agenda because the objective conditions of revolution had yet to mature. Second, it showed the indelible imprint of Mao Tse-Tung's method of dissecting the complex and multiple contradictions of class society.

In his 1937 essay "On Contradiction," Mao argued that the contradiction between the bourgeoisie and proletariat in China was the key to understanding the entire network of class contradictions. Among the secondary contradictions that had become subordinated to the principal contradiction were those between the semifeudal landed oligarchy and the bourgeoisie, the monopoly and nonmonopoly sectors of the bourgeoisie, the bourgeoisie and the petite bourgeoisie, and the proletariat and the petite bourgeoisie.[40] In China the relationship between the principal contradiction and these secondary contradictions presented a complicated picture.

Mao posed a question that attested to his originality as a Marxist thinker: "In any given contradiction, whether principal or secondary, should the two contradictory aspects be treated as equal?" His answer was that the development of these contradictory aspects was almost invariably uneven, that their appearance of equilibrium could only be momentary. "Of the two contradictory aspects, one must be principal and the other secondary."[41] The nature of a given structure of class domination is "determined mainly by the principal aspect of a contradiction, the aspect which has gained the dominant position."[42] If the bourgeoisie has the upper hand, then its members can afford the luxury of quarreling with one another. If it does not have to maintain a solid front against the working class, then intrabourgeois contradictions will prevail. Morales believed that this was what had happened in his country.

But the principal aspect of a contradiction cannot prevail forever. Whatever had been the principal aspect then becomes secondary, which changes the structure of domination.[43] "The proletariat which is more numerous than the bourgeoisie and grows simultaneously with it but under its rule, is a new force which, initially subordinate to the bourgeoisie, gradually gains strength, becomes an independent class playing the leading role in history."[44] From having been the principal aspect, the bourgeoisie is reduced to the secondary aspect of the principal contradiction. Morales believed that matters had yet to reach this point in Nicaragua.

In studying the complexities of a given structure of domination, Mao insisted, it is necessary to investigate both the principal and secondary contradictions, and the principal and secondary aspects of each.[45] This is precisely what distinguished Morales's investigation from Fonseca's. Mao further insisted that "the study of the various states of unevenness in contradictions . . . constitutes an essential method by which a revolutionary political party correctly determines its strategic and tactical policies both in political and military affairs."[46] This method had worked miracles in China and then in Vietnam. Morales hoped that it might likewise make a difference in Nicaragua.

The Emergence of a Proletarian Vanguard

Jaime Wheelock joined the FSLN in 1969, the year Morales became a member of the National Directorate. But his studies took him to Chile during the Allende period and to the German Democratic Republic after the reactionary military coup that toppled Allende's government in September 1973. He did not return to Nicaragua until 1975. Because of his extended absence from the country and his subsequent leadership of a disaffected current within the FSLN, the so-called Proletarian Tendency, he did not become a member of the National Directorate until the major divisions within the FSLN were overcome in March 1979. Today Wheelock is minister of agricultural development in the new government and director of the Nicaraguan Institute of Agrarian Reform (INRA).

In Leipzig, Wheelock completed his first book on the roots of the anticolonial struggle in Nicaragua followed by his most important work on imperialism and the Somoza dictatorship.[47] Both books (published in Mexico) were prohibited from entering Nicaragua. Even so, they were influential in building the Proletarian Tendency, which stressed the mobilization of Nicaraguan workers and the importance of building a vanguard party of the proletariat rather than a guerrilla force in the countryside.

Wheelock's analysis was based on the premises of Latin American dependency theory. Under the direction of Brazilian political exile Theotônio Dos Santos, the Center of Socioeconomic Studies (CESO) in Santiago de Chile had brought together a distinguished group of Marxist political economists and historians. From 1967 to 1973, when the center was dissolved by the military dictatorship, Dos Santos conducted seminars on dependency theory along with André Gunder Frank, Fernando Henrique Cardoso, Enzo Faletto, Aníbal Quijano, and Wheelock's own compatriot Edelberto Torres-Rivas. Dependency theory has been characterized as an amalgam of

Marxist political economy and the radical economics of the New Left, stemming from André Gunder Frank.[48] Its principal contribution has been to supplement Lenin's theses concerning imperialist exploitation with an analysis of Latin American underdevelopment as the outcome of a particular relationship to the capitalist world market.

The extent to which the Latin American countries have been victimized by the imperialist metropolises goes beyond Lenin's focus on the export of capital and the search for cheap labor and raw materials. Their internal development has been retarded by political and economic initiatives taken by the advanced countries, a condition exacerbated by the oligarchical origins and structure of the Latin American economies. Dependent development is a reflex of the development of the dominant nations. It is geared to meeting foreign rather than national needs, and the important decisions are made abroad. Dependence on the economies of Spain and Portugal, then on Great Britain and the United States, has been a constant for all of Latin America. What has varied from period to period, according to dependency theory, have been the internal structures and external forms of dependence.[49]

Among the Latin American originators of this theory was Edelberto Torres-Rivas, to whom Wheelock dedicated his major work. Published in Chile in 1969, Torres-Rivas's analysis of Central American dependence served as a starting point for Wheelock's investigation. Its core concepts of "dependent industrialization," the "industrial associate model of growth," the "industrial associate status" of the Central American bourgeoisie, and a "developmentalist dictatorship" were used by Wheelock in his own study.[50] Also basic to Wheelock's investigation was Torres-Rivas's thesis that the enclave status of the Central American economies was not overcome through industrialization, and that their development from agro-export enclaves to industrial-associate enclaves did not change their dependence on the United States.[51]

Wheelock argued that Nicaragua's economic dependence had resulted in a weakening of the bourgeoisie along with an erosion of secondary contradictions among different sectors of the business class.[52] Unlike Morales Avilés, who played down the unity of the bourgeoisie vis-à-vis the proletariat by emphasizing their respective internal contradictions, Wheelock stressed the internal unity of both classes and their immediate as well as fundamental opposition. What united the various sectors of the business class was their lack of independence, political power, or even a government they could call their own. Because the Nicaraguan bourgeoisie had to serve American interests to advance its own, Wheelock defined it as a "consular bourgeoisie."[53] Political hegemony was not held by the bourgeoisie nor even by its most powerful sector, the Somoza clique. Since the Somoza regime represented mainly the interests of the Pentagon, the State Department, and the U.S. multinationals and only secondarily those of Nicaragua's capitalists, Wheelock contemptuously characterized it as a "military dictatorship directed through telecommunications by the State Department!"[54]

The Somoza clan developed from a bureaucratic-despotic clique, Wheelock noted, into a bourgeois-despotic one. The family's vast wealth stemmed less from business acumen than from "political-military power and the no less important power of hired assassins of imperialism at the local level."[55] Referred to as the "Group of Loaded Dice," the Somoza clique got rich through dirty tricks. It monopolized Nicaragua's institutional contacts with U.S. government and business circles; it transformed the National Guard into the family's private army. Its embezzlement of public funds and revenues from state enterprises, its extortionate salaries for public administrators, and its gangsterlike methods applied to various business ventures stamped this group as a political-military or state bourgeoisie. It was able to perpetuate these abuses because it also served imperialist interests at the local level.[56] "The incalculable riches the Somozas succeeded in accumulating throughout forty years of outrages in Nicaragua were more than the outcome of a structured series of frauds. . . . The armed interventions of imperialism and its other more subtle forms of aggression were the determining factor in the continuity of the Somozas' military dictatorship."[57]

Wheelock concluded his work by disputing the "theses concerning the alleged 'crisis' within the Nicaraguan bourgeoisie"— an indirect reference to Morales's assessment of Nicaraguan reality, which had become adopted by the FSLN's National Directorate.[58] Intrabourgeois contradictions, he argued, were marginal to understanding what was happening in Nicaragua. The Conservative bourgeois had sided with the Somoza regime far more often than not, even though they strove to make it more "representative."[59]

The crisis had to be sought elsewhere, in the impediments to economic development resulting from the dependent character of Nicaraguan capitalism.[60] Besides the fetters on economic growth imposed by the structure of dependency, two contradictions with U.S. imperialism were undermining the local hegemony of Nica-

ragua's bourgeoisie: first, financial resources were under tight control by the U.S. banks and their local branches; second, native
enterprises could not compete with the subsidiaries of the multinationals that were making inroads into the domestic market.[61]
Since there was no feasible alternative to imperialist hegemony,
Wheelock believed, the outcome of these contradictions was to
make the native bourgeoisie ever more dependent:

> The crisis of the Nicaraguan bourgeoisie lies in its incapacity to re-
> solve the contradictions resulting from aggressive North American in-
> tervention in the economy—since that intervention is beneficial and
> indispensable politically and militarily to the bourgeoisie—and, at the
> same time, its incapacity to overcome the obstacles to the "free" pur-
> suit of its business interests stemming from the huge volume of in-
> vestments by the Somoza clan, whose monopoly of political power,
> despite its dynastic character, is the strongest guarantee of the con-
> tinued stability of the bourgeois regime.[62]

What were the political consequences of Wheelock's analysis?
Since the multinationals were riding roughshod over the Nicaraguan economy, they were responsible for "enormous social in-
stabilities."[63] Their increasing domestic role had intensified the
fundamental contradiction between the foreign and associated
bourgeoisie at one pole and the mass of exploited workers and peasants at the other. Because of the concentration and centralization of
capital in some twenty Nicaraguan superfamilies, Wheelock believed, the fundamental contradiction had become the immediate
focus of the class struggle.[64] Politically, the popular forces had
broken their ties with Nicaragua's two-party system to develop an
independent alternative that heightened the crisis. Wheelock thus
concluded that "the struggle against the system of exploitation in
Nicaragua takes on the character primarily of a confrontation with
its political form: the Somoza military dictatorship."[65]

Here was a new emphasis by a minority current within the
FSLN. For it an agrarian and anti-imperialist prolonged people's war
in the countryside had become increasingly irrelevant to the primary confrontation between a growing industrial proletariat and
Nicaragua's dependent bourgeoisie in the major urban centers. In
effect, Wheelock agreed with Dos Santos's diagnosis of the political
consequences of the new structure of dependence in Latin America:
"Everything now indicates that what can be expected is a long process of sharp political and military confrontations and of profound
social radicalization, which will lead these countries to a dilemma:
governments of force that open the way to fascism, or popular revo-

lutionary governments that open the way to socialism. Intermediate solutions have proved to be, in such a contradictory reality, empty and utopian."[66]

In 1976 Wheelock teamed up with Luis Carrión to produce a popular exposition of the Proletarian Tendency's version of Nicaragua's economic and political dependence. Along with other cadres of the Christian Revolutionary movement (MCR), Carrión had joined the FSLN in 1973 to become part of its first Christian cell. A leader of the Proletarian Tendency with Wheelock, he, too, became a member of the FSLN's Joint National Directorate in March 1979. Today Carrión is vice-minister of defense under Humberto Ortega.

Together, they characterized the Somoza dictatorship as a regime of exception, as a relatively autonomous power in relation to the rest of the business class. "In Nicaragua the bourgeoisie does not take over the administrative and political functions of the state but has instead delegated them to the Somoza dictatorship." That is because the business class believed the tremendous contradictions generated by Nicaragua's economic dependence could only be contained by military force. Under Nicaragua's form of dependent capitalism the bourgeoisie, too, suffered the adverse effects of paternalism: "The shade of two paternal trees has sheltered the growth of the bourgeoisie: imperialism and the Somoza dictatorship."[67]

The key to Nicaragua's dependence was traced to its agro-export economy and industrial platform geared to export.[68] Because production was directed outwards, the growth of the country's economy depended increasingly on uncontrollable external factors, such as prices on the world market, international loans, and export quotas imposed by the hegemonic centers of world capitalism. Both the agricultural and industrial sectors produced mainly for a foreign market, having been equipped to do so by foreign companies.

At the same time the agro-export sector had appropriated the best lands, so that cultivation for the internal market found itself displaced to backward regions worked under precapitalist conditions of production. Direct investment by U.S. companies in Nicaragua's basic industries had internalized the structure of dependence, Carrión and Wheelock contended, until it resembled Che Guevara's earlier depiction of underdevelopment. "The dependent and deformed development of Nicaraguan society finds concrete expression in the monsterlike growth of the agro-export sector, in the enormous backwardness of agricultural production for domestic consumption, and in the loss of national control over industrial production."[69]

During the thirties, when coffee was the principal agro-export commodity, the Depression-induced collapse of coffee prices had been accompanied by intensified exploitation and unemployment.[70] In this way the coffee magnates compensated themselves for the fall in their rate of profit. In 1956 when cotton replaced coffee as the principal product for export, the cyclical crisis and the fall in cotton prices had similar repercussions.[71] Thousands of rural workers found themselves without jobs or working for depressed wages.

The crisis of the agro-export sector, according to Wheelock and Carrión, led to a shift of investment capital to the industrial sector as the only remaining source of high profits. This shift resulted in a deterioration of petty artisan production from its leading position in 1963, when it represented 80 percent of the total value of industrial production, to barely 10 percent a decade later.[72] The country's internal market for industrial goods passed into the control of the multinationals, further aggravating Nicaragua's dependence on foreign interests. By the end of 1974, American enterprises dominated the strategic areas of petrochemicals, metallurgy, mining, and timber, and the principal sources of banking and commercial capital were also controlled from abroad.[73]

These changes shifted the social composition of Nicaragua's work force. The number of industrial workers increased several times since the early sixties, to about 70,000 in 1972.[74] Considering that the total work force was approximately 500,000 at the beginning of the seventies, and that a decade earlier the agricultural proletariat had already reached 180,000, according to figures cited by Wheelock, the bulk of the workers had become proletarianized.[75] By 1972 peasants had ceased to be the most numerous class.[76] Precisely this shift prompted Wheelock and Carrión to organize the Proletarian Tendency.

Since the workers were more concentrated, better organized, and more politically aware than the peasants, Wheelock and Carrión believed that the shift in the composition of the labor force portended an intensification of the class struggle. The collapse of cotton prices in 1956 had been accompanied not only by increasing levels of exploitation and unemployment, but also by massive labor unrest, by government repression, and by workers and students taking to armed struggle in protest.[77] For the first time the class contradiction between the bourgeoisie and the proletariat, the two contended, began to rival the class contradictions internal to the capitalist class.

Gradually, the contradiction between the bourgeoisie and the

Somoza dictatorship became subordinated to their common objective of containing the popular forces. The bourgeoisie as a whole was unable to achieve political power because it increasingly depended on the Somoza regime to guarantee internal order and a stable investment climate.[78] Meanwhile, Nicaragua's wage earners were becoming the vanguard in the people's struggle against the dictatorship: "Already by the end of the sixties and the beginning of the seventies, the proletarian struggle becomes the most important of all popular struggles."[79] For Wheelock and Carrión, this signified that the rivalry between the Somoza clique and the bourgeois opposition had finally given way to a confrontation between the bourgeoisie and the proletariat, led by the FSLN.

The Development of a Revolutionary Situation

To the FSLN's National Directorate, the thesis put forth by the Proletarian Tendency in 1975–1976 was based on a confusion of present tendencies and future expectations. But at the same time the FSLN's official assessment, as represented in the pamphlet by Ricardo Morales Avilés, appeared to an influential minority of the National Directorate as having underrated both the weaknesses of the Nicaraguan bourgeoisie and the growing strength of Nicaragua's working class. Whereas it seemed premature to suppose that the contradiction between the bourgeoisie and the proletariat had moved to the center of the stage, it seemed safe to conclude that the intrabourgeois struggle had moved toward the sidelines. A momentary equilibrium seemed to have been reached between these two kinds of class contradiction.

Humberto Ortega Saavedra (currently minister of defense and commander-in-chief of the Sandinista army) belonged to the minority that questioned both Morales's and Wheelock's assessments of what was happening in Nicaragua. Stationed in Havana as the National Directorate's representative from 1970 onward, Ortega assimilated both the lessons of the Cuban Revolution and the political thought of its leader, Fidel Castro. Although his most important work is mainly concerned with military-political and strategical issues, it also assesses Nicaragua's politico-economic situation.[80] In fact, his analysis rapidly gained the support of a majority of the National Directorate to become the basis of the FSLN's new insurrectional strategy.

Although it would be a mistake to conclude that Ortega made no independent assessment of the correlation of social forces, his interpretation was mainly an effort to mediate the contradictory claims made by Morales and by Wheelock and Carrión. Its composite character is indicated by the factors he considered basic to understanding the political crisis: "a revolutionary climax, an intrabourgeois struggle, and the brutal repression by Somoza."[81]

In Ortega's account, the political crisis indicated a contradiction between the Somoza dictatorship and the bourgeois opposition (Morales), and between the bourgeoisie as a class and the masses of workers and peasants (Wheelock and Carrión).[82] He traced its causes to two sets of factors: unequal investment opportunities and disproportionate shares of the economic surplus (Morales); and a fall in the prices of Nicaragua's chief exports and a decline in the rate of profit compensated by intensified exploitation (Wheelock and Carrión).[83] In effect, there were two interlocking crises tantamount to what Lenin would have called a revolutionary situation in Nicaragua: a crisis from above because of the incapacity of the bourgeoisie to continue governing in the old way; and a crisis from below because the oppressed and exploited classes refused to suffer in the old way.[84] The outcome was a nationwide political crisis affecting both the ruling class and the ruled.

This was not the only novel element in Ortega's analysis. He rejected the exaggerated depictions of the Somoza regime as an armed sector of the bourgeoisie in power and as an instrument of the State Department controlled by telecommunications from Washington. He considered it a "bourgeois military dictatorship" based on a coalition of the Somoza state bourgeoisie and the bureaucratic National Guard.[85] Although the Somoza regime exercised a despotic control over the rest of the bourgeoisie, it in turn enjoyed relative autonomy vis-à-vis U.S. imperialism.[86] In short, it was not a consular bourgeoisie.

To this depiction of the Somoza regime, Ortega added that it had a "fascist character."[87] Politically, it practiced an extreme demagogy while simultaneously persecuting and incarcerating the independent leaders of organized labor. It also exercised a generalized control over society that antagonized most of the bourgeoisie. The regime had given birth to a cultural movement that allegedly represented national values, but those values were really those of the ruling clique headed by Somoza. Ortega believed these ideological props of the regime could likewise be characterized as "fascist."[88]

By "fascist" Ortega meant that the brutal and gangsterlike methods of the Somoza clique had gradually deprived it of all legitimacy. Fascism was its last recourse. For Ortega, fascism appears only when the bourgeoisie can no longer rule in the old way by peaceful and constitutional methods. He conceived of the fascist syndrome and its causes as it had been characterized by Fidel Castro: "It is the desperation of the reactionaries, the desperation of the exploiters in today's world . . . that contributes to the most brutal and barbaric forms of violence and reaction . . . , there is nothing more unconstitutional, illegal, unrepresentative, repressive, violent, and criminal than fascism."[89]

Ortega modeled his analysis of the balance of social forces on Castro's Second Declaration of Havana: "The actual world correlation of forces and the universal movement for the liberation of the colonial and dependent peoples points out to the working class and the revolutionary intellectuals of Latin America their true role, which is to place themselves resolutely in the vanguard of the struggle against imperialism and feudalism."[90] In agreement with the communist parties in the hemisphere, Castro stressed the immediate anti-imperialist and agrarian character of the revolution while playing down its long-range socialist objectives. Although he concurred with Guevara that "the national bourgeoisie cannot lead the antifeudal and anti-imperialist struggle," he agreed with the established communist parties on the need for a broad front that would include the "most progressive layers" of the national bourgeoisie along with "progressive elements of the armed forces."[91] Guevara had discounted both elements. So did Fonseca in his assessment of Nicaragua.

Ortega disagreed with Fonseca's perspective and with Wheelock and Carrión for focusing on the socialist objectives of the struggle when, in his judgment, the immediate and urgent issue was to present a united front against imperialism and the landed oligarchy. At the same time, he rejected Morales's analysis for discounting the presence of a revolutionary situation and for stressing the enforced peace of repression instead of the stirrings of mass discontent beneath the surface.[92] In effect, Morales's assessment had failed to keep pace with the changing character of class contradictions, and Wheelock and Carrión's assessment had made the opposite mistake of leaving the facts behind.

These analyses of Nicaraguan reality provided the theoretical groundwork for the successive strategies adopted by the FSLN in the course of its struggle against the dictatorship. In disputing Fonseca's interpretation and the corresponding strategy influenced by Che Guevara, Morales gave a Chinese-type rationale for the strategy of prolonged people's war that had been successfully applied in Vietnam. Finding this rationale to be unsatisfactory,

Wheelock and Carrión applied dependency theory to Nicaragua and, on the basis of their new analysis, recommended a strategy for mobilizing the proletariat modeled on resistance to the military dictatorship in Chile. Taken separately, these last two theories acknowledged the existence of only a limited number of revolutionary conditions in Nicaragua. Only together did they recognize the presence of a revolutionary situation. Thus Ortega combined them as the basis of still another strategy, that of a nationwide general insurrection.

7. Reflections on Strategy

The intellectual foundations of Sandinista strategy are to be found, first, in the FSLN's political assessments and, second, in its reflections on the revolutionary experience and strategies for revolution in other Third World countries besides Nicaragua. How did these reflections influence the Sandinistas in their choice of alternative strategies?

The FSLN experimented with four different grafts of Third World strategies onto the body of Sandino's original practice. The first step was taken by Fonseca in combining Guevara's practice with Sandino's. The second step was the assimilation of the lessons of Vietnam and its revolutionary strategy based on Mao Tse-Tung's concept of prolonged people's war. Ricardo Morales and Tomás Borge were among its principal exponents. The third step marked a return to classical Leninism in the lessons culled from the proletarian and popular resistance to the Chilean military dictatorship. Jaime Wheelock and Luis Carrión were mainly responsible for this development. Finally, there was a return to the combined lessons of the Cuban Revolution involving the assimilation of Castro's widely misunderstood Moncada strategy. This strategy of general insurrection, or the people in arms, had Humberto Ortega for its chief spokesman.

By piecing together the fragments relating to the internal history of the FSLN, we can see how its strategy evolved. From 1961 to the end of 1967 the FSLN relied mainly on Guevara's manual of guerrilla warfare. From 1968 to the middle of 1977 it followed a different course of prolonged guerrilla war, although by October 1975 this new strategy was giving way to a proletarian strategy of popular resistance. From approximately May 1977 to the victory over Somoza in July 1979, the prevailing strategy was insurrectional. Although traces of these several strategies were present in the FSLN's practice from the beginning, they did not prevail all at once nor did they crystallize into rival tendencies until somewhat later.

The Original "Foco" Strategy

The initial strategy of the FSLN represented a continuation of the strategy adopted by the guerrilla forces at El Chaparral in 1959. The new guerrilla movement organized by the FSLN in 1962–1963, in the Honduran mountains some thirty miles from the border with Nicaragua, resembled the earlier one in several respects. Che Guevara had originally planned to participate in both and each was partly financed and armed with his help. In both instances he offered military advice. Both were organized on Honduran soil as expeditionary forces. The combatants at El Chaparral had been picked from elements of the PSN youth and the survivors of Gen. Ramón Raudales's abortive 1958 campaign—also launched from Honduras. The FSLN combatants consisted of former militants of the PSN and the survivors of El Chaparral under the military direction of a veteran Sandinista, Col. Santos López. Thus Sandino's influence was felt along with Guevara's.

The launching of armed actions was preceded by a year and a half of military training in Honduras combined with a year's political work on the Nicaraguan side of the border in the zone where the guerrillas expected to go into action—the area of Wiwilí where Sandino had established his headquarters in 1933 and the population was receptive to his ideas.[1] A logistical and communications network was established with the help of local sympathizers, and contacts were made with armed peasants prepared to join the guerrillas. Additional contacts were established with two other guerrilla groups operating farther south, in the vicinity of Matagalpa.[2]

The political work of preparing for armed struggle included the founding of a weekly review, *Trinchera*, whose first number in August 1962 called on the Nicaraguan people to support the coming offensive.[3] In its campaign to boycott the February 1963 presidential elections, *Trinchera* applauded the Conservative party's decision not to participate in the electoral farce while simultaneously pressuring it to take a more belligerent stand.[4] In May 1963 it announced the preparation of armed actions on an enlarged scale aimed at an eventual popular uprising.[5]

The FSLN's first armed action was launched in the capital in March. It took over a radio station and began to diffuse Sandinista slogans.[6] This action was followed in May by an assault on a local branch of the Bank of America in which four armed guerrillas escaped with thirty-five thousand córdobas.[7] Since the FSLN was the tenth in a series of insurrectional movements between 1958 and

1963, all aimed at overthrowing the Somozas, it could claim to be carrying on the work of its predecessors.[8]

"We spent more than a year and a half in those mountains," Borge recalled of the military preparations undertaken between the Patuca and Coco rivers in Honduran territory.[9] There the FSLN trained an invasion force of some sixty men, who reentered Nicaragua in the summer of 1963.[10] But instead of crossing the Coco River in the vicinity of Wiwilí, where they had already politicized the peasants and were familiar with the terrain, they changed their plans at the last moment because of the torrential rains and the huge distance they would have to cover from their training camp in Honduras. They chose a shortcut and the warmer climate to the east near Raití, without being familiar with either the people or the terrain. To make matters worse, the original column divided into three groups, which were unable to maintain contact. This almost completely dissipated their strength, in addition to which the guerrillas commanded by Borge became lost in the mountainous jungles and almost perished from hunger. Isolated from each other and pursued by the National Guard, which had become alerted to their presence in the area, they were forced to retreat across the border.

After this disaster, the FSLN temporarily shelved its strategy of armed struggle in favor of political agitation and propaganda in alliance with the PSN. Its immediate objective was to improve the workers' living conditions.[11] What saved it from backsliding altogether was its foresight in assigning Rigoberto Crus to continue the work of politicizing the peasants in the mountain zones of Matagalpa and Jinotega.[12] There, in the role of a healer and dispenser of medicines for various ailments, he made contact with hundreds of families whom he organized into bases of support for the FSLN. When Carlos Fonseca and Víctor Tirado returned clandestinely to Nicaragua in the summer of 1966, it was to intern themselves in the organizational network that had been prepared by Rigoberto Cruz for launching the second group of guerrillas in the mountains of Pancasán, some fifty kilometers east of Matagalpa.

From December 1966 to August 1967, the guerrillas were able to train in secret and to dominate the area politically.[13] With support from the local population, an effective logistical and information network was established throughout the zone of operations. Although there were only half as many guerrillas with far fewer arms than in 1962–1963, they were better prepared politically. For the first time the FSLN had an organized rear guard in Matagalpa,

León, and Managua; it had developed close ties with students in high schools and universities; it had working-class support; and it had contacts with religious opponents of the regime and with the political parties in opposition.[14] It had expanded its system of alliances, and by 1967 it had armed cadres in the cities specializing in robberies and bank assaults to finance the guerrillas in the mountains. It had a transportation and communications network by which its urban cadres channeled arms, munitions, medicines, and other provisions into the mountains. In short, it was the first armed movement by the FSLN that was completely trained, armed, financed, and launched inside the country.[15] Che Guevara was busy in Bolivia commanding a guerrilla movement of his own, so that he had neither the means nor the opportunity to assist the armed movement in Pancasán.

But the guerrillas made some serious mistakes. Once again, they divided into three groups, one led by Fonseca, one by Mayorga, and another by Borge. When the National Guard finally discovered their presence in August and organized a mop-up operation, Mayorga's group became isolated from the other guerrillas, unable to reestablish contact with them, and finally encircled. Mayorga was killed along with Rigoberto Cruz and the entire group of thirteen combatants.[16] In the other groups some were hunted down and killed, and others deserted because of the difficult conditions. The few remaining cadres returned to the cities.

Even so, the experience was not a total failure. The FSLN had learned a crucial lesson: how to prepare and launch an armed force inside Nicaragua relying on its own resources instead of on help from a neighboring country. Moreover, it did not retreat from armed actions, as in 1963, but began preparing for renewed armed struggle within the same general area.[17] Although the FSLN was modifying its strategy in response to new situations, the strategy it adopted at Pancasán was actually closer to Guevara's model of guerrilla warfare than was the strategy carried out by the expeditionary forces in 1963.

The original strategy was summarized in a December 1963 issue of *Trinchera* distributed in mimeograph form. "We have never maintained that a few men . . . could make . . . the insurrection. . . . What is needed is the intervention of the masses. A vanguard detachment and the popular forces [must] combine roles. . . . The detachment is at the head of the people's struggle. The masses do not actively join the fray in a single day . . . first one sector joins, then another . . . until finally all the popular forces are on a war footing."[18]

This strategy satisfied the conditions specified in Guevara's manual for launching an insurrectionary guerrilla nucleus or *foco*. First, the people had to be shown that it was clearly impossible for them to achieve needed social legislation through electoral or other legally prescribed channels.[19] Second, they had to back up their conviction that the government was illegitimate by acts of defiance, massive demonstrations, and armed resistance to official provocation.[20] Both of these conditions were present in Nicaragua in the middle fifties. The unpopular dictator was assassinated in 1956 after which a rash of armed struggles began in response to the government repression that came in retaliation.

The *foco* was distinguished from other armed organizations by being a tightly knit group whose members both lived and fought together. Guevara set the minimum at thirty guerrillas and the maximum number at one hundred.[21] Thus a moment would arrive when the guerrilla nucleus would have to split into two, and so on—each one highly concentrated like the first.

The *foco* was intended to serve the people as an example and to orient them ideologically.[22] As a social reformer, the guerrilla was to be a propagandist of the deed, a catalyst of revolutionary awareness, and a detonator of mass insurrection. The guerrilla was also to be a propagandist of the word. It was preferred that the guerrilla be an inhabitant of the zone of operations, since that was where he had made friends and could best influence people, and where he could most likely succeed militarily owing to his knowledge of the terrain.[23] Although Guevara repeatedly violated this last injunction, as did the FSLN in 1963, the operation at Pancasán did incorporate the local peasants into the guerrillas.

As Guevara defined the *foco*, it was the "armed nucleus, the fighting vanguard of the people."[24] In fact it consisted exclusively of guerrillas. Although it had a civilian organization and was backed by a variety of support groups in the cities, these performed a subordinate role.[25] Guerrilla warfare was upheld as the most advanced expression of the people's struggle, without whose cooperation Guevara believed the guerrillas were doomed.[26]

But was the FSLN a guerrilla *foco*? Its vanguard detachment did not consist solely of armed fighters, nor did its armed fighters consist solely of men. It also included cadres "outside the mountain zones, revolutionaries who mobilized the popular forces . . . because it is not only with bullets that we are fighting the Somoza tyranny."[27] Although the guerrillas lived and fought together in small concentrated units of more than thirty but less than one hundred men and women, the rest of the vanguard detachment engaged in organizational and political work in the cities. Although the *foco* was an indispensable part of the FSLN, the vanguard detachment had a body, not just a head.

On three occasions Tomás Borge expressly denied that the FSLN had ever adopted a *foco* strategy. Its first armed operations at the juncture of the Coco and Bocay rivers was not the work of a guerrilla *foco*, he claimed, because the FSLN had established links with several mass organizations.[28] A year of political education among the peasants in the area disqualified it from being an example of *foquismo*.[29] "We were never greatly influenced by the thesis of the guerrilla *foco*, we did not commence as a *foquista* organization . . . , we were not a guerrilla group but rather a revolutionary organization that applied guerrilla warfare as a method of struggle."[30] That was why the FSLN survived even when the guerrillas were destroyed—unlike the situation in the rest of Latin America, where revolutionary movements disappeared with the destruction of their armed cadres. Far from disappearing, the FSLN lost only one arm, which could be replaced with a new one because the revolutionary torso was still intact.[31]

Although denying that the first armed actions were those of a guerrilla *foco*, Borge claimed that the FSLN's second operation, at Pancasán, signified the end of its *foquista* remnants.[32] Apparently, the FSLN had incorporated at least some features of Guevara's strategy. But at Pancasán whatever traces remained had been allegedly overcome through concentrated political work. "In the same guerrilla zone we became involved in actions that presumed the existence of extraguerrilla factors. We continued our political work in the peripheral zones of Managua and other cities, we gave heed to student and trade union activity, we established connections with leaders of the traditional political parties, with priests and intellectuals."[33]

However, Guevara's strategy also recognized the importance of political work, as long as it was geared to building the guerrilla forces—the FSLN's main concern in Nicaragua. Thus the FSLN's campaigns of propaganda and agitation in the factories, poor neighborhoods and universities, the establishment of three political cells in Managua, and contacts with peasants on the capital's periphery are not enough to confirm Borge's claim.

Borge's mistake was not to have carefully distinguished Guevara's original strategy from its subsequent development by the chief disseminator of Guevarism throughout Latin America, the French philosopher and political activist, Régis Debray. The error was initially made by Debray who, after having correctly characterized Guevara's strategy in two major essays published in 1965, followed them in January 1967 with his celebrated *Revolution in the Revolution?* in which he ceased to be true to the original.[34]

Initially, Debray gave priority to political considerations in the preparation of the guerrillas. "The *foco* aspires to conquer power with and through the masses, that is to say with the poor and medium peasants and with the workers . . . , classes which have always been isolated from political life [and] require a long practical experience in order to gain consciousness of their exploited condition, and to organize and move into action."[35] He also claimed that the lengthy work of building a *foco* could only be done on the spot where it planned to go into action, that only a force that was politically rooted in an agrarian zone could seize the offensive at the appropriate moment.[36] Furthermore, the guerrillas must establish links with the cities not only to assure a steady supply of arms, funds, and fresh recruits, but also to maintain the required political contacts.[37] Basically, this was the strategy Guevara developed in his manual on guerrilla warfare and the FSLN applied in 1967, and in part in 1963 through a *foco* implanted from outside Nicaragua after doing political work inside the country.

But in *Revolution in the Revolution?* Debray gave priority to military factors. He reinterpreted the *foco* as an alien presence in the midst of the peasants it sought to mobilize. Considerations of military security as well as common sense called for distrust of the civilian population and for the maintenance of a certain aloofness.[38] The best form of political work was a show of military strength, because the "destruction of a troop transport truck or the public execution of a police torturer is more effective propaganda than a hundred speeches."[39] He concluded that the military detachment created the political vanguard, not conversely: "In most countries where conditions for armed struggle exist it is possible to move from a military *foco* to a political *foco*, but to move in the opposite direction is virtually impossible."[40] Such was the strategy that passed as *foquismo* in left-wing circles during the late sixties and early seventies, a military caricature of Guevara's original strategy but in principle opposed to it—an exotic "ism" divorced from political realities.[41]

On the basis of this distinction it seems reasonable to conclude that the FSLN was never a guerrilla *foco*, and that its armed detachments in 1963 and 1967 were virtually free of *foquismo*. But this is not to say that the FSLN did not establish guerrilla *focos* on both occasions or did not rely on a corresponding strategy. Phrased somewhat differently, the FSLN adapted Guevara's original strategy to its own novel revolutionary organization. Its leader, Carlos Fonseca, was the general secretary of its political apparatus even when he was not the commander of its military forces. Although the FSLN was not formally a vanguard party, it shared several of the attributes of one.

The Strategy of Prolonged People's War

The FSLN began a series of discussions in 1968 aimed at reassessing the abortive armed actions beginning at El Chaparral and ending at Pancasán. Self-reflection led to the question, "What are we: a party, an armed group, or a *foco?*"[42] In particular, the FSLN began "to question the famous *foco* strategy and to consider . . . where we were headed and what we wanted."[43] It was a turning point.

Fonseca's summary of the ten-year-old *foco* strategy (1959–1968) reads like a compendium of errors. These included the lack of an effective revolutionary organization tied to the people and especially to the peasants, the failure to combine conspiratorial work with political activity, the absence of an irregular guerrilla force of peasants for assisting the regular or full-time guerrillas, and the overestimation of purely military considerations.[44] The gist of Fonseca's criticism was that the FSLN had not made any serious progress, that its growth had been stunted, that its successive armed efforts, like its backsliding into legal work in 1964–1965, had "failed to accumulate forces" at an "accelerated rhythm."[45] These mistakes, which were being made by Guevarist groups all over Latin America, pointed to the limitations of a *foco* strategy. That is why it was abandoned in favor of a new strategy aimed at the patient accumulation of forces toward a prolonged people's war.

As one FSLN militant recalled, the FSLN did not come of age until "a [new] period opened in 1969–70 of the accumulation of forces."[46] What kind of strategy was that? "The accumulation of forces proposes first of all to set up a national organization, to build regional committees of the FSLN throughout the national territory, to establish links between these regional committees and the workers, and to do something also for international solidarity."[47] Fonseca was made responsible for obtaining this international support.

After the defeat at Pancasán and the adoption of a new strategy based on the accumulation of forces, Borge tells us, special efforts were made to build links between the revolutionary vanguard and the masses through so-called intermediate organizations. These served as transmission belts, recruiting agencies, and support groups for the guerrillas: "We had student organizations, neighborhood committees, Christian movements, artistic organizations, etc."[48] This marked the beginning of a nationwide subversive network that came to include students, workers, peasants, and other sectors of society under the leadership of the FSLN.

At the same time preparations for launching a new guerrilla force were being made in the mountains outside Zinica, about one hundred kilometers north of Pancasán. Precautions were taken to assure that most of the regular guerrillas as well as the irregulars would be peasants familiar with the region. FSLN cadres proceeding from the cities were instructed to integrate themselves into the people's daily lives. Except for those cadres destined to receive military training as urban guerrillas, the others were expected to remain in the mountains, "never to return," to win the confidence of the peasants.[49]

The forging of these links proved decisive for the survival and continuity of the guerrilla forces established in the area. Thus in February 1970, when patrols of the National Guard discovered the Sandinista camp near the Waslala River, the guerrillas were warned in advance by peasants and were not taken by surprise.[50] For the first time they were able to withdraw into another zone and to maintain their organization intact.[51] The FSLN established a new camp at El Bijáo in the mountains between Zinica and Pancasán, where it continued to build its forces in silence. This became the core of the guerrillas rediscovered by the National Guard at Zinica in November 1976, when Fonseca and two other militants were surprised and killed in an ambush. But the guerrillas were now firmly entrenched in the mountains and could not be dislodged. The strategy of prolonged people's war survived whereas the *foco* strategy had failed.

An authoritative account of the new strategy by one of its original formulators, Henry Ruiz, appeared in an interview published in *Nicaráuac* (May–June 1980). Ruiz joined the FSLN in 1967 but left Nicaragua to become a student in political economy at Patrice Lumumba University in Moscow. When he returned in 1969 he went directly into the mountains at Zinica, where he remained until the end of the war a decade later. In 1975 he was appointed a member of the FSLN's nine-man National Directorate.

He tells us that in the days following the defeat at Pancasán, which coincided with the annihilation of Guevara's Bolivian *foco* in October 1967, the FSLN reassessed both guerrilla movements.[52] It sought a new synthesis that would give greater weight to organizational matters, to political agitation among workers and peasants, to the combination of armed actions in the cities and the countryside, and to improvements in military skills. The National Directorate began talking of an accumulation of forces and of the organization of clandestine armed actions going beyond bank assaults and other economic "recuperations."[53] For the first time the struggle against the Somoza regime came to be formulated on the premise of a prolonged people's war: "In the balance sheet drawn up on Pancasán, prolonged people's war was mentioned. . . . That idea took shape from studying a little of the Vietnamese and the Chinese experiences. Without leaning toward the Cuban experience . . . we involved ourselves in the urban question at the same time that we did organizational work in the countryside."[54]

Impressed by the example of the guerrillas in Vietnam, who were holding up against the powerful U.S. military machine while those in Latin America were succumbing to the local forces of repression, the FSLN adopted a strategy of protracted warfare aimed at massively incorporating the peasants into the armed struggle. The problem the FSLN faced at that moment, according to Ruiz, was how to overcome its weakness as an organization of cadres by transforming the war into a total one.[55] For that, it would be necessary to mobilize the masses directly, not just indirectly through the actions of a guerrilla *foco* catalyzing them from a distance. The new strategy meant performing specialized political and military work simultaneously in the cities and the mountains.[56]

Nevertheless, the proponents of the new strategy insisted that the nucleus of the future army of liberation could only be created in the mountains.[57] Experience had shown that urban cadres slated to do political work in the cities could become steeled as revolutionaries only by sharing the hardships of the peasants and by participating in armed actions in the countryside. That was where the best cadres were being formed.

In considering the lessons of Pancasán, the FSLN realized that the war would be won or lost depending on the extent of popular support.[58] This raised the question of which sectors of the population were most likely to be won over by revolutionary propaganda. It was not enough for them to be exploited; they also had to be willing and able to make the sacrifices required of a long, drawn-out struggle.[59] Ruiz recalled that industrial workers at that time were too few numerically to make a difference and that rural day-laborers also failed to fit the bill—perhaps because their wages paid in money had effectively integrated them into the market economy. This left only the impoverished peasants tied to the soil, those for whom modern civilized existence was still fundamentally alien to their way of life.[60]

How were the peasants to be mobilized? The first step, Ruiz recalled, was to obtain their trust. This was achieved by working together in the same fields, by sharing and resolving problems together, by becoming their friends, and by being welcomed into their families.[61] The key to successful ties with the peasants was to become a godparent to their children.[62] In the event of the death of the family head, the *compadre,* or substitute father, was obliged to provide for the offspring. In the effort to solidify the peasants' support for their struggle, the guerrillas refused to accept any recruits who did not bring in other members of their family. This change in approach marked a great advance over the armed propaganda advocated by Che Guevara. It helped the guerrillas discover what Ruiz called the "secret" of how to organize peasants and of getting them to cooperate with the FSLN.[63]

The new strategy was applied with vigor by Carlos Agüero. Nephew of the Conservative party's candidate for president in 1967 and reputed to have Maoist sympathies, he became the military commander of the FSLN from 1968 to 1976, when Fonseca was outside the country.[64] In September 1968 Fonseca was detained in San José, Costa Rica, and imprisoned on charges of having participated in a bank assault. Agüero led a military operation for his release in December 1969, but, after being freed, Fonseca was recaptured and imprisoned anew with Humberto Ortega and two other Sandinistas involved in the action.[65] Fonseca was finally freed and flown to Cuba in October 1970, after Agüero directed the successful hijacking of a plane carrying executives of the United Fruit Company, who were released in exchange.[66] Although Agüero did not become a member of the FSLN's National Directorate until 1975, the application of the new strategy was actually the work of a new group of leaders consisting of Agüero, Ruiz, and Borge.

Under this new leadership the FSLN began the task of building a nationwide support network for the guerrillas. Borge recalled that "the process of accumulation of forces began showing results when the FSLN began organizing regional branches throughout the country."[67] There were strong regional branches in León and Managua, along with others in the North and the East.[68] Eduardo Contreras, appointed to the National Directorate in 1975, headed the Managua branch.[69] From his base in the capital, he established direct lines of communication with the FSLN's branches in Juigalpa, Rivas, Jinotepe, and the guerrillas in the North.[70] As a result of his organizational work, the FSLN also became the political-military vanguard of several student, worker, and peasant organizations that until then had engaged in isolated and uncoordinated struggles against the dictatorship. Especially influential was the Revolutionary Student Front (FER), which kept alive hope in the armed struggle by systematically disseminating the FSLN's propaganda.[71]

Between 1970 and 1974 the FSLN assiduously avoided armed engagements in an effort to build up its forces.[72] Armed combat would ensue not when the enemy chose, but when the FSLN determined that the moment was propitious for launching an uninterrupted political and military offensive. So successful was this strategy that during 1974 the National Guard was unable to capture even a single militant among the dozens of cadres tactically dispersed throughout the northern mountains.[73] Guardsmen also failed to demoralize the peasants or to dismantle their organizations.

The day finally arrived when, after quietly accumulating forces, the FSLN was ready to launch a spectacular armed action, which it hoped would accelerate its growth.[74] In December 1974 a group of commandos led by Contreras seized the house of José María Castillo in a Managua suburb and held hostage a dozen or so prominent supporters of the regime, including several foreign dignitaries and members of Somoza's family. These were subsequently ransomed and exchanged for imprisoned FSLN cadre members who, together with the commandos, were then flown to Cuba.

As part of the exchange agreement, an FSLN message was transmitted by the press, radio, and television on 30 December 1974. "The limitations of the guerrilla struggle of 1963," said the message, "were due to erroneous conceptions of how to develop a revolutionary war and, above all, to the absence of a strategy of Prolonged People's War."[75] This statement was followed by the claim that, after the guerrilla struggle of 1967, an entirely new phenomenon appeared in Nicaragua: the peasants themselves had taken to armed actions to confront the abuses of the landowners.[76]

This statement suggests that it was growing peasant support for the FSLN's rural guerrillas that prompted the shift from a purely defensive strategy to an offensive one. But this was not the only factor. The Christmas 1974 commando raid came in response to a combination of circumstances favorable to the development of the FSLN.

Although the revolutionary student movement of the late fifties and early sixties had subsided, as the U.S. Alliance for Progress began implementing token reforms in Nicaragua with a hint of coming liberalization, it revived in 1969 and the early seventies. In 1969 the pro-Sandinista FER gained control of student government at the National Autonomous University's campuses in Managua and León. In 1972 Father Uriel Molina founded the Christian Revolutionary movement (MCR), and the next year these Catholic activists went over to the FSLN. Mounting student support for the Sandinistas came in response to the increasing ruthlessness, corruption, and political incompetence of the third figure in the Somoza dynasty, Anastasio Somoza Debayle. Elected president in 1967, he had himself reelected in 1974 with some 40 percent of the eligible electorate abstaining. The massive Managua earthquake of December 1972, which killed eighteen thousand persons and completely shattered the downtown area, added to his unpopularity when his embezzlement of international relief funds was exposed.

The Vietnamese source of the FSLN's strategy of protracted warfare was Gen. Vo Nguyên Giap's *People's War, People's Army* (1962), based on Mao's earlier strategy. Supported by self-governing bases or liberated territories within the guerrillas' zone of operations and by massive popular resistance in the areas under enemy control, this strategy had for its basis a worker-peasant alliance in the struggle against foreign intervention and the landed oligarchy.[77]

The reason the struggle had to be protracted, Giap contended, was that the balance of forces initially favored the enemy. "Only a long-term war could enable us to utilize to the maximum our political trump cards, to overcome our material handicaps and to transform our weakness into strength."[78] This was called the accumulation of forces: "To maintain and increase our forces was the principle to which we adhered, contenting ourselves to attack when success was certain, refusing to give battle likely to incur losses to us or to engage in hazardous actions."[79] To strike swiftly in search of a shortcut to victory was considered a dangerous undertaking that played into the hands of the enemy.[80]

The people's forces can defeat a regular army, Giap argued, even though they lack a sophisticated military capability, because the enemy is confronted with an insuperable dilemma: it must either concentrate its forces or disperse them. If it concentrates them, it loses ground; if it disperses them, it loses strength. In either case, it can be overcome, whether by seizing territory or by sapping its energies in a war of attrition. Thus at Dien Bien Phu the French colonial forces surrendered to the Viet Minh. As Giap summarized the French predicament, "Without scattering his forces it was impossible for him [the enemy] to occupy the invaded territory; in scattering his forces . . . [the enemy] would fall easy prey to our troops, his mobile forces would be more and more reduced and the shortage of troops would be all the more acute."[81]

The rationale behind this strategy had originally been worked

out by Mao in his 1938 lectures, "On Protracted War." Although
the enemy is strong and the people are weak militarily, he noted,
"in other respects the enemy has shortcomings and we have advantages."[82] Hence the fundamental task of people's war is to accentu-
ate the enemy's weaknesses and to enhance the people's strong
points. Among the enemy's shortcomings were the reactionary and
barbarous features of his war and the lack of international support;
among the people's advantages was the progressive and humane
character of their resistance, the size of the territory invaded by the
enemy, and strong international support.[83] Under those conditions,
the strategy required for victory hinged on a protracted struggle
that would gnaw away at the enemy's resources and morale while
simultaneously enlarging the scope of the war through a fluid
rather than fixed front covering the entire country.[84]

The origins of this strategy in China's resistance to Japanese
imperialism provided fuel for the Maoist tendency within the
FSLN. This tendency surfaced in the wake of the Sino-Soviet split
and was further strengthened by the example of the Chinese Cultural Revolution. The Maoists in the FSLN were the most insistent
promoters of the new strategy; however, they broke away in the
early seventies to organize their own People's Action movement
(MAP), which persistently criticized the Sandinistas for their
Cuban connections and for being "pro-Soviet."[85]

One of the curiosities of the FSLN's political legacy is that its
strategy of prolonged people's war can be traced to Sandino as well
as to Mao. At the time Mao's guerrillas were chalking up their first
victories against Chiang Kai-shek, Sandino was applying a similar
strategy in Nicaragua. He demonstrated that a people's army organized in highly mobile columns with the support of the local population could hold out indefinitely against the superior military
forces of a modern industrial giant. His strategy was "tantamount
to what other peoples and countries have conceived as a prolonged
people's war, a war of liberation amounting to a war of attrition."[86]
Like Mao, Sandino believed that the peasants constituted the fundamental force of the revolution but should be led by a proletarian
vanguard. "Sandino made it a condition of his war of attrition that
the workers in the mines would participate; Sandino did not go
to work initially with peasants but rather with laborers, understanding well that they were the fundamental [guiding] force of
the revolution. That is what Sandino teaches and we share the
same view!"[87]

The shift to a Vietnamese-type strategy signified a downgrad-
ing of Guevara's earlier legacy. However, he, too, benefited from the

Vietnamese example by ultimately incorporating the strategy of protracted warfare and modifying his original version of the guerrilla *foco*. Impressed by the Vietnamese experience, he subsequently acknowledged that a shortcut to revolution in Latin America was out of the question. Within a given country the people's struggle might be decided in two or three years of continuous fighting, as in Cuba, but the war would be protracted on a continental scale.[88] The *foco* strategy continued to apply insofar as the immediate enemy in Latin America was not imperialism but the landed oligarchy supported by unpopular dictatorships or oligarchical regimes. But in the event of American military intervention, Giap's strategy would also apply, because its immediate objective was the struggle against foreign occupation.

In 1964 Guevara publicly defended the Vietnamese strategy in his prologue to the Cuban edition of Giap's book. The problems presented by Giap, he wrote, had particular importance for the people of Latin America assaulted by the North American leviathan. Without knowing Giap's writings and the experience of the Vietnamese and Chinese revolutions, Cuba had charted its road to liberation by adopting similar methods.[89] In Vietnam the struggle was defined as a war by the people and its army; mass struggle was an integral part of the war, with the result that the war became a total one.[90] Several times in his discussion of Giap's book, Guevara conceded the advantages of protracted warfare. It was precisely such a strategy, he concluded, that summarized the general characteristics that wars of liberation should take in dependent countries—in Latin America as well as in Asia.[91]

Ironically, on the heels of Debray's *Revolution in the Revolution?* which attacked the Vietnamese strategy as inapplicable to Latin America, Guevara affirmed its feasibility.[92] At the very moment when he seemed to embody the most extreme features of *foquismo* in Bolivia, his message to the Tricontinental Conference appeared in Havana extolling the road of Vietnam, the road that would be followed in Latin America.[93] The Cuban Revolution had assigned the Latin American people a task of great importance, to create "a Second or Third Vietnam, or the Second and Third Vietnam of the world."[94] This was not the task of a *foco* strategy, which favored a swift victory in what amounted to a limited war. Even on a national scale, "the struggle will be long, harsh, and its front shall be in the guerrilla's refuge, in the cities, in the homes of the fighters . . . in the massacred rural population, in the villages or cities destroyed by the bombardments of the enemy."[95] It would be a total war waged with relentless cruelty. "We must carry the war into every corner the enemy happens to carry it: to his home, to his centers of entertainment."[96] The strategic end of this struggle was to be the complete destruction of imperialism by a war extended in space and time, a war that had ceased to be peculiar to Vietnam.

The Strategy of Popular Resistance

As a consequence of the spectacular seizure of hostages, including the Chilean ambassador, in December 1974, the FSLN's popularity began to soar. But it was unable to assimilate successfully the influx of new recruits, among them intellectuals and academics with diverse educational backgrounds.[97] When theoretical and strategical differences began asserting themselves within the movement, the National Directorate was unprepared for the confrontation. "Since it was a strange and new phenomenon," Borge recalled, "we had no experience in dealing with it. We adopted authoritarian positions and tried to resolve the problem by decree. Although we said we would, we did not permit the development of a political and ideological discussion of the issues."[98] The leadership wanted to discuss the issues, but at the same time there were breaches of discipline. Sanctions were imposed, one group was expelled from the organization, and others interpreted the sanctions as reprisals aimed at silencing criticism of the leadership.

Instead of resolving differences, the disciplinary measures had the opposite effect. In 1975 the first major organized faction crystallized, the so-called Proletarian Tendency. It demanded to be heard at the national level and hoped to change the FSLN's strategy to fit the new economic and social conditions of Nicaragua in which the focus of class struggle had allegedly shifted to the cities. The armed struggle in the mountains no longer accomplished anything, it claimed, and should be abandoned for organizational work in the factories and other centers of production. The National Directorate agreed with the need to organize a resistance movement in the factories and working-class neighborhoods, but refused to give up its strategy of prolonged people's war in the countryside.[99]

There were those in the national leadership who disagreed with the theses of the Proletarian Tendency but questioned the disciplinary measures against it. The members of the National Directorate inside the country favored sanctions, but the comrades abroad opposed them. Moreover, the latter, too, began to question the priority assigned to armed struggle in the mountains. Soon they were developing a faction of their own within the National Directorate, "another tendency that was already projecting a different kind of struggle by means of armed actions in the cities."[100] Although both factions represented minorities, together they threatened to disrupt the movement and to replace the old leadership. The Proletarian Tendency was thus ultimately responsible for the process that culminated in the displacement two years later of the strategists of prolonged people's war, the heirs of the FSLN's original rural organization, from their position of control over the movement. And when this group ceased to represent a majority of the FSLN, it, too, became reduced to the status of a faction or separate tendency.

Initially, the Proletarian Tendency was directed by Jaime Wheelock, Luis Carrión, and Carlos Roberto Huembes. When Huembes was killed in November 1976, he was replaced by Carlos Núñez Téllez. Núñez, who represented his faction in the FSLN's Joint Coordination of the Internal Front during 1979, is the author of *El pueblo en armas*, the authoritative account of the urban uprisings in Managua and Masaya that contributed to the fall of the dictatorship. Along with Wheelock and Carrión, he became a member of the Joint National Directorate in March 1979, and today heads the FSLN's Department of Propaganda and Political Education.

In a March 1979 interview, Wheelock reviewed the events leading to the strategy adopted by the Proletarian Tendency. The expansion of cotton production and the emergence of the Central American Common Market had created a new working force consisting in 1975 of approximately 250,000 agricultural wage-hands plus an industrial proletariat of 60,000 in manufacturing and construction.[101] An incipient class struggle between bourgeois and proletarians had surfaced without a vanguard party to lead and organize the workers. This failure on the urban front had finally motivated the organization of the new tendency in October 1975.[102] Convinced that the struggle against the dictatorship required a new set of priorities, the Proletarian Tendency began devoting its energies to building a vanguard organization of the working class.

At its inception the FSLN consisted mainly of university students who concentrated on organizing peasants. But, Wheelock observed, the changed composition of the work force required that the FSLN be transformed into an organization of the agricultural and industrial proletariat, and that top priority be given to organizing wage hands. The organization of peasants, students, and intellectuals would come later, followed by the organization of office employees and the petite bourgeoisie.[103] The fundamental program of the FSLN, therefore, had to represent the interests of the vanguard class. Wheelock summarized those interests as the struggle for democracy and social progress, and the overcoming of Nicaragua's economic and political dependence.[104]

The Proletarian Tendency gave priority to building trade unions under FSLN leadership and to organizing a new Marxist-Leninist party of the proletariat. It favored a long-term strategy aimed at preparing the workers for a nationwide political strike supported by local uprisings and armed actions.[105] The transmission belts linking the party to the people were to include intermediary organizations such as student groups, parent-teacher associations, neighborhood councils, and the like. Because the bourgeois opposition collaborated with U.S. imperialism and the Somoza dynasty in economic matters, it was pointless to enter into political alliances with it. Although a broad popular resistance was considered indispensable in combatting the dictatorship, Wheelock added, under no circumstances should bourgeois elements be allowed to impose their objectives on the movement.[106]

Within the FSLN's national leadership the Proletarian Tendency found a responsive hearing from those whose initial concern was not to take sides. But during 1976 and 1977 the balance of power shifted to the moderators, who by then had evolved from a strategy of urban guerrilla warfare to a strategy of general insurrection. With protracted-warfare stalwarts like Fonseca dead, Borge in prison, and Ruiz isolated in the mountains, Humberto Ortega with his brother Daniel was able to win over Víctor Tirado and then other members of the National Directorate to his insurrectionary views. So the Proletarian Tendency had to reorient its polemics toward a confrontation with the Insurrectionalists.

In an April 1978 document put out by the Proletarian Tendency, the Insurrectionalists were attacked for ultraleft or "adventurist" as well as right-wing or "opportunist" errors.[107] In earlier polemics these criticisms had been based on the Insurrectionalists' professed strategy and published declarations, but this document made a point of criticizing their deeds.

The new Insurrectionalist leadership of the FSLN was rebuked for having launched an armed uprising prematurely. In October 1977 the FSLN had attempted a nationwide insurrection that failed because of the absence of intensive political work among the masses and the low level of political awareness and organization.[108] The Insurrectionalists were censured for subjectivism, for having failed to wait for the objective conditions of revolution to appear before inciting the people to take over entire cities. Another example of revolutionary irresponsibility was their attack on the military garrison at San Carlos, described as a *cuartelazo* (barracks coup) in the bourgeois tradition. Although the insurrection aimed at dividing the National Guard and at provoking frictions within Somoza's political apparatus, it had been launched without first healing the divisions within the FSLN.[109]

By the beginning of 1978 the political initiative had passed from Somoza's military-civilian regime to the bourgeois opposition, which meant that armed actions by the FSLN could be preparing the ground for a palace coup. The Insurrectionalists were chided for having become the armed instrument of the bourgeois opposition and the Carter administration, which were jointly seeking to get rid of Somoza for violations of human rights. The outcome, the Proletarian Tendency argued, would be a civilian government in place of the military-bureaucratic regime, one that would perpetuate Nicaragua's system of dependent capitalism and subordination to U.S. economic interests.[110] Furthermore, the Insurrectionalists were criticized for engaging in a national dialogue not as Marxists-Leninists but as alleged noncommunists and professed democrats. This was supposedly evidence of their "self-serving interests as a fraction of the petite bourgeoisie."[111]

What, then, was the alternative? The Proletarian Tendency decided against a general offensive in favor of a defensive strategy: "The tactic adopted by proletarian Sandinismo is to launch a POPULAR RESISTANCE to contain the aggression of the dictatorship and the exploiters."[112] Only in the long run would this popular resistance lead to a counteroffensive aimed at overthrowing both the dictatorship and the capitalist class. The Proletarian Tendency insisted that the immediate task was to strengthen the people's organizations by doing political work among the masses.[113] This meant refusing to engage in dialogue with the bourgeoisie and refusing to accept a policy of alliances with the bourgeois opposition.[114] It meant affirming the Marxist-Leninist character of the FSLN as the political vanguard of the proletariat. It meant cementing the unity of the popular forces on the basis of the class interests of the exploited in opposition to the exploiters. Meanwhile, conditions were not ripe for armed actions on a large scale, when these were helping the bourgeoisie to destabilize the Somoza regime.[115]

Although the military-bureaucratic dictatorship constituted the immediate enemy of the Nicaraguan people, the tactics of the exploiters also had to be combatted. Because the bourgeois opposition had seized the initiative, the Proletarian Tendency called on the FSLN "to undertake within the framework of the Popular Resistance a resolute and vigorous political activity destined to withstand bourgeois maneuvers." These maneuvers were aimed at preventing the people from putting forth demands of their own. "The tactic of Popular Resistance opposes at this juncture two facets of the same class enemy: the instrument of oppression momentarily disconnected from its class support; and this same class, which expects to cheat the Nicaraguan people."[116]

The inspiration for this strategy was neither Cuban nor Vietnamese but Chilean. The Popular Unity coalition led by the Socialist and Communist parties took on the form of a popular resistance movement after Salvador Allende's government was overthrown in September 1973. In July 1974 the resistance was formally organized by the principal parties of the Chilean Left, including the Movement of the Revolutionary Left (MIR), which had become progressively disillusioned with Allende's government because of concessions to the bourgeoisie.[117] The MIR was the Chilean equivalent of the FSLN. Wheelock, who had organized a Sandinista cell with other Nicaraguans studying in Chile during the Allende period and had kept abreast of Chilean events, patterned his strategy on the MIR's.[118] Convinced that a Vietnamese-type strategy had no application to Chile, he also questioned its application to Nicaragua, where the brunt of class struggle was no longer in the countryside.

By 1974 the MIR had temporarily shelved its socialist objectives for the more urgent tasks of restoring democracy and defending the workers' elementary rights. Because the working class was regarded as the principal force of the resistance, the MIR's urban guerrillas agreed to limit their armed actions to defending the workers' demands.[119] This meant avoiding armed confrontations with the military and providing firepower for workers' strikes and demonstrations. Clandestine committees of popular resistance were organized with MIR support. The conditions of repression in Chile were suddenly like those in Central America, calling for a strategy of collective self-defense.

The MIR's strategy of popular resistance was reaffirmed in a major document issued in February 1975 in reply to a call by the Communist party for joint action against the military junta. The Party insisted that the only way to combat what it called "fascism" was an antifascist popular front. Since that would have effectively subordinated the workers' movement to the bourgeois opposition, the MIR rejected the policy as "suicidal."[120] First, it would contribute to strengthening the big bourgeoisie and imperialism. Second, it would perpetuate the military junta by depriving the resistance of its most effective weapon—the workers in arms. "Only a determined Popular Resistance independent of any bourgeois faction can accelerate the fall of the dictatorship and the contradictions within the bourgeoisie, since it will demonstrate that the gorillas [reactionary generals] . . . are incapable of performing successfully the bloody repressive role assigned them by the owners of big capital both native and foreign." Since a political front even with the Christian Democratic party would confuse the working class and virtually disarm the Left, the MIR concluded, "the bourgeoisie and each of its factions must be unmasked before the masses, must be clearly shown to be enemies, and must be fought without concessions."[121]

This was the strategy applied by the Proletarian Tendency in Nicaragua, a strategy that gave top priority to political work within the intermediate organizations of the workers along with professional associations, neighborhood councils, and local churches. It focused on the recovery of trade union rights, the right of collective bargaining, the right to present grievances, and the right to strike. It called for a struggle against unemployment, for the organization of the unemployed, and for communal kitchens to feed them; for better housing and rent controls; for cheap credit and price controls for small and medium-sized proprietors against the big monopolies on which they were dependent; and for solidarity with the thousands of political prisoners and their families.[122] These demands would be supported by committees of popular resistance in conjunction with Marxist-Leninist armed cadres.[123]

We have seen that underlying the proposal for a broad antifascist front in Chile was the Communist party's characterization of the military regime as "fascist."[124] But this was not an accurate description of the Chilean situation nor, according to the Proletarian Tendency, was it the situation in Nicaragua. Implanted by a feeble and dependent bourgeoisie in the midst of a world economic crisis, the MIR contended, "the Chilean dictatorship is that of a bankrupt and impoverished bourgeoisie that is obliged to pay the costs of the crisis suffered by the imperialist powers."[125] It did not have the backing of the petite bourgeoisie, much less of a mass political movement including a sector of the working class, as in the case of European fascism. Thus it was more accurate to characterize the military junta as a Bonapartist regime or "state of exception," in which a virtual stalemate between the bourgeoisie and the working class had permitted the armed forces to step between them and to assume momentarily an independent role.[126] Efforts to "fascistize" the Chilean state had failed precisely because the military lost the support of the petite bourgeoisie, which had initially backed the coup. Although the military junta had surpassed in savagery the brutal repression of European fascism, it was incapable of destroying the autonomous organizations of the working class. Consequently, conditions were ripe for developing the resistance under proletarian leadership without the workers' having to moderate their demands under pressure from the bourgeois opposition.[127]

These were the basic ingredients of the strategy adopted by the Proletarian Tendency, including part of its rationale. It was a fundamentally "classist" strategy, as it was called in the Southern Cone, which distinguished it from the ideologically heterodox and multiclass "movementist" strategy favored by the established communist parties and by populist and nationalist currents on the Left.[128] Although a movementist strategy ultimately prevailed in Nicaragua because of the imposition of the Insurrectional Tendency, it did so under conditions in which the FSLN assumed a hegemonic role.

The Strategy of General Insurrection

The Insurrectionalists' perception of the divisions that surfaced in the FSLN at the end of 1975 differed from that of the strategists of both the GPP—the hard-line rural guerrilla faction that supported a *guerra popular prolongada* (prolonged people's war)—and the Proletarian Tendency. Daniel Ortega Saavedra, the head of the Revolutionary Junta from 1979 to 1984 and a member of the National Directorate along with his brother Humberto since 1971, traces the origins of this third tendency as far back as 1973. It first emerged from efforts to find an ideological-organizational alternative to pragmatic tendencies within the FSLN at one pole and sectarian tendencies at the other.[129] Those efforts resulted in the first major division within the movement, "the GPP and ourselves, with different conceptions concerning the development of the struggle aimed at overthrowing the dictatorship."[130] As for the so-called Proletarian Tendency, he said it "really didn't represent the traditions and the content that had characterized the FSLN since its inception . . . [but] had emerged as a small group of highly educated cadres who wanted to organize an orthodox-type political party . . . [and] had not transcended propagandism."[131]

The solution finally reached by this third tendency combined the strategies of prolonged people's war in the countryside with massive popular resistance in the cities. Several novel ingredients were added: a general insurrection, backed up by urban guerrilla warfare, and the mobilization of Nicaragua's middle sectors in a political confrontation with the dictatorship. As we have seen, the GPP focused on recruiting peasants for the armed struggle and the Proletarian Tendency addressed the material interests of the workers but was led mainly by intellectuals. Now it became the turn of the Insurrectionalists to represent not only those interests, but also the alienated middle sectors opposed to the Somoza regime.[132]

Unlike the GPP, the Insurrectionalists believed the center of armed struggle should be in the cities. Unlike the Proletarian Tendency, they favored immediate armed action by the workers. In addition, they proposed a new type of diplomatic offensive aimed at creating a broad alliance with the bourgeois opposition both within the country and abroad. Toward this end they revived the ideological pluralism that had been a feature of the FSLN during the interim between its first armed defeat in 1963 and the launching of its second armed operation in 1967.

Humberto Ortega was perhaps the first to perceive that a third social force, the so-called middle sectors of self-employed workers, salaried professionals, petty bureaucrats, small proprietors, and career-minded students, was ready to move against the regime. By the beginning of 1977 Nicaraguan society had become so polarized over the issue of the continuation of the tyranny, Ortega believed, that if the FSLN did not capitalize on the growing anti-Somoza sentiments the bourgeois opposition would. Realizing that President Carter's government was favorably disposed to getting rid of Somoza and replacing him with the moderate reformers centered around Pedro Joaquín Chamorro, Ortega argued that the FSLN's only hope for success was to build a multiclass anti-Somoza coalition of its own. This meant going beyond the FSLN's past reliance on a worker-peasant coalition in favor of wooing the middle sectors and giving primary attention to their immediate concerns and aspirations.

It was this new orientation that would eventually mislead the bulk of the Nicaraguan people and the Western media into equating the Insurrectional Tendency with its social democratic allies, personified by Edén Pastora. Thus the FSLN mistakenly became identified with a noncapitalist, noncommunist, and nonaligned "third position" in domestic and foreign policy. Although it did adopt such a position, its motive for doing so was purely strategical.

In May 1977 the National Directorate, by then firmly under the control of the Insurrectional Tendency, issued its first political-military platform spelling out the implications of the new strategy.[133] The Machiavellian character of this document is evident in directives aimed at avoiding leftist rhetoric, at developing a mini-

mum program of government acceptable to virtually everyone opposed to the Somoza regime, at creating a broad anti-Somoza front,
including the democratic and bourgeois opposition groups, and at
securing undisputed control of this front while preempting organizational efforts by other groups opposed to the dictatorship. In the
event of U.S. intervention, FSLN cadres were directed to resume a
strategy of protracted warfare based on "an openly socialist position, with the direct support of the socialist camp!" This last directive brings out the Insurrectional Tendency's commitment to the
new Marxism otherwise concealed behind its reformist rhetoric.

A year later, in April 1978, the National Directorate issued its
second major statement concerning strategy. The emphasis this
time was on an alliance with the bourgeois opposition together
with a global approach aimed at coordinating different methods of
struggle.

The first major thesis in this new statement, based on an assessment of Nicaragua's political and economic conditions, was
that the popular forces by themselves were incapable of overthrowing the dictatorship. Consequently, it became imperative to establish a temporary alliance with the bourgeois opposition. It was
anticipated that this alliance would continue after the seizure of
power, but that it would soon break down because of internal contradictions.[134] Meanwhile, it was critical for the popular forces to
take advantage of the favorable historical conjuncture in which U.S.
imperialism was being momentarily restrained by the new human
rights policy of the Carter administration and by support for that
policy from social democratic governments in Western Europe and
Latin America. Such a conjuncture could not last. "Therefore,
we favor the overthrow of the dictatorship in the shortest possible time."[135]

This strategy required a flexible policy of alliances not only
with the bourgeois opposition to Somoza, but also with liberal elements abroad. A diplomatic offensive had to be launched on the
external front parallel to and simultaneous with the guerrilla offensive.[136] A dialogue with these bourgeois elements required an intermediate organization of representatives from all social classes as
the FSLN's mouthpiece. The Group of Twelve was assembled for
presenting the FSLN's demands in a respectable light and for neutralizing the fears of the bourgeoisie and its supporters concerning
a future Marxist-Leninist takeover. In the role of a moderating
force, the Group of Twelve was also given the task of radicalizing
the petite bourgeoisie and other intermediate sectors.[137]

The Insurrectionalists' second major thesis was that the dictatorship could be overcome only by a continuous and generalized offensive combining all forms of struggle. At the decisive moment the people would have to be armed as the condition of a general insurrection. This global approach included plans for a nationwide general strike involving street barricades and widespread sabotage, the paralysis of transportation, the occupation of factories, workshops, churches, and commercial malls, and the takeover of entire neighborhoods.[138] The actions of guerrillas in the countryside would be coordinated with those of urban commandos and mobile strategic forces alternating from one battle zone to another in support of the FSLN's mass organizations.[139] This would keep the National Guard immobilized while the popular forces extended the radius of their operations and control over the principal urban centers.

The FSLN's minimum program of twenty-five points, formulated on the eve of its second insurrectional attempt in September 1978, called simply for the replacement of the dictatorship by a democratic and popular government.[140] It made a point of defending not only the class interests of workers and peasants, but also the interests of small farmers, small businessmen, teachers, government workers, commercial employees, professionals, and technicians. Thus it made a definite bid for support from these intermediate sectors. In this minimum program neither the goal of socialism nor a transitional regime based on people's power was even mentioned.

The origins of this strategy, like the one it displaced, are traceable to Sandino. Thanks to Fonseca, the FSLN made its first serious attempt to assimilate the lessons of Sandino's political-military experience. But it was Humberto Ortega who crowned this effort. Wounded in both arms during the action aimed at liberating Fonseca from a Costa Rican prison in 1969, he lost the mobility of his right hand and some in the left. Unable to bear a rifle after his exchange for hostages in 1970, he dedicated himself to the study of military strategy and to representing the FSLN's interests in Havana. It was his strategy that guided the FSLN's first partial offensive in October 1977, the insurrection of September 1978, and the general insurrection that toppled the Somoza regime in July 1979.

Ortega argued that Sandino's strategy combined protracted warfare, aimed at wearing down the enemy and sapping its morale, with a rudimentary insurrectional strategy of the people in arms.[141] From the beginning the peasants were organized to participate not only as part of a logistical rear guard, but also in actual combat. "From the military aspect, these armed actions had the characteristics of *partial insurrections,* in which a small force of *regular guerrillas* directed the actions of *large masses.*"[142] One example was the battle of Ocotal (July 1927), where Sandino led a partial insurrection of eight hundred peasants armed only with knives and machetes. Another was the battle of Bromodero (February 1928), when a sizable part of Sandino's troops had been recruited from the neighboring villages shortly before the engagement, after which they returned to their homes and their daily chores to await his next call.

In 1931, according to Ortega, Sandino's columns reached the Atlantic coast in what was tantamount to his first general offensive.[143] By then the revolutionary war of liberation had become a war of movement extending beyond its original base of operations in the Segovias to most of Nicaragua's populated regions. As Ortega characterized this higher phase of the armed struggle, "The war of movement reflects the military leap made by Sandinista troops after a number of years of intense guerrilla activity during which they gradually became transformed into large columns with the characteristics of a regular army. . . . Practically speaking, these were tantamount to *strategic mobile forces.*"[144] Moreover, they were supported by smaller bands of guerrillas and local part-time guerrillas.

Sandino's operational strategy during this higher phase of armed struggle consisted of a continuous offensive against the enemy, but without a frontal line of attack or struggle for positions. The difference between this phase of mobile warfare and the preceding phase of guerrilla skirmishes, Ortega noted, was that the guerrillas had no regular troops but only small bands operating within a comparatively narrow radius with hit-and-run tactics.[145] During the later phase the offensive character of Sandino's struggle became more pronounced, and military engagements became of greater consequence.

To reach this higher phase became the immediate objective of Ortega's insurrectional strategy. Bearing in mind the lessons of Sandino's struggle, he called for the transformation of guerrilla warfare into a popular insurrection supported by regular mobile columns in a war of movement extending throughout the entire country.

Until December 1974 the FSLN pursued a defensive strategy, including armed propaganda in the countryside and bank robberies in the cities, that barely kept the movement alive.[146] This strategy corresponded to the initial stage of Sandino's struggle between 1927 and 1931, but on a much smaller scale. Although the FSLN had the advantage of a clandestine urban apparatus, which Sandino did not have, it lacked his base of support among the peasants. Nonetheless, with the intensification of political-organizational work in the cities and the development of a support network for the guerrillas in the mountains, "the Sandinista war made a great leap forward . . . with the aim of preparing the political-military offensive that began with the successful action of 27 December 1974."[147]

To this point the FSLN's strategy was not to fight unless compelled to do so. This strategy helped the vanguard to survive and kept the enemy disconcerted. It contributed to building a basis of mass resistance in the cities, to diffusing the ideology of Sandinismo through the FSLN's intermediate organizations, and to alerting the people to a revolutionary alternative. But the time had come "to break with the defensive posture and pass to an uninterrupted political and military offensive."[148]

The operation launched in December 1974 did not achieve its main objective of strengthening the guerrilla forces in the mountains that were in the stage of organizing mobile columns.[149] The terrible repression unleased by the government in retaliation for the seizure of hostages prevented the guerrillas from carrying out their plan of a continuing offensive. Thus a period of relative stagnation followed until the offensive launched by the Insurrectional Tendency in October 1977, when the people began responding to the FSLN's initiatives.[150]

Why did the Nicaraguan people respond to the FSLN in 1977 but not before? The answer lies in the FSLN's adoption of a new and broader strategy and in the changed political situation in Nicaragua and the corresponding change in the people's perceptions, which occurred independently of the FSLN.

The conjunction of two originally unrelated series of events set the stage for the 1977–1979 insurrection. The first began with Somoza's imposition of martial law and press censorship in December 1974 in retaliation for the successful commando raid that obliged the regime to release FSLN prisoners and to pay one million dollars in ransom for the FSLN's hostages. The state of siege suspended civil liberties and gave the National Guard a virtual license to terrorize the civilian population. The resulting human rights violations coincided with the election of a new U.S. president committed to a strong human rights policy. In an effort to appease the Carter administration, Somoza lifted the state of siege and press censorship in September 1977. But by then it was too late. Mounting popular hostility to the regime suddenly erupted in successive waves that could not be contained. It reached a point of frenzy with the news in January 1978 that Pedro Joaquín Chamorro, the Conservative leader of the democratic opposition, had been assassinated by Somoza agents. The Monimbó rebellion in a neighborhood of Masaya was indirectly a response to this assassination.

Concurrently, other events helped the Insurrectional Tendency to prevail in the National Directorate. In a statement in April 1978 the Insurrectionalists reported that in the early months of 1975 only five remained of the original nine-man National Directorate dating from 1969.[151] But as a result of the imprisonment of José Benito Escobar and Daniel Ortega, it had been reduced in practice to three: Fonseca, Borge, and Humberto Ortega. Since Fonseca and Humberto Ortega were in Cuba, the functioning heads of the movement, except for Borge, were not members of the national leadership. A similar situation had occurred in 1970–1971, when Oscar Turcios was the only member of the National Directorate operating freely inside the country. Only after the exchange of the December 1974 hostages for Escobar and Daniel Ortega was this situation remedied. A majority of the National Directorate met in the early part of 1975 to replace the dead leaders. Seven new members were added: Carlos Agüero, Henry Ruiz, Pedro Arauz, Víctor Tirado, Plutarco Hernández Sancho, Eduardo Contreras, and Jacinto Hernández.[152]

The replenished leadership divided into two tendencies. Borge claimed that he, Fonseca, and Ruiz defended the GPP line, that Tirado and the Ortega brothers represented the Insurrectional Tendency, and that Contreras's position was unknown.[153] From another source we know that Plutarco Hernández belonged to the Insurrectional Tendency and that Escobar vacillated between both camps.[154] Jacinto Hernández's position remains unclear, but both Agüero and Arauz were GPP.[155] The picture we get at the end of 1975 is the following: five supporters of the GPP, four supporters of the Insurrectionalist Tendency, two unknown quantities, and one straddler. Thus the GPP had one more vote than the Insurrectionalists when the divisions became further accentuated in 1976.

Between November 1976 and October 1977 the new leadership was in turn decimated. Five members were killed and not replaced: Fonseca (GPP), Agüero (GPP), Arauz (GPP), and the two unknowns, Jacinto Hernández and Contreras.[156] Borge, who had been captured and imprisoned at the beginning of 1976, was held incommunicado until his exchange for new hostages in August 1978.[157] This left an effective National Directorate in which the Insurrectionalists held a clear majority. An official FSLN communiqué in October 1977, for example, contained the signatures of only six members: four Insurrectionalists (Tirado, Plutarco Hernández, and the Ortega brothers), one GPP (Ruiz), and the only straddler (Escobar).[158] Although Bayardo Arce had been chosen as Arauz's successor in the event of death, when Arauz was killed in October 1977 Arce was promoted to the GPP leadership but blocked from becoming a member of the National Directorate. The Insurrectionalists were thus firmly in control and could begin to apply their strategy of a general insurrection.

Actually, they had begun preparing for an insurrection at the beginning of 1977. As Sergio Ramírez noted, he was assigned the task of organizing "an alliance with democratic sectors of the national bourgeoisie through a group that would provide political support for the Sandinista Front and that eventually might be included in a government backed by the FSLN."[159] By June 1977 the core of the future Group of Twelve had already been organized for that purpose. Several months later Humberto Ortega informed it of the proposed plan to seize the military garrisons of San Carlos, Rivas, Masaya, Ocotal, and possibly Estelí, all in a single day. He also let it know that "during that same operation, on the same day, the establishment of a provisional government in Nicaraguan territory might be announced that would be headed by the Group of Twelve."[160] In Mexico, Ramírez's group raised one hundred thousand dollars to finance the insurrection. However, after arriving in Costa Rica preparatory to setting up a provisional government, it was told that the insurrection would not have the results originally anticipated and that the National Directorate had therefore resolved to relieve the Group of Twelve of any further responsibility.[161]

What actually transpired was the following. On October 13 the FSLN captured the National Guard garrison at San Carlos near the Costa Rican border. The attack on the garrison at Ocotal was unsuccessful. Moreover, not until several days later were these actions followed by an attack on the main garrison in Masaya, less than twenty kilometers from the capital.[162] A week later three squads from an FSLN column took San Fernando, only ten kilometers from a previous operation at Mozónte near the Honduran border. Armed actions in the extreme north were thus coordinated with those in the south and west-central regions. As the Nicaraguan equivalent of Fidel Castro's attack on the Moncada garrison in Santiago de Cuba on 26 July 1953, Ramírez concluded, "it had the same political effect, which is to say that the October offensive really paved the way toward victory."[163]

The time chosen was especially propitious because Somoza had just lifted the state of siege in an effort to improve his image.

Convinced that the FSLN had been all but eliminated, he decided to launch a democratic opening in the face of the bourgeois opposition. The FSLN struck to upset this maneuver. "We regained the initiative we had taken on 27 December 1974," Humberto Ortega noted, "but this time we resolved not to lose it."[164]

The original plan was to organize the masses to support the guerrillas, but a different strategy emerged in which the guerrillas provided armed support for the people. Originally, it was thought that the guerrillas might defeat the National Guard, but it was discovered that only the armed people could do so. Alone, the guerrillas could never match the enemy's numbers and firepower. Ortega concluded that, "to win, we had to mobilize the masses and get them to participate actively in the armed struggle."[165]

The October offensive was launched as part of an insurrectional strategy, but it did not lead to an insurrection. At best it was a partial offensive in which armed actions served as propaganda for a mass uprising. Realizing afterward that the offensive had not produced the desired result, the FSLN's National Directorate began giving priority to armed actions by the masses. Said Ortega, "We realized that our chief source of strength lay in a state of total mobilization that would disperse the technical and military resources of the enemy."[166] The October offensive was not entirely a failure, because it contributed to deepening a political crisis at a moment when all outward signs indicated it was over. Abandoning the vaunted democratic opening, the dictatorship adopted a series of indiscriminately repressive measures that alienated still further the bourgeois opposition.[167]

In January 1978 the new wave of repression peaked when government agents assassinated Pedro Joaquín Chamorro, editor of the Conservative newspaper *La Prensa* and leader of the bourgeois opposition. Only then did the masses occupy the streets of the capital in protest, thus manifesting for the first time their determination to do something concrete.[168] At that point, said Ortega, the people began acting on their own initiative instead of responding to a call from the FSLN—a situation nobody had foreseen.[169] When trade unions and employers alike called a general strike against the dictatorship, the FSLN decided to make its presence felt with armed actions of its own. In February Rivas and Granada in the south were captured. At the same time an antiguerrilla camp was successfully encircled and immobilized in the north.

These combined actions on several fronts redoubled the people's enthusiasm and determination to overthrow the dictatorship. They kindled the spark of the first popular insurrection in Masaya's In-

dian suburb of Monimbó. Organized and planned by the local inhabitants, it was assisted only incidentally by those Sandinistas
who were present. That insurrection lasted for almost a week, Ortega recalled, until it was crushed by the National Guard on February 26.[170]

Following is his account of the insurrection and his vindication
of the new strategy:

> The people of Monimbó, a neighborhood of Masaya with some twenty
> thousand inhabitants and both urban and rural zones, began in a spon-
> taneous fashion to prepare for the insurrection. They began to organize
> block by block and to take over the key spots, to execute henchmen of
> the regime, to apply people's justice for the first time. They began to
> work as a Sandinista unit when they still lacked the organized leader-
> ship of the Sandinista movement. . . . This Indian sector responded
> immediately to the capture of the cities several days before.[171]

The actions in Monimbó showed that the FSLN had finally reached
the point of reproducing its own armed actions through the people
in arms. Although this first partial insurrection failed because of
its purely local character, it became the model for all subsequent
ones. Henceforth the problem would be to set up a clandestine
radio station in direct contact with the people for the purpose of
launching several Monimbó-type uprisings simultaneously.[172]

The next major action occurred in August 1978, when the
FSLN's Operation Pigsty catalyzed the first such uprising on a national scale by capturing the National Palace.[173] The congressmen
who were held as hostages were released in exchange for political
prisoners, a ransom of half a million dollars used to finance the
final offensive, and press and radio transmission of FSLN messages
calling for a nationwide insurrection. The point of this operation
was to foil a planned coup to replace Somoza with a civilian-
military regime that would have effectively nullified a revolutionary alternative.[174]

The popular uprising that followed Operation Pigsty, like the
one in Monimbó, went beyond the vanguard's limited manpower
and capacity to lead it. But at the same time the FSLN had to maintain momentum to avoid losing the political initiative.[175] During
the last week in August in an action that caught the nation by surprise, teenagers in Matagalpa responded to its call for insurrection.[176] It took a week of savage battles before the National Guard
could retake the captured positions and restore order.

The Matagalpa uprising, a kind of second Monimbó, was the
signal for the FSLN's large-scale September offensive.[177] The people
poured into the streets to seize the department capitals of Chinan-

dega, León, Estelí, and the village of Yali, supported by barely 150 armed FSLN militants. The National Guard had to use Sherman tanks and the air force to quell the uprising. In Estelí alone there were several thousand dead. Militarily, the offensive failed, according to Ortega, because none of the National Guard centers could be captured. This was not altogether accurate. Missing from his account was the successful assault on a National Guard station that occurred for the second time at Monimbó.[178]

Once again the masses had moved faster than the vanguard. Despite the military setback, the people's response to the resulting genocide helped to make a victory of defeat. As Ortega commented, "Our forces were multiplied several times over: three- or fourfold, plus the potential for recruiting thousands of others."[179] The FSLN grew in firepower because of the weapons captured from the enemy and it also learned how to retreat successfully with a minimum of casualties.

This was not the GPP's assessment. Both the October 1977 offensive and the September 1978 popular insurrection were launched, according to GPP commander Henry Ruiz, without the minimum conditions required for a military victory.[180] Since these conditions had yet to be created, he called for the abandonment of the insurrectional strategy and a return to guerrilla warfare. He criticized the Insurrectionalist strategy for being counterproductive. This "great wave of attacks on military garrisons," he contended, this "beachhead strategy," assumed that the defeat of the National Guard was a military-technical problem when it was really a social one.[181] He argued that the ebb of the revolutionary tide after the 1978 offensive resulted from having launched it prematurely, when the FSLN was still divided organizationally and lacked a unified political-military command.

The Insurrectionalists insisted that their choice of strategy had been correct, because the masses had actively joined the struggle. The key to victory, according to Ortega, was to give precedence to mobilizing the people for an urban insurrection from the start. In this perspective the September offensive had been a big step forward: "We had struggle in the cities, struggle for control of the means of communication, and struggle in the rural and mountain areas. But the columns were not the determining factor of victory; they were simply a part of a greater determining factor, which was the armed struggle of the masses."[182]

A single political-military command was finally established in March 1979, with the unification of the three tendencies. The new National Directorate consisted of three representatives from each:

Humberto Ortega, Daniel Ortega, Tirado (Insurrectionalists); Borge, Ruiz, and Arce (GPP); and Wheelock, Carrión, and Núñez (Proletarian Tendency). The Coordinating Commission of the new unified leadership, consisting of Humberto Ortega, Borge, and Wheelock, was assigned the task of supervising the daily conduct of the struggle. Each faction put aside its differences with the others by recognizing the importance of everybody else's work. According to Ortega, "unity was achieved on the basis of a single conception without each having to cede ground to the others . . . on a strategy that upheld the insurrectional nature of the struggle, the need for a flexible policy of alliances, and the need for a broad program."[183] This was precisely the Insurrectionalists' own strategy. In effect, the other tendencies decided to make common cause with the Insurrectionalists, whose strategy was broad and flexible enough to encompass their own.

A united FSLN became the cue for a new series of partial and uncoordinated offensives beginning with the capture of El Jícaro in March, when the enemy garrison was overpowered by guerrillas.[184] In April 1979, Estelí was taken by a guerrilla column without a popular uprising. Although these actions were followed by a military setback in Nueva Guinea in southeastern Nicaragua, Jinotega was captured in May. That same month El Naranjo, where the National Guard had stationed a large force, was taken. But these offensives were poorly coordinated, narrow in scope, and only sporadically supported by the people.

At this point the leadership concluded that, if the struggle continued in this way, the enemy would cut the movement to pieces.[185] If El Naranjo fell, the initiative would pass to Somoza. Moreover, the FSLN would have lost the opportunity of scoring a short-term military victory. It was then, said Ortega, that plans were laid for the final offensive.[186]

The final assault began in June 1979, when the Southern Front was instructed to capture and hold the important city of Rivas. By then the regime found itself in a dilemma that the FSLN hoped to use to advantage: "If the enemy left the cities, the mass movement would get the upper hand; if it remained, this would help the guerrilla columns."[187] Accordingly, efforts were made to bog down the National Guard with popular insurrections in the cities combined with a nationwide general strike.

The insurrection had to last at least two weeks to give the columns in the northwest and east a chance to regroup and launch a coordinated attack at the right moment. Several days after the battles in El Naranjo, Ortega recalled, "our forces in Masaya, Granada, and Carrazo were to go into action, cutting off the means of communication with Somoza's forces on the Southern Front. The uprising in Managua was to start as soon as fighting had begun on all those fronts."[188] That is basically what happened. It became possible to coordinate in the same time and space the three essential factors of a successful strategy: an urban mass insurrection; an offensive by the FSLN's military forces; and a nationwide general strike. The final offensive beginning in June 1979 could not have succeeded, Ortega claimed, without the combination of these different forms of struggle.[189]

Ortega traced the origins of the Insurrectionalist strategy to Sandino, but there is a more immediate origin in the Cuban Revolution. The elements of Ortega's synthesis may also be found in Fidel Castro's Moncada strategy.[190]

In his speech on the twentieth anniversary of the assault on Moncada (26 July 1973), Castro revealed what the enemies of the Cuban Revolution had long suspected. Even before Batista's coup of 10 March 1952, Castro had concluded that the solution to Cuba's problems was revolution, that power had to be seized by the people in arms, and that socialism had to be the final objective.[191] He then sketched the strategy of the insurrection applied during the assault on the Moncada barracks:

> The first revolutionary laws would be decreed as soon as the city of Santiago de Cuba was in our hands. . . . The people would be exhorted to struggle against Batista and to make these laws a reality. The workers throughout the country would be called on to declare a revolutionary general strike over the heads of the yellow trade unions and the leaders who had sold out to the government. . . . In the event of not being able to hold onto the city with the thousand arms taken from the enemy, we would launch the guerrilla struggle in the Sierra Maestra.[192]

Recourse to a guerrilla war in the mountains would be a last resort, a means of holding out and repeating the same strategy at a later date.

The same strategy was applied when Castro returned to Cuba from exile at the head of an armed force in November 1956. It called for a coordinated and simultaneous popular insurrection in Santiago and other cities in the province of Oriente, based on the capture of the principal military barracks and police stations. For the second time this strategy failed. Nonetheless, the victory over the regular army after little more than two years of fighting demonstrated "the extent to which the revolutionary conception of the July 26 Movement was correct."[193] After converging on Santiago a third time, on 1 January 1959, Castro continued, "we called for a general revolutionary strike by the workers."[194] The entire country was paralyzed, despite government control over the trade unions. Within forty-eight hours all the military installations in the country had surrendered to his minuscule forces, the people had armed themselves, and a military coup in the capital was aborted. As he recalled, "This was the same strategy of a general strike we thought of launching on 26 July 1953, after taking the city of Santiago."[195]

In a manifesto issued from the Sierra Maestra on 12 March 1958, Castro summarized the strategy guiding the July 26 movement from its inception, "the strategy of the final blow . . . based on the general revolutionary strike, to be seconded by military action."[196] Not until the failure of the general strike movement in April 1958 did he revise the original strategy of urban insurrection by giving the initiative to the guerrillas.

At the same time other civic forces and opposition parties were incorporated into the revolutionary process. This new twist in the Moncada strategy was reflected in the Unity Manifesto, also known as the Caracas Pact, broadcast by Radio Rebelde on 20 July 1958: "Aware that the coordination of human resources, civic forces, political and revolutionary sectors of the opposition, including civilians, military men, workers, students, professionals, businessmen, and citizens in general is necessary to overthrow the dictatorship through a supreme effort, we pledge our united efforts . . . to create a large revolutionary, civic coalition . . . to defeat the dictatorship by means of armed insurrection."[197] Thousands of Cubans willing to fight for freedom would be mobilized along with labor, civic, professional, and economic associations, culminating in a general strike. This amplified strategy of urban insurrection proved to be more effective than the original one in combining and coordinating all forms of struggle. Such was the insurrectional strategy also successfully applied in Nicaragua from 1977 to 1979—exactly two decades later.

In "History Will Absolve Me!" Castro's speech at his trial in October 1953, he cited evidence indicating that the Cuban people were ready to respond to his call for a general insurrection—to be broadcast by radio after the capture of the Moncada barracks. Between May and December 1952, unemployment had reached one million in a country of only 5.5 million.[198] Cubans were blaming Batista for their economic ills, not just for having made a mockery of the constitution. Because popular resentment had peaked, virtually all of the conditions for a revolutionary situation were present at the moment of launching the assault in July 1953. The detonator of a popular explosion would be the seizure of a major garrison and the distribution of arms to the people—not a guerrilla *foco* or armed column operating in the mountains.[199]

Castro's July 26 movement had proved successful owing in large part to its strategy of broad alliances and the absence of any publicly identifiable and doctrinaire "ism." The movement exemplified the importance of political pluralism in the support it received not only from rival political parties, but also from rival ideologies.

Following Castro's example, the Insurrectionalists organized in February 1979 the National Patriotic Front (FPN). This network of alliances included the Independent Liberal party (PLI); the Popular Social Christian party (PPSC); a major 1978 split-off from the Nicaraguan Socialist party, also calling itself the PSN; an earlier splinter group from the PSN calling itself the Communist Party of Nicaragua (PC de N); the Group of Twelve; and the United People's movement (MPU)—a massive coalition of revolutionary trade unions under FSLN leadership.[200] By then even the Insurrectionalists' own ranks contained ideologically heterogeneous elements with independent liberal, social democratic, and Social Christian beliefs. As Borge later acknowledged, "ours was neither a Marxist nor a Christian revolution . . . [but] a revolution in which Marxism and Christianity were integrated with all other ideologies."[201]

Sandino had shown the way with his ideological pastiche of liberalism, populism, communism, and liberation theosophy, behind which he kept the public confused about his own views. Castro seems to have followed Sandino's example. A few months after the overthrow of Somoza in July 1979, he confessed that he had become a communist at least a decade prior to his December 1961 speech announcing his acceptance of Marxism-Leninism: "You can say that beginning with my reading of the Communist Manifesto [throughout 1949 he attended Marxist study courses offered by the Communist party at the University of Havana], . . . I rapidly became a communist . . . a devoted communist, except that I was not a member of the Party . . . because I had already conceived of a different revolutionary strategy . . . without any talk of communism, but with a revolutionary program whose final objective would be socialism."[202] It was his Moncada strategy.[203]

The strategy of dissimulation was among the most important lessons of the Cuban Revolution the Insurrectionalists and their converts assimilated, notably Borge, who has since become a leading FSLN spokesman on ideological matters. "In order not to capitulate before our enemies," Borge recalled, "we had to capitulate before our secondary differences. . . . To triumph in Nicaragua it was necessary to neutralize a sector of the bourgeoisie and to attract the intermediate layers of the population."[204] Such was the pragmatic purpose served by the advocacy of ideological pluralism.

In deciding to organize urban guerrilla commandos in addition to carrying on the struggle in the mountains, Humberto Ortega assimilated the lessons not only of Castro's Moncada strategy but also of the urban guerrillas in Uruguay, Argentina, and Brazil. The Uruguayan Tupamaros and the Argentine Montoneros rejected Che Guevara's thesis that urban guerrilla warfare is at best auxiliary to the main struggle in the countryside. Under the influence of Abraham Guillén's *Strategy of the Urban Guerrilla* (1966), they came to favor an insurrectional strategy that increasingly corresponded to Castro's.[205]

Guillén's theses on urban guerrilla warfare were well known when Ortega launched the new insurrectional strategy in October 1977. Omar Costa's *Los Tupamaros* contains a long interview with Guillén.[206] In the literature concerning the Tupamaros, Guillén's manual was frequently cited as an alternative to Guevara's and Debray's views of the insurrectional *foco*.[207] And selections from his manuscript "The People in Arms" had been published in Mexico in *Revaloración de la guerrilla urbana* more than six months before the FSLN's October offensive.[208]

A Spanish Civil War veteran and exile in Argentina and then in Uruguay, Guillén became a mentor to urban guerrillas in the Southern Cone. I have noted the importance of Col. Alberto Bayo for an understanding of the Nicaraguan Revolution. It now appears that his fellow Spaniard also indirectly shaped its strategy. Guillén, who fought in every major battle during the Spanish Civil War, began his revolutionary career as an anarcho-syndicalist in the urban struggles in Madrid against the local military garrisons loyal to General Franco. That experience was decisive for his political-military strategy, first applied in Argentina and then in Uruguay and Brazil.

Guillén believed that the guerrillas must spread out among the people like spots on a leopard—his favorite metaphor. They must have the active, not just the passive, support of a majority of the population. His strategy of an urban-based insurrection gave priority to a popular uprising over tactical armed actions against the enemy. The mistake of most urban guerrilla movements in Latin America, he argued, was to exaggerate the importance of tactical victories instead of relying on the people to make a generalized insurrection.[209] "As much as 80 percent of the population is needed for combined urban and rural guerrillas to carry forward a general insurrection, a vast surface revolutionary war in all parts of a national territory."[210] The fundamental problem of the guerrillas is to achieve that support. "A popular insurrection can only extend itself in space, like the spots on a leopard's skin, when the guerrillas are the armed fist of the people, the people's justice, the people's hope, in sum, the people in arms." He then attributed this strategy to Fidel Castro.[211]

We have seen that differences over the foregoing strategies and their intellectual foundations were not peculiar to Nicaraguan Marxists. However, elsewhere these strategies corresponded to rival revolutionary movements rather than to competing tendencies within the same organization. Moreover, disputes over strategy were seldom resolved.[212] Not until the principal revolutionary organizations in El Salvador merged in 1980 in the Farabundo Martí National Liberation Front (FMLN), for example, did they finally agree on a strategy of general insurrection.[213] This important development encouraged by Fidel Castro was prompted by the victory of the FSLN.

Unquestionably, the Nicaraguan Revolution represents an original revolutionary experience. The FSLN's experience differed from the Cuban in its collective as opposed to individual leadership and the massive level of popular participation on the side of the revolutionaries.[214] But there is a temptation to exaggerate these differences. At issue is whether the originality of the Nicaraguan Revolution is to be traced to a new revolutionary model of popular insurrection or to the so-called idiosyncrasy of peoples, to differing historical conditions and national and geographical characteristics. The strategy of popular insurrection was not unique to the Nicaraguan experience; only its particular application by the FSLN was original.

8. Ideologies of the Revolution

The struggle against Somoza was waged against almost insuperable odds under conditions that defied most efforts to predict the outcome and to vindicate the risks based on a selfish calculation of the gains, losses, and trade-offs of those who militated in the FSLN. As Pascal said, "The heart has its reasons which reason knows nothing of." We can say as much for those Sandinistas who gave their lives for a revolution in whose triumph they did not share.

In September 1978, barely nine months before launching the final offensive, the FSLN could boast of some 250 fully armed and trained combatants against a professional army of 14,000. For each guerrilla there were approximately 50 National Guardsmen equipped with Sherman tanks and a modern air force unequaled in Central America. To challenge this military Frankenstein took more than strong nerves and guts. It required mass participation. The people in arms evidently made the difference.

Faced with mounting insecurity and repression, the Nicaraguan people revolted against the Somoza regime. The government retaliated with aerial bombardments that leveled entire neighborhoods. Was it ideology that led the people to revolt or a sober calculation of ends and means? It was a little of both.

We have seen how Sandino's ideology had two principal components. Ethically, he appealed to the values of patriotism and articulated a doctrine of human rights tied to the word *sacred*. Theologically, he mounted a system of beliefs predicated on a continuing war between the forces of good and evil, a final holocaust, and the victory of divine justice. These nonrational sources of motivation gave a tremendous impetus to his movement by strengthening the will to sacrifice.

The FSLN also had need of a justifying set of myths. To salvage Sandino's ideology and adapt it to the people's Catholicism, the FSLN had to get rid of its theosophical content. It incorporated the ethical leftovers into its cult of the new man and doctrine of human rights. But these were not the only ideologies of the revolution. A Christian version of the new man based on a reinterpretation of the moral values of Christianity developed alongside the FSLN's version and partly coalesced with it. In addition, a movement to reinterpret the Christian faith in the light of the revolutionary process gave rise to a liberation theology, which has filled the void left by Sandino's now obsolete theosophy.

The Cult of the New Man

What are the ethical values that Fonseca and the FSLN explicitly invoked as inspiration for their revolutionary struggle? What was their ideal of the new man who would make the Nicaraguan revolution?

Among the publications of the FSLN is a pamphlet entitled *¿Qué es un sandinista?* (*What Is a Sandinista?*). It contains three brief statements concerning the qualities of the new man, each dating from the early seventies. The first is by Carlos Fonseca, the second by Oscar Turcios, and the third by Ricardo Morales Avilés. Their purpose is stated on the cover: "to rescue and spread among our people the best qualities and virtues of the revolutionaries who have fought in the ranks of our organization . . . to rescue the mystique of the FSLN, that daily attitude of constant sacrifice for our people, of respect for our leaders and comrades, of fraternity, humility, and simplicity." In the prologue by Carlos Núñez we read that the Sandinista is a revolutionary with a great sense of humanity. He is the most dedicated to the just cause of the people, "his generosity is boundless, his interests as an individual are subordinated to the collective interest represented by the vanguard, and his political activity and militancy are guided by political and ideological principles."[1]

Fonseca's statement begins by stressing the importance of integrating revolutionary theory with concrete practice in close connection with the masses. The Sandinista, he says, must have an authentically critical judgment.[2] Besides this fundamental, eminently intellectual trait, the revolutionary must demonstrate qualities of character, among which Fonseca lists modesty, respect, sincerity, and fellow-feeling.[3] "Above all else, the Sandinista possesses revolutionary modesty."[4] Modesty, which might not seem to be that important, restrains individual assertiveness and defers to the collective consciousness required for collective action.[5] For the most part, Fonseca's statement dispenses with the standard assortment of moral crutches or appeals to what is right, just, good, and virtuous. It was the social and individual psychology of the revolutionary that interested him more than the inculcation of a revolutionary morality. Nonetheless, traces of a moral ideology appear in his concluding observation: "The revolutionary knows that wherever he is, as long as he struggles for humanity, he will be doing his duty."[6]

The much shorter code by Oscar Turcios, a member of the National Directorate killed in 1973 along with Ricardo Morales, stresses the role of class interest in the makeup of the Sandinista. What is fundamental is "the capacity of analysis and the careful determination of the correct path for taking power."[7] Although he adds to this an intransigent revolutionary courage and audacity, there is no indication that these are moral ideals. Turcios's statement is completely devoid of moral language—courage and audacity are psychological traits rather than specifically moral ones. The Sandinista is motivated less by moral appeals than by the Machiavellian advice "to think and act with a strategic mentality."[8] One is advised to stay close to the masses as part of the "conditions for victory."[9]

The sacrificial and moral element is evident mainly in Ricardo Morales's sketch of the new man. Among his appeals to nonrational motives is the following: "A Sandinista is one who recognizes the happiness that comes from fertilizing with blood the soil of the Fatherland."[10] Even more telling is his concluding sentiment: "The Sandinista has hands for laboring with peasants . . . , he has a breast prepared to be a martyr!"[11] Oddly enough, these and other implicit appeals to a higher principle than intelligent self-interest are not presented in the language of morals. They are presented as part of an "art of revolution . . . that unites and educates the people, that combines revolutionary realism with revolutionary romanticism."[12] Although Morales also noted the need for a proletarian, interest-oriented, scientific approach to social change, he appealed mainly to sentiment.

More recently, Tomás Borge has tried to answer the question, "What is a Sandinista?" In a speech in commemoration of the forty-sixth anniversary of Sandino's death (20 February 1980), he distinguished the militants of the FSLN by their superior moral qualities. "A Sandinista is one who concerns himself more for the people's well-being than his own . . . , who does everything possible to overcome egoism, the aversion to work, and a domineering attitude." The militants in the new Sandinista party slated to replace the FSLN "must be an example in everything . . . : THEY MUST

HAVE A SUPERIOR MORALITY TO BE THE SONS OF SAN-
DINO"—not just in critical moments but twenty-four hours
a day.[13]

Borge delineated the specific duties of the militant in a follow-
up speech on the Party of the Sandinista Revolution (September
1980). The militants in the Sandinista party must accept work as a
reward rather than as punishment, must regard discipline as an
honor, must overcome envy, vanity, and other base desires, must invariably tell the truth, must conscientiously serve and remain close
to the people, and must persist in the effort to change themselves
and society.[14] They will do this in their capacity as representatives
of the people's interest, regardless of the consequences. Sandinistas
are those "who are capable of suffering, of enduring pain, of challenging the enemy no matter how powerful he may be—precisely
those are the true sons of Sandino, the real brothers of Carlos Fonseca, and the only ones worthy of being militants."[15] This is the
moral ideology of the Sandinista directly expressed as a matter of
revolutionary principle. Borge is saying that the duty of the revolutionary is to become a new man.

Elsewhere, Borge affirms that the key to liberation is not economic or political but moral; it consists of liberating oneself from
egoism.[16] The fundamental human problem is to overcome alienation from others and self-alienation, a dehumanized condition accentuated by contagion with the "American way of life!"[17] Only by
ridding oneself of egoism, according to Borge, is it possible to build a
new society. Thus it is not the transformation of the economic in-
frastructure but the creation of a new man that "in our judgment is
the most important aspect of national reconstruction."[18]

That the creation of a new man is a key to Nicaragua's revolution was brought out in the speeches at the First Conference of
Cultural Workers, held in the capital in February 1980. Bayardo
Arce, a former leader of the protracted warfare tendency, focused on
the question of ideology. Noting that a people's democratic revolution on the cultural front must concentrate on creating a new man,
Arce added that one should look for new values in figures like Sandino and those who have best served the people.[19] The new values
should also be communicated in such a way that, without sacrific-
ing artistic quality, they can be understood by ordinary workers and
peasants: "Whenever the artist sets out to paint, to write a poem,
to publish a book, to compose a song, we want him to consider the
extent to which his work will be understood by people, the extent
to which it will help the people to transform themselves."[20] The

task of cultural workers is not only to formulate the values of the new man, but also to communicate them effectively to others.

Cultural activity, which "recovers, reproduces, develops, and transmits the values, ideas, and customs of a society," is essentially ideological.[21] We know, said Arce, that the principal type of domination that had to be overcome was economic, but at the same time there was the need to combat a whole series of ideological values, transmitted by the educational apparatus and mass media, that contributed to supporting economic domination. In the struggle on the cultural front, Arce insisted, it is imperative to break the ideological power of the bourgeoisie.[22] This requires that obsolete theological beliefs be replaced by a new religious mentality committed to changing the world; and that "disco" music, insipid, frivolous, and syrupy verse, and formal and costly theater be replaced by art having a revolutionary content.[23]

The most difficult revolution to make and that which takes the longest, Arce continued, is the cultural revolution. This includes a struggle against the imposition of Yankee values and the archaic values remaining from the Spanish conquest. The cosmopolitan values of the slick "jet set," expressed through the sophisticated techniques of contemporary music, film, and television, are especially obnoxious.[24] The Nicaraguan people still regard these foreign values as "normal." In their place Arce recommended the diffusion of patriotic and humane values forged in the image of Sandino. He despised the shallow materialism of modern society, rejected egoism and individualism in favor of collective life, but also spurned the remnants of feudal servility and backwardness.[25] Embodied in the figure of Sandino were the new values required to make the ideological revolution in the arts, literature, journalism, and so on.

The objective of the Sandinista cultural revolution was discussed by the minister of culture, Ernesto Cardenal. Commenting on Marx's eleventh thesis on Feuerbach, Cardenal agreed that "philosophy should have no other task than that of transforming reality," which means that knowledge does not exist for its own sake. Similarly, theology, literature, music, and the arts should have an ultimately practical aim: "I believe that theology also should serve to transform reality. And that poetry should serve to transform reality, and also the theater and every intellectual artistic creation. And that culture exists to transform reality." The only justification of culture, then, is to create the new man who will make the revolution.[26] Expressed by almost anybody else, this might be dismissed as propaganda insensitive to both art and the artist. But coming from the leading poet and theologian of the Sandinista revolution, these thoughts are hardly those of a cultural philistine.

Cardenal outlined what he believed to be necessary to make the cultural revolution in Nicaragua. In opposition to the dominant bourgeois values under Somoza, the FSLN must develop revolutionary values in education, art, literature, music, history, and the social sciences. The new culture, Cardenal continued, will stress popular and folkish themes that were systematically ignored by artists in the past. The new culture will not subscribe to or diffuse the values of a supercilious and educated elite; it will not be art for art's sake. It will be a popular culture not in the sense of a commercialized and vulgar "pop art" but in the sense of promoting authentic human values in place of the induced and contrived values of the mass media.[27] The new culture will be national instead of cosmopolitan; it will focus on the nation's history and on the development of the national character; it will take into account the different geographical regions, races, and languages of Nicaragua. The new culture will be anti-imperialist in rejecting U.S. culture imports such as "disco," *Star Wars,* "Dallas," *Reader's Digest, Playboy.* It will replace them with the folklore and folk art of Nicaragua and the rest of Central America.

How did this Catholic priest in trouble with church authorities square his religious faith with these revolutionary pronouncements? As he noted in the introduction to his speech, those with a Christian upbringing believe that everything should be subordinated to God. This includes literature, music, and the arts. But authentic Christianity also teaches that God is love—love for others. "Therefore we have to say that everything should be subordinated to the love for man. . . . Art must be subordinated to the love for man, along with everything else. That is the Revolution."[28] In this latter-day revival of Tolstoy's thesis concerning art and religion we see the confluence of the two most powerful movements in Western history, Marxism and Christianity, which Marx believed to be fundamentally antithetical.[29]

We are familiar with the personification of the new man as Che Guevara, but thanks mainly to Nicaragua's minister of culture the new man is also publicly equated with Jesus Christ—still the most revered example of love and sacrifice for the world's poor and oppressed. During Christmas 1980, posters in the Nicaraguan capital celebrated the birth of the new man, picturing the Christ child in a manger with the Virgin Mary protected by Sandinista armed guards!

As Sergio Ramírez acknowledged in a major address on the

first anniversary of the Revolution (19 July 1980), Sandinismo and
Christianity are two vital and complementary aspects of Nicaraguan life. The moral values of each had become amalgamated in a
single revolutionary option aimed at liberating the humiliated, the
oppressed, and the exploited. In praise of the Sandinistas who had
worked in the Literacy Crusade as militants of the Popular Army of
Alphabetization, Ramírez likened their values to Christian values:

> You who have gained through the hardships of this struggle the right
> to be Sandinistas have accomplished this Crusade on the basis of true
> Christian values that do not contradict Sandinista values: love with-
> out limit, humility, the disposition to sacrifice, the preferential option
> for the poor. . . . The new man, the new woman, who scorn the accu-
> mulation of material goods and see with clarity that the future be-
> longs to all, that there will be no humiliation in the future, are that
> way because they are Sandinistas, because they are Christians.[30]

In Nicaragua the cult of a new man has an independent Christian as well as Marxist origin. Theologians of liberation extracted
from the Epistles of St. Paul the doctrine of a new man in Christ
counterposed to the Adam in all men before Christ. Just as sin entered the world with Adam, so grace and everlasting life were made
possible by Christ's expiation of Adam's sin.[31] We are resurrected or
born again in Christ, according to St. Paul, when "our old self has
been crucified with Him in order to crush the sinful body and free
us from any further slavery to sin."[32] There is a new humanity
in accepting Christ as our savior: "There is a new creation whenever a man comes to be in Christ; what is old is gone, the new
has come."[33]

The principal Marxist source of the cult of a new man is Marx's
"Economic and Philosophic Manuscripts of 1844," which predated
his and Engels's scientific socialism. But its immediate inspiration
was Che Guevara, who, attracted by Sorel's vision of a morally regenerated proletariat, modeled his own humanism on Marx's prescientific works.[34] In his essay "Socialism and Man in Cuba,"
Guevara claims that the authentic revolutionary is guided by
strong feelings of love, that love for the people is a sacred cause,
that to this strong dose of fellow feeling is added an equally strong
sense of justice, that there should be ties of friendship only with
comrades completely dedicated to the revolution, that there must
be no life for him outside the revolution, that there is no sacrifice
too great to make for the people, and that sacrifices must be made
on a continual and daily basis.[35] The objective of this moral code
was to fashion the revolutionary vanguard. "The human person-

ality plays the role of mobilization and direction insofar as it incarnates the highest virtues and aspirations of the people."[36]

Guevara recognized the vanguard's need to combine a cool head with a passionate spirit, but he was also concerned with arousing the revolutionary expectations of the masses. He hoped to instill heroic attitudes in everyday life:

> The vanguard group is ideologically more advanced than the masses, who are insufficiently acquainted with the new values. While in the former a qualitative change takes place that permits it to make sacrifices as a function of its vanguard character, the latter see only by halves and must be subjected to incentives and pressures of some intensity. Thus the dictatorship of the proletariat is exercised not only on the defeated class, but also individually on the victorious class.[37]

Guevara's essay aimed at making every Cuban a revolutionary. He began by idealizing the guerrilla or freedom fighter as the prototype of the new man, and then the Communist party militant as the builder of a new society.[38]

The confluence in Nicaragua of Marxist and Christian conceptions of the new man should not blind us to their differences, however. For most Christians these differences are crucial. Three months after victory five hundred evangelical pastors, representing about half the Protestant ministers in Nicaragua, signed a declaration of support for the new revolutionary government. They did so with the understanding that the end of this revolutionary process is the cultivation of the new person, of a just and fraternal society inspired by Jesus Christ.[39] For the bulk of the FSLN's Christian followers, the formation of a new person depended on faith in the Christian revelation of Jesus as the Son of God, in conjunction with the Old Testament belief that man is created in God's image.

Certainly, this new person in Christ is not the vanguard's conception of the revolution's objective, nor is the notion of a "just and fraternal society" sufficiently precise to satisfy the vanguard's criterion of socialism based on a Marxist or materialist interpretation of history. For the vanguard the new person is the party militant who belongs to the elite corps of the revolution. Everybody else is "malleable clay," to use Che Guevara's expression.[40]

The Guevarist conception of the new man is profoundly elitist although seldom recognized as such: "The party is a minority but the quality of its cadres gives it great authority. . . . The party is the living example, its cadres must . . . lead the masses . . . against . . . class enemies, the defects of the past, imperialism."[41] This is the context of Guevara's call for sacrifice, love, and dedication to the revolution, including "hatred as an element of struggle, relentless hatred of the enemy that . . . transforms us into effective, violent, selective, and cold killing machines!"[42] The focus of the role personality plays is the party cadre, the individual who inspires trust in "the masses that make history . . . a great mass that follows its leaders because it has faith in them . . . because these leaders have known how to interpret the longings of the masses."[43] If there is any worship in this new humanism, it is not of the person regenerated in the image of God, but created in the image of the vanguard.

The Defense of Human Rights

To the FSLN's cult of the new man must be added its defense of human rights. This ideology came in response to the escalating repression, martial law, and state of siege imposed by Somoza in December 1974 in the name of saving democracy and human freedom. The state of siege remained in effect until September 1977. During this period government repression accounted for a weekly toll in human lives that did not spare women, children, or the aged. In addition, torture became common. Aimed at annihilating the "internal enemy" physically as well as socially, the repressive measures that had been successfully tested in Brazil and Chile were also applied to Nicaragua.

In 1975 the International Federation of the Rights of Man published its first report on government-sanctioned atrocities in Nicaragua, and in August of that year the FSLN made its first public statement on human rights. It published a manifesto condemning the institutionalized violence, the official terrorism, and the laws condoning censorship of the press, radio, and television.[44] On the pretext that the country was becoming infiltrated by international communism, the FSLN declared, Somoza had strangled what little remained of Nicaraguan liberties.[45] Through the Somoza regime, U.S. imperialism and the local oligarchy had violated the basic rights of the Nicaraguan people: "the right to life, to work, to health, to housing, to the wealth produced by one's own hands, to free association."[46]

The FSLN's position on human rights was reaffirmed in January 1978 in response to a new series of atrocities. That same month the popular leader of the Conservative party and one of the most persistent critics of the Somoza regime, Dr. Pedro Joaquín Chamorro, was assassinated by government agents. In the prologue to what was tantamount to a human rights manifesto, the FSLN drew attention to the defensive character of its struggle. In an appeal to all reasonable and humane persons it condemned the government's violations of basic human rights, the disappearance and assassination of thousands of innocent and defenseless peasants, and the continuing torture of city people without regard to social class, political belief, or party affiliation.[47] The manifesto provided a list of what the FSLN considered basic rights. "The most elementary *human rights*, such as respect for life, do not exist and have not existed in *Nicaragua* during the 45 years of the Somozas' dictatorship. This situation has become exaggerated during the last few years when the people have begun to struggle, with more force than ever, for their *right to live*, for their *right to work*, for their *right to think freely*, for their *right to organize a government* that represents their true interests."[48]

Another document of importance, Borge's "Declaration on Human Rights," was presented at the Inter-American Commission on Human Rights, which met in Managua in October 1980. "The political thrust of this revolution and this government," Borge declared, "is unshakeably and irreversibly in favor of human dignity and human rights."[49] This policy reversed Somoza's policy of institutionalized violence, which was responsible for Borge's own torture and the death of his wife. "I remember when we captured those who tortured me. I told them: I am going to get back at you; now comes the hour of my revenge. And my revenge is that we are not going to harm a single hair on your heads. You didn't believe us before, but now we are going to make you believe us!"[50] The slightest sign or hint from the Sandinista leadership would have resulted in a bloodbath. But the National Directorate took great pains to protect the Guardsmen's lives and to guarantee that they were not maltreated.

Borge then explained why the revolution was so lenient toward its former enemies. First, Fonseca taught them to be merciful rather than vindictive. Second, the FSLN was also thinking of the impact of its behavior on revolutions elsewhere in Latin America. "If we made a revolution here that was bloody and vengeful, with firing squads and beatings, we would hurt the chances of revolutionary movements in other places. We would make it harder for them to find allies, we would frighten people in other countries." Borge concluded by noting that the defense of human rights is a primary rather than a secondary concern of the Nicaraguan Revolution. "We want to become a shining example for the whole continent in the area of human rights, and we are going to be. When people talk about human rights, when people talk about respect for human rights, we want them to say—*as in Nicaragua*."[51]

Borge summarized his moral ideology in an interview with Julio Scherer García, director of the Mexican weekly *Proceso*, in November 1980. First, he believes in human dignity. "Either one is on the side of the dignity of man and respect for man and human rights or one is against human rights . . . , the political leadership of this revolution and this government has taken the firm and irrevocable decision to be on the side of the dignity of man." Second, although an atheist, he supports the moral principles of Christianity. If Somoza had accepted them, he would not have taught children to become torturers. "Perhaps the worst crime committed by Somoza and his son was . . . that of having converted children into criminals, children who specialized in scooping out the eyes of prisoners with a spoon"—children who were deliberately transformed into monsters. Third, he defends the moral faith of Sandino and the Sandinistas: "I believe in justice in this world. . . . Man is an instrument of the Monster. The Monster is pride. . . . It invents deceptions. The victims of pride dream they are superior. Superior is he who kills, who rapes, who rules, who lays waste, who raises children to become torturers. Superior is he who believes . . . that he is above the rules of human conduct."[52]

Here is the Sandinistas' countermorality of the tortured, of the victims of those who violated human rights and Christian moral principles. Borge is the revolutionary leader who has suffered most from torture. The first time, in 1956, when he was imprisoned for two and a half years, he was beaten by Guardsmen until he screamed; he was also locked up in a cell lined with ice. The second time, in benevolent and democratic Costa Rica, where he had gone to buy arms, he was questioned with the aid of electrical prods for three consecutive days and nights. The third time was the worst because Anastasio Somoza Debayle had vowed to drive him mad by reducing him to an animal on four legs: nine months in chains and completely covered by a hood; nine months completely naked and cold; nine months on a diet of crumbs.[53] When he was released he was skin and bones and too weak to stand. His sufferings account in part for his high regard for human rights.

Unlike the FSLN's cult of the new man, which testifies to the influence of both Che Guevara and the new Christianity, its doctrine of human rights is indebted to the liberal tradition in the West and to established church doctrine. The concept of human rights is not a Marxist but a liberal concept. Although Marxists show a healthy respect for legal rights that are strictly enforceable, Marx considered moral or human rights to be based on wishful thinking. The adaptation of the liberal doctrine of rights to revolutionary struggles in the twentieth century began with anarchists like Flores Magón and Sandino. It was Sandino's example that predisposed the FSLN to recast its political objectives in the language of human rights.

The timing of the FSLN's human rights declarations was tied to a unique set of circumstances: the escalation of repression by the Somoza regime after December 1974, and the simultaneous emergence of a new Sandinista leadership concerned with broadening the FSLN's strategy of alliances. By January 1978 its immediate motivation was to strengthen support for the anti-Somoza struggle from mainstream Christians inside the country and from liberals outside the country, in the United Nations and the Carter administration.

The fervor over human rights since World War II has come in response to their systematic violation. Following the revulsion over the atrocities committed under Hitler and Stalin, there were the revelations of the use of official torture and death squads under the repressive military regimes in Brazil, Chile, Uruguay, and Argentina during the seventies. In response to the charges of U.S. genocide in Vietnam and complicity in the violations of human rights in Latin America, President Carter sought to reestablish a credible moral posture for the U.S. government by reaffirming the 1948 U.N. Universal Declaration of Human Rights. By recasting its political objectives in the same language, the FSLN hoped to neutralize the role of the United States in Nicaragua and to obtain international support for its struggle against Somoza.

The other major factor shaping the FSLN's doctrine of human rights was the Catholic church in Latin America. Whereas much of the church's practical work was involved in relief for political prisoners and their immediate families and in efforts to curb the death squads and the widespread use of official torture, the doctrinal basis for this work was Pope John XXIII's encyclical *Pacem in Terris* (*Peace on Earth*). It appeared on the eve of the Second Vatican Council (1962–1965) and contained the most developed statement on human rights in official Catholic doctrine.

Unlike the U.N. declaration, which gives precedence to individual or personal rights vis-à-vis the state, John XXIII stressed the importance of social and economic rights.[54] Among these were the right to work, the right to a decent wage in keeping with human dignity, and the right to shape the social system under which one lives. Thus he steered a middle course between the classical liberal doctrine of human rights reaffirmed by the United Nations and the modification of this doctrine in the socialist countries, where social and economic rights take precedence over the rights of individuals.

The FSLN's January 1978 manifesto paid serious homage to both sets of rights, to the right to live and to think freely as well as to the right to work and to organize a government that represents the people's real interests. But its recommendations for implementing those rights went considerably beyond the liberal tradition and Vatican II's proposals for reform. Besides establishing a common ground with liberals and mainstream Catholics in the face of the Somoza regime's human rights abuses, its ultimate purpose was a socialist revolution in Nicaragua.

The Sandinista leaders have a well-deserved reputation for being keen critics of traditional ideologies. Yet they believe in at least two ideologies of their own: an ideal of a new man, and a doctrine of human rights. Although they have publicly confessed to being atheists, none has admitted to being beyond good and evil. They are not amoral and are apparently ignorant of both Marx's and Nietzsche's critiques of morality as a form of self-alienation, as a secular form of superstition, and as a rival to religious opiates in dulling man's social awareness.[55] Instead, they profess a countermorality based on the slippery notions of revolutionary ideals and human rights. Although this countermorality has proved itself politically, so has the new Christianity and its theology of liberation. Both are eminently useful, but are there any intellectual grounds for believing in one rather than the other? The FSLN has yet to answer this question.

The Religious Policy of the FSLN

In a major interview with the editor of the Mexican weekly *Proceso* in November 1980, Borge was asked, "What is the gravest threat to the Revolution?" He replied that it was not President Reagan but the "mistake of those who would have the world believe that this revolution is communist and atheist." In a country of Christians, he observed, it would be stupid and would ignore history to undertake a revolution of that nature.[56]

Yet the Sandinista leaders and a growing number of intermediate cadres are atheists. As Jaime Wheelock publicly admitted in a 1984 May Day address in Chinandega before a crowd of some thirty thousand, a speech also broadcast live on radio and television, "They [the enemies of the revolution] may say you are atheists. Okay, we acknowledge this. But here in the past there was José Santos Zelaya, the Masons; that is, atheism. Here in Nicaragua atheism is something of almost folkloric dimensions. . . . We state openly that there are some in the Sandinista National Liberation Front who, on the basis of their ideas, their ideology [sic] their studies, their questions, have begun to believe that God does not exist!"[57]

This was a formidable admission, which might easily have provoked a hostile response were it not for the FSLN's religious policy. Despite the Sandinista leaders' atheism, they are staunch defenders of religious freedom: "But who is it that permits religious freedom here? Isn't it us? There are many more religious schools here now than in the time of somocismo. Who led the literacy campaign? A priest. Who is responsible for Nicaraguan culture? A priest." And if that were not enough, Wheelock added, "This is a government of Christian and revolutionary principles, a government oriented by Christians. So there is no contradiction [between atheism and Christianity], because the Christians are also in power!"[58]

Among contemporary revolutions led by Marxist-Leninist vanguards, the Nicaraguan is unique in involving the massive participation of Christians. As the prologue to the FSLN's official communiqué on religion states, "Christians have played an integral part in our revolutionary history to a degree unprecedented in any other revolutionary movement in Latin America and possibly the world. This fact opens new and interesting possibilities for the participation of Christians in the revolutions of other latitudes not only during the struggle for power, but also afterward, during the stage of constructing a new society."[59]

Fonseca was the first to update Sandino's theosophy of liberation by appealing directly to Christians to join in the struggle against Somoza. His message broadcast during the takeover of a radio station in 1970 began with the words, "Two thousand years ago there appeared a redeemer who said that his brothers were those who did the will of one in heaven from whom proceeded justice and truth. . . . Brother was [also] the term of address used by Augusto César Sandino toward those who accompanied him with their rifles in the resistance against the Yankee aggressors." He then added that the members of the FSLN had no other brothers than those willing to share the same martyrdom.[60] Fonseca was saying that Sandino and the FSLN were both following in Christ's footsteps.

The study of Sandino's life and thought has taught the leaders of the Sandinista movement to respect the vital role of religion in preparing the masses for revolution. For a Catholic country like Nicaragua, Sandino's theosophy of liberation was useful in challenging the prevailing theology of domination that had kept the people subjugated since the Spanish conquest, but it could not compete with the new Christian theology that had developed since the Cuban Revolution. The evangelical work of the new Christianity was not, like that of Sandino's mystical brotherhood, outside the religious mainstream in Latin America.

The official Sandinista policy toward Christianity was enunciated in a nine-point document released by the National Directorate in the fall of 1980. The FSLN (1) guarantees the "inalienable right" to religious freedom; (2) has learned from experience that religion need not be an opiate but can become an impulse to revolution; (3) does not close its doors to religious believers as long as they accept its fundamental policies and objectives; (4) prohibits proselytizing among its members as a divisive and factious tendency but permits it elsewhere; (5) has profound respect for religious ceremonies and celebrations but condemns their use for politicking and commercial purposes; (6) is a lay organization without any religious beliefs of its own; (7) refrains from giving any opinion concerning doctrinal matters; (8) guarantees to priests the right of every Nicaraguan citizen to be active politically and to become a member of the government; (9) considers the revolutionary state to be a lay state that cannot adopt any religion because it represents the interests of both believers and nonbelievers.[61]

As evidence of the FSLN's positive approach to religion the document notes that three Catholic priests have been members of the Sandinista Assembly, a consulting body designed to assist the National Directorate in formulating state policies.[62] Other Sandinista priests have been rewarded with top government positions for their services to the Revolution. Father Miguel D'Escoto was made minister of foreign relations; Father Fernando Cardenal was placed in charge of the government's Literacy Crusade and has since become minister of education; and his brother Ernesto was made minister of culture. That responsibility for the cultural and educational revolution has been placed in the hands of Catholic priests is an indication of the extent to which Nicaragua's Marxist-Leninist vanguard relies on the revolutionary potential of Christians and their capacity to mobilize the masses.

Some revolutionary priests made the ultimate commitment of bearing arms for the revolution. One of them, Father Gaspar García Laviana from Spain, rose through the ranks to become a "guerrilla commander"—the next highest rank to "commander of the revolution" and reserved for members of the National Directorate. On 11 December 1980 the armed forces held a special commemoration on the occasion of the second anniversary of his death in battle. Daniel Ortega read some of Father Gaspar's poems of social protest dedicated to Third World peoples who struggle for their liberation. Collected under the title *Songs of Love and War* and published by the Ministry of Culture, they offer further testimony to the revolutionary impulse in Christianity. Here is one extract:

> Landlord!
> I'm going to cut my flesh into pieces
> And hang them
> On your fence posts
> Until the flesh rots
> And you cannot stand the stench
> But must go
> Elsewhere.[63]

In a symposium on the theme "What does the FSLN expect from Christians and what do Christians expect from the FSLN?" (28 September 1979), Luis Carrión argued that, as a religious and moral faith, Christianity is compatible with Sandinismo. But at the same time he noted that the established churches represent a deformed Christianity that has served the interests of ruling classes.[64] Sandinismo is patently incompatible with that type of Christianity. Carrión then related how his adoption of a Marxist worldview was made possible by his Christian upbringing and concern for human suffering, which he later tried to explain in scientific terms.[65] Since he had personally arrived at Marxism through his experience of the Christian faith, he hoped to encourage others to travel the same road.

The leaders of the FSLN have in different ways shown a profound respect for the Christian faith. Borge himself took the initiative in requesting eight hundred thousand popular-language New Testaments for Nicaragua—a request met mainly by the United Bible Societies, headquartered in the United States.[66] The request was tied to the Literacy Crusade in 1980, which generated a corresponding need for new reading materials. Apparently, the Soviet Union's readiness to help with Spanish-language editions of the Marxist-Leninist classics was deemed inappropriate, even assuming the masses were sufficiently politicized to understand them. In any event, the choice of reading materials was based on the premise that Christianity, like Sandinismo, provided ideological support for the revolution.

The effort to nurture the seeds of revolutionary struggle in the consciousness of the people, taking the masses as they are rather than as they should be, is basic to the FSLN's approach to the religious question. The FSLN has encouraged the new Christianity by officially recognizing that people can be both Christians and revolutionaries, thus breaking with a tradition going back to Marx. It has also diverged significantly from the policy toward religion adopted by Cuban Marxists. Whereas the Cuban Communist party specifically excludes religious believers, the FSLN accepts as members even those whose religious beliefs contradict the premises of Marx's philosophical materialism.

Besides the FSLN's official policy toward religion, it has an informal or unofficial policy. In an interview in March 1983, Daniel Ortega revealed what is tantamount to the FSLN's informal position. He said he wanted the church in Nicaragua to "opt for the poor, for the workers, for the humble, for the dispossessed." In effect, he hoped that Christians who were not Sandinistas would understand that the FSLN was not trying to divide the church, but rather "to demand from the church, which we understand is one, a positive attitude toward social change."[67] The church hierarchy interpreted this demand as blatant interference in religious matters, in violation of the FSLN's official policy. It felt threatened by Ortega's comment that one sector of the church was closely allied to the FSLN.[68]

The FSLN's informal policy toward religion has been to support actively what Borge calls the "church of the poor," or, more precisely, the liberating current in Catholicism. "Everyone knows that there are two churches. . . . The other church is tied to the past; it is the church of the rich. This is not something new, because Christ also . . . found that there were two churches . . . : the church of the temple, where he went with a whip, and his own church of fishermen and humble people." Borge further claimed that the church of the rich was also that of the "pharisees." It had sacrificed Christ to the Romans, and that history was repeating itself in Nicaragua— ominous words from a member of the National Directorate. Although the so-called universal church attends to the needs of both the poor and the rich, in effect there were two churches. Thus Borge testified to two different policies toward Christians: "We have great sympathy for the church of the poor, though we also respect that of the rich and even dialogue with it, as we do with businessmen and owners of the means of production."[69]

Borge's Manichaean vision of two opposed churches within the universal church is far from accurate. The Jesuit Alvaro Argüello, a prominent Sandinista and director of the Central American Historical Institute for the documentation of the role of Christians in the Nicaraguan Revolution, insists that there is only one universal church but admits to three rival tendencies within it. Besides the liberating current supported by the FSLN, he distinguishes a reform current within contemporary Catholicism and a traditional current.[70]

The traditional current is authoritarian, ritualistic, and sacramental. It professes a profound moral concern for the family and for education, and it has yet to pay more than lip service to the church's internal reforms. Originally allied to the landed oligarchy and today to the hegemonic sector of the bourgeoisie and the multinationals, it has turned its back on the human rights doctrine of Pope John XXIII, which is now official church policy. In sharp contrast, the reform current is pastoral in orientation and supportive of the changes recommended by the Second Vatican Council. As the mainstream of the Catholic church, neither left nor right but Social Christian or Christian Democratic in political matters, it is allied to the bourgeois opposition and to the petite bourgeoisie.

Actually, the principal organized opposition to the Sandinista government comes not from traditional but from reform Catholicism, which speaks for the so-called universal church. Rather than a "church of the rich," to use Borge's metaphor, it is the church of the pharisees or moral reformers within the Catholic church.[71] The FSLN certainly has no respect for traditional Catholics who supported Somoza's genocidal regime. Its policy of conciliation is aimed at reform Catholics and at the church hierarchs who opposed the dictatorship, but who today reject the Marxist policies of the revolutionary government.

Respect for the reformed church but at the same time aid and comfort for revolutionary Christians who want to change it—that is the double-edged religious policy favored by Daniel Ortega and Tomás Borge. Given an already divided church, they hope that revolutionary Christians may gradually gain ascendancy over those Borge unceremoniously calls "false Christians" and "pharisees."[72]

Borge's diatribes against the perverters of Christianity, against their passivity in the face of oppression, against their theology of domination, which consecrates the poor's being always with us, have fooled some into believing that he is a recent convert to Christianity. His support of bibles as the basic reading material in the Literacy Crusade instead of the classics of Marxism-Leninism has further strengthened this image. Among his favorite literature he lists erotic poetry first, and the Bible next. Why the Bible? Because of his friendship for Fernando Cardenal, the Jesuit priest and theologian who directed the Literacy Crusade, the man Borge cares for most.[73]

Borge is conversant not only with liberation theology as it emerged in the early seventies, but also with its recent development as a theology of life opposed to the theology of death. Whereas the theology of death looks for salvation beyond the grave, the theology of life affirms the possibility of salvation in this world. Said Borge in an address to the Second Latin American Conference of Christians for Peace (1 June 1982), "True Christians have confronted the theology of death with a theology of the resurrection . . . not of the dead but of the living!"[74] Here again we have Borge's two churches in mortal conflict: a church that has made its peace with the slow and premature death of millions of human beings from hunger, misery, and exploitation versus a church of life that believes in revolution and "struggles so that the Christ of the poor is not crucified again."[75]

Borge agrees with the theologians of liberation that genuine Christians show their respect for Christ in deeds rather than words. "Have not the Sandinistas profoundly respected that extraordinary exponent of love for man who is Jesus Christ?" Although Sandinistas do not shout Christian slogans, those who do shout "Christ yesterday, Christ today, Christ forever!" are not thinking of Christ but of how to combat the Revolution and thus "mishandling the image they claim so much to adore, so much to respect, by reducing everything to a slogan." Then comes the punch line: "I sincerely believe that we Sandinistas are much more respectful of Christ than those false Christians, pharisees, and traitors to the real cause and thought of Christ!"[76] Just as Christ died for the poor, so the Sandinista revolution was made by those willing to give their lives for them.[77] Certainly, there can be no reasonable doubt concerning Borge's support for the new Christianity and theology of liberation.[78]

Borge shows a familiarity with liberation theology that is unique among members of the National Directorate, but it is not a recent acquisition. In a December 1982 interview by the Peruvian journalist Ricardo Gadea, Hilda Gadea's brother, Borge recalled the several months he spent in Peru under the populist military regime of Velasco Alvarado. There he became a close personal friend of Father Gustavo Gutiérrez, whose seminal work on the theology of liberation helped launch the new theology.[79]

Among the distinguishing features of liberation theology, says Father Gutiérrez, is a critical reflection based on the Gospel in response to the struggle for liberation by the oppressed and exploited peoples of Latin America.[80] At the same time it is a form of action, "a theology which does not stop with reflecting on the world, but rather tries to be part of the process through which the world is transformed."[81] It has what Gutiérrez calls a *locus theologicus*, a privileged theological datum in the life, preaching, and historical commitment of Christians involved in the great liberating movements in Latin America, where it came in response to structural poverty, economic dependence, and changes brought about by the Cuban Revolution.[82] Besides actual struggles of liberation, the new theology is a response to the thinking of Latin American revolutionaries, a response to the new Marxism that began with Mariátegui and was later revived by Che Guevara and Fidel Castro.[83]

Another feature of liberation theology is the recovery of the original revolutionary beliefs of Christianity. Unlike the traditional and reform currents in Roman Catholicism, liberation theology speaks with the voice of the poor and oppressed, who are raised to the status of God's Chosen People. Salvation is projected onto the screen of history, and thus ceases to be otherworldly or metaphysical. Its focus is not the personal longing for eternal life but the collective longing for a new society without exploitation.

In Nicaragua the development and diffusion of liberation theology have been the principal task of the Antonio Valdivieso Center, created one month after the Sandinista victory in memory of the sixteenth-century Nicaraguan bishop killed by a conquistador for defending the rights of native Indians. Besides being a think tank, it elaborates training courses for pastoral leaders of Nicaragua's *comunidades de base*, or Christian grass-roots communities.

These communities have sprung up all over Nicaragua. Father José de la Jara organized one of the first in 1966 in San Pablo parish, a squatter settlement on the outskirts of Managua, as did Ernesto Cardenal in the Solentiname archipelago.[84] More important than bishops' conferences in shaping the new Christianity have been the popular roots of rebellion in these Christian communities.

Their role in the Revolution has been described by Father Francisco Solana of the Capuchin order in eastern Nicaragua. After the bishops' conference at Medellín, Colombia (August 1968), says Father Solana, assemblies of parish delegates of the Word were held in the southern zone of Zelaya, just south of Bluefields.[85] That was the first step to recruit lay religious leaders through whom the priesthood might organize Christian grass-roots communities. At these assemblies lay leaders were given a basic biblical orientation. They then returned to their parishes to organize the struggle for human rights and justice. In 1981 the Department of Zelaya alone had more than six hundred such communities.[86]

The FSLN's formal and informal policies on religion are a carryover from its earlier strategy of setting up intermediate organizations for reaching out to and mobilizing the masses. Although grass-roots Christian activism was a mass phenomenon in Nicaragua and emerged independently of the FSLN, by mutual agreement it became part of the anti-Somoza movement and the insurrection. On the one hand, grass-roots Christianity was introduced into the anti-Somoza movement not by the revolutionary vanguard but by its followers. On the other hand, the vanguard attempted to mold it to its own far-reaching political purposes. Although the FSLN did not create the Christian Revolutionary movement (MCR) in Nicaragua, it did attempt to direct it. As Bayardo Arce recalled the vanguard's efforts to win over Christians for the FSLN, "Luís Carrión, Joaquín Cuadra, Alvaro Baltodano, and Roberto Gutiérrez made up the first Christian cell. They were assigned the task of organizing a progressive Christian movement that might bring Christians together and perform intermediate tasks for the Front."[87] Thus there is a grain of truth in Archbishop Miguel Obando y Bravo's remark during a 1983 interview, that the "church that they call 'popular' is a church wedded to Marxist ideology."[88]

The emergence of grass-roots Christianity reinforced by a theology of liberation was sparked in Latin America by the Latin American Bishops' Conference at Medellín, Colombia, in August 1968. Although this conference had its beginnings in the Second Vatican Council in 1962, convened under the progressive Pope John XXIII, it was at Medellín that the church hierarchy sought to apply the reforms of Vatican II to Latin America. The development of a progressive Christian movement in Nicaragua dates from this historic conference.[89]

Most scholars trace the emergence of the new Christian activism of the late sixties and early seventies to this post-Medellín development. But this derivation undercuts the importance of the pre-Medellín Marxist-Christian currents centered around Father Camilo Torres of Colombia. Camilo Torres was the first priest to bear arms for a Marxist-Leninist revolutionary vanguard in Latin America, the first guerrilla-priest in the hemisphere. His death in combat in February 1966, as a militant of the Guevarist-oriented

National Liberation Army (ELN), inspired Father Gaspar García Laviana to join its Nicaraguan equivalent, the FSLN.[90]

Six months before the Medellín Conference, the first Camilo Torres Latin American Encounter occurred in Montevideo, Uruguay, attended by delegations from the already established Camilo Torres movements of Colombia, Uruguay, Chile, and Argentina.[91] Following Father Torres's lead, these movements combined Christ's and Guevara's mandates to liberate the oppressed: the duty of every Christian is to be a revolutionary; the duty of every revolutionary is to make the revolution.[92] It was this pre-Medellín rather than post-Medellín development that helped shape the new Marxist policy toward Christians, first formulated by Fidel Castro as early as 1969 in response to the example set by Father Torres.[93]

An Episcopalian pastor, Sergio Arce Martínez, has written a book on the living Christ in Cuba that testifies to the origins of this new policy. In Cuba, unlike in Nicaragua, the revolution was made without the active support of Christians. Guevara was perhaps the first to state, "When Christians dare to give full testimony to the revolution, then the Latin American revolution will be invincible . . . [but] until now they have allowed their doctrine to be used as an instrument by reactionaries."[94] Castro went considerably farther. Reiterating to representatives of the Catholic church in Jamaica what he had publicly declared during his visit to Chile in 1971, he said, "There are no contradictions between the proposals of religion and the proposals of socialism. . . . We have to make an alliance, but not a tactical one. I say a strategical alliance between religion and the revolution!"[95]

Fernando Cardenal gives an example of such a strategical alliance: when he made his first contacts with the FSLN, Oscar Turcios told him, "It shouldn't concern me if you believe there is something after death, nor should it interest you if I think that after death I'm going to rot here. What should concern us is that we can both work together to build a new Nicaragua."[96] If the FSLN hoped to use Christians for political purposes, then Christians might be able to use the FSLN for religious ends. As Fernando Cardenal notes, "the Sandinista Front has been the channel that has enabled me to live my Christian faith more authentically, that is, with actions."[97] He might have added that it was a channel through which revolutionary Christians hoped to transform Nicaragua in the image of Christ and of the new Christian man.

Wheelock's account of the strategic alliance between the FSLN and progressive Christians stresses its purely political character. Speaking of the incorporation of Catholic activists and even priests into the FSLN, he said in a May 1983 interview with Marta Harnecker, "We did not give either the students or the priests the task of using their religious message to gain sympathy. What we did was to link up with them as combatants, as representatives of part of our people . . . we agreed on common objectives."[98] There was a political coincidence of views. Marxists and Christians participated in a common struggle, but on their own terms and "with their own perspective."[99]

Initially, the FSLN anticipated that Christians who might walk part of the way would abandon the revolution when it entered the final stretch. But what began as a strategical alliance ended in a solid embrace. In a symposium at the Central American University in Managua in September 1979, Luis Carrión acknowledged on behalf of the FSLN that "it is not a matter anymore of establishing a strategical alliance because if we are already revolutionaries we definitely belong in the same camp, we are brothers and comrades, which signifies much more than allies."[100] In a nutshell, this was the crucial difference between the FSLN's policy toward Christians and that of the Cuban Communist party. In Cuba acceptance of the principles of dialectical materialism is a condition of party membership.[101]

In Nicaragua the FSLN had as collaborators two different kinds of Christian revolutionaries. They shared a similar theology of liberation, but differed on the issue of whether to embrace or reject Marxism: "Among such Christians one may still make a distinction between two kinds: revolutionary Christians who are Marxists, and revolutionary Christians who are not."[102] Although the National Directorate was bound to feel a closer affinity toward those Christians who accepted Marxism than toward those who rejected it, there was a single policy that included both.

The FSLN's policy on religion was shaped in response to the supportive role of Christian grass-roots communities in the struggle against Somoza. But it was also a Nicaraguan adaptation of the new Marxism going back to Mariátegui's break with the classical Marxist treatment of religion.[103]

Unlike his fellow communists, who rejected religion as an opiate of the masses, Mariátegui believed that religion might become an impulse to revolution. "The days of anticlerical a priori reasoning, when free-thinking criticism contented itself with a sterile and cursory dismissal of all dogmas and churches, have been completely surpassed."[104] The contribution of pragmatic philosophers like William James, he noted, had been to find a place for the religious spirit: "The historic experience of the past decades shows that the present revolutionary or social myths may deepen human awareness in the same way as did the religious myths of antiquity."[105]

Mariátegui believed that Marxist criticism had made the mistake of identifying religion with obscurantism and of underestimating its past services to humanity.[106] Christianity should be taken for what it is, he admonished, an integral part of the people's consciousness in Latin America. It would be used for one purpose or another—if not for revolution, then for reaction. Not to seek control of this powerful lever would be to abandon it to the enemy. Enlightened snobs, not the people, are atheists, and they, too, can play a reactionary role.[107] Anticlericalism is no longer revolutionary but a substitute for revolution, Mariátegui concluded. In practice, it frequently means contempt for the people.[108]

To sum up, the religious policy of the FSLN is unique in the history of Marxist movements. Ernesto Cardenal recalls that during the years underground, the founders of the FSLN continually sought his advice about "how we could create a truly Christian revolution in Nicaragua."[109] This effort was not just strategical. As Sergio Ramírez has acknowledged, "our revolution did *not* consider religion a backward element, something we had to leave behind."[110]

Ernesto Cardenal's Tour de Force

Although Ernesto Cardenal's theology is far from representative of liberation theology in Nicaragua, it is the closest to representing the political and ideological views of the FSLN. It is one of the few theologies of liberation to give a religious significance to the new Marxism, and its extreme communist orientation makes it the only living substitute for Sandino's communist theosophy.

Father Cardenal has made two significant contributions to the ideology of the Nicaraguan Revolution: first, the development of a unique theology of liberation whose key to the Scriptures is humanity's collective rather than personal existence; second, the adaptation of this theology to the Marxist class struggle. Together they provide a religious justification of the Nicaraguan Revolution for those Sandinistas who are both Christians and Marxists.[111]

Cardenal admits to having had two spiritual conversions: "In 1970 I made my first trip to Cuba and there I had what I call my second conversion: after my conversion to God, my conversion to the revolution."[112] He then describes how this second conversion led him to incorporate himself into that current of liberation theol-

ogy that was, practically speaking, a Marxist theology. Thus he
not only adopted liberation theology, but also became, in his own
words, a "Marxist Christian"—the contemporary equivalent of
Sandino's "rational communist."

The principal statement of Cardenal's theology is *The Gospel
in Solentiname*. It consists of four volumes of Gospel discussions
recorded from 1971 to 1976 with minor editorial changes by the author. The discussants belonged to a fishing and peasant community
on an island of the Solentiname archipelago at the southern extremity of Lake Nicaragua. Cardenal became an ordained priest in
1965 and, with several friends, moved to the island in January 1966
and founded a Christian grass-roots community. There he practiced
conscientization for more than a decade before joining the FSLN
with his entire congregation in the middle seventies. The elucida-
tion of the revolutionary message implicit in the Gospels is the
guiding thread of his major work. It presents Jesus Christ as the
Savior not only from the wages of sin, but also from the wages of
labor defined by Marxists as a form of exploitation.

Cardenal's key to the Gospels is a depersonalized and collectivist interpretation of the fundamental concepts of Christianity. In
adapting the new Christianity and its theology of liberation to
Nicaragua, he has altered its fundamental beliefs in God the Father,
the Son, the Second Coming, and Resurrection.

Commenting on the passages from Mark 12 : 28–34, where
Jesus says that the most important commandments are to love God
and your neighbor as yourself, Cardenal explains why these make
up one commandment rather than two: "God appears before the
people of Israel freeing them from the slavery of Egypt . . . he wants
the people to be faithful to him and not to recognize other gods of
other societies, which do not represent any liberation. So to love
him is to love liberation and justice and that's the same thing as to
love your neighbor."[113] In effect, the first commandment tells us
there is no other God than love, and the second commandment
tells us that love exists only when we show it toward others. The
conclusion is inescapable: "God is love among people. . . . God
doesn't exist in another way separated from love among people, as
God is usually imagined."[114]

This means that outright atheists who love the poor and oppressed are really obeying the first commandment, whether they
like it or not.[115] "In the Bible the opponent of God isn't atheism; it's
the idols."[116] The idols are the enemies of love. Since God can be
loved only in one's neighbor, not through worship, prayer, and rit-
ual, according to Cardenal, God is a collective phenomenon like

love and not an individual being or person. Although not a novel thesis, this explains how atheists can be religious even though they do not believe in a Supreme Being.

Concerning the nature of Christ, Cardenal says, "The fact is that as God became man, now man is God. First God became flesh in a person, Jesus Christ, to become flesh afterwards in all the poor and oppressed."[117] For Cardenal the "people," in the Marxist sense of the exploited and oppressed classes, have become God through Christ Jesus. Commenting on the parable in Matthew 25 : 31–46, where a king says that whoever feeds and clothes the poor also feeds and clothes their lord, he explains that Christ is the poor.[118] He then cites approvingly Mao's parable of the foolish old man who was so persistent in removing a mountain that God intervened and removed it for him: "Mao says: 'The same thing will happen to us if we persist obstinately, but in reality, for us, God is the masses.'"[119] In this interpretation both God the Father and Christ his Son are collective beings.

As for Christ's Second Coming, when he will judge the world, Cardenal interprets it as the coming of a new society and of a new humanity. "The Son of Man will not come as an individual, as he did the first time; he will be a collective Christ, he will come as a society, or rather a new species, the New Person [or new man]. . . . Christ is the society of the poor, the proletariat, as we say today. And this people is the one that's going to judge."[120]

Cardenal also interprets the Christian doctrine of resurrection in collectivist terms bordering on heresy for the traditional church. Marxism tells us that matter is eternal, which suggests to Cardenal that consciousness must also be eternal, since it, too, is an essential part of nature. "And when we die, we can go to form part of that universal consciousness, depending on the degree of evolution that we have reached; or else we can remain eternally separated. . . . [In any case] we can understand the resurrection of our bodies this way: that since we're part of the consciousness of the universe, our bodies will be the whole universe."[121]

This interpretation follows from an earlier discussion that concluded, "In reality all of us are a single organism, and all together we are a single I. That's why each one of us must love the others as part of our own person (that means 'as oneself'). If we don't, we don't belong to the complete Man, we are cut off from humanity."[122] For Cardenal there is no individual soul in need of salvation but only a collective one. And this implies that sin is not personal but structural or collective. It also implies that grace is a collective gift and that the people must be converted en masse to deserve it.

Cardenal did not get his inspiration for these theosophical nostrums from Sandino. Nonetheless, his theology of liberation stresses humanity's collective salvation based on its collective nature as a single organism, as did Sandino's.

Cardenal's adaptation of his theology to the Marxist class struggle takes several forms. He has accepted a position in the revolutionary government and has encouraged like-minded priests to do likewise in the conviction that the Sandinista government is objectively Christian. He has interpreted the Christian faith as a pre-scientific precursor of Marxism containing the germs of Marxist revolutionary theory. And he has disseminated a Christianized version of what life would be like in Marx's communist society.

In August 1980 Father Cardenal was interviewed by the Austrian sociologist Leo Gabriel, coordinator of the Alternative Information News Agency (APIA) in Managua. In this unpublished interview Ernesto Cardenal presented his views on the role of the revolutionary priest in politics.

He began by recalling how his religious community in the archipelago of Solentiname became an integral part of the FSLN, first as a political cell and then as an armed unit. To Gabriel's question concerning voices in the church who say that priests may not occupy government positions, he replied, "I believe the pope should be the first to give up his political position as head of the Vatican State and its armed forces. If priests should give up their jobs in government, the pope should be the first to do so."[123] He added that he saw no contradiction in performing the will of God and serving the Nicaraguan Revolution as the new government's minister of culture.

Father Cardenal said further that the union of Marxist and Christian currents in the FSLN is a lesson for other peoples who want to make a revolution. The Sandinista government is basically a Christian one. "Even its leaders who do not consider themselves Christians are really Christians because they carry out the Gospel word. What is important for the Gospel is not what these leaders say but what they do."[124] In this perspective, the members of the National Directorate are among the most deserving Christians because they fulfill the word of the Bible without so much as a thought of personal salvation. For Father Cardenal, Christians are in power in Nicaragua for the first time in that nation's history, even though they do not profess the Christian faith.

Some may object that a Christian is someone who believes not only in obeying Christ's commandments, but also in Christ's divinity as the son of God. To be precise, Christianity means considerably more than the acceptance of Christian ideals or morality, which would make Christians of nearly everybody. By pushing liberation theology to its limits, Cardenal provides a rationale for Christianity without Christ. No wonder Pope John Paul II has been concerned with uprooting what he perceives to be the growth of a heretical movement within the church.

The new Christianity is nominally based on Christ's divinity and moral teachings, but Cardenal's version smacks of idiosyncrasy. Although he affirms the divinity of Christ, which to that extent makes him an authentic Christian, his liberation theology would make Christians of atheists. Moreover, Cardenal's claim to believe in Christ's divinity may be reasonably disputed. It is one thing to believe that Christ personifies the people and something quite different to claim, as Cardenal does, that Christ *is* the people. For the uniqueness of Christ is effectively undermined when millions of ordinary persons also become sons of God. Either Christ was a person or he is the people. He cannot be both except in the form of a new mystery and a new doctrine of the incarnation challenging the traditional one.

In line with the theologically accepted view of the "communist" nature of early Christianity, Cardenal believes that primitive Christianity was an unscientific precursor of Marxist revolutionary thought. In a March 1978 tape recording of a mass for FSLN guerrillas, Cardenal noted that Christ identified himself with the proletariat and championed fundamentally the same cause as Marxism. The seeds of Marxism are implicit in Christ's revolutionary message even though they are not expressed scientifically: "Christ did not speak in scientific language, but spoke in that simple form understandable to the people, saying that the sheep would be separated from the goats. Actually, he was presenting Marxist revolutionary thought . . . by dividing humanity into two classes: the oppressors and the oppressed."[125] And because Christ identifies himself with God, one can also say that wherever there is a revolution, God's judgment has already begun. "This judgment is what today is called the class struggle, the struggle that must occur between the exploited and exploiters, from which the exploited and oppressed will emerge as victors as we see them presented in the Final Judgment."[126]

The thrust of this commentary is that, contrary to the professed beliefs of most Marxists and Christians, their doctrines are basically similar, because Christianity expresses in religious terms what Marxism came to express later in scientific language. Cardenal suggests that Christ was thinking about the Marxists because revolutions generally have *not* been made in the name of Christ, and they have *not* been made from religious motives: "Christ was foreseeing that revolutions would be made for the people and that revolutionaries would not know that they were making revolutions for Christ. That is why Christ says that they will be surprised when they afterwards learn that it was precisely for Christ that they made the revolution."[127] If past revolutions made people atheists, it was because existing Christianity had become reactionary. Because the new Christianity contains the germs of Marxism, it makes people revolutionaries. Thus for Father Cardenal the Marxist science of revolution was a belated response almost two millennia later to the message of biblical salvation.

It follows that those who conceive of God after the manner of the established church, which has traditionally been on the side of the oppressors, have betrayed God as well as the people by presenting Christ in a false light. There are two churches rather than one. There is the reactionary church presenting God as a dictator like Somoza, and there is the revolutionary church presenting God as the proletariat.[128] In effect, there is a religious class struggle between the church of the oligarchy and that of the guerrillas. The God of Somoza cannot be the God of the Bible, Father Cardenal was saying, because the God of the Bible is the God of Marxism-Leninism, the God of subversion.

Father Cardenal points out that Christ met his death in the struggle against Roman imperialism.[129] This is the traditional Marxist interpretation of Jesus, as presented in Karl Kautsky's *Foundations of Christianity.*[130] In Solentiname, Cardenal recalls, the Sunday commentaries on the Gospel were made in the light of the new revolutionary struggles in Latin America. "There the peasants discovered the radical and revolutionary message of the Gospel as it had not been discovered by theologians who had studied it over the centuries. In those commentaries it is very clear how Christ's message on earth was that of revolution: the total revolution of humanity not only against Roman imperialism and slave societies, but also against the future oppression of humankind in the form of feudalism, capitalism, and North American imperialism."[131]

As Engels indicated in his own studies of Christianity as a movement of social protest, it was the form in which rebellion was possible within the historical limitations of the times. Stressing the similarities between the early Christian and modern working-class movements, he noted that both were originally made up of oppressed people, both preached deliverance from human bondage, both were despised and persecuted, and both forged irresistibly ahead.[132] The religious and unscientific form historically taken by the rebellion of the oppressed meant postponing actual liberation. Projected to another or heavenly world, religious rebellion became a cultural substitute for political and economic liberation.[133] But it was also a preview of modern socialism—a prescientific anticipation. This is also Father Cardenal's thesis.

Although Engels was the first Marxist theologian, he was not a Christian. Father Cardenal claims to be both, but only after tinkering with their generally accepted definitions. He is on safer ground when he upholds the usefulness of Christianity to Marxism and shows how Marxism is useful to Christianity.

Finally, Cardenal offers a Christianized version of Marx's communist society. "The goal the Gospel affirms is none other than the perfect communist society. That is very clear in almost all the Gospel texts. And with their simplicity and their great political wisdom the peasants began discovering it, Sunday after Sunday, in those commentaries we made on the archipelago of Solentiname."[134]

The Kingdom of God on earth, Father Cardenal continues, is communism. Although he notes that Saint Matthew calls it the Kingdom of Heaven out of respect for Jewish tradition and the name of God, "this does not mean that God's kingdom is in the skies." On the contrary, it is a society on earth. Christ teaches his disciples to pray "Thy Kingdom come," to pray for the Kingdom to come on earth. "He does not say they should pray for us to go to the Kingdom, but rather that the Kingdom should come to us . . . a society without exploitation of man by man, without domination of any kind, which will be the complete fraternity of perfect love among men."[135]

How does one reconcile this interpretation of the Kingdom of God with that other statement attributed to Christ by the Gospel texts, in which he says that his Kingdom is not of this world? In the past, says Father Cardenal, such statements were misinterpreted and used to disparage the people's struggle against injustice and oppression. "During this century linguistic studies of the Bible have shown that in the Gospel of Saint John the 'world' means what we today understand by the 'system' or what North Americans call the 'establishment.' And Saint John elsewhere portrays Christ as making indictments against the 'world.' The 'world' is the enemy, but the 'world' means injustice, the Roman Empire, the status quo. That is why Jesus says to Pilate that his kingdom is not of this world."[136]

During a Sunday mass a member of Cardenal's congregation angrily questioned the assertion that Jesus was a communist.

Said Cardenal, "The communists try to achieve a perfect society
where each one contributes his labor and receives according to his
need. . . . You can refuse to accept communist ideology [atheistical
materialism] but you do have to accept what you have here in the
Gospels. And you might be satisfied with this communism of the
Gospels." He was then asked if this meant that those who follow
the word of God are therefore communists. Yes, replied Cardenal,
"because we seek the same perfect society."[137] But he was using the
word *communist* loosely. Elsewhere he adds that the first Christians called the Eucharist by the Greek word *Koinonia*, which is
the same word they used for the community of goods; "that is because communism and Communion are the same thing."[138] Again,
these words mean something different to most Marxists.

In the epilogue to *The Gospel in Solentiname*, Cardenal claims
it was the study of the Gospel that most radicalized his community politically. In a new kind of mass based on dialogue with the
peasants, they came to understand the core of the Gospel message:
"the announcement of the Kingdom of God, that is, the establishment of a just society, without exploiters or exploited, *with all
goods in common, just like the society in which the first Christians lived.*"[139] Cardenal had in mind the description of the early
Christian communities in the Book of Acts: "The believers all kept
together . . . , not one of them considered anything his personal
property, they shared all they had with one another. There was not
a needy person among them, for those who owned land or houses
would sell them and bring the proceeds of the sale, laying the
money before the feet of the apostles; it was then distributed according to each individual's need."[140] Such was the life led by Cardenal and his companions before his community was destroyed
by the National Guard for having led the attack on the San Carlos
garrison in October 1977. However, Cardenal has no intention of
resurrecting that small paradise: "I think of a task much more
important that we all have—the reconstruction of the whole
country."[141]

Besides the early Christian communities, Cardenal finds examples of the perfect society in monasteries and convents, until recently the only way of practicing a community of goods. But, he
adds, "we see that the time is now coming when it [Jesus's message]
should be made *public*—in political life and in social life. Now the
historical conditions allow the change of attitude to be a change in
society as a whole."[142]

Cardenal's political ideology and corresponding morality of
love for the poor and oppressed have actually little in common with

Marxism. They share instead the political morality of Marx's immediate predecessor, Wilhelm Weitling, who also appealed to the Gospel in defense of the perfect society of communism. Weitling's *The Poor Sinner's Gospel*, published in 1843, belongs to the same genre as *The Gospel in Solentiname*. As the principal mouthpiece of the League of the Just before Marx and Engels took over and transformed it into the Communist League in 1847, Weitling represented what they characterized as a prescientific, crude, leveling or egalitarian communism without any real possibility of being implemented in the modern world.[143]

Weitling believed that nineteenth-century communism was the successor to the communist tendencies of early Christianity. Because Christianity was the religion of freedom, it must not be destroyed but used to free humanity.[144] The practical question was how to implement Christ's teaching. Weitling's answer was through "the most perfect form of communism."[145] The core doctrine of the Gospels is that of the Kingdom of God, Weitling claimed, and communism is that kingdom on earth, "the victory of the poor and oppressed, the overthrow of the rich and the oppressors . . . , the abolition of property [as] the necessary condition for putting the teaching of Jesus into practice."[146] Because communism is a state of equality and justice among all persons capable of working, stealing is the test of a communist society: "Every man can have as much as another, and this makes stealing impossible. . . . Those who are in positions of government have no greater merit and [will have] no greater material advantages than the rest."[147]

Marx had no patience for this strain of sentimentality in Weitling's thought. They eventually quarreled. The outcome was Marx's emphatic repudiation of any form of communism based on love and of any effort to justify communism by appeals to religion.

Traditionally, Marxists have argued that the only realistic way of overcoming social inequality is to raise the material and cultural conditions of wage earners to the level of professional, administrative, and scientific workers. This is called "leveling upwards." In this perspective the communist principle of distributing to each according to one's needs must be postponed until the society known as socialism has had an opportunity to develop on the basis of the quite different principle of rewarding each according to one's work. This is a far cry from Ernesto Cardenal's communism, which, like Weitling's, shows an all-consuming concern for equality that, in practice, leads to "leveling downwards."

It is this anarchist component of Christian communism that Marxists find politically unacceptable, because it alienates potential supporters among the college-educated by disregarding differences based on merit. It was given classic expression during the final stage of the French Revolution in Sylvain Maréchal's *Manifesto of the Equals* (1796): "Let all the arts [and sciences] perish, if necessary, as long as real equality remains!"[148] His mentor, François Noël Babeuf, provided the rationale at his trial in 1797: "The superiority of talents and efforts is only a chimera and specious trap, which has always unduly served the schemes of conspirators against equality. . . . It is both absurd and unjust to pretend that a greater recompense is due someone whose task demands a higher degree of intelligence, a greater amount of application and mental strain. . . . No grounds whatever can justify pretension to a recompense beyond what is sufficient for individual needs."[149]

Ernesto Cardenal's principle that all men must behave as brothers has in practice a leveling effect tantamount to socializing poverty. But we have seen that this principle is not shared by the Sandinista leadership. In Nicaragua the struggle to implement it is being carried on by Marxist Christians without support from other Marxists or other Christians. The Marxists in the National Directorate are sympathetic to theological communism mainly because it supports their position on other crucial issues.

The Ideological Pluralism of the FSLN

One must take care not to misinterpret the FSLN's policy on ideological matters. The ideology of Sandinismo is a composite of the national and patriotic values of Sandino and of the ethical recasting of Marxism-Leninism in the light of the philosophical humanism of the young Marx.[150] At the same time it coexists with other independent social and political doctrines. It shares with the Liberal tradition a belief in basic human rights but interprets them differently. It shares with the new Christianity a special bond based on belief in the ultimate redemption of the poor and oppressed. And it shares with the Marxist philosophical tradition the cult of a new socialist man predicated on Marx's early discussions of alienation— before he became a communist and developed his materialist interpretation of history.[151]

The following picture emerges of the FSLN's vaunted ideological pluralism. Its ideology consists of a cult of the new man and a doctrine of human rights that is consistent with Sandino's ideology. This official Sandinista ideology is buttressed by several unofficial ideologies wedded to liberation theology but also claiming to be Sandinista. As for the country as a whole, the FSLN's policy is to tolerate ideological diversity even when some ideologies are hostile to the FSLN.

There are two Sandinismos: one popular and folkloric, and the other intellectual and systematic. The first boasts of an ideology; the second relies on this ideology to mobilize the masses. But there is more than one expression of popular Sandinismo. Besides the official version propagated by the FSLN, there is that of revolutionary Christians who are Marxists and that of revolutionary Christians who are not. These ideologies are also rooted in popular belief and are to that extent folkloric. But they are fundamentally religious in conception and ideologically independent of the FSLN.

In Nicaragua these Sandinista ideologies coexist and are believed to be consistent with one another. At a symposium at the Central American University in Managua (August 1980), Fernando Cardenal acknowledged that, although the FSLN's leaders are convinced Marxists, "one should not forget that the revolution in Nicaragua has produced something profoundly original, which is the reconciliation of Marxism and Sandinismo."[152] Several months later he made a comparable case for the new Christianity: "Since I began working with the Sandinista Front I have never—never!—at any moment met anything that contradicts my Christian faith, or that clashes with my Christian morals."[153]

Ernesto Cardenal goes somewhat farther in testifying to being a Marxist, a Christian, and a Sandinista. But are they compatible, as they are alleged to be? Should one completely discount Marx's characterizations of religion and, by implication, Christianity, as a "perverted world consciousness" and as the "opium of the people?"[154] To his death Marx remained not just an atheist but an intransigent enemy of all religion, convinced that the "abolition of religion as the *illusory* happiness of the people is required for their *real* happiness."[155] The sentiments on which religion is based are a poor substitute for knowledge, according to Marx, and rather than helping they tend to hamper the workers in their struggle for liberation.

In addition to the holy form of self-alienation in religion, Marx criticized self-alienation in its unholy forms—the secular counterpart of religious devotion. Belief in God is not the only form of superstition. Moral superstition arises when man submits to an ideal or sacrifices his personal interests for what is right and just.[156] These are human creations made in man's image; he was not created to serve them. The *Communist Manifesto* stresses that the fundamental motive for revolution is not altruism but collective self-help or class egoism: "The workers have nothing to lose but their chains. They have a world to win!"[157] Thus, to the extent that they tolerate religion, the Sandinistas have abandoned Marx.

Marx likened moral values to the mist-enveloped creations of the religious world. "In that world the productions of the human brain appear as independent beings endowed with life, entering into relation with one another and the human race."[158] So it is with moral values that acquire magical properties when they appear to lead a life of their own. History abounds with examples of those who sacrificed their lives not so much for other people as for the sake of righteousness. Moral values acquire the character of a fetish when they begin to be considered for their own sake.

Unlike Marxism, Sandinismo thrives on moral faith. The patriotic and national values defended by the FSLN are far from being purely instrumental. In its folkloric dimension Sandinismo is an expression of moral rather than economic interests. Sandinista ideology encourages belief in both a new man and a doctrine of human rights that spurs men and women to acts of sacrifice incompatible with self-interest. Since one form of idealism opens the door to others, it is not surprising that the FSLN, in a striking departure from classical Marxism, seeks support for its moral values from the new Christianity and a theology of liberation.

The division within contemporary Sandinismo between religious and nonreligious Sandinistas resembles the division during Sandino's time. To the peasants in his Defending Army Sandino was both a political and a spiritual leader. Belausteguigoitia reported that he was revered as a prophet and holy man, and we know from Sandino's correspondence that several of his generals, themselves of peasant origin, shared his beliefs. Those who questioned Sandino's theosophy, such as Farabundo Martí and the other international volunteers who joined his army, came from a different cultural background and were usually better educated. If they did not desert his cause before it turned into a holy war, they barely tolerated his theosophy because the rest of his program—driving the Americans out of Nicaragua—suited their purpose.

Today history is repeating itself. The FSLN's National Directorate has become Sandino's political heir, and Ernesto Cardenal has become Sandino's religious heir as the spiritual father to Nicaragua's Marxist Christians. Cardenal's theology of liberation is hardly less exotic or bizarre than Sandino's. Its importance stems from its Marxistoid version of the Christian faith and from its communist interpretation of the Christian moral tradition. Although the Sandinista leaders do not share Father Cardenal's communist theology, its hybrid of Marxism and Christianity serves the

singular purpose of breaking down the barriers that have traditionally separated Marxists from Christians.

But are the FSLN's efforts to establish the consistency of Sandinismo, Marxism, and Christianity convincing? No, because the
evidence attested is highly selective. Liberation theology is marginal to Christian doctrine, and Cardenal's version is marginal
within liberation theology. Although the new Christianity and the
new Marxism are consistent with Sandinismo, the old Marxism
and the old Christianity are not. Moreover, the new Marxism and
the new Christianity have different and opposed interpretations of
communism. But these observations are mostly academic. What
counts in practice is the mutual reinforcement of Sandinismo,
Marxism, and Christianity, despite their inconsistency on selected
issues. The ideological pluralism of the FSLN has had a strategical
objective—the forging of a broad alliance for revolution unob-
structed by ideological differences.

Conclusion

What is the relevance of the philosophy of Sandino and the Sandinistas to the future of the Nicaraguan Revolution? The revolution's critics insist that the FSLN has betrayed Sandino's legacy. What stock should we give to this claim? We have seen where the Sandinistas would like to lead the revolution. But the outcome of contemporary revolutions has seldom, if ever, conformed to expectations.

To recapitulate, there are two main currents within contemporary Sandinismo: a popular and folkloric current, and an intellectual and systematic one. Today the enemies of the revolution claim that the popular current, which they identify with Sandino, is incompatible with the intellectual current backed by the Sandinista leadership. For them the future of the revolution lies with the popular current rather than with the new Marxism of the FSLN.

The conviction that Sandino's democratic and populist program has been "betrayed" by the revolutionary government provides sustenance to the Nicaraguan *contras*. In 1981 there were fewer than fifteen hundred *contras* operating within Nicaraguan territory and they consisted mostly of former members of Somoza's National Guard. Only after Pastora's defection in 1982 did counterrevolutionary sabotage escalate into a full-scale war. It was Pastora who appealed for popular support in defense of Sandino's principles. The Jeane Kirkpatrick Brigade of American volunteers shares Pastora's conviction that the *contras* rather than the Sandinista government are the legitimate heirs of Sandino. If they knew what Sandino really stood for, they would not be invoking his name.

In a statement to the U.N. Security Council (26 March 1982), Ambassador Kirkpatrick quoted at length from a statement by Pedro Joaquín Chamorro, former editor and publisher of the conservative *La Prensa*, in support of her thesis that Sandino had been betrayed by the Marxist-Leninist leadership of the FSLN. Wrote Chamorro, "There is a great difference between the Communist

Fidel Castro who in his false battle for the independence of his country has filled it with Russian rockets, soldiers, planes and even canned goods, and a Sandino who defended the sovereignty of his ground with homemade bombs but without accepting the patronage of another power."[1] Kirkpatrick relied on this statement for her thesis that Sandino was at most a national liberation hero operating within the parameters of the liberal democratic tradition.

This statement was followed by a second one to the Security Council (2 April 1982) accusing the FSLN of a policy of revolution by obfuscation. Besides posing as democrats, the Sandinistas "pretended not to be Marxist-Leninists, and today they pretend there is no contradiction between Sandinism and Marxism-Leninism." The Mexican Communists, she recalled, rejected Sandino's program as bourgeois and counterrevolutionary.[2] Again, this was supposed to confirm her thesis that Sandino was really a liberal democrat whose legacy had been "betrayed."

That there was and still is a contradiction between Marxism-Leninism and Sandino's thought has been confirmed by my discussion of his philosophy of liberation. But the contradiction is not what Kirkpatrick and the *contras* imagine. They mistakenly identify Sandino's thought with the popular and folkloric image of him. We have seen that this interpretation is the one farthest removed from Sandino's underlying views.

Unknown to Kirkpatrick and those who share her views, Sandino's occult philosophy of liberation falls outside the dichotomy between his liberal-democratic image and the image compatible with Marxism-Leninism. Both of these images, I have argued, are mistaken. Sandino's philosophy of liberation consisted of an anarchist version of communism. Unknown to Kirkpatrick, Sandino's philosophy challenges Sandinismo from a position situated to the political left of the FSLN. Ideologically, Kirkpatrick has more in common with the FSLN than with Sandino's revolutionary extremism.

Yet Sandino was a political realist who sought support wherever he could get it. It was not he who betrayed the Comintern; its Mexican representatives betrayed his struggle in Nicaragua. International communism has since learned from its mistakes. Cuba has become the principal supporter of the Nicaraguan Revolution and the Soviet Union is not far behind. Today Sandino's followers have little cause to complain that their struggle to build a new society is being blocked by Soviet interests.

There remains the accusation by Sandino's cobelievers in the Magnetic-Spiritual School of the Universal Commune, especially from its headquarters in Buenos Aires, that his austere rational communism has been permanently scrapped.[3] This is true, but it now has a Christian equivalent reinforced by the anarchist component in Sandino's thought that was rescued by the FSLN and wedded to the new Marxism disseminated by Che Guevara. Moreover, Guevara's own Marxism had an anarchist dimension traceable to the influence of Georges Sorel and his Peruvian counterpart, José Carlos Mariátegui.

Historically, the major intellectual contribution of Sorel and his followers was to preserve the legacy of charismatic communism or communist anarchism eclipsed by Marx's and Engels' scientific socialism. This workers' communism survived in a variety of forms, including the unusual synthesis of Marxism and anarchism developed by Sorel, by Ricardo Flores Magón, and by the social movements they influenced. It became the communism of Sandino and that of thousands of rank-and-file Sandinistas and grass-roots Christian organizers who helped make the Nicaraguan Revolution. Intellectually, the revolution rests on this novel foundation.

Although Sandino repudiated Christianity in all its forms, the new theology of liberation encouraged by the FSLN represents the single most important carrier of his anarcho-communism. It, rather than the philosophy of the Magnetic-Spiritual School, is a major spiritual force in the new Nicaragua. For the first time in history, revolutionary Christians are in a position to guide society along a communist path that does not come to a dead end under socialism.

The FSLN is unique among revolutionary vanguards in having a Christian left wing. Its Christianity without Christ has proved to be a more effective means of mobilizing the masses than Sandino's philosophy of liberation. Today this Christian-anarchist component of Sandinismo cannot be purged without undermining the FSLN's credibility as the vanguard of the revolution. The spread of the new theology signifies not the future liberalization but the communization of Nicaragua.

Because of their commitment to political pluralism and a mixed economy, the Sandinistas have become the darling of the Socialist International. Socialist support for the Sandinista government, however, has obscured the fact that Christian communists and anarchists also support it, but for quite different reasons. They defend political pluralism as their sole protection against Marxist-Leninist regimes intent on stamping out "infantile leftism."[4]

Kirkpatrick has stressed what she calls the "exhaustion of Marxism as an ideology."[5] She has in mind the challenge of Solidarity, above all, its demands for greater internal and external freedom for Poland. But she slights the anarchist and communist component in Solidarity and the historical roots of its ideology.[6] Marxism-Leninism may be exhausting itself, but it is not being replaced by what other neoconservatives have aptly characterized as the "pigmy ideologies" of liberalism and social democracy.[7]

In Nicaragua one finds a three-cornered ideological contest in which the liberal-democratic and new Marxist legacies are still the principal contenders. Nonetheless, Sandino's communism dressed up in Marxist-Leninist phraseology and a theology of liberation has a magnificent opportunity to replace the worn-out and exhausted liberalism of the Nicaraguan opposition.

According to one North American commentator whose views coincide with those of the State Department, the "force that really stands between the Sandinistas and the fulfillment of their ideology is the popular nature of the Nicaraguan Revolution."[8] What precisely is that popular force? He identifies it with the reformist currents within Christian democracy and with the liberal-democratic and social democratic currents within the revolution. Numerically, this force supposedly outweighs support for the new-style Leninism of the FSLN. But is this a significant factor? Old ideas are bound to persist during and after a major social and political upheaval. In Nicaragua they are being gradually eroded by those of a new generation formed in the crucible of the revolution.

This brings me to the question of the likely outcome of the Nicaraguan Revolution in view of these intellectual foundations. The syncretistic character of Sandinista ideology fits nicely with the revolutionary government's plans for political pluralism and a mixed economy. Relying heavily on support from the Socialist International and the social-democratic governments of Western Europe, Nicaragua is unlikely to fall under the hegemony of the Soviet Union. Short of a military invasion by the United States or by its Central American allies, one may reasonably expect the present stage of people's democracy to continue for a long time. Although Cuba rushed through this stage in little less than a decade, it is unlikely that Nicaragua will.

That Nicaragua will not become another Cuba, however, tells us next to nothing about its future. Although there are as many different roads to socialism as there are separate national states, the important point is that they are headed in the same general direction. Those North American scholars who look askance at the Soviet Union while insisting that the Nicaraguan Revolution is unique because of its political pluralism and a mixed economy are apt to forget that a multiparty system is also a feature of such

Soviet-bloc countries as the German Democratic Republic and Czechoslovakia as well as Poland. A small but significant capitalist sector survives in several of those countries, including Yugoslavia, which makes them mixed economies also. Thus Nicaragua already shares features common to these kindred revolutions in Eastern Europe.

These are not the only traits that Nicaragua's revolution shares with its East European counterparts. Much has been written of late on the emergence of a "new class" of professional, managerial, and scientific workers especially within the Soviet bloc.[9] The revolutions of the twentieth century have led to something quite different from anything Marx anticipated, to so-called actually existing or real socialism. Although some observers have distinguished a lower stage of socialism from a higher stage of workers' self-management, neither stage resembles the lower and higher stages of communism originally sketched by Marx and Engels.

The phenomenon of a "new class" is far from peculiar to the Soviet Union and Eastern Europe. Jeane Kirkpatrick observes that it is a universal phenomenon tied to the bureaucratization of contemporary societies whether capitalist or socialist. Since World War II the demand for the services of college graduates and intellectuals has mushroomed, and with it the initiation of the new class into politics. New-class politics, she notes, manifests a generally negative orientation toward the status quo rooted in the "relatively low income and status of intellectuals in capitalist, democratic societies (as compared to their much greater power in contemporary revolutionary regimes)."[10]

The new revolutionary politics featuring privileged roles for intellectuals, as in Cuba and Nicaragua, according to Kirkpatrick, leads to what she calls the "totalitarian temptation."[11] This is the temptation of the new class to rearrange the institutions and the lives of people in conformance to rationalist blueprints of an ideal social order. Although she acknowledges her own membership in the new class along with the leaders of the Nicaraguan Revolution and members of the New Left in the United States, she concludes that a monopoly of power, meaning, and purpose by this new class is incompatible with social well-being. As Henri Weber anticipates, the long-term threat to the revolution is that the FSLN vanguard will be tempted to "substitute itself for the people" in the form of "an oppressive bureaucratic caste."[12]

One may agree with Kirkpatrick's thesis concerning the rise of a new class without sharing her animadversions on revolutionary regimes.[13] Specifically, one may agree that under existing conditions the Nicaraguan Revolution cannot do more than replace the business class's monopoly of power and wealth with that of a new class whose fundamental asset is knowledge rather than ownership of the means of production. As Kirkpatrick's neoconservative ally, Irving Kristol, observes, "The simple truth is that the professional classes of our modern bureaucratized societies are engaged in a class struggle with the business community for status and power. Inevitably, this struggle is conducted under the banner of 'equality.'"[14] In Nicaragua, it is carried on with Marxist-Leninist phraseology under the banner of the FSLN.

Although this thesis concerning the new class contributes to undermining the pretensions of revolutionaries and their goal of a classless society, it has a revolutionary pedigree. One is apt to forget that it has an anarchist source in the writings of Michael Bakunin. As early as 1872 he predicted the advent of a new postcapitalist order based on the reign of scientific intelligence: "There will be a new class, a new hierarchy of real and counterfeit scientists and scholars, and the world will be divided into a minority ruling in the name of knowledge and an immense ignorant majority."[15] Should his own anarchist project fail, he believed, this class of salaried intellectual and professional workers rather than the class of wage-earning manual workers was slated to become the principal beneficiary in a new socialist order.

Understandably, the new socialist regimes since World War II find this thesis downright counterrevolutionary. A recent comment in *The Progressive* focuses on the plight of Ariel Hidalgo, a Cuban leftist writer and educator, serving a sentence of one to eight years for inciting against the socialist state. The prosecutor's case relied on testimony by a local neighborhood defense committee that accused him of "talking too much." What about? About the ideas contained in an unpublished manuscript that had been seized by the police, a manuscript in which "Hidalgo called for opposition to the 'new class' that he said had come to power in Cuba."[16]

Within the newly formed socialist societies, political opposition to the privileges of such a class has come not only from anarchists, but also from discontented members of the working class, as in Poland. This opposition from the left, unlike that from the liberal center, has been growing rather than diminishing since Milovan Djilas first published his inside account of Yugoslav socialism in 1957—an important source of Hidalgo's ideas.[17]

A salient difference between the Cuban and Nicaraguan revolutions is that in Nicaragua this anarcho-communist current has enjoyed the backing of the new Christianity and its theology of liberation. Ernesto Cardenal's theology belongs to the same genre as Sandino's philosophy of liberation and Wilhelm Weitling's *The Poor Sinner's Gospel.* It is governed by the same premises: God is love; the people are God; we are his children; therefore, all men and women are brothers and sisters. These are anarchist, not Marxist or Leninist, motifs. As the Mexican theologian José Porfirio Miranda has acknowledged concerning his own theology of liberation, it was not necessary for him to have a knowledge of Marxism to arrive at the equation of Christianity and communism—the anarchist component within the New Testament sufficed.[18]

Unlike the Cuban and other communist parties, which have forcibly uprooted this anarchist current from their midst, in Nicaragua it survives alongside the new Marxism of the FSLN. If this tendency persists, it will have a significant effect on the future of the Nicaraguan Revolution in circumscribing, if not the authority, at least the privileges of the new class.

Notes

Preface

1. Humberto Ortega Saavedra, *50 años,* 5, 9.
2. See Jeane Kirkpatrick's twin addresses on "The Betrayal of Sandino" in *The Reagan Phenomenon.* David Nolan, an active-duty officer in the U.S. Foreign Service, has authored a monograph providing documentary evidence for Kirkpatrick's interpretation of the FSLN as a Marxist-Leninist vanguard. He argues that each of the FSLN's three main tendencies or branches, as well as its trunk, is rooted in Marxism-Leninism. See his *The Ideology of the Sandinistas,* 19, 37–38, 50, 55, 65, 120, 123–124.
3. See Thomas A. Walker's "Introduction," *Nicaragua in Revolution,* 20–21; and John A. Booth, *End and Beginning,* 138, 146–147, 216.
4. Kirkpatrick, *The Reagan Phenomenon,* 196, 204; Thomas A. Walker, *Nicaragua,* 22–23; and Booth, *End and Beginning,* 42, 145, 237.
5. Kirkpatrick, *The Reagan Phenomenon,* 196, 204.
6. The National Directorate used Pastora for propaganda purposes. He helped to convince the public that the FSLN shared his social-democratic convictions. See Nolan, *The Ideology of the Sandinistas,* 91–92.
7. "An Exclusive Interview with Arturo Cruz," 7, 12.
8. Ibid., 8.
9. This characterization of the role of theory in Sandinista thought challenges Nolan's interpretation, according to which the Sandinistas' interpretation of Nicaraguan reality is "subjectivist" in reflecting their particular "faith." He argues that a nonrational ideology is their starting-point, as it was for Sandino. See *The Ideology of the Sandinistas,* 106, 107, 111, 122–123.

1. The Making of a Revolutionary

1. Gregorio Selser, *Sandino, general de hombres libres* (Mexican ed.), 110. Unless otherwise indicated, all references to this work will be to the Mexican edition. Translations are mine, unless otherwise noted.
2. José Román, *Maldito país,* 46.
3. Ibid.
4. Ibid., 45.
5. Ibid., 47.
6. Ibid., 49.

7. Augusto César Sandino, *Pensamiento*, 217. Unless otherwise indicated, all references to this work will be to the 5th edition.

8. Ibid., 218.

9. Román, *Maldito país*, 55.

10. Gregorio Selser, "Sandino, el guerrillero," 29.

11. Neill Macaulay, *The Sandino Affair*, 52.

12. Interview with Mónico Rodríguez. Rodríguez lived in both Tampico and Cerro Azul, where his father worked in the oil fields and raised his son on the lore of Ricardo Flores Magón's *Semilla libertaria*. Sandino also worked in Cerro Azul at that time.

13. César Escobar Morales, *Sandino*, 56.

14. Valentín Campa, *Mi testimonio*, 25–26.

15. Sandino, *Pensamiento*, 53.

16. Kaja Finkler, "Dissident Sectarian Movements," 282.

17. Sandino, *Pensamiento*, 132.

18. Ibid., 53.

19. Ibid., 54.

20. Ibid.

21. Román, *Maldito país*, 57.

22. Anastasio Somoza García, *El verdadero Sandino*, 83–84.

23. Ibid., 83.

24. Pierre Joseph Proudhon, *What Is Property*, 37–41.

25. Somoza, *El verdadero Sandino*, 83.

26. Sandino, *Pensamiento*, 85.

27. Somoza, *El verdadero Sandino*, 84.

28. Selser, "Sandino, el guerrillero," 44.

29. Cited by Escobar Morales, *Sandino*, 62–63.

30. Gregorio Urbano Gilbert, *Junto a Sandino*, 265.

31. Somoza, *El verdadero Sandino*, 200.

32. Ibid., 239.

33. Letter from Sandino to Joaquín Trincado dated 12 November 1932; reproduced in Trincado's fortnightly *La Balanza* 1:4 (1933).

34. Ibid.

35. Joaquín Trincado, *Filosofía austera racional*, 74–75, 796–797.

36. Cited by Somoza, *El verdadero Sandino*, 141.

37. Román, *Maldito país*, 88.

38. Ibid., 87–88. Román mistook "Martín" for "Joaquín."

39. Somoza, *El verdadero Sandino*, 239–240.

40. Augusto César Sandino, *Manifiesto a los pueblos*, 16.

41. See the excerpts from Ramón de Belausteguigoitia's February 1933 conversations with Sandino in Sandino, *Pensamiento*, 285–289.

42. So did another biographer: see Román, *Maldito país*, 85, 184–185.

43. Sandino, *Pensamiento*, 287.

44. Ibid., 287–288.

45. Ibid., 285.

46. Ramón de Belausteguigoitia, *Con Sandino*, 143.

47. Sandino, *Pensamiento*, 204–206.

48. Ibid., 213–214.
49. Ibid., 122.
50. Belausteguigoitia, *Con Sandino*, 130.
51. Ibid., 132.
52. Ibid., 142.
53. Ibid., 145–146.
54. Ibid., 41–42. See also Somoza, *El verdadero Sandino*, 467.
55. Somoza, *El verdadero Sandino*, 501–505, 552–557.
56. Selser, *Sandino*, 288–289.
57. Somoza, *El verdadero Sandino*, 227, 238.
58. Interview with Luis Sánchez Sancho.
59. Macaulay, *The Sandino Affair*, 53.
60. Booth, *End and Beginning*, 42, 145, 237.
61. See Richard Millett, *Guardians of the Dynasty*, 64–65; and Thomas W. Walker, *Nicaragua*, 22–23.
62. North American scholars have been especially prone to this confusion because they hesitate to attribute Machiavellian designs to Sandino. See, for example, Macaulay, *The Sandino Affair*, 53, 157–160, 226, 247; Millett, *Guardians of the Dynasty*, 64–65; Booth, *End and Beginning*, 42, 49; Walker, *Nicaragua*, 22–23; and Harry E. Vanden, "The Ideology of the Insurrection," 44–45.
63. Sergio Ramírez, "Análisis histórico-social," 15.
64. Ibid., 14.
65. Although Sandino was a careful reader, his memory was occasionally inaccurate. One instance was his confusion of what Trincado called the "century of lights" with the twentieth instead of the nineteenth century. Compare Sandino, *Pensamiento*, 214, with Trincado, *Filosofía austera racional*, 142, 163. Another instance was his confusion of Sarabasti, misspelled "Sarabatista," with Zoroaster's mother instead of Brahma's. Compare Sandino, *Pensamiento*, 306, with Trincado, *Filosofía austera racional*, 24.
66. Ramírez, "Análisis histórico-social," 14.
67. Román, *Maldito país*, 183.

2. *Activating Ideologies*

1. Macaulay, *The Sandino Affair*, 53.
2. Sandino, *Pensamiento*, 293.
3. The stereotype of Sandino popularized by the Argentine Gregorio Selser, in his two-volume biography, *Sandino, general de hombres libres* (Cuban ed.).
4. Joaquín Trincado, *Los cinco amores*.
5. Ibid., 378.
6. Ibid., 419.
7. Ricardo Flores Magón, *Semilla libertaria*, 2:210–213.
8. Andrés García Salgado, *Yo estuve con Sandino*, 47.

9. Ethel Duffy Turner, *Flores Magón*, 343–345.

10. Ibid., 348.

11. Ricardo Flores Magón, *Antología*, 77–82.

12. Turner, *Flores Magón*, 359.

13. David Poole, ed., *Land and Liberty*, 143–144.

14. Turner, *Flores Magón*, 353–354.

15. Armando Bartra, ed., *"Regeneración,"* 29 n19.

16. Ibid., 314.

17. Ibid.

18. Ricardo Flores Magón, *Epistolario*, 1:32.

19. Bartra, *"Regeneración,"* 415–416.

20. Ibid., 435.

21. Ibid., 247.

22. Ibid., 307, 314, 323, 327.

23. Ibid., 421.

24. Flores Magón, *Epistolario*, 1:39.

25. Bartra, *"Regeneración,"* 304, 326–327, 411, 414, 415–416, 435, 436–437.

26. Sandino, *Pensamiento*, 177, 232; Ricardo Flores Magón, *Tribuna roja*, 33.

27. See Sandino's letter dated 12 May 1931, reproduced by Somoza, *El verdadero Sandino*, 227–231; and Flores Magón, *Semilla libertaria*, 1:33–39.

28. Somoza, *El verdadero Sandino*, 230; Flores Magón, *Semilla libertaria*, 1:164, and *Tribuna roja*, 34–35.

29. Sandino, *Pensamiento*, 204–206, 213–214, 286–287; Flores Magón, *Semilla libertaria*, 2:45, and *Tribuna roja*, 34–35. For Flores Magón's concept of "universal love," see *Epistolario*, 3:45.

30. Flores Magón, *Tribuna roja*, 22.

31. Flores Magón, *Semilla libertaria*, 1:13–15, 132–135, and 2:73–75.

32. Sandino, *Pensamiento*, 213–214.

33. Flores Magón, *Semilla libertaria*, 1:105.

34. Ibid., 1:137.

35. Ibid., 2:37–38, 91. This Marxist component in Flores Magón's thought was subsequently played down. Instead of his original ordering of the enemies of the working class—capital, authority, clergy—he returned to the tenets of classical anarchism when he listed them as authority, capital, clergy. See *Tribuna roja*, 84; and Bartra, *"Regeneración,"* 435.

36. Flores Magón, *Semilla libertaria*, 1:101.

37. Ibid., 2:134.

38. Ibid., 2:40.

39. Sandino, *Pensamiento*, 122.

40. Ibid.

41. Finkler, "Dissident," 281–282.

42. R. Laurence Moore, *In Search of White Crows*, 70–71.

43. Ibid., 71 note, and 258 n3.

44. Finkler, "Dissident," 278–279.

45. Ibid., 282.

46. Ibid. For a discussion of Joachim's philosophy of history, see Karl Lowith, *Meaning in History*, 145–159.

47. Finkler, "Dissident," 282.

48. Ibid., 283.

49. Fredrick B. Pike, "Visions of Rebirth," 481.

50. Ibid., 479–480.

51. H. F. Ellenberger, *The Discovery*, 65.

52. R. Darnton, *Mesmerism*, 15.

53. Sandino, *Pensamiento*, 288.

54. Ibid.

55. Escobar Morales, *Sandino*, 56.

56. John Robison, *Proofs of a Conspiracy*, 233.

57. Ibid., 58, 62–63, 76.

58. Ibid., 91.

59. Ibid., 92–93.

60. Ibid., 78. For the theosophical component of Freemasonry, see 87.

61. Sandino, *Pensamiento*, 173.

62. Bruce F. Campbell, *Ancient Wisdom Revived*, 53.

63. Ibid., 54.

64. Belausteguigoitia, *Con Sandino*, 88.

65. Sandino, *Pensamiento*, 306.

66. "Oráculos de Zoroastro," *Zoroastro: El Zend-Avesta.* From the library of Karl T. Duda, director of the Centro Mazdaznan de México, Cuernavaca.

67. Somoza, *El verdadero Sandino*, 200.

68. Ibid.

69. Sandino, *Pensamiento*, 286.

70. For Sandino's trinity of "Reason, Justice, and Right" or "Justice, Right, and *Reason*," see his open letter to President Hoover (6 March 1929) and his letter to Gen. Francisco Estrada (20 May 1929), the latter in the 8th rev. ed. of ibid., 294. For Sandino's references to "Divine Justice," both before and after his second trip to Mexico in 1929, see ibid., 166, 191, 222, 226.

71. Ibid., 287.

72. Ibid., 306.

73. Ibid.

74. R. C. Zaehner, *Dawn and Twilight*, 42–43.

75. Ibid., 45–46.

76. Robert O. Ballou, ed., "From the Gathas," *World Bible*, 209.

77. Sandino, *Pensamiento*, 213. See also Sandino's letter to Abraham Rivera (14 October 1930), ibid., 204.

78. Zaehner, *Dawn and Twilight*, 40, 271–272.

79. Ibid., 51.

80. Ibid., 146, 274.

81. Sandino, *Pensamiento*, 209. See also Sandino's letter to José Hilario Chavarría (12 May 1931), in Somoza, *El verdadero Sandino*, 228.

82. Zaehner, *Dawn and Twilight*, 254.

83. Sandino, *Pensamiento*, 205–206.

84. Ibid., 287.

85. Zaehner, *Dawn and Twilight*, 292.

86. Bernhard W. Anderson, *Understanding the Old Testament*, 538–539.

87. Zaehner, *Dawn and Twilight*, 308–310.

88. Ibid., 315–318.

89. Ibid., 58.

90. Sandino, *Pensamiento*, 205–206.

91. Zaehner, *Dawn and Twilight*, 308.

92. Ibid., 278.

93. Interview with Karl T. Duda. See note 66.

94. Campa, *Mi testimonio*, 27.

95. Julio A. Mella, *Documentos y artículos*, 266.

96. For these biographical data and subsequent data covering the Magnetic-Spiritual School I am indebted to a series of interviews with Joaquín Trincado's son, Juan D. Trincado, at the school's headquarters in Buenos Aires in March and April 1985.

97. Trincado, *Filosofía austera racional*, 764.

98. Escuela Magnético-Espiritual de la Comuna Universal, "Declaración de principios."

99. Trincado, *Filosofía austera racional*, 764.

100. Ibid.

101. Ibid.

102. Escuela Magnético-Espiritual de la Comuna Universal, "Declaración de principios," 1.

103. Ibid., 3.

104. Ibid., 4.

105. Ibid.

106. Escuela Magnético-Espiritual de la Comuna Universal, "Reglamento interno," 11–12.

107. Ibid., 12.

108. Ibid., 15.

109. Ibid., 14.

110. Alfonso Alexander M. and Ramiro Molla Sanz, "Un 'caballero andante.'"

111. Ibid.

112. Joaquín Trincado, "Augusto César Sandino."

113. Joaquín Trincado, "1934—Febrero 22—1935."

114. *La Balanza* 1 : 4 (1933).

115. Augusto César Sandino, *Escritos literarios*, 67.

116. Trincado, *Filosofía austera racional*, 27.

117. Ibid., 76–77, 83.

118. Ibid., 27, 186–187.

119. Ibid., 27–28, 130, 642–643.

120. The cosmology of the Kabbalah was not original but derived from the ideas of neoplatonic philosophy. On this point, see Gershom Scholem, *Kabbalah*, 87–88. Neoplatonism received its classic expression in the philosophy of Plotinus (A.D. 205–270), an Egypto-Roman philosopher whose principal debt was to Zoroaster. It is noteworthy that Plotinus had traveled to Persia. There he acquired a firsthand knowledge of Zoroastrianism before moving to Rome in A.D. 245, where he founded his own school of philosophy. Plotinus had been a student of Ammonius Saccus, who taught in Alexandria and was the first to coin the term "theosophy."

121. Trincado, *Filosofía austera racional*, 76–77, 83, 87–92, 104, 110–111, 788.

122. Ibid., 92.

123. Ibid., 89–90, 92.

124. Ibid., 27.

125. See the Italian seventeenth-century Kabbalistic drawing reproduced in Scholem's *Kabbalah*, 364.

126. *Hebraic Literature*, 273.

127. Trincado, *Filosofía austera racional*, 87.

128. Ibid., 24, n85, 117, 231 note.

129. Somoza, *El verdadero Sandino*, 205.

130. Hippolyte Léon Denizard Rivail (Allan Kardec, pseud.), *El libro*, 406.

131. Hippolyte Léon Denizard Rivail (Allan Kardec, pseud.), *The Spirits' Book*, 19.

132. Ibid., 19–20.

133. Trincado, *Filosofía austera racional*, 187.

134. Ibid., 736–737; and Rivail, *El libro*, 16–17, 28.

135. Trincado, *Filosofía austera racional*, 537–539, 736–737; and Rivail, *El libro*, 16, 22.

136. Hippolyte Léon Denizard Rivail (Allan Kardec, pseud.), *El evangelio*, 52–53.

137. Ibid., 58.

138. Ibid., 41.

139. Orlando S. Suárez, *La ruta*, 420–421.

140. Rivail, *El evangelio*, 34, 37–39.

141. Trincado, *Filosofía austera racional*, 532–533, 784–785.

142. Ibid., 805–807.

143. Ibid., 74–76.

144. Ibid., 214, 233.

145. Joaquín Trincado, "*Los extremos*," 194.

146. Interview with Trincado's son, Juan D. Trincado, 6 April 1985.

147. Trincado, *Filosofía austera racional*, 24, 27.

148. Ibid., 26.

149. Ibid., 74.

150. Ibid., 74–75.

151. Sandino, *Pensamiento*, 306.

152. Ibid., 287, 306. See Trincado, *Filosofía austera racional*, 13, 25–26, 46–49; and Trincado, *"Los extremos,"* 55–58.

153. Somoza, *El verdadero Sandino*, 155. The title of Cañadas's work was *El sindicalismo*.

154. Georges Sorel, *Reflections on Violence*, 142–145, 250–259. For these ideas Sorel was indebted to the German philosopher Friedrich Nietzsche, and to the French philosopher Henri Bergson.

155. Somoza, *El verdadero Sandino*, 155.

156. Ibid., 155–156.

157. Sorel, *Reflections on Violence*, 142–145, 250–259.

158. Heleno Saña, *El anarquismo*, 191.

159. Ibid., 191–192.

160. Ibid., 192.

161. Cited in ibid., 191.

162. George Woodcock, *Anarchism*, 381.

163. Ibid., 382.

164. Cited in ibid.

165. Trincado, *Filosofía austera racional*, 114–119.

166. Ibid., 125–126.

167. Ibid., 138, 141.

168. Ibid., 116–117.

169. Ibid., 173.

170. Ibid., 118, 123, 125–128, 805.

171. Ibid., 162, 805.

172. Trincado, *"Los extremos,"* 346.

173. Trincado, *Filosofía austera racional*, 73–74.

174. Ibid., 162.

175. Ibid., 75.

176. Ibid., 134.

177. Ibid., 135.

178. Ibid., 117.

179. Ibid., 166.

180. Ibid., 760.

181. Ibid.

182. Ibid., 761.

183. Ibid., 254.

184. Ibid. See chapter 7 of Lenin's "Imperialism, the Highest Stage of Capitalism," *The Lenin Anthology*, 243–251.

185. Trincado, *Filosofía austera racional*, 653.

186. Ibid.

187. Ibid., 762–763.

188. Ibid., 762.

189. Ibid., 763.

190. Ibid.

191. Ibid., 771.

192. Ibid., 773.

193. Ibid., 770.
194. Karl Marx and Friedrich Engels, *Marx-Engels Reader*, 529–531.
195. Trincado, *Filosofía austera racional*, 769–770.
196. Ibid., 772; Sandino, *Pensamiento*, 306.
197. Trincado, *Filosofía austera racional*, 221, 223.
198. Ibid., 225.
199. Ibid., 224, 764.
200. Ibid., 224.
201. Ibid., 306. See Jean Jacques Rousseau, *Social Contract*, 13–14.
202. Trincado, *Filosofía austera racional*, 223.
203. Ibid., 219; Rousseau, *Social Contract*, 49.
204. Rousseau, *Social Contract*, 49–50; emphasis mine.
205. Ibid., 50.
206. Trincado, *Filosofía austera racional*, 223.
207. Charles William Heckethorn, *The Secret Societies*, 2:140.
208. Ibid., 2:140–141.
209. Trincado, *Filosofía austera racional*, 225.
210. Ibid., 762.
211. Ibid., 224.
212. Ibid.
213. Ibid., 221, 230, 749.
214. Trincado, "*Los extremos*," 353.
215. Sandino, *Pensamiento*, 306.
216. Ibid., 286.
217. Ibid.
218. Ibid., 168; and idem, *Escritos literarios*, 48.
219. Sandino, *Pensamiento*, 213.
220. Ibid.
221. For Trincado's doctrine of the holocaust, see *Filosofía austera racional*, 764, 767–771.
222. Sandino, *Pensamiento*, 214.
223. Ibid., 217.
224. Ibid., 221.
225. Ibid., 223.
226. Ibid., 222–223.
227. Ibid., 289.
228. Ibid., 287.
229. Ibid., 287–288.
230. Ibid., 289.
231. Letter to Abraham Rivera dated 14 October 1930, in ibid., 205.
232. Ibid.
233. Ibid., 206.
234. Ibid., 205–206.
235. Ibid., 206.
236. Letter to Dr. Humberto Barahona, in ibid., 306.
237. Ibid., 286–287.
238. The world-historical contribution of Islam, according to Trincado,

was to have contained the advance of Christianity. Where the extremes of Roman Catholicism and Oriental religions touched, Islam inserted itself as a neutral force preserving the equilibrium between Christ and Krishna. See Trincado, "*Los extremos*," 213–217.

239. Sandino's letter is almost entirely a paraphrase of passages taken from the following pages of Trincado's *Filosofía austera racional*: 12, 14, 18–19, 22–23, 28, 54, 73–74, 83, 104–105, 114–115, 119–120, 123–126, 134, 136, 138, 167. I have deliberately omitted references to the most obscure passages, involving the identification of such personages as Peris, Fulo, and Aitekes. For a clarification of the "fifth essence of nature," see ibid., 544–546.

240. Letter to José Hilario Chavarría dated 12 May 1931, cited by Somoza, *El verdadero Sandino*, 227–228.

241. Ibid., 228.

242. Ibid.

243. Ibid., 228–229. For Adam and Eve's redemptive mission, see the complete text of Sandino's letter to Abraham Rivera dated 22 February 1931, cited in full by Somoza, *El verdadero Sandino*, 210.

244. Ibid., 229.

245. Ibid.

246. Ibid.

247. Ibid., 230.

248. Ibid.

249. Ibid. The Spanish word for "common" is *común*, so *comunista* can mean either "commonist" or "communist."

250. Sandino, *Pensamiento*, 214.

251. Ibid., 233.

252. Ibid., 237.

253. Manifesto dated 15 November 1931, in ibid., 238.

254. Belausteguigoitia, *Con Sandino*, 108.

255. Ibid., 80.

256. Román, *Maldito país*, 166.

257. Letter dated 30 March 1931, in Sandino, *Pensamiento*, 220.

258. Ibid. See also 222.

259. Somoza, *El verdadero Sandino*, 239.

260. Ibid., 239–240.

261. Letter to Jose Idiáquez dated 10 August 1931, in Sandino, *Pensamiento*, 234.

262. Somoza, *El verdadero Sandino* (cited from Sandino's "Pauta del Ejército Autonomista de Centro América," dated 18 August 1933), 527.

263. Ibid., 529.

264. Ibid. (cited from Sandino's "Suprema proclama de unión centroamericana," dated 16 August 1933), 524.

265. Ibid., 525.

266. Ibid.

267. Ibid.

268. Ibid., 530.

269. Ibid., 526–527.

270. Macaulay, *The Sandino Affair*, 226, 302 n16. See also the statement by the poet Guillermo Valencia from Popayán, Colombia (December 1931), concerning Ramiro Molla Sanz's book of recollections, "Un 'caballero andante.'"

271. Sandino, *Pensamiento*, 297.

272. Trincado, *Filosofía austera racional*, 173.

273. Ibid., 172.

274. Sandino, *Pensamiento*, 297.

275. Letter dated 16 July 1933, in Sandino, *Escritos literarios*, 67.

276. Cited by Selser, *Sandino*, 256.

277. Macaulay, *The Sandino Affair*, 226.

3. Strategy for Subversion

1. On the connection between occult wisdom and political subversion among the intellectual currents shaping Sandino's thought—the Jewish Kabbalah, the German Illuminati, and French Revolutionary Masonry—see Nesta H. Webster, *Secret Societies*, 177–268.

2. Macaulay, *The Sandino Affair*, 9–10, 99–100, 121–122, 267.

3. See Sandino's letter to Froylán Turcios (10 June 1928) and his "Letter to the Governors of America" (4 August 1928) in Sandino, *Pensamiento*, 139–144. See also his "Plan de realización del supremo sueño de Bolívar," *Escritos literarios*, 77–79, 90–91.

4. Sandino refused to sign the peace terms of 2 February 1933 until the representatives of the Liberal and Conservative parties had agreed to remove the stain from his name by acknowledging the patriotism of his cause and his complete disinterest in acquiring wealth or material advantages for himself. See Sandino, *Pensamiento*, 280. For the Nicaraguan government's characterization of Sandino as a "bandit," see the interview with former president Adolfo Díaz in *La Balanza* 1:20 (1933); and Somoza, *El verdadero Sandino*, 85–86, 164–165, 226–227.

5. Manifesto dated 1 July 1927, in Sandino, *Pensamiento*, 87.

6. Booth, *End and Beginning*, 42, 49. Booth's assessment follows Ramírez's biographical account of Sandino, "El muchacho de Niquinohomo," Sandino, *Pensamiento*, lxviii–lxix. As we shall see in a later section, Ramírez's interpretation is rejected by members of the National Directorate of the FSLN.

7. Sandino, *Escritos literarios*, 33.

8. Sandino, *Pensamiento*, 103.

9. Ibid., 181.

10. Ibid., 96.

11. Sandino, *Escritos literarios*, 37.

12. Ibid., 43.

13. Sandino, *Pensamiento*, 123.

14. Ibid., 87.

15. Ibid., 180.
16. Sandino, *Escritos literarios*, 51–53.
17. Macaulay, *The Sandino Affair*, 57.
18. Sandino, *Pensamiento*, 169.
19. Ibid., 139.
20. Ibid., 144.
21. Ibid., 170.
22. Ibid., 179.
23. Ibid., 180.
24. Ibid., 202–203.
25. Ibid., 222.
26. Ibid., 230.
27. Ibid., 209.
28. Ibid.
29. Román, *Maldito país*, 70.
30. Sandino, *Pensamiento*, 214.
31. Ibid.
32. Ibid., 228.
33. Ibid., 232.
34. Ibid., 82–83.
35. Ibid., 88.
36. Ibid., 89–90.
37. Ibid., 89.
38. Flores Magón, *Tribuna roja*, 15.
39. Flores Magón, *Antología*, 65–66.
40. Ibid. See also Sandino, *Pensamiento*, 87–88, 99–101.
41. Sandino, *Pensamiento*, 92, 209; Flores Magón, *Tribuna roja*, 33, 35, 63.
42. Flores Magón, *Antología*, 66–69.
43. "Programa del Partido Liberal Mexicano," in Rafael Carrillo, *Ricardo Flores Magón*, 23–30.
44. Turner, *Flores Magón*, 71–72.
45. Flores Magón, *Semilla libertaria*, 1:136–140, 2:36–45.
46. Sandino, *Pensamiento*, 168.
47. James D. Cockroft, *Intellectual Precursors*, 114–115.
48. Diego Abad de Santillán, *Ricardo Flores Magón*, x.
49. Abelardo Ojeda and Carlos Mallén, *Ricardo Flores Magón*, 79–82; Bartra, "*Regeneración*," 29.
50. Escobar Morales, *Sandino*, 62.
51. Bartra, "*Regeneración*," 23–25, 29–30.
52. Flores Magón, *Semilla libertaria*, 1:167.
53. Sandino, *Pensamiento*, 295.
54. Ricardo Flores Magón, *Ricardo Flores Magón*, 203.
55. Flores Magón, *Semilla libertaria*, 2:90.
56. Ibid., 2:91.
57. Abad de Santillán, *Ricardo Flores Magón*, xi.

58. Letter from Froylán Turcios to Sandino, dated 28 December 1928, in Sandino, *Pensamiento*, 158.

59. Letter from Froylán Turcios to Sandino, dated 17 December 1928, in ibid., 157.

60. Ibid., 139–140.

61. Ibid., 128.

62. Ibid., 143.

63. Ibid., 157.

64. Ibid., 138–139.

65. Ibid., 139.

66. Ibid., 117–118.

67. Ibid., 149.

68. Ibid., 149, 328–329.

69. Somoza, *El verdadero Sandino*, 391.

70. Ibid., 393–394.

71. Ibid., 394.

72. Sandino, *Pensamiento*, 156–157.

73. Ibid., 158.

74. Gregorio Urbano Gilbert, *Junto a Sandino*, 131–143.

75. Ibid., 136.

76. Ibid., 137–138.

77. Ibid., 137.

78. Ibid., 140–141.

79. Ibid., 141–143.

80. Macaulay, *The Sandino Affair*, 131.

81. Sandino, *Pensamiento*, 143.

82. Ibid.

83. Sandino, *Escritos literarios*, 54; emphasis mine.

84. Ibid., 51–54.

85. Sandino, *Pensamiento*, 170.

86. Sandino, *Escritos literarios*, 77, 87, 89.

87. Ibid., 79–80.

88. Sandino, *Pensamiento*, 180.

89. Ibid., 51.

90. Macaulay, *The Sandino Affair*, 157.

91. Víctor Raúl Haya de la Torre, *El antimperialismo*, 33; and idem, *Pensamiento político*, 1:34. Haya's racial mystique, like Sandino's, was derived from José Vasconcelos's notion of a "cosmic race" fusing Indian, Iberian, Latin, and black elements. See José Vasconcelos, *La raza cósmica*, 28–30.

92. Macaulay, *The Sandino Affair*, 157.

93. Haya de la Torre, *El antimperialismo*, 16.

94. Mella, *Documentos y artículos*, 370.

95. Felipe Cossio del Pomar, *Haya de la Torre*, 117–118.

96. Luis Alberto Sánchez, *Haya de la Torre*, 156–157.

97. Sandino, *Pensamiento*, 8th ed., 550.

98. Mella, *Documentos y artículos*, 365–367, 370, 379, 381, 396–397.

99. Selser, *Sandino, General de hombres libres* (Cuban ed.), 2:32–33. The letter is dated 31 July 1928.

100. "Biographical Sketch," 6.

101. Ibid., 7. See also García Salgado, *Yo estuve con Sandino*, 106.

102. Mella, *Documentos y artículos*, 379.

103. "Biographical Sketch," 21.

104. Román, *Maldito país*, 137.

105. Victor Alba, *Politics*, 127–128.

106. Sandino, *Pensamiento* (October 1929 interview), 184.

107. Macaulay, *The Sandino Affair*, 157–158.

108. Ibid., 158.

109. Sandino, *Pensamiento*, 198.

110. Macaulay, *The Sandino Affair*, 285–286.

111. Campa, *Mi testimonio*, 68–69.

112. Macaulay, *The Sandino Affair*, 160.

113. García Salgado, *Yo estuve con Sandino*, 98.

114. Ibid., 101.

115. Ibid., 102.

116. Ibid.

117. Ibid., 102–103.

118. Ibid., 103.

119. Robert J. Alexander, *Communism*, 379.

120. Luis E. Aguilar, ed., *Marxism in Latin America*, 119.

121. Ibid., 122.

122. Ibid., 123.

123. Alexander, *Communism*, 378.

124. Selser, *Sandino, General de hombres libres* (Cuban ed.), 1:272.

125. Sandino, *Pensamiento*, 202. See also Sandino's autobiographical sketch, dated 4 August 1932, in which he favors a worker, peasant, and student alliance, ibid., 261.

126. Mella, *Documentos y artículos*, 615–616, 619–626.

4. The War in Nicaragua

1. Selser, "Sandino el guerrillero," 29.

2. Macaulay, *The Sandino Affair*, 10.

3. Mao Tse-tung, *Selected Works*, 1:13, and 4:417.

4. Sandino, *Manifiesto a los pueblos*, 2.

5. February 1933 interview with Belausteguigoitia, Sandino, *Pensamiento*, 297–298.

6. Trincado, *Filosofía austera racional*, 168–173.

7. Sandino, *Manifiesto a los pueblos*, 2–3.

8. For further uses of the term "pirates," see Sandino, *Pensamiento*, 100, 142, 165, 194, 199, 247, 256; and idem, *Escritos literarios*, 17, 43.

9. Sandino, *Manifiesto a los pueblos*, 3.

10. Ibid.

11. Ibid.

12. Ibid.

13. Frederic Rosengarten, Jr., *Freebooters Must Die!* 11.

14. Sandino, *Pensamiento*, 193; idem, *Manifiesto a los pueblos*, 4.

15. William Walker, *War in Nicaragua*, 250–254.

16. Ibid., 271–274.

17. Ibid., 430.

18. Ibid.

19. Cited by Rosengarten from a May 1857 speech, *Freebooters Must Die!* 178–179.

20. Walker, *War in Nicaragua*, 254–256.

21. Ibid., 254.

22. Ibid., 259–260, 265.

23. Ibid., 259.

24. Ibid., 258, 272.

25. Sandino, *Pensamiento*, 78.

26. Ibid., 88.

27. Ibid., 88–89.

28. Ibid., 100. He used almost the same words in a follow-up letter on 24 September 1927.

29. Ibid., 140.

30. Letter dated 29 April 1928, in Macaulay, *The Sandino Affair*, 119.

31. Sandino, *Pensamiento*, 193.

32. Ibid.

33. Isidro Fabela, "Augusto César Sandino," 45.

34. Ibid., 44.

35. Ibid., 45.

36. Ibid., 46.

37. Sandino, *Pensamiento*, 194.

38. Sandino, *Escritos literarios*, 77–78.

39. Sandino, *Pensamiento*, 88–89, 100, 103, 140–142.

40. Ibid., 82, 95, 145–146, 244.

41. Sandino, *Pensamiento*, 140–142.

42. Somoza, *El verdadero Sandino*, 93.

43. Sandino, *Pensamiento*, 100.

44. Ramiro Guerra, *Expansión*, 492–493.

45. On the literature of Yankeephobia, see the discussion by Miguel Jorrín and John D. Martz, *Political Thought*, 388–394.

46. Sandino, *Pensamiento*, 132.

47. Ibid., 226, 228.

48. Ibid., 196.

49. Ibid., 140.

50. Ibid., 291. Americans were also welcome; see 297.

51. Sandino, *Manifiesto a los pueblos*, 3.

52. Ibid. See also Booth, *End and Beginning*, 23–24.

53. Sandino, *Manifiesto a los pueblos*, 3.

54. Ibid., 4.
55. Ibid., 23.
56. Sandino, *Escritos literarios*, 49–50, 58–59; idem, *Pensamiento*, 165–167.
57. Sandino, *Escritos literarios*, 8.
58. Sandino, *Pensamiento*, 194, 223.
59. Sandino, *Escritos literarios*, 49.
60. Ibid., 7.
61. Sandino, *Pensamiento*, 165.
62. Ibid., 165–166.
63. Guerra, *Expansión*, 433–434.
64. Sandino, *Pensamiento*, 194.
65. Ibid., 142.
66. Sandino, *Escritos literarios*, 58.
67. Sandino, *Pensamiento*, 194.
68. Sandino, *Escritos literarios*, 58.
69. Sandino, *Manifiesto a los pueblos*, 23.
70. See Lenin on the new role of the banks and the nature of finance capital and the financial oligarchy in chapters 2 and 3 of his "Imperialism, the Highest Stage of Capitalism," *The Lenin Anthology*, 214–225. In his March 1929 "Plan for Realizing Bolívar's Supreme Dream," Sandino warned that, because "North American capitalism has arrived at its highest stage of development, thereby transforming itself into imperialism," strong measures were needed to prevent "North American finance capital from penetrating the Latin American states in the form of investments" (*Escritos literarios*, 77, 88).
71. Selser, *Sandino*, 57–58 n8.
72. Samuel Guy Inman, *América revolucionaria*, 17.
73. Booth, *End and Beginning*, 28.
74. Guerra, *Expansión*, 432–433.
75. Ibid., 432. See also Macaulay, *The Sandino Affair*, 119.
76. Sandino, *Pensamiento*, 136.
77. Gregorio Selser, *Ejército loco*, 77–79.
78. Open letter to President Hoover, Sandino, *Pensamiento*, 167.
79. Mayo Antonio Sánchez, *Nicaragua, año cero*, 44–45.
80. Ibid., 42–45.
81. Sandino, *Escritos literarios*, 59.
82. Sandino, *Pensamiento*, 226.
83. Ibid., 216.
84. Ibid., 215.
85. Ibid., 226.
86. Ibid., 228.
87. Ibid., 255.
88. Ibid., 193–194.
89. Juan José Arévalo, *The Shark*, 60.
90. Sandino, *Pensamiento*, 232.
91. Ibid., 88.

92. Sandino, *Manifiesto a los pueblos*, 4.
93. Ibid.
94. Sandino, *Escritos literarios*, 57.
95. Ibid., 58.
96. I have corrected the date, reported incorrectly in Sandino, *Pensamiento*, 166.
97. Ibid.
98. Sandino, *Escritos literarios*, 59.
99. Sandino, *Pensamiento*, 167.
100. Sandino, *Escritos literarios*, 59.
101. Sandino, *Pensamiento*, 56.
102. Sandino, *Escritos literarios*, 59.
103. Ibid.
104. Sandino, *Pensamiento*, 140.
105. Ibid., 141–142.
106. Ibid., 140.
107. Ibid., 142–143.
108. Selser, *Ejército loco*, 10–11.
109. Ibid., 57–62, 77–78.
110. Enrique Krause, "Convicción y responsabilidad," cited by Sánchez, *Nicaragua, año cero*, 43.
111. Sandino, *Pensamiento*, 255.
112. Ibid.
113. Ibid., 54 (repeated verbatim on p. 261).
114. Ibid., 100, 165–166. See also Sandino, *Manifiesto a los pueblos*, 6; and idem, *Escritos literarios*, 43–44, 49–51.
115. Sandino, *Pensamiento*, 168.
116. Ibid., 234.
117. Sandino, *Escritos literarios*, 57.
118. Sandino, *Pensamiento*, 132.
119. Ibid., 88.
120. Sandino, *Manifiesto a los pueblos*, 4.
121. Sandino, *Pensamiento*, 141–142.
122. Ibid., 142.
123. Sandino, *Escritos literarios*, 50.
124. Arévalo, *The Shark*, 62.
125. Ibid.
126. Sandino, *Escritos literarios*, 8.
127. Sandino, *Pensamiento*, 228.
128. Ibid., 132.
129. Sandino, *Escritos literarios*, 58.
130. Ibid., 58–59.
131. Ibid., 256.
132. Ibid.
133. Ibid., 70.
134. Ibid., 70–71.
135. Ibid., 71.

136. Ibid.
137. Sandino, *Escritos literarios*, 43–44.
138. Sandino, *Pensamiento*, 74.
139. Ibid., 72.
140. Ibid.
141. Ibid., 78.
142. Ibid.
143. Ibid., 79.
144. Ibid., 82.
145. Ibid., 55.
146. Ibid.
147. Macaulay, *The Sandino Affair*, 161.
148. Sandino, *Pensamiento*, 247–248.
149. Ibid., 308; see also 314, 316, 318.
150. Ibid., 196; emphasis mine.
151. Sandino, *Manifiesto a los pueblos*, 6.
152. Sandino, *Pensamiento*, 308.
153. Ibid., 95–96.
154. Román, *Maldito país*, 134; see also 110, 135–138.
155. *El sandinismo*, 186, 190.
156. Román, *Maldito país*, 110, 137.
157. Sandino, *Manifiesto a los pueblos*, 4.
158. Sandino, *Pensamiento*, 260.
159. Ibid., 54.
160. Emigdio Maraboto, *Sandino ante el coloso*, 9.
161. Ibid., 9–10.
162. Claribel Alegría and D. J. Flakoll, *Nicaragua*, 51.
163. Escobar Morales, *Sandino*, 57.
164. Alegría and Flakoll, *Nicaragua*, 54.
165. Ibid., 54–55.
166. Ibid., 55.
167. Ibid., 56.
168. Sandino, *Pensamiento*, 258.
169. Ibid., 260.
170. Ibid., 79.
171. Ibid., 83.
172. Ibid., 88.
173. Ibid., 95.
174. Ibid., 117–118.
175. Ibid., 128.
176. Sandino, *Escritos literarios*, 43–44.
177. Ibid., 44.
178. Sandino, *Pensamiento*, 150.
179. Ibid., 151.
180. Ibid., 92.
181. Ibid., 94.
182. Sandino, *Manifiesto a los pueblos*, 16.

183. Ibid.
184. See figures cited by Carlos Fonseca, *Sandino*, 3.
185. Fabela, "Augusto César Sandino," 63. Booth estimates the number at one thousand: *End and Beginning*, 44.
186. Sandino, *Pensamiento*, 231.
187. Letter to Alemán Bolaños, dated 16 July 1931, ibid., 230.
188. Macaulay, *The Sandino Affair*, 214.
189. Sandino, *Pensamiento*, 213–214.
190. Ibid., 204.
191. Ibid., 242–243.
192. Ibid., 261.
193. Ibid., 263.
194. Ibid.
195. Ibid., 267.
196. Selser, *Sandino*, 247.
197. Sandino, *Pensamiento*, 268–269.
198. Sandino, *Manifiesto a los pueblos*, 18–20.
199. Ibid., 22.
200. Letter to the wife of Dr. Humberto Barahona, dated 15 March 1933, Sandino, *Pensamiento*, 300.
201. Letter to Alemán Bolaños, dated 16 March 1933, ibid., 301.
202. Fabela, "Augusto César Sandino," 88.
203. Selser, *Sandino*, 275–276.
204. Jaime Wheelock Román, *Imperialismo y dictadura*, 123–124.
205. Ortega, *50 años*, 62–63.
206. Sandino, *Manifiesto a los pueblos*, 22.
207. Ortega, *50 años*, 64.
208. Sandino, *Manifiesto a los pueblos*, 23.
209. Sandino, *Escritos literarios*, 77–91.
210. Sandino, *Pensamiento*, 220.
211. Sandino, *Pensamiento*, 304–305.
212. Ibid., 307–308.
213. Ibid., 307.
214. Ibid.
215. Ibid., 308.
216. Ibid., 309.
217. Ibid., 311.
218. Ibid.
219. Somoza, *El verdadero Sandino*, 467, 470–473, 477–478, 556–557.
220. Sandino, *Pensamiento*, 316.
221. Ibid.
222. Sandino, *Escritos literarios*, 72–73.
223. Henry L. Stimson, *American Policy*, 92–93, 104–107, 111–112.
224. Ibid., 94–95.
225. Ibid., 97.
226. Ibid., 116.
227. Ibid., 15.

228. Ibid., 23.
229. Ibid., 26.
230. Ibid., 29.
231. Ibid., 33.
232. Ibid., 36.
233. Ibid., 38–39.
234. Ibid., 34.
235. Ibid., 88–89.
236. Ibid., 30.
237. Ibid., 65–66.
238. Ibid., 67.
239. Ibid., 70.
240. Ibid., 75.
241. Ibid.
242. Ibid., 75–76.
243. Ibid., 77.
244. Ibid., 72–73.
245. Ibid., 76.
246. Ibid., 79.
247. Ibid., 85.
248. Ibid. That Stimson believed this fabrication is evident from his account of Sandino in Henry L. Stimson and McGeorge Bundy, *On Active Service*, 114–115.
249. Ibid., 114.
250. Guerra, *Expansión*, 449–450.
251. Selser, *Sandino*, 297n.

5. From Sandino to Sandinismo

1. Selser, *Sandino*, 290–291.
2. Jesús Miguel Blandón, *Sandino y Fonseca*, 10–13.
3. Carlos Fonseca, "¡Con la revolución siempre!" 132.
4. "Biografía," 24.
5. Guillermo Rothschuh Tablada, *Los guerrilleros*, 19–20, 68–69. See also Tomás Borge, "Carlos," 104.
6. Blandón, *Sandino y Fonseca*, 200.
7. For the following account, see "Biografía," 24–25.
8. Víctor Manuel Tirado López, "Pensamiento político," 18–20.
9. Borge, "Carlos," 104.
10. Daniel Waksman Schinka, "Entrevista con Tomás Borge," 20.
11. Borge, "Carlos," 104.
12. Ibid.
13. Ibid., 106.
14. Rothschuh Tablada, *Los guerrilleros*, 69.
15. Tirado López, "Pensamiento político," 18.
16. Ibid., 20.

17. Alegría and Flakoll, *Nicaragua*, 166–168. On the JPN, see also Blandón, *Sandino y Fonseca*, 204–208.

18. Alegría and Flakoll, *Nicaragua*, 168. See also Borge, "Carlos," 106.

19. Víctor Manlio Tirado, *La revolución sandinista*, 24.

20. Ibid., 25. Based on Borge's testimony.

21. Borge, "Carlos," 107.

22. Alegría and Flakoll, *Nicaragua*, 171–172.

23. Juan Colindres, *Anastasio Somoza*, 87.

24. Ibid., 88.

25. Ibid., 88, 90.

26. "Carlos Fonseca," 23.

27. Carlos Fonseca, *Ideario político*, 137–176.

28. Fonseca, *Sandino*, 3.

29. Ibid., 5.

30. Ibid., 6.

31. Ibid., 5.

32. Ibid., 4.

33. Fonseca's interpretation of Sandino as a revolutionary and not just a radical nationalist was reaffirmed by José Benito Escobar, another member of the FSLN's National Directorate. Wrote Escobar in his own biographical sketch of Sandino, "Sandino's class outlook is evident from the moment he organized the Liberal column under his command in 1926. . . . Without being a Marxist, Sandino knew how to apply nationalism in a creative, revolutionary way" (*Ideario sandinista*, 132, 135).

34. For the following biographical data, see Robert K. Brown's preface to Alberto Bayo's *150 Questions*, ii–xvi.

35. Ibid., ii, xi, xvii.

36. Ibid., 15.

37. Ibid., 30–31.

38. Ibid., xiv.

39. Blandón, *Sandino y Fonseca*, 100–113. See also the account by Alegría and Flakoll, *Nicaragua*, 153–156.

40. For an account of Gen. Ramón Raudales's campaign, see Blandón, *Sandino y Fonseca*, 67–81.

41. Borge, "Carlos," 108.

42. See Ernesto Che Guevara's acknowledgment in his introduction to Bayo's book, *Mi aporte a la revolución cubana* (Havana, 1960), reproduced at the beginning of Bayo's *150 Questions*.

43. Macaulay, *The Sandino Affair*, 262.

44. Hilda Gadea, *Ernesto*, 47, 56–57.

45. Macaulay, *The Sandino Affair*, 263.

46. Ibid., 263–266.

47. Blandón, *Sandino y Fonseca*, 103–104, 106–109. See also Alegría and Flakoll, *Nicaragua*, 154.

48. Macaulay, *The Sandino Affair*, 260–261.

49. Ibid., 261.

50. Herbert L. Matthews, *Fidel Castro*, 90. See also Matthews's *Revolution in Cuba*, 70.

51. Vania Bambirra, *La revolución cubana*, 39–42.

52. Macaulay, *The Sandino Affair*, 262.

53. See note 42.

54. Alegría and Flakoll, *Nicaragua*, 156–157.

55. Ernesto Che Guevara, *Obras 1957–1967*, 1:31.

56. Bayo, *150 Questions*, 19.

57. Ibid., 31.

58. Ibid., 46.

59. Macaulay, *The Sandino Affair*, 76.

60. Guevara, *Obras 1957–1967*, 1:41.

61. Bayo, *150 Questions*, 32.

62. Blandón, *Sandino y Fonseca*, 109.

63. Alegría and Flakoll, *Nicaragua*, 156.

64. Ibid., 157.

65. Carlos Fonseca, *Nicaragua: hora cero*, 37–38. See also his "Por la lucha armada," 167.

66. Carlos Fonseca, *Un nicaragüense*, 7, 46, 61.

67. Fonseca, "Por la lucha armada," 166.

68. Fonseca, "¡Con la revolución siempre!" 139.

69. Frederick Engels, *Socialism*, 51–53. For a lengthier presentation of the same thesis, see idem, "Speech at the Graveside of Karl Marx," Marx and Engels, *The Marx-Engels Reader*, 681–682.

70. Lenin, *The Lenin Anthology*, 644.

71. Fonseca, "¡Con la revolución siempre!" 139.

72. The first is from "The Second Declaration of Havana" (4 February 1962), *Fidel Castro Speaks*, 104; the second is from "Speech" (13 March 1967), ibid., 131.

73. Ibid., 131–132. See also Fidel Castro's "Discurso" (26 July 1966), *Lecturas de Filosofía*, 2:389.

74. Guevara, *Obras 1957–1967*, 2:92.

75. Fidel Castro, *Fidel Castro Speaks*, 131.

76. Interview with Ricardo Napurí (pseud. Silvestre Condoruma), co-founder of Peru's Vanguardia Revolucionaria, concerning his conversations with Che Guevara.

77. Guevara, *Obras 1957–1967*, 2:206.

78. Ibid., 1:61.

79. Ibid., 2:372.

80. Fidel Castro, "The Duty of Marxist-Leninists," 219.

81. Castro, "Discurso" (26 July 1966), *Lecturas de filosofía*, 2:389.

82. Ibid.

83. Castro, *Fidel Castro Speaks*, 130.

84. Ibid.

85. Ibid., 131.

86. Castro, "Discurso" (26 July 1965), *Lecturas de filosofía*, 2:542.

87. Guevara, *Obras 1957–1967*, 2:677.
88. Ibid., 678.
89. Ibid.
90. Fidel Castro, "Discurso" (1 May and 26 August 1966), *Lecturas de filosofía*, 2:546–547, 552–553.
91. Ibid., 552.
92. Ibid.
93. Ibid., 553.
94. From an interview with the editors of *Pensamiento Crítico* at the journal's offices in Havana, November 1968.
95. Ibid.
96. Gadea, *Ernesto*, 5.
97. "José Carlos Mariátegui (1895–1930)," 1.
98. José Carlos Mariátegui, *Defensa del Marxismo*, 59–60.
99. José Carlos Mariátegui, *El alma matinal*, 33.
100. Ibid., 32.
101. Ibid., 35.
102. Ibid., 29.
103. Ibid.
104. Sorel, *Reflections on Violence*, 142–144, 264.
105. Ibid., 144–145.
106. Mariátegui, *Defensa del Marxismo*, 21.
107. "*The intellect is characterized by a natural inability to comprehend life*"—Henri Bergson, *Creative Evolution*, 182. In the same vein, William James asserted that "to compare the *worths*, both of what exists and what does not exist, we must consult not science, but what Pascal calls the heart." See "The Will to Believe" in his *Essays on Faith and Morals*, 53.
108. Mariátegui, *Defensa del Marxismo*, 21.
109. Ibid., 57. The Sorelian content of Mariátegui's reconceptualization of Marxism is brought out by Luis Villaverde, "El sorelismo de Mariátegui," republished in José Aricó, *Mariátegui*, 145–154.
110. Mariátegui, *Defensa del Marxismo*, 57.
111. Ibid., 114–115.
112. Ibid., 21, 43.
113. Sorel, *Reflections on Violence*, 145.
114. Ibid., 253.
115. Mariátegui, *Defensa del Marxismo*, 59–60.
116. *Lecturas de filosofía*, 1:213–220, 263–281, 2:705–718.
117. Luciano Pellicani, *Gramsci*, 61. Quotation from Antonio Gramsci, *Quaderni del carcere*.
118. Ramírez, "Análisis histórico-social," 15.
119. Ibid., 15–16.
120. Cited by John M. Cammett, *Antonio Gramsci*, 254 n 7.
121. Ibid., 125.
122. Pellicani, *Gramsci*, 4.

123. Ibid., 7, 45.
124. H. Portelli, *Gramsci*, 199.
125. Cammett, *Antonio Gramsci*, 204–205.
126. The reference to Croce is from Mariátegui, *Defensa del Marxismo*, 56.
127. Antonio Gramsci, *The Modern Prince*, 85.
128. Ibid., 58–64.
129. Ibid., 135.
130. Tomás Borge, "Interview," 714.
131. Deirdre English, "'We Are Sandinistas,'" 23.
132. José Luis Balcárcel, "El Sandinismo," 115.
133. Ibid.
134. Michael Baumann, "Year at War," 885.
135. Ibid.
136. Balcárcel makes the mistake of reducing Sandinismo to an application of the principles of classical Marxism to Nicaragua: "El Sandinismo," 117–118.
137. Borge, "Carlos," 104.
138. Carlos Fonseca, *Desde la cárcel*, 6–9.
139. Ibid., 7.
140. Ibid.
141. Ibid.
142. Ibid., 9.
143. Fonseca, *Nicaragua: hora cero*, 27.
144. Ibid., 27–28.
145. Fonseca, "¡Con la revolución siempre!" 139.
146. Ibid., 129–131.
147. Ibid., 133.
148. Fonseca, "Por la lucha armada," 166.
149. Ricardo Morales Avilés, *La Dominación*, 39.
150. Ibid., 40.
151. Humberto Ortega, *La lucha de Sandino base de la revolución sandinista*, 9.
152. Ibid., 11.
153. Ibid., 13.
154. Víctor Tirado López, "Crecerá la ofensiva," 144.
155. Ibid.
156. Tirado López, "Pensamiento político," 20–21.
157. Ibid.
158. Interview with Luis Sánchez Sancho.
159. Tirado López, "Pensamiento político," 20–21.
160. Karl Marx, *Selected Works*, 2:606.
161. Ibid., 2:567.
162. Lenin, *The Lenin Anthology*, 667–668.
163. Interview with Bayardo Arce, in English, "'We Are Sandinistas,'" 22.

164. Ibid., 23.
165. Walker, *Nicaragua in Revolution*, 20–21.
166. Booth, *End and Beginning*, 216.
167. Humberto Ortega, "Diálogo abierto a la asamblea," 175.
168. Ibid., 174, 177.

6. *Political Assessments*

1. See "The Second Declaration of Havana" (4 February 1962), the single most important statement concerning the theory and practice of the Cuban Revolution and the common denominator of the new Marxism, Castro, *Fidel Castro Speaks*, 103.
2. Fonseca, *Nicaragua: hora cero*, 10.
3. Ibid., 18–19.
4. Ibid., 11.
5. Ibid., 13.
6. Ibid., 35.
7. Ibid., 35–36.
8. Guevara, *Obras 1957–1967*, 2:409.
9. Ibid.
10. Ibid., 409–410.
11. Ibid., 410–411.
12. Ibid., 412–413.
13. Ibid., 1:165–166.
14. Ibid., 178.
15. See André Gunder Frank's theoretical articulation of Che's views concerning "underdevelopment" and the role of the "national bourgeoisie" in *Latin America*, xiv, xviii, 371–373, and in *Lumpenburguesía: lumpen-desarrollo*, 14–15. In acknowledgment of the importance of Frank's contribution to the new Marxism, the Philosophy Department of the University of Havana included a translation of his essay "The Development of Underdevelopment" in its *Lecturas de Filosofía*, 2:421–430.
16. Guevara, *Obras 1957–1967*, 1:174.
17. Lenin, *The Lenin Anthology*, 129–130.
18. Fonseca, *Nicaragua: hora cero*, 12.
19. Guevara, *Obras 1957–1967*, 2:588.
20. Fonseca, *Nicaragua: hora cero*, 21.
21. Ibid., 22–23.
22. Ibid., 26.
23. Morales Avilés, *La dominación*, 5.
24. Ibid., 5–7.
25. Ibid., 44.
26. Ibid., 7.
27. Ibid.
28. Ibid., 9–10.

29. Ibid., 11–12, 20, 22.
30. Ibid., 11–12.
31. Ibid., 10–12, 18.
32. Ibid., 16.
33. Ibid., 12, 17.
34. Ibid., 12, 19, 22–23.
35. Ibid., 22–24.
36. Ibid.; see also p. 13 on the effects of "polarization."
37. Ibid.
38. Ibid., 23.
39. Ibid., 24.
40. Mao Tse-tung, *Selected Works*, 1:331.
41. Ibid., 1:333.
42. Ibid.
43. Ibid.
44. Ibid., 1:334.
45. Ibid., 1:336.
46. Ibid., 1:337.
47. Jaime Wheelock Román, *Raíces indígenas*; and idem, *Imperialismo y dictadura*.
48. Susanne Jonas (Bodenheimer), "Dependency and Imperialism," 156–165, 168–169.
49. Theotônio Dos Santos, "The Structure of Dependence," 227–233.
50. Edelberto Torres-Rivas, *Procesos y estructuras*, 141, 153, 164, 179, 185. For Torres-Rivas's intellectual debt to his colleagues at CESO, see ibid., 13. CESO was instrumental in publishing not only his book, but also the works of his colleagues through Ediciones Prensa Latinoamericana in Santiago de Chile.
51. Ibid., 164–165, 178–179, 185–186. Torres-Rivas owes a special debt to the work of Fernando Henrique Cardoso and Enzo Faletto. See especially their discussion of the new character of dependence, *Dependencia y desarrollo*, 130–160.
52. Wheelock, *Imperialismo y dictadura*, 105, 176, 180–189, 195.
53. Ibid., 147.
54. Ibid., 119.
55. Ibid., 164.
56. Ibid.
57. Ibid., 163–164.
58. Ibid., 180.
59. Ibid., 187.
60. Ibid., 188.
61. Ibid., 188–189.
62. Ibid., 189.
63. Ibid.
64. Ibid.
65. Ibid., 195.
66. Dos Santos, "The Structure of Dependence," 236. The political con-

sequences of dependency theory for revolutionary movements in Latin America were also under investigation at CESO, principally by Vania Bambirra, *Diez años.*

67. Jaime Wheelock and Luis Carrión, *Apuntes,* 14.
68. Ibid., 10.
69. Ibid.
70. Ibid., 26.
71. Ibid., 31.
72. Ibid., 67, 70–71.
73. Ibid., 70.
74. Ibid., 67, 72.
75. Ibid., 72; and Wheelock, *Imperialismo y dictadura,* 82.
76. Because "peasants" are typically self-employed workers cultivating their own small plots, I have included agricultural day laborers within the category of a "rural proletariat."
77. Wheelock and Carrión, *Apuntes,* 31–33, 35.
78. Ibid., 14.
79. Ibid., 35.
80. Ortega's analysis paved the way toward a study by a team of FSLN sociologists who investigated the correlation of social forces in detail. See Julio C. López et al., *La caída* (originally published as articles between November 1978 and May 1979).
81. Ortega, "Diálogo abierto a la asamblea," 89.
82. Ibid., 68–76.
83. Ibid., 77–79.
84. Lenin, *The Lenin Anthology,* 275–276, 602–603.
85. Ortega, "Diálogo abierto a la asamblea," 68, 70–71.
86. Ibid., 89–91.
87. Ibid., 71–72.
88. Ibid., 71.
89. Fidel Castro, *Hoy somos un pueblo entero,* 162.
90. Castro, *Fidel Castro Speaks,* 103.
91. Ibid., 103–104.
92. Castro makes the same point in ibid., 102.

7. Reflections on Strategy

1. Tomás Borge, "Historia político-militar," 40–41.
2. Ibid.
3. Manlio Tirado, *La revolución sandinista,* 26.
4. Ibid.; from *Trinchera,* no. 15.
5. Ibid., 26–27; from *Trinchera,* no. 36.
6. Ibid., 27; from *La Prensa* (Managua), 22 March 1963.
7. Ibid., 27–28; based on Borge's account.
8. Fonseca, *Nicaragua: hora cero,* 24.
9. Waksman Schinka, "Entrevista con Tomás Borge," 20.

10. Borge, "Historia político-militar." The guerrillas survived for roughly two months (July and August 1963) in the Nicaraguan jungles. See Manlio Tirado, *La revolución sandinista*, 28–30.

11. Waksman Schinka, "Entrevista con Tomás Borge," 21.

12. Ibid.

13. Ibid.

14. Borge, "Historia político-militar," 44.

15. Waksman Schinka, "Entrevista con Tomás Borge," 21.

16. Manlio Tirado, *La revolución sandinista*, 41.

17. Borge, "Historia político-militar," 44

18. Manlio Tirado, *La revolución sandinista*, 35; from *Trinchera*, no. 37.

19. Guevara, *Obras 1957–1967*, 1:32.

20. Ibid.

21. Ibid., 1:74, 131.

22. Ibid., 1:62.

23. Ibid., 1:63.

24. Ibid., 1:33.

25. Ibid., 1:102–107.

26. Ibid., 1:33, 39.

27. Manlio Tirado, *La revolución sandinista*, 35; from *Trinchera*, no. 37.

28. Borge, "Carlos," 109.

29. Borge, "Historia político-militar," 41.

30. Tomás Borge, "La formación," 30.

31. Ibid.

32. Borge, "Carlos," 113.

33. Ibid., 113–114.

34. See "Castroism: The Long March in Latin America," and "Problems of Revolutionary Strategy in Latin America," in Régis Debray, *Strategy for Revolution*, 27–81, and 113–152, respectively.

35. Debray, *Strategy for Revolution*, 40.

36. Ibid., 43.

37. Ibid., 54.

38. Debray, *Revolution in the Revolution?* 42.

39. Ibid., 53, 56.

40. Ibid., 120.

41. See the special issue of *Monthly Review*, "Régis Debray and the Latin American Revolution" (July–August 1968), esp. the essay by Eqbal Ahmad, "Radical but Wrong," 72–73, 76–77. In *The Marxism of Regis Debray*, 63, Hartmut Ramm makes a corresponding distinction between what he misleadingly labels *"foquismo* I" and *"foquismo* II," more accurately designated as *"foco* I" and *"foco* II."

42. Pilar Arias, ed., *Nicaragua*, 46; recollected by Jacinto Suárez.

43. Ibid.

44. Fonseca, *Nicaragua: hora cero*, 25–34.

45. Ibid., 28–29.
46. Alegría and Flakoll, *Nicaragua*, 208; from a speech by Jacinto Suárez at the Catholic University in Managua, November 1979.
47. Ibid.
48. Waksman Schinka, "Entrevista con Tomás Borge," 21.
49. Henry Ruiz, "La montaña," 14.
50. Alegría and Flakoll, *Nicaragua*, 200.
51. Ibid., 204–205.
52. Ruiz, "La montaña," 10.
53. Ibid., 11.
54. Ibid., 14.
55. Ibid.
56. Ibid., 16.
57. Ibid., 17–18.
58. Ibid., 13.
59. Ibid., 14.
60. Ibid., 13.
61. Ibid., 14–15.
62. Ibid., 16.
63. Ibid., 14.
64. Ibid., 13; and Borge, "Carlos," 120.
65. Borge, "Carlos," 114.
66. Alegría and Flakoll, *Nicaragua*, 206.
67. Borge, "Historia político-militar," 44.
68. Ibid.
69. Alegría and Flakoll, *Nicaragua*, 227.
70. Ibid., 228.
71. Ortega, *50 años*, 108.
72. Ibid.
73. Ibid., 108–109.
74. Borge, "Historia político-militar," 44.
75. FSLN, "Iniciamos una nueva etapa," 171.
76. Ibid., 171–172.
77. Vo Nguyên Giap, *People's War*, 27–33.
78. Ibid., 29.
79. Ibid.
80. Ibid., 169–170.
81. Ibid., 159.
82. Mao Tse-tung, *Selected Works*, 2:134.
83. Ibid., 2:123–124.
84. Ibid., 2:119, 124.
85. "Who Are the MAP/FO," 136.
86. Gabriel García Márquez, "Entrevista," 154; from a 1978 interview with Orlando Loaiziga.
87. Ibid.
88. Guevara, *Obras 1957–1967*, 1:177.
89. Ibid., 1:180.
90. Ibid., 1:182.

328   *Notes to Pages 232–241*

91. Ibid., 1:185.
92. Debray, *Revolution in the Revolution?* 48–53.
93. Guevara, *Obras 1957–1967*, 2:593.
94. Ibid., 2:594.
95. Ibid., 2:595.
96. Ibid., 2:596.
97. Waksman Schinka, "Entrevista con Tomás Borge," 22.
98. Ibid.
99. Ibid.
100. Ibid.
101. Jaime Wheelock, "Entrevista al FSLN."
102. Ibid.
103. Ibid.
104. Ibid.
105. Ibid., 25.
106. Ibid.
107. Gabriel García Márquez et al., eds., *"Los Sandinistas,"* 181–182.
108. Ibid.
109. Ibid., 182.
110. Ibid.
111. Ibid., 182–183.
112. Ibid., 185.
113. Ibid.
114. Ibid., 186.
115. Ibid., 183.
116. Ibid., 186.
117. Donald C. Hodges, *Legacy of Che Guevara*, 147–149.
118. For data on Wheelock, see Arias, *Nicaragua*, 221.
119. MIR, *Correo*, September 1974.
120. MIR, "Respuesta," 4.
121. Ibid., 5.
122. Ibid., 11.
123. Ibid., 12–13.
124. Ibid., 7.
125. Ibid., 8.
126. Ibid.
127. Ibid., 9.
128. For this distinction, see Donald C. Hodges, *Argentina*, 65–66, 87–88.
129. FSLN, "Sandinistas hablan," 226. This interpretation of the divisions within the FSLN was reaffirmed in a major document by the Insurrectionalist Tendency, idem, "La situación general del FSLN," 194–195.
130. FSLN, "Sandinistas hablan," 226.
131. Ibid., 227.
132. Orlando Núñez Soto, "Third Social Force," 5–6, 12.
133. Nolan, *The Ideology of the Sandinistas*, 78–79.
134. FSLN, "Algunas consideraciones estratégicas," 203.

135. Ibid., 204.
136. Ibid., 205.
137. Ibid., 205–206.
138. Ibid., 208–209.
139. Ibid., 209.
140. FSLN, "Programa mínimo del FSLN," 225–233.
141. Ortega, *50 años*, 40, 44, 98.
142. Ibid., 46.
143. Ibid., 54, 58–59.
144. Ibid., 54–55.
145. Ibid., 56.
146. Ibid., 107–109.
147. Ibid., 108.
148. Ibid., 109.
149. Humberto Ortega, "La insurrección," 33; based on an interview with Marta Harnecker in January 1980.
150. Ortega, *50 años*, 110.
151. FSLN, "La situación general del FSLN," 198.
152. Ibid., 199.
153. Waksman Schinka, "Entrevista con Tomás Borge," 22.
154. FSLN, "La situación general del FSLN," 200–201.
155. Ibid., 189–190; and Alegría and Flakoll, *Nicaragua*, 248, 270.
156. FSLN, "La situación general del FSLN," 199.
157. Ibid., 201.
158. FSLN, "El FSLN," 191.
159. Arias, *Nicaragua*, 129.
160. Ibid., 130.
161. Ibid., 131.
162. H. Ortega, "La insurrección," 34.
163. Arias, *Nicaragua*, 130.
164. H. Ortega, "La insurrección," 35.
165. Ibid., 36.
166. Ibid.
167. Ibid., 37.
168. Ibid.
169. Ibid., 39.
170. Ibid., 40.
171. Ibid., 41.
172. Ibid., 42.
173. Ibid.
174. Ibid., 45.
175. Ibid.
176. Ibid., 27; addendum to the Harnecker interview in response to questions at the Ministry of Culture in Managua, February 1980.
177. Ibid., 28.
178. See Anastasio Somoza Debayle's account of the September offensive in *Nicaragua Betrayed*, 184.

179. H. Ortega, "La insurrección," 44.
180. FSLN, "Sandinistas hablan," 237–238.
181. Ibid., 239.
182. H. Ortega, "La insurrección," 46.
183. Ibid., 56.
184. Ibid., 46.
185. Ibid., 49.
186. Ibid., 51.
187. Ibid., 48.
188. Ibid., 51.
189. Ibid., 48–49.
190. See the equation of Castro's Moncada strategy with a strategy of general insurrection in Bambirra, *La revolución cubana*, 40–42, 100–102.
191. Castro, *Hoy somos un pueblo entero*, 103.
192. Ibid., 104–105.
193. Ibid., 106.
194. Ibid.
195. Ibid.
196. Fidel Castro, *Revolutionary Struggle 1947–1958*, 1:376.
197. Ibid., 1:387.
198. Ibid., 1:188–189.
199. Ibid., 176–177.
200. Booth, *End and Beginning*, 115–116, 154.
201. "Playboy Interview," 64.
202. Fidel Castro, "Reflexiones," 82, 84. For an account of his early Marxist studies and their influence on his original program in "History Will Absolve Me," see Baudilio Castellanos, "La historia me absolverá."
203. Castro, "Reflexiones," 84.
204. Tomás Borge, *Los primeros pasos*, 281.
205. Abraham Guillén, *Philosophy of the Urban Guerrilla*, introduction, 8–14, 19–20, 25–26.
206. Omar Costa, *Los Tupamaros*, 149–159.
207. See bibliography, Guillén, *Philosophy of the Urban Guerrilla*, 304–305.
208. Abraham Guillén and Donald Hodges, *Revaloración*, 69–130.
209. Guillén, *Philosophy of the Urban Guerrilla*, 234–235.
210. Ibid., 253.
211. Guillén and Hodges, *Revaloración*, 70.
212. For a discussion of earlier efforts to combine these alternative but complementary strategies of revolution, see Bambirra's introduction to *Diez años*, 1:27–75. Although the introduction was completed in 1969, it shows an unusual grasp of the problems that the FSLN did not begin to tangle with until the middle seventies.
213. For data on the armed organizations in El Salvador prior to their unification in 1980, see the discussion of their respective strategies in *El Salvador*, 5–6, 9–14, 39–40, 45–46; and the interviews by Mexican jour-

nalist Mario Menéndez Rodríguez, published in the English-language edition of *Granma* (Havana), 16 March–5 June 1980.

214. Ricardo E. Chavarría, "The Nicaraguan Insurrection," 37–38.

8. *Ideologies of the Revolution*

1. Fonseca et al., *¿Qué es un sandinista?* 5.
2. Ibid., 7.
3. Ibid., 8–9.
4. Ibid., 7.
5. Ibid., 7–8.
6. Ibid., 12.
7. Ibid., 14.
8. Ibid., 13.
9. Ibid.
10. Ibid., 17.
11. Ibid.
12. Ibid., 15.
13. Tomás Borge, "¡Hay que aprender," 29.
14. Tomás Borge, "Hacia el partido," 47–48.
15. Ibid., 48.
16. Borge, *Los primeros pasos*, 192–193.
17. Ibid., 194.
18. Ibid., 199.
19. Bayardo Arce, "El difícil terreno," 156.
20. Ibid., 157.
21. Ibid., 153.
22. Ibid.
23. Ibid., 153–154.
24. Ibid., 154.
25. Ibid., 155.
26. Ernesto Cardenal, "Cultura revolucionaria," 165.
27. Ibid., 164.
28. Ibid., 163.
29. For Tolstoy the only good art and the only art that is not fake art is Christian art, that which unites people and is based on love. See Leo Tolstoy, *What Is Art?* 226–227, 241–242.
30. Sergio Ramírez, "Junta de Gobierno," 23.
31. Rom. 5:12–18. All biblical references are to the translation by James Moffatt.
32. Ibid., 6:6.
33. 2 Cor. 5:17. See also Eph. 4:22–24.
34. Guevara, *Obras 1957–1967*, 2:251–253.
35. Ibid., 2:382.
36. Ibid., 2:384.

37. Ibid., 2 : 374.
38. Hodges, *Legacy of Che Guevara*, 16–17.
39. Cited by Michael Dodson and T. S. Montgomery, "The Churches," 176.
40. Guevara, *Obras 1957–1967*, 2 : 380.
41. Ibid., 2 : 381.
42. Ibid., 2 : 596.
43. Ibid., 2 : 381.
44. FSLN, "Represión y lucha de clases," 178–179.
45. Ibid., 180.
46. Ibid., 178.
47. García Márquez et al., "*Los Sandinistas*," 171.
48. Ibid., 172.
49. "Tomás Borge Speaks," 248.
50. Ibid., 249.
51. Ibid., 255.
52. Julio Scherer García, "La peor acechanza," 6.
53. Ibid., 7.
54. Phillip Berryman, *The Religious Roots*, 323–326.
55. Donald C. Hodges, *Socialist Humanism*, 137, 150–165, 170–175.
56. Scherer García, "La peor acechanza," 6.
57. Jaime Wheelock, "The Sandinista Front," 286–287.
58. Ibid., 287.
59. "Comunicado oficial," 70.
60. Fonseca, "Por la lucha armada," 165.
61. "Comunicado oficial," 70–73.
62. Ibid., 71.
63. "Gaspar García Laviana," 9.
64. Luis Carrión, "La revolución," 334.
65. Ibid., 338.
66. Borge subsequently set this figure at one million. See *Los primeros pasos*, 203.
67. Kevin McKiernan, "Shrines and Slogans," 33.
68. Ibid., 47.
69. Borge, "Interview," 713.
70. Alvaro Argüello, *Fe cristiana*, 82–84.
71. McKiernan, "Shrines and Slogans," 31.
72. Borge, *Los primeros pasos*, 197–198.
73. Scherer García, "La peor acechanza," 9.
74. Raúl Macín, ed., "El evangelio," 25.
75. Ibid., 26.
76. Borge, *Los primeros pasos*, 198.
77. Ibid., 212.
78. Ibid., 197, 199.
79. Tomás Borge, "Interview with Nicaraguan Leader," 119.
80. Gustavo Gutiérrez, *A Theology of Liberation*, ix.
81. Ibid., 15.

82. Ibid., 8, 12, 89.

83. Ibid., 90–91, 98 n45, 120 n10, 123 n20.

84. Berryman, *The Religious Roots*, 7–8, 59–60.

85. Francisco Solana, "Nicaragua," 12.

86. Ibid. See also Berryman on the role of Christian grass-roots communities during the Revolution, *The Religious Roots*, 59–64, 70–74, 82, 88.

87. From a statement by Bayardo Arce included in Arias, *Nicaragua*, 87.

88. McKiernan, "Shrines and Slogans," 31.

89. Dodson and Montgomery, "The Churches," 162–163.

90. Max Azicri, "A Cuban Perspective," 364.

91. Hodges, *Legacy of Che Guevara*, 63–65.

92. Juan García Elorrio, "Bases," 193.

93. See the discussion of Castro's speeches of 14 July 1969 and 22 April 1970, in Donald C. Hodges, *The Latin American Revolution*, 145–146.

94. Sergio Arce Martínez, *Cristo vivo en Cuba*, 27.

95. Ibid., 170.

96. Fernando Cardenal, "Como cristiano revolucionario," 103.

97. Ibid.

98. Jaime Wheelock, "The Great Challenge," 139.

99. Ibid., 140.

100. Cited by Roberto Rivera Mendizábal, "Introducción," 20.

101. Ibid., 21.

102. A distinction made by Father Alvaro Argüello, "Posturas de los cristianos," 84.

103. See the references to Mariátegui in the anthology of Borge's speeches, *Los primeros pasos*, 151, 280.

104. Mariátegui, *7 ensayos*, 162.

105. Ibid., 193.

106. Ibid., 162.

107. Ibid., 187.

108. Ibid.

109. "Playboy Interview," 60.

110. Ibid., 188.

111. The orthodox Marxist interpretation is that Christian Sandinismo is at most an auxiliary ideology, which excludes it from being an integral part of the ideology of the Revolution. See Harry E. Vanden, "The Ideology of the Insurrection," 52–53.

112. From an interview with Claribel Alegría and D. J. Flakoll, *Nicaragua*, 275.

113. Ernesto Cardenal, *The Gospel in Solentiname*, 4:112–113.

114. Ibid., 4:114.

115. Ibid., 4:114–115.

116. Ibid., 4:119.

117. Ibid., 1:10.

118. Ibid., 4:56.

119. Ibid. See also Mao Tse-tung, *Selected Works*, 3:272.

120. Cardenal, *The Gospel in Solentiname*, 4:50, 54.

121. Ibid., 4:58–59.

122. Ibid., 1:244.

123. Leo Gabriel, interview with Ernesto Cardenal, August 1980, unpublished, 3.

124. Ibid., 8.

125. Ernesto Cardenal, "Ernesto Cardenal comenta," 127.

126. Ibid., 131.

127. Ibid., 133.

128. Ibid., 132.

129. Manuel Pereira, "Conversación inconclusa," 31.

130. Karl Kautsky, *Foundations of Christianity,* 397–405.

131. Pereira, "Conversación inconclusa," 31.

132. Friedrich Engels, "On the History of Early Christianity," in Marx and Engels, *Basic Writings,* 168.

133. Ibid., 169.

134. Pereira, "Conversación inconclusa," 31.

135. Ibid.

136. Ibid.

137. Cardenal, *The Gospel in Solentiname,* 1:179–180.

138. Ibid., 4:128.

139. Ibid., 4:272; emphasis mine.

140. Acts 2:44–45 and 4:32–36.

141. Cardenal, *The Gospel in Solentiname,* 4:275.

142. Ibid., 1:257.

143. Friedrich Engels, "History of the Communist League," in Marx and Engels, *Basic Writings,* 460–461, 464–468; and Marx, "Economic and Philosophic Manuscripts," in Marx and Engels, *The Marx-Engels Reader,* 82–84.

144. Wilhelm Weitling, *The Poor Sinner's Gospel,* 10.

145. Ibid., 17.

146. Ibid., 75, 79.

147. Ibid., 185–186.

148. Sylvain Maréchal, "Manifesto of the Equals," 52, 53.

149. François Noël Babeuf, "Defense," 65.

150. For the assimilation of Marx's early humanism by the new Marxism, see Guevara, *Obras 1957–1967,* 2:251–253.

151. The materialist interpretation of history dates from *The German Ideology* (1845–1846), the watershed between Marx's early philosophical humanism and what he called his new scientific worldview. This was the work in which he and Engels "resolved to work out in common the opposition of our view to the ideological view of German philosophy, in fact, to settle accounts with our erstwhile philosophical conscience." See Marx, "Preface to *A Contribution to the Critique of Political Economy,*" in Marx and Engels, *The Marx-Engels Reader,* 5.

152. Fernando Cardenal, "La campaña de alfabetización," 151.

153. Cardenal, "Como cristiano revolucionario," 103.

154. Marx, "Introduction to *Toward the Critique of Hegel's Philosophy*

of Right," in Marx and Engels, *Basic Writings,* 262–263.

155. Ibid., 263.

156. See the relevant citations by Marx on morality and my commentary in Hodges, *Socialist Humanism,* 137, 150–165, 170–175.

157. Marx and Engels, *Basic Writings,* 41.

158. Karl Marx, *Capital,* I, 183.

Conclusion

1. Kirkpatrick, *The Reagan Phenomenon,* 196.

2. Ibid., 204.

3. Interview with Juan D. Trincado Riglos, 8 April 1985.

4. Lenin's term for left-wing communists who share common ground with anarchists. See *The Lenin Anthology,* 567, 568–569.

5. Kirkpatrick, *The Reagan Phenomenon,* 36.

6. Jacek Kuron and Karol Modzelewski, "An Open Letter to the Party."

7. James Burnham's characterization in a special preface to the 1963 edition of *The Machiavellians: Defenders of Freedom.* Cited by George H. Nash, *The Conservative Intellectual Movement in America,* 91–92.

8. Nolan, *The Ideology of the Sandinistas,* 126.

9. See the discussion of this literature in Donald C. Hodges, *The Bureaucratization of Socialism,* 35–45, 92–102.

10. See her essay "Politics and the New Class," in Jeane J. Kirkpatrick, *Dictatorships and Double Standards,* 194.

11. Ibid., 203.

12. Henri Weber, *Nicaragua: The Sandinist Revolution,* 120–121.

13. See my discussion of revolutionary regimes in *The Bureaucratization of Socialism,* 174–189.

14. Quoted from the chapter on Irving Kristol in Peter Steinfels, *The Neoconservatives,* 95.

15. Michael Bakunin, *Bakunin on Anarchy,* 319.

16. "Even in Havana," *The Progressive* (March 1985), 12.

17. Milovan Djilas, *The New Class,* 37–62.

18. From a letter to Linda Damico dated 14 January 1983, cited in her Ph.D. dissertation at Florida State University, "The Anarchist Dimension of Liberation Theology," 127 n 25.

Bibliography

The history of the Nicaraguan Revolution and its intellectual biography in particular continue to be fragmentary. We still lack a complete edition of Sandino's writings. Although the most complete and useful compilation is Sergio Ramírez's *El pensamiento vivo de Sandino*, it went through seven editions before including Sandino's important *Manifiesto a los pueblos de la tierra y en particular al de Nicaragua* and still leaves out some of his most controversial letters. Besides Sandino's own account of his ideas, there are the reports by some who participated in his struggle: one by Gregorio Urbano Gilbert, a Dominican member of Sandino's general staff; and another by Andrés García Salgado, a Mexican volunteer. Santos López, a colonel in Sandino's army, has left us his recollections of some of Sandino's battles but he tells us next to nothing about Sandino's thought.

There are several biographies of Sandino, of which three deserve special mention. They were the only ones based on extensive interviews and impromptu conversations with Sandino. To these he provided the documentation and gave his imprimatur. The earliest, by the Mexican writer Emigdio Maraboto, *Sandino ante el coloso* (Veracruz, 1929), covers the liberal origins and populist orientation of Sandino's Defending Army.

Sandino revealed his philosophical and theosophical ideas to only two of his biographers, and then only after his military campaign had come to an end. Their works provide the most candid and accurate accounts of his thought. The first, by the Basque writer and journalist Ramón de Belausteguigoitia, *Con Sandino en Nicaragua* (Madrid, 1934), includes several lengthy conversations with Sandino along with the most exhaustive account of his theosophical beliefs. The second, by the Nicaraguan journalist José Román, *Maldito país* (Managua, 1983), is valuable mainly for Sandino's stories about his early life and otherwise unavailable data concerning his Defending Army. Although the manuscript was completed in February 1934, for political reasons Román could not find a publisher until almost half a century later.

Among other sources on Sandino's thought the most detailed account is Gregorio Selser's two-volume *Sandino, general de hombres libres.* (An English translation of Selser's condensed version of this work, which includes long excerpts from Sandino's writings, has recently been published by Monthly Review Press.) At the same time, one should not discount Anastasio Somoza García's ghost-written and poisonous biography of Sandino for the light it sheds on his relationship to the Communist International and on the anarcho-syndicalist origins of his thought, but above all for the controversial correspondence it contains on Sandino's bizarre theosophy, correspondence that is missing in other anthologies.

There are two general accounts of the origins and formative stages of the FSLN by its founders: Carlos Fonseca's *Nicaragua: hora cero* and Tomás Borge's prison notes, "Carlos, el amanecer ya no es una tentación." Daniel Waksman Schinka's interview with Borge contains additional information. Humberto Ortega, the artificer of the Sandinistas' strategy for victory, provides the most thorough description of the political-strategical aspects of the struggle that began with Sandino. Although his *50 años de lucha sandinista* was completed in the early months of 1977, the interview conducted by Marta Harnecker covers the period until victory in July 1979. (This interview is also available in English from *Intercontinental Press.*) Jesús Miguel Blandón's *Entre Sandino y Fonseca Amador* is indispensable to understanding the historical linkage between Sandino's movement and the FSLN. Two anthologies of Sandinista writings also deserve attention: Fernando Carmona's *Nicaragua: la estrategia de la victoria;* and Gabriel García Márquez's *"Los Sandinistas."* These works along with Waksman's interview are especially valuable for their commentaries on the FSLN's internal conflicts after 1975. For understanding the political thought of the present leaders of the FSLN, the most important source is still *La revolución a través de nuestra dirección nacional,* the first major statement of their views since seizing power in July 1979.

INTERVIEWS

Gabriel, Leo. Interview with Ernesto Cardenal, Managua, August 1980.
Hodges, Donald C. Interviews with Adolfo Alfaro, director of Importaciones y Exportaciones Literarias, S.A. (IMELSA), Managua, 24 and 27 December 1980.

————. Interview with José Bell Lara and the editors of *Pensamiento Crítico*, Havana, November 1968.

————. Interview with Valentín Campa, presidential candidate of the Mexican Communist party in 1976, Cuernavaca, Mexico, 3 January 1978.

————. Interview with Theotônio Dos Santos, Marta Harnecker, and other members of CESO, Santiago de Chile, February 1969.

————. Interview with Karl T. Duda, director of the Centro Mazdaznan de México, Cuernavaca, Mexico, 15 April 1982.

————. Interview with Onofre Guevara, editor of *Barricada*, official organ of the FSLN, Managua, 26 December 1980.

————. Interview with Ricardo Napurí (pseud. Silvestre Condoruma), cofounder of Peru's Vanguardia Revolucionaria, Lima, February 1969.

————. Interviews with Mónico Rodríguez, anarcho-communist, Magonist activist, and organizer for the Mexican Communist party during the 1950s, Chiconcuac, Mexico, January 1978, May 1982, and June 1983.

————. Interview with Luis Sánchez Sancho, general secretary of Partido Socialista Nicaragüense (PSN), Managua, 26 December 1980.

————. Interviews with Juan D. Trincado Riglos, director of the Escuela Magnético-Espiritual de la Comuna Universal, Buenos Aires, 12 March, 6 and 8 April 1985.

PUBLISHED SOURCES

Abad de Santillán, Diego. *Ricardo Flores Magón: el apóstol de la revolución social mexicana.* Mexico City: Grupo Cultural Ricardo Flores Magón, 1925.

Aguilar, Luis E., ed. *Marxism in Latin America.* New York: Knopf, 1968.

Ahmad, Eqbal. "Radical but Wrong." *Monthly Review* (July–August 1968):70–83.

Alba, Victor. *Politics and the Labor Movement in Latin America.* Stanford, Cal.: Stanford University Press, 1968.

Alegría, Claribel, and D. J. Flakoll. *Nicaragua: la revolución sandinista. Una crónica política, 1855–1979.* Mexico City: Era, 1982.

Alemán Bolaños, Gustavo. *Sandino el libertador.* Mexico City: Ediciones del Caribe, 1951.

Alexander, Robert, ed. *APRISMO: The Ideas and Doctrines of Víctor Raúl Haya de la Torre.* Kent, Oh.: Kent State University, 1973.

Alexander M., Alfonso. "Notas para la historia de Nicaragua." *La Balanza* (Buenos Aires) 1:2 (1933).

Alexander M., Alfonso, and Ramiro Molla Sanz. "Un 'caballero andante': España aun tiene Quijotes. Desde New York a Buenos Aires a pie y sin dinero." *La Balanza* (Buenos Aires) 1:2 (1933).

Althusser, Louis. "Acerca de Gramsci." In *Para leer El capital,* by Louis Althusser and Etienne Balibar, pp. 13–17. Mexico City: Siglo XXI, 1969.

Anderson, Bernhard W. *Understanding the Old Testament.* Englewood Cliffs, N.J.: Prentice-Hall, 1957.

Antología de la economía política. Managua: Secretaría Nacional de Propaganda y Educación Política del FSLN, 1980.

Arce Castaño, Bayardo. "Como debe ser la educación en la revolución." In *La revolución a través de nuestra Dirección Nacional,* pp. 85–95. Managua: Secretaría Nacional de Propaganda y Educación Política del FSLN, 1980.

————. "El difícil terreno de la lucha: el ideológico." *Nicaráuac* (Managua), no. 1 (May–June 1980): 152–157.

————. "La intervención extranjera en Nicaragua y el proceso de autodeterminación nicaragüense." *Revolución Sandinista y Educación.* Special issue of *Encuentro* (Managua), no. 15 (September 1980): 56–64.

————. "Los medios de comunicación en un proceso revolucionario caen en la esfera de la actividad ideológica." *Patria Libre* (Managua) (February 1980): 37–39.

————. *La revolución nicaragüense: historia y perspectiva.* Managua: Secretaría Nacional de Propaganda y Educación Política del FSLN, 1980.

————. "Unidad nacional y poder popular." *Cuadernos del Tercer Mundo,* no. 39 (August–September 1980): 32–35.

Arce Martínez, Sergio. *Cristo vivo en Cuba.* San José: Departamento Ecuménico de Investigaciones, n.d.

Arévalo, Juan José. *The Shark and the Sardines.* New York: Lyle Stuart, 1961.

Argüello H., Alvaro. "Posturas de los cristianos frente al proceso revolucionario nicaragüense." *Fe cristiana y revolución sandinista en Nicaragua,* pp. 81–98. Managua: Instituto Histórico Centroamericano, 1979.

————, et al. *Fe cristiana y revolución sandinista en Nicaragua.* Managua: Instituto Histórico Centroamericano, 1979.

Arias, Pilar, ed. *Nicaragua: Revolución—relatos de combatientes del Frente Sandinista.* Mexico City: Siglo XXI, 1980.

Aricó, José, ed. *Mariátegui y los orígenes del marxismo latinoamericano.* Mexico City: Siglo XXI, 1978.

Assmann, Hugo. *Teología desde la praxis de la liberación.* 2d ed. Salamanca: Sígueme, 1976.

Azicri, Max. "A Cuban Perspective on the Nicaraguan Revolution." In *Nicaragua in Revolution,* edited by Thomas W. Walker, pp. 345–373. New York: Praeger, 1982.

Babeuf, François Noël. "Defense (From the Trial at Vendôme, February–May 1797." In *Socialist Thought: A Documentary History,* edited by Albert Fried and Ronald Sanders, pp. 56–71. Garden City, N.Y.: Anchor, 1964.

Bakunin, Michael. *Bakunin on Anarchy.* Edited and translated by Sam Dolgoff. New York: Random House, 1972.

Balcárcel, José Luis. "El sandinismo, ideología de la revolución nicaragüense." *Nicaráuac* (Managua), no. 2 (July–August 1980): 112–119.

Ballou, Robert O., ed. *World Bible.* New York: Viking, 1950.
Bambirra, Vania [Clea Silva], ed. *Diez años de insurrección en América Latina.* 2 vols. Santiago de Chile: Prensa Latinoamericana, 1971.
———. "The Errors of the *Foco* Theory." *Monthly Review* (July–August 1968): 18–35.
———. *La revolución cubana: una reinterpretación.* Mexico City: Nuestro Tiempo, 1970.
Barreto, Pablo Emilio. *El repliegue de Managua a Masaya.* Mexico City: Cártago, 1980.
Bartra, Armando, ed. *"Regeneración" 1900–1918: la corriente más radical de la revolución mexicana de 1910 a través de su periódico de combate.* 3d ed. Mexico City: Era, 1981.
La batalla por Nicaragua: Cuadernos de Unomásuno. Mexico City: Editorial Uno, 1980.
Bauman, Michael. "Year at War Steels Mass Organizations: Sandinistas Put 'Borrowed Time' to Good Use." *Intercontinental Press* (27 December 1982): 884–888.
Bayo, Alberto. *150 Questions for a Guerrilla.* Boulder, Colo.: Panther Publications, 1965.
Beals, Carleton. *Banana Gold.* Philadelphia: Lippincott, 1932.
Belausteguigoitia, Ramón de. *Con Sandino en Nicaragua.* Madrid: Espasa-Calpe, 1934.
Bergson, Henri. *Creative Evolution.* Authorized translation by Arthur Mitchell. New York: Random House, 1944.
Berryman, Phillip. *The Religious Roots of Rebellion: Christians in Central American Revolutions.* Maryknoll, N.Y.: Orbis, 1984.
"Biografía del jefe de la revolución." *Patria Libre* (Managua) (October–November 1980): 24–25.
"Biographical Sketch of Agustín Farabundo Martí." Mimeographed. Committee in Solidarity with the People of El Salvador, n.d.
Black, George. *Triumph of the People: The Sandinista Revolution in Nicaragua.* London: Zed Press, 1981.
Blandón, Jesús Miguel. *Entre Sandino y Fonseca Amador.* Managua: Talleres de Impresiones y Troquela, 1980.
Booth, John A. *The End and the Beginning: The Nicaraguan Revolution.* Boulder, Colo.: Westview Press, 1982.
Borge, Tomás. "Carlos, el amanecer ya no es una tentación." In *Nicaragua: la estrategia de la victoria,* edited by Fernando Carmona, pp. 103–122. Mexico City: Nuestro Tiempo, 1980.
———. "La formación del FSLN." In *La revolución a través de nuestra Dirección Nacional,* pp. 25–36. Managua: Secretaría Nacional de Propaganda y Educación Política del FSLN, 1980.
———. "Hacia el partido de la revolución sandinista." *Patria Libre* (Managua) (October–November 1980): 45–49.
———. "¡Hay que aprender de las masas para educar a las masas!" *Patria Libre* (March 1980): 26–30.
———. "Historia político-militar del FSLN." *Revolución Sandinista y*

Educación. Special issue of *Encuentro* (Managua), no. 15 (September 1980): 39–46.

———. "Interview with Nicaraguan Leader Tomás Borge." *Intercontinental Press* (28 February 1983): 118–119.

———. "Interview with Tomás Borge: 'We Will Not Take a Single Step Backward.'" *Intercontinental Press* (6 July 1981): 713–715.

———. *El partido sandinista y las cualidades del militante*. Managua: Secretaría Nacional de Propaganda y Educación Política del FSLN, 1980.

———. *Los primeros pasos: la revolución popular sandinista*. Mexico City: Siglo XXI, 1981.

———. "Tomás Borge Speaks on Human Rights in Nicaragua." *Intercontinental Press* (16 March 1981): 248–255.

Brandon, S. G. F. *Jesus and the Zealots*. New York: Scribner's, 1967.

Burbach, Roger, and Tim Draimin. "Nicaragua's Revolution." *NACLA: Report on the Americas*, no. 3 (May–June 1980): 2–35.

Cabezas Lacayo, Omar. *La montaña es algo más que una inmensa estepa verde*. Havana: Casa de las Américas, 1982.

Calderón Ramírez, Salvador. *Ultimos días de Sandino*. Mexico City: Ediciones Botas, 1934.

Callcott, Wilfrid Hardy. *Liberalism in Mexico, 1857–1929*. Hamden, Conn.: Archon Books, 1965.

Câmara, Dom Helder. *Church and Colonialism*. London: Sheed & Ward, 1968.

Camejo, Pedro, and Fred Murphy, eds. *The Nicaraguan Revolution*. New York: Pathfinder, 1979.

Cammett, John M. *Antonio Gramsci and the Origins of Italian Communism*. Stanford, Cal.: Stanford University Press, 1967.

Campa, Valentín. *Mi testimonio: experiencias de un comunista mexicano*. Mexico City: Cultura Popular, 1978.

Campbell, Bruce F. *Ancient Wisdom Revived: A History of the Theosophical Movement*. Berkeley & Los Angeles: University of California Press, 1980.

Cannabrava, Paulo. *Tras los pasos de Sandino: Nicaragua 1978*. Madrid: Ediciones Encuentro, 1978.

Cardenal, Ernesto. "Cultura revolucionaria, popular, nacional, antimperialista." *Nicaráuac* (Managua), no. 1 (May–June 1980): 163–168.

———. "Ernesto Cardenal comenta el evangelio entre rifles M-1." Report by Pedro Meyer, in *La batalla por Nicaragua: Cuadernos de Unomásuno*, pp. 126–133. Mexico City: Editorial Uno, 1980.

———. *The Gospel in Solentiname*. 4 vols. Translated by Donald D. Walsh. Maryknoll, N.Y.: Orbis, 1976–1982.

———. *La santidad de la revolución*. Salamanca: Sígueme, 1976.

Cardenal, Fernando. "La campaña de alfabetización y la revolución." *Encuentro*, no. 15 (September 1980): 147–153.

———. "Como cristiano revolucionario encontré un nuevo camino." *Nicaráuac* (Managua), no. 5 (April–June 1981): 99–108.

Cardoso, Fernando H., and Enzo Faletto. *Dependencia y desarrollo en América Latina*. Mexico City: Siglo XXI, 1969.

"Carlos Fonseca: héroe nacional." *Patria Libre* (Managua) (October–November 1980): 23–24.

Carmona, Fernando, ed. *Nicaragua: la estrategia de la victoria*. Mexico City: Nuestro Tiempo, 1980.

Carrillo, Rafael. *Ricardo Flores Magón*. Mexico City: n.p., 1945.

Carrión, Jorge. "Socialdemocracia y reformismo en América Latina." *Estrategia* (Mexico City) no. 31 (January–February 1980): 65–80.

Carrión, Luis. "Nicaragua: el sello de un nuevo ejército." *Casa de las Américas* (Havana), no. 117 (November–December 1979): 191–193.

———. *El patriotismo: base de la unidad nacional*. Managua: Departamento de Propaganda y Educación Política del FSLN, 1981.

———. "La revolución y los cristianos." In *Nicaragua: la estrategia de la victoria*, edited by Fernando Carmona, pp. 333–338. Mexico City: Nuestro Tiempo, 1980.

Castañeda, Jorge G. *Nicaragua: contradicciones en la revolución*. Mexico City: Tiempo Extra, 1980.

Castellanos, Baudilio. "La historia me absolverá, documento esencialmente marxista." *Revolución* (Havana) (18 July 1962).

Castro, Fidel. "La acción guerrillera es el único camino para la mayoría de los pueblos de Latinoamérica." In *Lecturas de filosofía*, vol. 2, pp. 387–390. Havana: Instituto del Libro, 1968.

———. "Discurso en el acto central conmemorativo del XXVI aniversario del asalto al cuartel Moncada." *Casa de la Américas* (Havana), no. 117 (November–December 1979): 4–13.

———. *Discursos, 1965–1968*. Havana: Instituto del Libro, 1968.

———. "The Duty of Marxist-Leninists." In *Marxism in Latin America*, edited by Luis E. Aguilar, pp. 218–220. New York: Knopf, 1968.

———. *Fidel Castro Speaks*. Edited by Martin Kenner and James Petras. New York: Grove, 1969.

———. *Fidel in Chile: Selected Speeches*. New York: International Publishers, 1972.

———. "History Will Absolve Me." *Revolutionary Struggle, 1947–1958: The Selected Works of Fidel Castro*. Vol. 1, pp. 164–221. Cambridge, Mass.: MIT Press, 1972.

———. *Hoy somos un pueblo entero (1953–1973)*. Mexico City: Siglo XXI, 1973.

———. "Reflexiones sobre la revolución cubana." *Estrategia* (Mexico), no. 31 (January–February 1980): 81–93.

———. *La revolución cubana 1953–1962*. Edited by Adolfo Sánchez Rebolledo. Mexico City: Era, 1972.

———. *Revolutionary Struggle, 1947–1958: The Selected Works of Fidel Castro*. Vol. 1. Edited by Rolando E. Bonachea and Nelson P. Valdés. Cambridge, Mass.: MIT Press, 1972.

———. *Socialismo y comunismo: un proceso único*. Santiago de Chile: Prensa Latinoamericana, 1970.

———. *Speeches: Cuba's International Foreign Policy, 1975–80.* New York: Pathfinder, 1981.

———. "Total War against Tyranny." *Revolutionary Struggle, 1947–1958: The Selected Works of Fidel Castro.* Vol. 1, pp. 373–378. Cambridge, Mass.: MIT Press, 1972.

Castro, Horacio. *Nicaragua: la lucha popular que cambió su historia.* Mexico City. Cártago, 1979.

Chavarría, Ricardo E. "The Nicaraguan Insurrection." In *Nicaragua in Revolution,* edited by Thomas W. Walker, pp. 25–40. New York: Praeger, 1982.

Chilcote, Ronald H. "Issues of Theory in Dependency and Marxism." *Latin American Perspectives,* nos. 30–31 (Summer–Fall 1981): 3–16.

Cockcroft, James D. *Intellectual Precursors of the Mexican Revolution, 1900–1913.* Latin American Monographs series, no. 14. Austin: University of Texas Press, 1968.

Colindres, Juan. *Anastasio Somoza: fin de una estirpe de ladrones y asesinos.* Mexico City: Editorial Posada, 1979.

"Con virulentos ataques a la política 'imperialista' en América Latina concluyó ayer la reunión de la IS." Declaration of Santo Domingo. *Unomásuno* (Mexico City) (30 March 1980): 8.

Cooper-Oakley, Isabel. *Masonry and Medieval Mysticism: Traces of a Hidden Tradition.* 2d ed. London: Theosophical Publishing House, 1977.

Cossio del Pomar, Felipe. *Haya de la Torre el indoamericano.* Lima: Editorial Nuevo Día, 1946.

Costa, Omar. *Los Tupamaros.* Mexico City: Era, 1971.

Crahan, Margaret E. "National Security Ideology and Human Rights." Paper presented at Tenth Interamerican Congress of Philosophy, Florida State University, Tallahassee, 18–23 October 1981.

Cueva, Agustín. *El desarrollo del capitalismo en América Latina.* Mexico City: Siglo XXI, 1979.

———. "A Summary of 'Problems and Perspectives of Dependency Theory.'" *Latin American Perspectives,* no. 11 (Fall 1976): 12–16.

Dalton, Roque. *"¿Revolución en la revolución?" y la crítica de derecha (una defensa y un balance).* Havana: Casa de las Américas, 1969.

Darnton, R. *Mesmerism and the End of the Enlightenment in France.* Cambridge, Mass.: Harvard University Press, 1968.

Debray, Régis. "Castroism: The Long March in Latin America." In *Strategy for Revolution,* edited by Robin Blackburn, pp. 25–81. New York: Monthly Review Press, 1969.

———. "Nicaragua: Radical 'Moderation.'" *Contemporary Marxism,* no. 1 (Spring 1980): 10–18.

———. *Prison Writings.* New York: Vantage, 1973.

———. *Strategy for Revolution.* Edited by Robin Blackburn. New York: Monthly Review Press, 1969.

Desarrollo de la sociedad nicaragüense. 3d ed. Managua: Ediciones Dávila Bolaños, 1980.

Díaz Soto y Gama, Antonio. *La revolución agraria del sur y Emiliano Zapata su caudillo.* Mexico City: El Caballito, 1976.

Djilas, Milovan. *The New Class.* New York: Praeger, 1957.

Dodson, Michael, and T. S. Montgomery. "The Churches in the Nicaraguan Revolution." In *Nicaragua in Revolution,* edited by Thomas W. Walker, pp. 161–180. New York: Praeger, 1982.

Dos Santos, Theotônio. *Dependencia económica y alternativas de cambio en América Latina.* Santiago de Chile: Centro de Estudios Socio-Económicos, 1969.

————. "The Structure of Dependence." In *Readings in U.S. Imperialism,* edited by K. T. Fann and Donald C. Hodges, pp. 225–236. Boston: Porter Sargent, 1971.

Droguett, Carlos. "Sandino: morir para seguir viviendo." *Casa de las Américas* (Havana), no. 117 (November–December 1979): 108–119.

Duncan, W. Raymond, and James N. Goodsell, eds. *The Quest for Change in Latin America.* New York: Oxford University Press, 1970.

Dussell, Enrique. "Derechos básicos: capitalismo y liberación." Paper presented at Tenth Interamerican Congress of Philosophy, Florida State University, Tallahassee, 18–23 October 1981.

————. *Método para una filosofía de la liberación.* Salamanca: Sígueme, 1974.

————. *Para una ética de la liberación latinoamericana.* 2 vols. Buenos Aires: Siglo XXI, 1973.

Eagelson, John. *Christians and Socialism: Documents of the Christians for Socialism Movement in Latin America.* Maryknoll, N.Y.: Orbis, 1980.

————. "Liberation Theology Flows from Reality." *Maryknoll* (July 1981): 54–57.

Ellenberger, Henri F. *The Discovery of the Unconscious: The History and Evolution of Dynamic Psychiatry.* New York: Basic Books, 1970.

El Salvador: Alianzas políticas y proceso revolucionario. Cuadernos de Coyuntura, no. 5. Mexico City: Ediciones SEPLA, 1979.

Engels, Frederick. *Anti-Duhring.* New York: International Publishers, 1972.

————. "Letter to Conrad Schmidt." In Karl Marx and Frederick Engels, *Selected Correspondence.* Moscow: Foreign Languages Publishing House, n.d.

————. *Socialism: Utopian and Scientific.* New York: International Publishers, 1935.

English, Deirdre. " 'We are Sandinistas': Conversations with Nicaragua's Embattled Leaders." *Mother Jones* (August–September 1985): 22–29, 51.

Escobar, José Benito. *Ideario sandinista.* Managua: Secretaría Nacional de Propaganda y Educación Política del FSLN, n.d.

————. *Roberto López Pérez: el principio del fin.* Managua: Secretaría Nacional de Propaganda y Educación Política del FSLN, 1980.

Escobar Morales, César. *Sandino en el panorama nacional.* Managua: Comités de Defensa Sandinista, 1979.

Escuela Magnético-Espiritual de la Comuna Universal. *Declaración de principios.* Buenos Aires: n.p., n.d.

———. *Reglamento interno,* 3d rev. ed. Buenos Aires: n.p., n.d.

El evangelio en la revolución. Managua: Instituto Histórico Centro-americano, 1979.

"Even in Havana." *The Progressive* (March 1985): 12.

"An Exclusive Interview with Arturo Cruz: An 'All-Out Struggle' for a Free Nicaragua" *Conservative Digest* (April 1985): 7–12.

"La experiencia sandinista demuestra que se puede ser creyente y al mismo tiempo revolucionario." *Patria Libre* (Managua) (October–November 1980): 69–70.

Fabela, Isidro. "Augusto César Sandino." In *Sandino, el rebelde de América.* 2d ed., pp. 37–93. Managua: Ediciones Monimbó, 1979.

Fajardo, José. "¿Quiénes son los sandinistas?" In *Los Sandinistas,* edited by Gabriel García Márquez et al., pp. 15–28. Bogotá: La Oveja Negra, 1979.

Fann, K. T., and Donald C. Hodges, eds. *Readings in U.S. Imperialism.* Boston: Porter Sargent, 1971.

Finkler, Kaja. "Dissident Sectarian Movements, the Catholic Church, and Social Class in Mexico." *Comparative Studies in Society and History* 25:2 (1983): 277–305.

Flores Magón, Ricardo. *Antología Ricardo Flores Magón.* Edited by Gonzalo Aguirre Beltrán. Mexico City: Universidad Nacional Autónoma de México, 1972.

———. *Epistolario revolucionario e íntimo.* 3 vols. Mexico City: Grupo Cultural Ricardo Flores Magón, 1925.

———. *Ricardo Flores Magón: epistolario y textos.* Edited by Manuel González Ramírez. Mexico City: Fondo de Cultura Económica, 1961.

———. *Semilla libertaria.* 2 vols. Mexico City: Grupo Cultural Ricardo Flores Magón, 1923.

———. *Tribuna roja.* Mexico: Grupo Cultural Ricardo Flores Magón, 1925.

Fonseca Amador, Carlos. *Bajo la bandera del Sandinismo.* Managua: Editorial Nueva Nicaragua, 1983.

———. "¡Con la revolución siempre!" In *Nicaragua: la estrategia de la victoria,* edited by Fernando Carmona, pp. 129–139. Mexico City: Nuestro Tiempo, 1980.

———. *Desde la cárcel yo acuso a la dictadura.* Managua: Secretaría Nacional de Propaganda y Educación Política del FSLN, n.d.

———. ed. *Ideario político del General Augusto César Sandino.* San José, Costa Rica: Editorial Porvenir, 1979.

———. *Nicaragua: hora cero.* Managua: Secretaría Nacional de Propaganda y Educación Política del FSLN, 1980.

———. *Un nicaragüense en Moscú.* Managua: Secretaría Nacional de Propaganda y Educación Política del FSLN, 1980.

———. "Por la lucha armada, a la hermandad internacionalista." In *Nicaragua: la estrategia de la victoria,* edited by Fernando Carmona, pp. 165–167. Mexico City: Nuestro Tiempo, 1980.

————. *Sandino: guerrillero proletario.* Managua: Secretaría Nacional de Propaganda y Educación Política del FSLN, n.d.

Fonseca, Carlos; Oscar Turcios; Ricardo S. Morales Avilés. *¿Qué es un Sandinista?* Managua: Secretaría Nacional de Propaganda y Educación Política del FSLN, 1980.

Frank, André Gunder. *Latin America: Underdevelopment or Revolution?* New York: Monthly Review Press, 1969.

————. *Lumpenburguesía: lumpendesarrollo.* Santiago de Chile: Prensa Latinoamericana, 1970.

Freire, Paulo, *Pedagogy of the Oppressed.* New York: Seabury, 1974.

Frente de Acción Popular Unificada (FAPU). "La ideología dominante: la doctrina de seguridad nacional." *Polémica Internacional* (San Salvador), no. 2 (April–May 1980): 22–37.

————. "La permanente intervención yanqui." *Polémica Internacional* (San Salvador), no. 2 (April–May 1980): 4–21.

Frente Patriótico Nacional (FPN). "Nace el Frente Patriótico Nacional." In *Nicaragua: la estrategia de la victoria,* edited by Fernando Carmona, pp. 249–254. Mexico City: Nuestro Tiempo, 1980.

Frente Sandinista de Liberacion Nacional (FSLN). "Algunas consideraciones estratégicas." In *"Los Sandinistas,"* edited by Gabriel García Márquez et al., pp. 202–210. Bogotá: La Oveja Negra, 1979.

————. "Alianzas de clase en la situación revolucionaria." In *Nicaragua: la estrategia de la victoria,* edited by Fernando Carmona, pp. 237–244. Mexico City: Nuestro Tiempo, 1980.

————. "Comunicado oficial de la Dirección Nacional del FSLN sobre la religión." *Patria Libre* (Managua) (October–November 1980): 70–73.

————. "El FSLN y el grupo de 'los doce.'" In *Nicaragua: la estrategia de la victoria,* edited by Fernando Carmona, pp. 188–191. Mexico City: Nuestro Tiempo, 1980.

————. "Iniciamos una nueva etapa." In *Nicaragua: la estrategia de la victoria,* edited by Fernando Carmona, pp. 169–177. Mexico City: Nuestro Tiempo, 1980.

————. "Manifiesto sobre los derechos humanos." In *"Los Sandinistas,"* edited by Gabriel García Márquez et al., pp. 171–176. Bogotá: La Oveja Negra, 1979.

————. "Proclama a la unidad." In *Nicaragua: la estrategia de la victoria,* edited by Fernando Carmona, pp. 263–265. Mexico City: Nuestro Tiempo, 1980.

————. "Programa mínimo del FSLN." In *Nicaragua: la estrategia de la victoria,* edited by Fernando Carmona, pp. 225–233. Mexico City: Nuestro Tiempo, 1980.

————. "Pronunciamiento del FSLN sobre las elecciones." *Patria Libre* (Managua) (August 1980): 19.

————. "Represión y lucha de clases." In *Nicaragua: la estrategia de la victoria,* edited by Fernando Carmona, pp. 178–183. Mexico City: Nuestro Tiempo, 1980.

————. "La reunificación del FSLN con las tendencias Guerra Popular

Prolongada y Tendencia Proletaria." In *"Los Sandinistas,"* edited by Gabriel García Márquez et al., pp. 210–218. Bogotá: La Oveja Negra, 1979.

———. "Sandinistas hablan de sus divergencias." In *"Los Sandinistas,"* edited by Gabriel García Márquez et al., pp. 224–241. Bogotá: La Oveja Negra, 1979.

———. "La situación general del FSLN. In *"Los Sandinistas,"* edited by Gabriel García Márquez et al., pp. 188–202. Bogotá: La Oveja Negra, 1979.

Freud, Sigmund. *Civilization and Its Discontents.* Translated by Joan Rivière. Chicago: University of Chicago Press, n.d.

Fried, Albert, and Ronald Sanders, eds. *Socialist Thought: A Documentary History.* Garden City, N.Y.: Anchor, 1964.

Gadea, Hilda. *Ernesto: A Memoir of Che Guevara.* Garden City, N.Y.: Doubleday, 1972.

Galich, Manuel. "Nicaragua 1933–1936: gestación y nacimiento de la dinastía." *Casa de las Américas* (Havana), no. 117 (November–December 1979): 65–75.

García Elorrio, Juan. "Bases of the Camilo Torres Latin American Encounter." In *Legacy of Che Guevara,* edited by Donald C. Hodges, pp. 192–194. London: Thames & Hudson, 1977.

García Márquez, Gabriel. "Entrevista a los Sandinistas." In *"Los Sandinistas,"* edited by Gabriel García Márquez et al., pp. 135–167. Bogotá: La Oveja Negra, 1979.

García Márquez, Gabriel, et al., eds. *La batalla de Nicaragua.* Mexico City: Bruguera Mexicana de Ediciones, 1979.

———, eds. *"Los Sandinistas."* Bogotá: La Oveja Negra, 1979.

García Salgado, Andrés. *Yo estuve con Sandino.* Mexico City: Bloque Obrero "General Heriberto Jara," 1979.

"Gaspar García Laviana: la semilla que ayudó a sembrar ya está dando frutas." *Patria Libre* (Managua) (December 1980): 8–11.

Giap, Vo Nguyên. *See* Vo Nguyên Giap.

Gibellini, Rossino, ed. *Frontiers of Theology in Latin America.* Maryknoll, N.Y.: Orbis, 1979.

Gilbert, Gregorio Urbano. *Junto a Sandino.* Santo Domingo: Universidad Autónoma de Santo Domingo, 1979.

Gilly, Adolfo. *La nueva Nicaragua: antimperialismo y lucha de clases.* Mexico City: Nuevo Imágen, 1980.

Gómez, J. "La traición de Sandino." Extracted by Adolfo Gilly, in *La nueva Nicaragua: antimperialismo y lucha de clases,* pp. 101–104. Mexico City: Nuevo Imágen, 1980.

Gramsci, Antonio. *Los intelectuales y la organización de la cultura.* Buenos Aires: Editorial Lautaro, 1959.

———. *El materialismo histórico y la filosofía de Benedetto Croce.* Buenos Aires: Editorial Lautaro, 1958.

———. *The Modern Prince and Other Writings.* Translated by Louis Marks. London: Lawrence & Wishart, 1957.

——. *Notas sobre Maquiavelo, sobre política y sobre el estado mo-derno*. Buenos Aires: Editorial Lautero, 1962.

Grigulevich, J., ed. *Nicaragua: glorioso camino a la victoria*. Moscow: U.S.S.R. Academy of Sciences, 1981.

Guerra, Ramiro. *La expansión territorial de los Estados Unidos a expen-sas de España y de los países hispanoamericanos*. 4th ed. Havana: Edi-torial de Ciencias Sociales, 1975 (1st ed. 1937).

Guevara, Ernesto "Che." *Obras 1957–1967*. 2 vols. Havana: Casa de las Américas, 1970.

Guido de López, Lea. "Movimientos y organizaciones políticas." *Revolu-ción Sandinista y Educación*. Special issue of *Encuentro* (Managua), no. 15 (September 1980): 81–88.

Guillén, Abraham. *Desafío al Pentágono*. Montevideo: Andes, 1969.

——. *Estrategia de la guerrilla urbana*. Montevideo: Manuales del Pueblo, 1966; 2d ed., Montevideo: Liberación, 1969.

——. *Philosophy of the Urban Guerrilla: The Revolutionary Writings of Abraham Guillén*. Edited by Donald Hodges. New York: William Mor-row, 1973.

Guillén, Abraham, and Donald Hodges. *Revaloración de la guerrilla ur-bana*. Edited by Donald Hodges. Mexico City: El Caballito, 1977.

Gutiérrez, Gustavo. *A Theology of Liberation*. Maryknoll, N.Y.: Orbis, 1973.

Harnecker, Marta. *Los conceptos elementales del materialismo histórico*. 5th ed. Mexico City: Siglo XXI, 1970.

——. *Cuba: Dictatorship or Democracy?* Westport, Conn.: Lawrence Hill, 1980.

Haya de la Torre, Víctor Raúl. *El antimperialismo y el APRA*. Santiago de Chile: Ercilla, 1936.

——. *Pensamiento político de Haya de la Torre: Indoamérica*. Vol. 1. Edited by Luis F. Rodríguez et al. Lima: Ediciones Pueblo, 1961.

——. *Por la emancipación de América Latina*. Buenos Aires: Glei-zer, 1927.

——. *Treinta años de Aprismo*. Mexico City: Fondo de Cultura Econó-mica, 1956.

Hebraic Literature: Translations from the Talmud, Midrashim and Kab-bala. Translated by M. H. Harris. New York: Tudor, 1936.

Heckethorn, Charles W. *The Secret Societies of All Ages and Countries*. 2 vols. New York: University Books, 1965.

Hinkelammert, Franz. *Las armas ideológicas de la muerte*. San José: DEI-EDUCA, 1977.

Hodges, Donald C. *Argentina, 1943–1976: The National Revolution and Resistance*. Albuquerque: University of New Mexico Press, 1976.

——. *The Bureaucratization of Socialism*. Amherst: University of Mas-sachusetts Press, 1981.

——. *The Latin American Revolution*. New York: William Mor-row, 1974.

———. *The Legacy of Che Guevara: A Documentary Study.* London: Thames & Hudson, 1977.

———. *Socialist Humanism: The Outcome of Classical European Morality.* St. Louis, Mo.: Warren Green, 1974.

Hodges, Donald C., and Ross Gandy. *Mexico, 1910–1982: Reform or Revolution?* 2d ed. London: Zed Press, 1983.

Horowitz, Irving L. *Radicalism and the Revolt against Reason: The Social Theories of Georges Sorel.* London: Routledge & Kegan Paul, 1961.

Inman, Samuel G. *América revolucionaria.* Madrid: Javier Morata, 1933.

Instituto de Estudio del Sandinismo. *El Sandinismo: documentos básicos.* Managua: Editorial Nueva Nicaragua, 1983.

"Izquierdización de la Internacional Socialista." *Unomásuno* (Mexico City) (30 March 1980): 8.

James, William. *Essays on Faith and Morals.* New York: Longmans, Green, 1947.

Jonas (Bodenheimer), Susanne. "Dependency and Imperialism: The Roots of Latin American Development." In *Readings in U.S. Imperialism,* edited by K. T. Fann and Donald C. Hodges, pp. 155–181. Boston: Porter Sargent, 1971.

Jorrín, Miguel, and John D. Martz. *Latin American Political Thought and Ideology.* Chapel Hill: University of North Carolina Press, 1970.

"José Carlos Mariátegui (1895–1930): medio siglo después" (editorial). *El Nuevo Diario* (Managua) (28 December 1980).

Kautsky, Karl. *Foundations of Christianity.* New York: Monthly Review Press, 1972.

Kirkpatrick, Jeane J. *Dictatorships and Double Standards.* New York: Simon & Schuster, 1982.

———. *The Reagan Phenomenon and Other Speeches on Foreign Policy.* Washington, D.C.: American Enterprise Institute for Public Policy Research, 1982.

Kohl, James, and John Litt, eds. *Urban Guerrilla Warfare in Latin America.* Cambridge, Mass.: MIT Press, 1974.

Konstantinov, F., et al. *Fundamentos de filosofía marxista-leninista.* 2 vols. Havana: Editorial de Ciencias Sociales, 1977.

Kossok, Manfred. *José Carlos Mariátegui y el desarrollo del pensamiento marxista en el Perú.* Lima: Ensayos, 1967.

Krause, Enrique. "Convicción y responsabilidad de nuestra diplomacia." *Proceso* (18 September 1978).

Kuron, Jacek, and Karol Modzelewski. "An Open Letter to the Party." *New Politics* (Spring 1966): 5–46; (Summer 1966): 72–99.

Las Casas, Bartolomé de. *Brevísima relación de la destrucción de las Indias.* Buenos Aires: Eudeba, 1966.

Lecturas de filosofía, 2d ed. 2 vols. Edited by Dept. of Philosophy of University of Havana. Havana: Instituto del Libro, 1968.

Lenin, V. I. *The Lenin Anthology.* Edited by Robert C. Tucker. New York: W. W. Norton, 1975.

———. *Marx-Engels-Marxism.* 5th ed. Moscow: Foreign Languages Publishing House, 1953.

———. *Selected Works.* 3 vols. New York: International Publishers, 1967.

Lin Piao. *Long Live the Victory of People's War!* Peking: Foreign Languages Press, 1965.

Liss, Sheldon. *Marxist Thought in Latin America.* Berkeley & Los Angeles: University of California Press, 1984.

López C., Julio, et al. *La caída del Somocismo y la lucha sandinista en Nicaragua.* 2d ed. San José: EDUCA, 1980.

López Oliva, Enrique. *El Camilismo en la América Latina.* Havana: Casa de las Américas, 1970.

Löwith, Karl. *Meaning in History.* Chicago: University of Chicago Press, 1949.

Lowy, Michael. *The Marxism of Che Guevara.* New York: Monthly Review Press, 1973.

La lucha de los dioses: los ídolos de la opresión y la búsqueda del dios liberador. San José: DEI, 1980; and Managua: Centro Antonio Valdivieso, 1980.

Luz Brum, Blanca. *Blanca Luz contra la corriente.* Santiago de Chile: Ercilla, 1936.

Macaulay, Neill. *The Sandino Affair.* Chicago: Quadrangle, 1967.

Macín, Raúl, ed. "El evangelio según el comandante de la revolución Tomás Borge." *¡Por Esto!* (15 July 1982): 23–26.

McKiernan, Kevin. "Shrines and Slogans: The Divided Church in Nicaragua." *Mother Jones* (April 1984): 28–33, 47–53.

Manlio Tirado, Víctor. *La revolución sandinista.* Mexico City: Nuestro Tiempo, 1983.

Mao Tse-tung. *Selected Works of Mao Tse-tung.* 5 vols. Peking: Foreign Languages Press, 1967–1977.

Maraboto, Emigdio. *Sandino ante el coloso.* Managua: Patria y Libertad, 1980 (orig. pub. Veracruz, 1929).

Marcus, Bruce, ed. *Nicaragua: The Sandinista People's Revolution (Speeches by Sandinista Leaders).* New York: Pathfinder, 1985.

Maréchal, Sylvain. "Manifesto of the Equals." In *Socialist Thought: A Documentary History,* edited by Albert Fried and Ronald Sanders, pp. 51–55. Garden City, N.Y.: Anchor, 1964.

Mariátegui, José Carlos. *El alma matinal. Obras completas.* 3d ed. Vol. 3. Lima: Biblioteca "Amauta," 1967.

———. *Defensa del Marxismo. Obras completas.* 3d ed. Vol. 5. Lima: Biblioteca "Amauta," 1967.

———. *7 ensayos de interpretación de la realidad peruana. Obras completas.* 16th ed. Vol. 2. Lima: Biblioteca "Amauta," 1969.

Marini, Ruy Mauro. "The Nicaraguan Revolution and the Central American Revolutionary Process." *Contemporary Marxism,* no. 3 (Summer 1981): 62–66.

———. "The Question of the State in the Latin American Class Struggle." *Contemporary Marxism,* no. 1 (Spring 1980): 1–9.

Marx, Karl. *Capital.* Edited by Friedrich Engels. 3 vols. Moscow: Foreign Languages Publishing House, 1961–1962.

Marx, Karl, and Friedrich Engels. *Basic Writings on Politics and Philosophy.* Edited by Lewis S. Feuer, Garden City, N.Y.: Anchor, 1959.

———. *The German Ideology.* Edited by S. Ryazanskaya. Moscow: Progress Publishers, 1964.

———. *The Marx-Engels Reader.* 2d ed. Edited by Robert C. Tucker. New York: W. W. Norton, 1978.

———. *Selected Correspondence.* Moscow: Foreign Languages Publishing House, n.d.

———. *Selected Works.* 2 vols. New York: International Publishers, 1933.

Matthews, Herbert L. *Fidel Castro.* New York: Simon & Schuster, 1969.

———. *Revolution in Cuba.* New York: Charles Scribner's Sons, 1975.

May, Robert E. *The Southern Dream of a Caribbean Empire, 1854–1861.* Baton Rouge: Louisiana State University Press, 1973.

Mella, Julio Antonio. *Documentos y artículos.* Havana: Instituto Cubano del Libro, 1975.

Memorias del Coronel Santos López. Managua: Secretaría Nacional de Propaganda y Educación Política del FSLN, n.d.

Mena, Luis. *Arquitectos de la victoria liberal (Augusto César Sandino).* Managua: n.p., n.d.

Míguez Bonino, José. *Doing Theology in a Revolutionary Situation.* Philadelphia: Fortress Press, 1975.

Millett, Richard L. *Guardians of the Dynasty.* Maryknoll, N.Y.: Orbis, 1977.

Miranda, José Porfirio. *Marx y la Biblia: crítica a la filosofía de la opresión.* 2d ed. Salamanca: Sígueme, 1972.

Moffatt, James, trans. *The Bible.* New York: Harper & Brothers, 1935.

Moncada, José María. *Estados Unidos en Nicaragua.* Managua: Tipografía Ateneas, 1942.

Moore, R. Laurence. *In Search of White Crows: Spiritualism, Parapsychology, and American Culture.* New York: Oxford University Press, 1977.

Mora Tavares, Guillermo. "Crea el FSLN su cuarto frente armado." In *La batalla por Nicaragua: Cuadernos de Unomásuno,* pp. 147–148. Mexico City: Editorial Uno, 1980.

Morales Avilés, Ricardo. *La dominación imperialista en Nicaragua.* Managua: Secretaría Nacional de Propaganda y Educación Política del FSLN, 1980.

———. *El pensamiento vivo de Ricardo Morales Avilés.* Managua: Asociación de Estudiantes de Sicología, n.d.

Movimiento de Izquierda Revolucionaria de Chile (MIR). *Correo de la Resistencia* (Mexico City) (September 1974).

———. "Respuesta del MIR a la dirección del Partido Comunista," *Correo de la Resistencia* (April 1975): 1–20.

Nash, George H. *The Conservative Intellectual Movement in America.* New York: Basic Books, 1976.

Natividad Rosales, José. *¿Qué hizo el Che en México?* Mexico City: Editorial Posada, 1973.

Nicaragua: combate de un pueblo. Presencia de los cristianos. Lima: Centro de Estudios y Publicaciones (CEP), 1978.

Nicaragua: elementos históricos, estratégicos y tácticos de la revolución. Mexico City: Cuadernos de Coyuntura (SEPLA), no. 4, 1979.

Nolan, David. *The Ideology of the Sandinistas and the Nicaraguan Revolution.* Coral Gables, Fla.: Institute of Interamerican Studies, University of Miami, 1984.

Núñez Soto, Orlando. "Del socialismo en libertad al socialismo por decreto." *Barricada* (Managua) (23 December 1980): 3.

————. "The Third Social Force in National Liberation Movements." *Latin American Perspectives*, no. 29 (Spring 1981): 5–21.

Núñez Téllez, Carlos. *Un pueblo en armas.* Managua: Secretaría Nacional de Propaganda y Educación Política del FSLN, 1980.

Ojeda, Abelardo, and Carlos Mallén. *Ricardo Flores Magón.* Mexico City: Secretaría de Educación Publica, 1967.

Oliveros Maqueo, Roberto. *Liberación y teología: génesis y crecimiento de una reflexión (1966–1976).* Lima: Centro de Estudios y Publicaciones (CEP), 1977.

Oráculos de Zoroastro. Translated by Pedro Font Puig. Appended to *Zoroastro: el Zend-Avesta.* Biblioteca de Teosofía y Orientalismo. Barcelona: B. Bauzá, n.d.

Ortega Saavedra, Daniel. "La realidad forzó nuestras respuestas adecuadas." *Casa de las Américas* (Havana), no. 117 (November–December 1979): 185–187.

Ortega Saavedra, Humberto. *50 años de lucha sandinista.* Managua: Ministerio del Interior, 1979.

————. "Diálogo abierto a la asamblea." *Revolución Sandinista y Educación.* Special issue of *Encuentro* (Managua), no. 15 (September 1980): 154–179.

————. "Discurso del comandante de la revolución y ministro de la defensa." *Patria Libre* (Managua) (August 1980): 12–18.

————. "Entrevista con el Comandante Humberto Ortega Saavedra." *Patria Libre* (Managua) (February 1980): 12–18.

————. "La guerra, no es sólo militar." *Casa de las Américas* (Havana), no. 117 (November–December 1979): 187–190.

————. "La insurrección nacional victoriosa." *Nicaráuac* (Managua), no. 1 (May–June 1980): 26–57.

————. "La lucha de Sandino base de la revolución sandinista." In *La revolución a través de nuestra Dirección Nacional*, pp. 7–13. Managua: Secretaría Nacional de Propaganda y Educación Política del FSLN, 1980.

Partido Socialista Nicaragüense (PSN). "Con la revolución por el socialismo" (editorial). *El Popular* (Managua) (6 November 1980).

————. "El PSN y la revolución popular sandinista." *El Popular* (Managua) (6, 15 November 1980).

Pascal, Blaise. *Pensées, the Provincial Letters.* Translated by W. G. Trotter and Thomas M'Crie. New York: Random House, 1941.

Pavletich, Esteban. "Perspectivas de la revolución nicaragüense." *Casa de las Américas* (Havana), no. 117 (November–December 1979): 94–96.

Pedro Arauz Palacios: datos biográficos. Managua: Secretaría Nacional de Propaganda y Educación Política del FSLN, 1980.

Pellicani, Luciano. *Gramsci: An Alternative Communism?* Translated by Mimi Manfrini-Watts. Stanford, Cal.: Hoover Institution Press, 1981.

Pereyra, Manuel. "Conversación inconclusa con Ernesto Cardenal." *Bohemia* (Havana), no. 42 (19 October 1979): 31.

Petras, James. "Nicaragua: The Transition to a New Society." *Latin American Perspectives,* no. 29 (Spring 1981): 74–94.

Pike, Fredrick B. "Visions of Rebirth. The Spiritualist Facet of Peru's Haya de la Torre." *Hispanic American Historical Review* 63 : 3 (1983): 479–516.

"Playboy Interview: The Sandinistas." *Playboy* (September 1983): 57–68, 188–200.

Plekhanov, George V. *The Development of the Monist View of History.* Moscow: Progress Publishers, 1956.

———. *Fundamental Problems of Marxism.* New York: International Publishers, 1975.

Poole, David, ed. *Land and Liberty: Anarchist Influence in the Mexican Revolution.* Sanday, Orkney: Cienfuegos Press, 1977.

Portelli, H. *Gramsci e la questione religiosa.* Milan: Mazzota, 1976.

Posada, Francisco. *Los orígenes del pensamiento marxista en Latinoamérica.* Havana: Casa de las Américas, 1968.

Poulantzas, Nicos. "Introducción al estudio de la hegemonía en el estado (fin)." *Pensamiento Crítico* (Havana), no. 8 (September 1967): 131–152.

———. *Poder político y clases sociales en el estado capitalista.* Mexico City: Siglo XXI, 1968.

Proudhon, Pierre Joseph. *What Is Property: An Inquiry into the Principle of Right and of Government.* Translated by Benjamin R. Tucker. London: William Reeves, n.d.

Ramírez Mercado, Sergio. "Análisis histórico-social del movimiento sandinista, desde el orígen hasta la maduración." *Revolución Sandinista y Educación.* Special issue of *Encuentro,* no. 15 (September 1980): 10–20.

———. "Breve historia contemporánea de Nicaragua." *Casa de las Américas* (Havana), no. 117 (November–December 1979): 17–39.

———. "Los intelectuales en el futuro revolucionario." *Nicaráuac* (Managua), no. 1 (May–June 1980): 158–162.

———. "Junta de Gobierno de Reconstrucción Nacional acepta llamado de la Dirección Nacional del FSLN." *Patria Libre* (Managua) (August 1980): 21–25.

———. *Mensaje de la Junta de Gobierno de Reconstrucción Nacional al pueblo nicaragüense.* Managua: Secretaría Nacional de Propaganda y Educación Política del FSLN, 1980.

————. "El muchacho de Niquinohomo." In Augusto César Sandino, *El pensamiento vivo de Sandino*, edited by Sergio Ramírez Mercado, 5th ed., pp. v–lxix. San José: EDUCA, 1980.

Ramm, Hartmut. *The Marxism of Regis Debray: Between Lenin and Guevara*. Lawrence: Regents Press of Kansas, 1978.

Ramos, Jorge Abelardo. *Historia de la nación latinoamericana*. Buenos Aires: A. Peña Lillo, 1968.

————. *Manuel Ugarte y la revolución latinoamericana*. Buenos Aires: Coyoacán, 1961.

Randall, Margaret. *"Somos millones . . ." (La vida de Doris María, combatiente nicaragüense)*. Mexico City: Extemporáneos, 1977.

Reissner, Will. "'Granma' Reports How El Salvadoran Groups View Struggle." In *Revolt in El Salvador*, pp. 23–40. New York: Pathfinder, 1980.

"Resolución sobre la América Latina del Congreso Antimperialista de Bruselas." In *Documentos y artículos*, by Julio Antonio Mella, pp. 636–642. Havana: Instituto Cubano del Libro, 1975.

La revolución a través de nuestra Dirección Nacional. Managua: Secretaría Nacional de Propaganda y Educación Política del FSLN, 1980.

Rivail, Hippolyte Léon Denizard [Allan Kardec]. *El evangelio según el espiritismo*. Barcelona. Visión Libros, 1979.

————. *El libro de los mediums*. Barcelona: Visión Libros, 1978.

————. *The Spirits Book*. Translated by Anna Blackwell. Boston: Colby & Rich, 1875.

Rivera Mendizábal, Roberto. "Introducción. Revolucionarios no creyentes y cristianos revolucionarios en Nicaragua: profundización en la alianza estratégica." In *Fe cristiana y revolución sandinista en Nicaragua*, pp. 9–25. Managua: Instituto Histórico Centroamericano, 1979.

Robison, John. *Proofs of a Conspiracy*. Boston: Western Islands, 1967 (orig. pub. 1798).

Rodó, José Enrique. *Ariel*. Boston: Houghton Mifflin, 1922.

Román, José. *Maldito país*. Managua: El Pez y la Serpiente, 1983.

Roth, Jack J. *The Cult of Violence: Sorel and the Sorelians*. Berkeley & Los Angeles: University of California Press, 1980.

Rothschuh Tablada, Guillermo. *Los guerrilleros vencen a los generales*. Managua: Ministerio de Educación, 1980.

Rousseau, Jean Jacques. *The Social Contract and Discourses*. Translated by G. D. H. Cole. New York: E. P. Dutton, 1950.

Ruiz, Henry. "Este es el Plan 80." *Patria Libre* (Managua) (February 1980): 20–24.

————. "La montaña era como un crisol donde se forjaban los mejores cuadros." *Nicaráuac* (Managua), no. 1 (May–June 1980): 8–24.

Ruiz, Henry, and Carlos Núñez Téllez. *Los trabajadores sandinistas y las tareas del momento*. Managua: Secretaría Nacional de Propaganda y Educación Política del FSLN, 1980.

Salazar Bondy, Augusto. *América Latina: filosofía y liberación.* Buenos Aires: Bonum, 1974.

Salvatierra, Sofonías. *Sandino o la tragedia de un pueblo.* Madrid: Europa, 1934.

Sánchez, Luis Alberto. *Haya de la Torre o el político.* 2d ed. Santiago de Chile: Ercilla, 1936.

Sánchez, Mayo Antonio. *Nicaragua, año cero.* Mexico City: Diana, 1979.

Sandino, Augusto César. "Boletín de noticias del E.D. de la S.N. de N. correspondiente al mes de julio del corriente año." *La Balanza* (Buenos Aires) 1 : 1 (1933).

———. "Credencial de representante de nuestro Ejército D. de la S.N. de N. y el suscrito en la República Argentina." *La Balanza* (Buenos Aires) 1 : 4 (1933).

———. *Escritos literarios y documentos desconocidos.* Edited by Jorge Eduardo Arellano. Managua: n.p., 1980.

———. *Manifiesto a los pueblos de la tierra y en particular al de Nicaragua.* Managua: n.p., 1979.

———. "Mensaje a los hombres del periódico Nicaragüense." *La Balanza* (Buenos Aires) 1 : 4 (1933).

———. *El pensamiento vivo de Sandino.* Edited by Sergio Ramírez Mercado. 5th ed. San José: EDUCA, 1980; 8th rev. ed. Managua: Nueva Nicaragua, 1981.

———. "Respuesta a la carta del Señor Don Joaquín Trincado." *La Balanza* (Buenos Aires) 1 : 4 (1933).

Saña, Heleno. *El anarquismo, de Proudhon a Cohn-Bendit.* Madrid: Indice, 1970.

Sartre, Jean-Paul. Preface to *The Wretched of the Earth,* by Frantz Fanon. Translated by Constance Farrington. New York: Grove, 1963.

Scherer García, Julio. "La peor acechanza para Nicaragua, la falacia de los ricos. Aún no preocupa Reagan a Borge: 'El poder no es absoluto.'" *Proceso* (Mexico) (17 March 1980) : 6–9.

Scholem, Gershom. *Kabbalah.* New York: New American Library, 1978.

Scroggs, William O. *Filibusters and Financiers.* New York: Macmillan, 1916.

Selser, Gregorio. *El pequeño ejército loco.* Havana: Imprenta Nacional, 1960 (orig. pub. Buenos Aires, 1958).

———. "El pre-Sandino: Benjamín F. Zeledón." *Casa de las Américas* (Havana), no. 117 (November–December 1979) : 57–61.

———. "Sandino el guerrillero." In Gregorio Selser, *Sandino,* pp. 5–50. Montevideo: Biblioteca de Marcha, 1970.

———. *Sandino, general de hombres libres.* 2 vols. Havana: Imprenta Nacional, 1960 (orig. pub. Buenos Aires, 1957).

———. *Sandino, general de hombres libres.* 1 vol. Mexico City: Diógenes, 1979.

"The Situation of the Latin American Communist Parties on the Eve of the Seventh Congress of the Comintern." In *Marxism in Latin America,* edited by Luis E. Aguilar, pp. 118–123. New York: Knopf, 1969.

Solana, Francisco. "Nicaragua: One Priest's View." *Guardian* (26 August 1981).

Somoza Debayle, Anastasio. *Nicaragua Betrayed*. Boston: Western Islands, 1980.

Somoza García, Anastasio. *El verdadero Sandino, o el Calvario de las Segovias*. Managua: Tip. Robelo, 1936.

Sorel, Georges. *Reflections on Violence*. New York: Peter Smith, 1941.

Steinfels, Peter. *The Neoconservatives: The Men Who Are Changing America's Politics*. New York: Simon & Schuster, 1979.

Stimson, Henry L. *American Policy in Nicaragua*. New York: Charles Scribner, 1927.

Stimson, Henry L., and McGeorge Bundy. *On Active Service in Peace and War*. New York: Harper & Brothers, 1948.

Suárez, Orlando S. *La ruta en la hora llegada*. Buenos Aires: Talleres Gráficos Editorial Mayo, 1954.

Tertullian's Treatise on the Incarnation. Edited and translated by Ernest Evans. London: Society for the Propagation of Christian Knowledge, 1956.

Tirado López, Víctor. "Crecerá la ofensiva del FSLN dice el Mexicano Tirado López." Interview by Guillermo Mora Tavares, in *La batalla por Nicaragua: Cuadernos de Unomásuno*, pp. 142–145. Mexico City: Editorial Uno, 1980.

———. "FSLN leader speaks on Karl Marx." *Intercontinental Press* (16 May 1983): 265–267.

———. "Improvement in the Situation of Workers is the Task of the Workers Themselves." In *Nicaragua: The Sandinista People's Revolution*, edited by Bruce Marcus, pp. 95–100. New York: Pathfinder, 1985 (orig. pub. as "The Road to Socialism," *Intercontinental Press*, 18 April 1983).

———. "El pensamiento político de Carlos Fonseca Amador." In *La revolución a través de nuestra Dirección Nacional*, pp. 15–24. Managua: Secretaría de Propaganda y Educación Política del FSLN, 1980.

Tolstoy, Leo. *What Is Art? and Essays on Art*. Translated by Aylmer Maude. London: Oxford University Press, 1950.

Torres, Camilo. *Camilo, el cura revolucionario: sus obras*. Edited by Juan García Elorrio. Buenos Aires: Cristianismo y Revolución, 1968.

Torres, Simón, and Julio Aronde. "Debray and the Cuban Experience." *Régis Debray and the Latin American Revolution*. Special issue of *Monthly Review* (July–August 1968): 44–62.

Torres-Rivas, Edelberto. *Procesos y estructuras de una sociedad dependiente (Centroamérica)*. Santiago de Chile: Prensa Latinoamericana, 1969.

Trías, Vivián. *Imperialismo y geopolítica en América Latina*. Montevideo: El Sol, 1967.

Trincado, Joaquín. "Augusto César Sandino: Con la bandera de la U.H.A.O." *La Balanza* (Buenos Aires) 3:2 (1935).

————. *Los cinco amores: ética y sociología.* Buenos Aires: Preusch & Eggeling, 1922.

————. "E. Unidos vs. Mexico: así los coloca el ex-presidente Díaz en el caso de Nicaragua." *La Balanza* (Buenos Aires) 1:20 (1933).

————. "*Los extremos se tocan": epílogo de la guerra y prólogo a la paz.* Buenos Aires: Talleres Gráficos Gasperini, 1930.

————. *Filosofía austera racional.* Buenos Aires: Imprenta López, 1965 (orig. pub. 1920).

————. "1934–febrero 22–1935." *La Balanza* (Buenos Aires) 3:2 (1935).

Tronti, Mario. "Algunas questiones en torno al Marxismo de Gramsci." In *Gramsci y el Marxismo,* by Palmiro Togliatti et al., pp. 60–75. Buenos Aires: Proteo, 1965.

Tunnerman, Carlos. "La nueva filosofía educativa del Gobierno de Reconstrucción Nacional." *Revolución Sandinista y Educación.* Special issue of *Encuentro* (Managua), no. 15 (September 1980):99–111.

Turner, Ethel Duffy. *Ricardo Flores Magón y el Partido Liberal Mexicano.* Morelia: Editorial "Erandi" del Gobierno del Estado, 1960.

Ugarte, Manuel. *El destino de un continente.* Madrid: Mundo Latino, 1923.

————. *El porvenir de la América española.* Valencia: Promoteo, 1920.

Urcuyo M., Francisco. *Solos: los últimos 43 horas en el bunker de Somoza.* Guatemala City: Editorial Académica Centro América, 1979.

Vanden, Harry. "The Ideology of the Insurrection." In *Nicaragua in Revolution,* edited by Thomas W. Walker, pp. 41–62. New York: Praeger, 1982.

————. *Mariátegui: influencias en su formación ideológica.* Lima: Biblioteca "Amauta," 1975.

————. "Mariátegui's Marxismo, Comunismo, and Other Bibliographic Notes." *Latin American Research Review* 14:3 (1979):61–86.

Vasconcelos, José. *La raza cósmica.* 3d ed. Mexico City: Espasa-Calpe, 1966.

Villaverde Alcalá-Galiano, Luis. "El Sorelismo de Mariátegui." In *Mariátegui y los orígenes del Marxismo latinoamericano,* edited by José Aricó, pp. 145–154. Mexico City: Siglo XXI, 1978.

Vo Nguyên Giap. *People's War, People's Army.* New York: Praeger, 1962.

Waksman Schinka, Daniel. "Entrevista con Tomás Borge." *Combate* (Stockholm) (July–September 1979):20–22.

Walker, Thomas W. *Nicaragua: The Land of Sandino.* Boulder, Colo.: Westview, 1981.

————, ed. *Nicaragua in Revolution.* New York: Praeger, 1982.

Walker, William. *The War in Nicaragua.* Mobile, Ala.: S. H. Goetzel, 1860.

Weber, Henri. *Nicaragua: The Sandinist Revolution.* Translated by Patrick Camiller. London: New Left Books, 1981.

Weitling, Wilhelm. *The Poor Sinner's Gospel.* Translated by Dinah Livingstone. London: Sheed & Ward, 1969.

Wheelock Román, Jaime. "Entrevista al FSLN (Tendencia Proletaria)." *Combate* (Stockholm) (July–September 1979):23–25.

————. "The Great Challenge." In *Nicaragua: The Sandinista People's*

Revolution (Speeches by Sandinista Leaders), edited by Bruce Marcus, pp. 125–172. New York: Pathfinder, 1985.

——. "The Sandinista Front Is the Organization of the Working People." In *Nicaragua: The Sandinista People's Revolution (Speeches by Sandinista Leaders)*, edited by Bruce Marcus, pp. 271–289. New York: Pathfinder, 1985.

——. *Imperialismo y dictadura: crisis de una formación social*, 5th ed. Mexico City: Siglo XXI, 1980.

——. "El movimiento sandinista y la lucha de clases." *Revolución Sandinista y Educación*. Special issue of *Encuentro* (Managua), no. 15 (September 1980): 21–38.

——. "No hay 2 reformas agrarias." *Nicaráuac* (Managua), no. 1 (May–June 1980): 58–75.

——. *Los raíces indígenas de la lucha anticolonial en Nicaragua*. Mexico City: Siglo XXI, 1975.

——. "La reforma agraria en marcha." *Cuadernos del Tercer Mundo*, no. 39 (August–September 1980): 44–50.

Wheelock Román, Jaime, and Luis Carrión. *Apuntes sobre el desarrollo económico y social de Nicaragua*. Managua: Secretaría Nacional de Propaganda y Educación Política del FSLN, 1979.

"Who Are the MAP/FO and 'El Pueblo'?" *Intercontinental Press* (18 February 1980): 136.

Woodcock, George. *Anarchism: A History of Libertarian Ideas and Movements*. New York: Meridian, 1962.

Woodward, Ralph Lee, Jr. *Central America: A Nation Divided*. New York: Oxford University Press, 1976.

Zaehner, Robert C. *The Dawn and Twilight of Zoroastrianism*. New York: Putnam, 1961.

——. *The Teachings of the Magi: A Compendium of Zoroastrian Beliefs*. London: Allen & Unwin, 1956.

Index

Additional cross-references may be found in the list of abbreviations, pp. vii–viii.